In solidarity with Ra...

# Orestes Pursued by the Furies

The Furies (also called Erinyes) were three netherworld goddesses who avenged crimes, particularly homicide, unfilial conduct, and perjury. A victim seeking justice could call down the curse of the Furies upon the criminal. The wrath of the Furies manifested itself in a number of ways. Offenders might suffer madness or disease; a nation harboring such a criminal could as well. The wrath of the Furies could only be placated with ritual purification and the completion of some task of atonement. Furies were depicted as ugly, winged women with hair, arms and waists entwined with poisonous serpents. This representation was painted by William-Adolphe Bouguereau in 1862 and is the keenest visual representation of my book that I have found.

Image courtesy of Wikimedia Commons

# Ida Bell Wells-Barnett

(1862–1931)

Was born a slave in Holly Springs, Mississippi.

Ida attended Shaw University but was expelled for her rebellious behavior after confronting the college president. She later attended LeMoyne College where she expressed strong political opinions and provoked many people with her views on women's rights.

On May 4, 1884, a train conductor ordered Wells to give up her seat to a White person and move to the smoking car, which she refused to do. She bit the conductor who tried to move her, and he retreated and got two other men to drag her out of the car.

In March 1892, three of her friends were lynched by a White mob. Their murder influenced her to research and document lynchings and their causes. She published her findings in a pamphlet entitled "Southern Horrors: Lynch Laws in All Its Phases" and hence started her international anti-lynching campaign.

She became a tireless worker for women's suffrage: in the suffrage parade of 1913 organized by Alice Paul's Congressional Union, black women were asked to march in a segregated unit. Ida refused, and slipped into her state's delegation after the start of the parade.

She was also a newspaper editor and publisher, the first black woman to be a paid correspondent for a mainstream white newspaper, an investigative journalist, co-founder of the NAACP, political candidate, mother, wife, and the single most powerful leader in the anti-lynching campaign in America.

# Inez Milholland

(1886–1916)

Came from wealthy and radical politics. As a student at Vassar College she started the suffrage movement, enrolled two-thirds of the students, and taught them the principles of socialism. After graduation she was refused admission at both Oxford and Cambridge law schools due to gender.

She worked for prison reform, world peace, and equality for African Americans. Milholland was a member of the NAACP, the Women's Trade Union League, the Equality League of Self Supporting Women in New York (Women's Political Union), the National Child Labor Committee, and England's Fabian Society. She was also involved in the National American Woman Suffrage Association, and the grass-roots radical National Woman's Party.

In 1913, she helped organize the suffrage parade in Washington D.C., which took take place the day before President Wilson's inauguration. She led the parade wearing a crown and a long white cape while riding atop a large white horse.

At the beginning of World War I, Milholland traveled overseas as a war correspondent where she composed pacifist articles, which led to her censure by the Italian government, which ousted her from the country.

In 1916, she went on a tour in the West speaking for women's rights despite suffering from deteriorating health. On October 22, 1916, she collapsed in the middle of a speech in Los Angeles, and died on November 25.

Milholland's last public words were, "Mr. President, how long must women wait for liberty?"

# Emily Wilding Davison

(1872–1913)

Was a militant activist who fought for women's suffrage in Britain. She joined the Women's Social and Political Union (WSPU) in 1906. Formed in 1903 by Emmeline Pankhurst, the WSPU brought together those who felt strongly that militant, confrontational tactics were needed in order to achieve women's suffrage. Wilding Davison gained a reputation as a militant and violent campaigner. On her own initiative and without WSPU approval, her actions developed from disrupting meetings to stone throwing and arson.

She was jailed on nine occasions and went on hunger strike and consequently force-fed 49 times. Many jailed suffragists went on hunger strikes to protest the government's refusal to classify them as political prisoners.

She is best known for stepping in front of King George V's horse Anmer at the Epsom Derby on 4 June 1913, sustaining injuries that resulted in her death four days later. Ms. Wilding Davison was known to keep her own counsel and so her intentions on that day are unknown. She may have decided to martyr herself; she may have intended to put a suffrage sash on the King's horse.

Her gravestone bears the WSPU slogan, "Deeds not words." Roughly 15 years after her death, Davison's dream was finally realized. Britain gave women the right to vote in 1928.

# introduction

The last time I was asked to make a public presentation about so-called domestic violence was to a medical school class where I was to sit on a panel of three adults—two women and me—and relate my experiences of being battered by my father.

That was the day I decided I could no longer contain my efforts to change the world within the neat confines of my personal story or to the subject for which I have been a much sought-after speaker—domestic violence perpetrator tactics. To continue to do so would be to selfishly fail the women and children to whom I am fiercely committed.

I was a social worker. I've given lectures and workshops across the country about "batterer tactics" and "batterer dynamics" and "batterer accountability." That's all fine, but it's not enough.

I did share some of the details of my past, and present, with the students that day—along with Khita and Elizabeth—two strong and brave women. It is crucially important these stories be told and heard.

Although I was battered, bullied and abused as a child by my father, I no longer find my story particularly noteworthy, compelling or even interesting.

What I do find compelling and noteworthy is the actual cause of domestic violence, and how that cause is in plain view for all to see who are foolhardy enough to take a peek.

I'm tired of women and children cowering, cringing, sobbing and begging for mercy while men rant, pontificate and rage as tyrants. I'm tired of women's bodies being used as human dart boards for men's arrogant gratification.

Batterers are men, only more so. I am on a course to address the "more so."

I'm tired of pleading with well-meaning audiences.

I'm tired of putting it in medical jargon so health professionals can "get it."

I'm tired of massaging it in therapeutic jargon so social workers can "get it."

I'm tired of crafting it in legalistic jargon so criminal justice professionals can "get it."

I'm tired of spoon-feeding it in palatable pap so men can "get it."

I'm tired of talking around the problem.

I'm sick to death of the problem, and the problem is Patriarchy, pure and simple. I'm sick to death of what Patriarchy has done to my family, our community, and our Earth.

I'm sick to death of NASCAR, Monday Night Football, the Elks, the military, the Catholics, the Taliban, the polygamists, the White supremacists and all of the other institutions whose primary purpose on this Earth is the perpetuation of patriarchal privilege and to groom me to ascend (descend?) to that throne.

I'm sick to death of wasting my life locking my doors and nagging my loved ones about the dangers men pose to us because Patriarchy has taught us men to think and behave like entitled, spoiled, cowardly blowhards.

I'm tired of husbands raping and strangling their wives and lovers, cutting them into pieces and throwing them into dumpsters along with the rest of their garbage.

I spent the first 18 years of my life surviving my father's relentless attempts, at the behest of Patriarchy, to crush the love, sensibility and kindness out of me so he could enjoy the throne of King and God in our household.

I've spent the last 30 years studying this rapacious, cruel and destructive parasitic organism called Patriarchy. I've done so by painfully peeling away the privileged layers of masculine veil from my eyes.

I have been an explorer of dangerous things. I have been, and am, a stranger in a familiar land. At this point in my journey, I am very proud to say I am ashamed to be a man under Patriarchy.

I see Patriarchy. I see it in the big things and I see it in the little things.

I have become a feminist. I have become a radical feminist. I am a hairy-legged radical feminist.

I have come to understand the only grace that has a chance of saving humans on earth, let alone the Earth herself, is feminism.

How many women reading this book can say with truthful certainty your father, brother, husband, male lover or son would choose to eat a bowl of live cockroaches rather than strike you or your children?

How miserable our world and reality is because of the worship of Patriarchy.

I will share some details of my life with you relating to my father's abuse of me and my family. I do so to explain how and what I am learning. But I refuse to leave my words and story on the doorstep of my childhood home—right where Patriarchy tells me to leave it.

I'm writing not to get your sympathy or your empathy. I'm writing to attempt to pull the veil from your eyes a little bit so you, too, can see the ugliness a little better.

You hereby enter the secret world of men—at your own peril. It is the foul, corrupt, privileged and cowardly world of men, masculinity and male privilege. It is those people and institutions that prop up His bloated undead corpse because it is expedient for them.

Although it is a secret world, it is not mysterious or even complex. No more so than a punch in the face. It is in fact our own reeling and disoriented brains that make it seem so—and so much the better for us men. The more confused, disheartened and ignorant are those who might otherwise challenge our privilege and demand justice, the better for the parasite that is Patriarchy.

I will not rest in my mission to hold Patriarchy accountable. I have no illusions I will be successful, but that won't stop me. I have no illusions I will escape paying a price, as I already have, but that won't stop me. I know Patriarchy will swat me like a harmless gnat, but I have a voice and I am going to use it.

I was battered by a man who enjoyed the benefits of Patriarchy. His tactics were the tactics of Patriarchy. This is where my education began. The tyrant teaches his traitor best. I am a traitor and this is what I have learned. I am limb by verse of the beast. His contemptible blood courses in my veins. When I gaze in the mirror, there he is. I am doomed to resist my habits, question my motives and look over my shoulder.

I deserve no special recognition because I am a man saying many of the same things women have been saying, and dying for saying, for literally centuries.

I want you to stand up from reading this book infuriated and trusting men a little less. I hope this book disturbs you.

# Speaking of Women

In education, in marriage, in religion, in everything, disappointment is the lot of women. It shall be the business of my life to deepen this disappointment in every woman's heart until she bows down to it no longer.

~ Lucy Stone
(1818–1882)

The more I see of men, the more I admire dogs

~ Jeanne-Marie Roland
(1754–1793)

To study psychological trauma is to come face-to-face both with human vulnerability in the natural world and with the capacity for evil in human nature. To study psychological trauma means bearing witness to horrible events. When the events are natural disasters or "acts of God," those who bear witness sympathize readily with the victim. But when the traumatic events are of human design, those who bear witness are caught in the conflict between victim and perpetrator. It is morally impossible to remain neutral in this conflict. The bystander is forced to take sides.

~ Judith Herman
(1942–)

Only when manhood is dead—and it will perish when ravaged femininity no longer sustains it—only then will we know what it is to be free.

~ Andrea Dworkin
(1946–2005)

One hundred women are not worth a single testicle.

~ Confucius
(551–479 BCE)

Reformers who are always compromising, have not yet grasped the idea that truth is the only safe ground to stand upon.

~ Elizabeth Cady Stanton
(1815–1902)

Ideally, what should be said to every child, repeatedly, throughout his or her school life is something like this: You are in the process of being indoctrinated. We have not yet evolved a system of education that is not a system of indoctrination. We are sorry, but it is the best we can do. What you are being taught here is an amalgam of current prejudice and the choices of this particular culture. The slightest look at history will show how impermanent these must be. You are being taught by people who have been able to accommodate themselves to a regime of thought laid down by their predecessors. It is a self-perpetuating system. Those of you who are more robust and individual than others will be encouraged to leave and find ways of educating yourself—educating your own judgments. Those that stay must remember, always, and all the time, that they are being molded and patterned to fit into the narrow and particular needs of this particular society.

~ Doris Lessing
(1919–)

The prolonged slavery of women is the darkest page in human history.

~ Elizabeth Cady Stanton
(1815–1902)

# in philogynous esteem

Feminism made a man out of me.

I thank the many women who have generously taught, inspired, and/or held me accountable. This does not imply any of them endorse what I've written or want to be associated with me, my opinions, or this book. I would have preferred to list all of their names but have chosen not to for a number of reasons.

The fact that so many strong, intelligent and assertive women have mentored and generally put up with me over the years is conclusive proof in itself feminists do have a bighearted sense of humor.

I dedicate this book to two women:

To *Mary Daly*: thank you for your intellect and courage, and for sharing it with us. I will never get over your passing, and I love you.

To *Elizabeth*: thank you for providing for my welfare in all ways as I follow this path. Thank you for loving me, inspiring me, putting up with me, and being a role model for all of us about what it takes and what it costs to treat women with respect and honor. I wish I were a big enough soul to love the world more than I love one person; alas, I am not.

## Speaking of Women

There are and will be those who think I have gone overboard. Let them rest assured that this assessment is correct, probably beyond their wildest imagination, and that I will continue to do so.

~ Mary Daly
(1928–2010)

I long to speak out the intense inspiration that comes to me from the lives of strong women.

~ Ruth Benedict
(1887–1948)

Feminism is hated because women are hated.

~ Andrea Dworkin
(1946–2005)

She [Mary Daly] taught us not only to think outside the box but then to ask, who put this box here and why?

~ Linda Barufaldi
(dates unknown)

My appreciation to MerAnoosh (Armenian for "Our sweet") who sat with me through the thick of the writing.

**Philogyny**: fondness, liking, or love for or of women.

# compendium of fulminations

*Feminism hasn't failed; it's just never been tried.*
~ Hilary Mantel
(1952-)

## premonitory

| | |
|---|---|
| frontispiece | 1 |
| title page | 3 |
| permission to use | 4 |
| introduction | 8 |
| in philogynous esteem | 11 |
| compendium of fulminations | 12 |
| admonitory & disclaimer | 14 |
| lexicon conjured in this fulmination | 16 |
| about the infidel | 20 |

## witnessing

| | |
|---|---|
| welcome to the penile colony | 23 |
| how would you like your Kryptonite | 27 |
| it's not dysfunctional if it's working | 36 |
| demaletarized zones | 42 |
| the metrics of ischogyny | 46 |
| my commitment to treason from Androputriarchy | 49 |
| take a walk on the reviled side | 54 |
| Androputriarchy played backward | 59 |
| the wall of fraudulence | 63 |
| which came first… the chicks or the fags | 74 |
| hate is overrated | 77 |
| bravely overcoming drunken deterrents | 83 |
| instant asshole | 88 |
| man robs bank – motive unknown | 93 |
| gender oppression full speed ahead | 98 |
| baby, why can't you just forgive and forget | 100 |
| who wears the pad in your family | 104 |
| mother's day proclamation | 106 |
| my abusive relationship was sent to prison | 108 |
| poppa quiz | 110 |
| are beavers victims of falling trees | 111 |
| i feel your pain | 114 |
| from sexual harassment to broad brushes | 118 |
| women trapped in brothel rescued after 1,873 days | 122 |
| is Patriarchy really malevolent | 124 |
| don't let him under your skin | 127 |
| operation peeved pencil | 132 |
| girls, boys, coons and bitches | 134 |
| if he quacks like a duck | 138 |
| bride burning | 142 |
| love and marriage | 145 |
| i know how you feel, man | 148 |
| unsinkable titanic | 151 |
| freeze frame | 154 |
| domestic homicide | 159 |
| he's a pedophile | 161 |
| sitting at the mall | 166 |
| batterers are men, only more so | 169 |
| what if she likes it | 172 |
| a most isolated incident | 175 |

wall street billionaire therapy group . . . . . . . .179
anger Mistermanagement . . . . . . . . . . . . . . . .182
which men should i trust . . . . . . . . . . . . . . . . .186
i have a communication problem, bitch . . . . . .190
seeing is believing -
    women should be believed . . . . . . . . . . . .192
i won't be seeing you . . . . . . . . . . . . . . . . . . . . 194
Androputriarchal semen-encrusted bliss . . . 203
goddam those fucking children. . . . . . . . . . . 207
are we leaving our men behind . . . . . . . . . . .214
i just don't understand, okay . . . . . . . . . . . . .219
bravery and knavery . . . . . . . . . . . . . . . . . . . .223
i can't believe he'd do something like that . . . 226

father knows best - price for sex . . . . . . . . . . 229
intimate patriarchal violence. . . . . . . . . . . . . 234
from the halls of montezuma . . . . . . . . . . . . .238
taking everything personally . . . . . . . . . . . . 242
are all clouds tornados . . . . . . . . . . . . . . . . . . 249
all women are: brave! strong! beautiful! . . . . . .251
am i a man hater . . . . . . . . . . . . . . . . . . . . . . 254
why, daddy . . . . . . . . . . . . . . . . . . . . . . . . . . 257
the slime trail less slithered . . . . . . . . . . . . . .261
how do we change Androputriarchy . . . . . . . 265
inoculating against Androputriarchy. . . . . . . 268
you can lead a batterer to help, but. . . . . . . . 272
what might male accountability look like . . . 277

*expositories*

the perfectly mangineered woman . . . . . . . . . .41
you don't have to be a feminist to
    hate Patriarchy. . . . . . . . . . . . . . . . . . . . . 45
feminist card carrying. . . . . . . . . . . . . . . . . . .53
straight white male for lesbian rights. . . . . . . 58
welcome to earth . . . . . . . . . . . . . . . . . . . . . . .81
instant assholes . . . . . . . . . . . . . . . . . . . . . . . 87
wanted by M.P.T.P.P. . . . . . . . . . . . . . . . . . . 97
yet another deadbeat dad. . . . . . . . . . . . . . . .103
take your son to brothel day . . . . . . . . . . . . . 117
burqa's or bikini's. . . . . . . . . . . . . . . . . . . . . .126
playing my r-ace card . . . . . . . . . . . . . . . . . .137
what do you get when you fall in love. . . . . . .141
roller dukes. . . . . . . . . . . . . . . . . . . . . . . . . . .147
Patriarchy - it doesn't get any better
    than this . . . . . . . . . . . . . . . . . . . . . . . . . .153
Sorry excuses. . . . . . . . . . . . . . . . . . . . . . . . .158
erectile dysfunction. . . . . . . . . . . . . . . . . . . . .165

till death do us part. . . . . . . . . . . . . . . . . . . . .171
pimp . . . . . . . . . . . . . . . . . . . . . . . . . . . . . . . .174
anger management strategies for men . . . . . . .185
this is what a feminist looks like. . . . . . . . . . .189
this is your brain on Patriarchy -
    women objectified . . . . . . . . . . . . . . . . . . .198
because i have a scrotum . . . . . . . . . . . . . . . . 206
guns for tots . . . . . . . . . . . . . . . . . . . . . . . . . .213
dilder's. . . . . . . . . . . . . . . . . . . . . . . . . . . . . . .233
all we need now is a button maker . . . . . . . . 247
this is your brain on Patriarchy -
    women silenced . . . . . . . . . . . . . . . . . . . .253
men are not pigs. . . . . . . . . . . . . . . . . . . . . . . 256
we can do it. . . . . . . . . . . . . . . . . . . . . . . . . . 260
on the job safety . . . . . . . . . . . . . . . . . . . . . . 267
draining lake Patriarchy. . . . . . . . . . . . . . . . . 276
this is your brain on Patriarchy -
    Earth raping . . . . . . . . . . . . . . . . . . . . . . 280

*lamentations*

daddy's little feminist . . . . . . . . . . . . . . . . . . .35
keepsakes . . . . . . . . . . . . . . . . . . . . . . . . . . . 82
fathers . . . . . . . . . . . . . . . . . . . . . . . . . . . . . .178

pleas and promises . . . . . . . . . . . . . . . . . . . . .218
hurricane . . . . . . . . . . . . . . . . . . . . . . . . . . . 222
you're next. . . . . . . . . . . . . . . . . . . . . . . . . . . 248

*sequent*

synthesis . . . . . . . . . . . . . . . . . . . . . . . . . . . .281
arcanum . . . . . . . . . . . . . . . . . . . . . . . . . . . 282

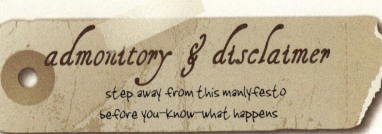

## admonitory & disclaimer
*step away from this manlyfesto before you-know-what happens*

**Admonitory** ~ Twenty reasons you might want to conceal the fact you are reading this book:

1. Your children will roll their eyes every time you start going on and on about "Androputriarchy."
2. Your husband/partner will add it to the list of why you shouldn't get child custody.
3. Your friends will start whispering you are a man-hating lesbian behind your back.
4. Your conservative friends and family will pray for your salvation and look upon your children with pity.
5. Your liberal friends and family will call you a punitive, sexist extremist.
6. Your creepy uncle George will think you are exotic and have all the more interest in forcing sex on you.
7. The police will say you had it coming.
8. Your mom will think you've been abducted by a cult.
9. Your brothers won't let you near their children unsupervised.
10. The Ku Klux Klan will burn a giant wooden vagina on your front lawn in the middle of the night.
11. The Pope and the Grand Ayatollah will issue a joint death fatwah on you.
12. The United States Air Force will discharge a "Hellfire" drone into your garage as a pre-emptive, collateral deterrent.
13. Your workplace will tactfully remind you that "kick him in the fucking nuts" is not on the list of customer service-approved responses.
14. Your gynecologist will politely and with decorum decline the invitation to join your witches' coven.
15. Your child's teacher will email to notify you the school board has voted unanimously to ban little Suzy's social studies poster based on this book.
16. Your probation officer will exasperatedly remind you one more door-blocking at the local "Gentleman's Club" will get you some serious time.
17. Your high school 20-year-anniversary organizing committee will "forget" to include your 5,000 word radical feminist polemic in the "What I'm thankful for now" section of the program.
18. You may be identified by the United States Centers for Disease Control as a geographic source-point for a calamitous outbreak of erectile dysfunction.
19. A friendly and oh-so-helpful social worker somewhere will concoct a personality disorder that remarkably resembles you, and unveil to the world a lengthy and quite expensive treatment regimen she/he will humbly offer to provide.
20. Having to wear the fake eyebrows, glasses and mustache outside of the house at all times will aggravate your isopropylidenebisphenol allergy.

## Disclaimer

The book you are about to read contains graphic language, distasteful scenarios and left of left-wing feminist vitriol. It is not suitable for all audiences. If you are under 18 years of age and not accompanied by a parent, guardian, or other adult you'll probably do a lot better than the rest of us chauvinistic dinosaurs.

Sitting through anything written by Mr. Marillynson has been demonstrated to cause irritation and vomiting in laboratory cockroaches, not to mention the following symptoms in human beings:

- elevated blood pressure
- vomiting
- dizziness
- tearing in the eyes
- excessive salivation
- increased heart rate
- sweating palms
- acute tourette's syndrome
- eye rolling
- labored breathing
- side to side shaking of head
- nausea
- itchy, swelling brain
- sudden evacuation of a room

If you experience any of these symptoms beyond 24 hours it is recommended you listen to right-wing radio until you achieve the effective stuporous dose, or until you feel like your old self again, whichever occurs first.

It is important to remember you should never attempt to duplicate anything presented here without proper training and supervision. Especially not on your unsuspecting, innocent little sister who never did anything to you except love and accept you.

In an attempt to respond therapeutically to the controversial nature of the comments you are about to read, I recommend you search the internet for Sensitive New-Age Guys (SNAG's) who are trained to "talk you down" should you begin to hyperventilate or have an overwhelming desire to write your Senator, agents of the Homeland Security Administration, or the person(s) or institution(s) who published this diatribe.

If, at any time during your reading, you imagine it helpful to request a listing of tedious research footnotes produced by humorless medical school dropouts with very thick eyeglasses whose only enjoyment in life is composing valid control groups, you will not find that in this book, I can assure you.

**Bon voyage!**

---

## Speaking of Women

Women may think like men, act like men, live the rules of the male world, and think they live in the male world until something happens that shows how wide the chasm really is.

~ Jessie Shirley Bernard
(1903–1979)

Revolution is the festival of the oppressed.

~ Germaine Greer
(1939–)

... the precision of all men whose souls do not exceed the limits of their uniforms.

~ Leslie Forbes
(dates unknown)

Our culture spends an inordinate amount of time and energy making sure girls become girls and boys become boys.

~ Mary Ellen S. Capek
(1980–)

# lexicon conjured in this fulmination

Androputriarchy controls our language, hence promoting words and their meanings which support the interests of male privilege, and omitting and/or discouraging words that could lead to awareness of reality and subsequent revolt. Given that fact, I have conjured some of my own words to help the process of insurrection along.

**Androconditional privilege:** some of the benefits of male privilege, entitlement, and oppression being conditionally extended by Androputriarchy and/or His agents to those who do not normally qualify: that is, women. For instance, a white, heterosexual woman who enjoys much affluence and power due to her marriage to a wealthy white, heterosexual male who will lose those conditional privileges upon being discarded by him.

**Androputriarchy:** [*andro* meaning male, man; *putrere*, meaning rotten, or proceeding from decay; *archy* meaning ruler] an alternative for "patriarchy" that attempts to make clearer the corruption, malevolence, and destructive blight that male supremacy has been in human history and remains to this day.

**Brotherhood refugee:** one who flees the wretched squalor of Androputriarchy in search of safety, sanity, and harmony in a merciful and conscientious world.

**Demaletarized zones:** 1. the embarrassing existence of any and all places on Earth that are better off in every way devoid of the presence of men and/or Androputriarchy; 2. a replacement for the insanely brilliant term "demilitarized zones" that unveils the truth about what these zones actually are; 3. a hope for the future when these zones are actually created, free of men, and exist for the welfare of women and children.

**Ecodestruction:** how our environment, identical to the treatment of women, has been and is being raped and plundered by Androputriarchy for the establishment, support, and perpetuation of necrophilic male-privileged values and interests.

**Horizontal hostility:** people of oppressed groups believing, acting on, or enforcing the dominant system of discrimination and oppression against themselves and others. This "hostility" can occur between members of the same group or between members of different, targeted groups. Basically, the old notion of "let's you and her fight."

**Intimate Patriarchal Violence (IPV):** a replacement for both "domestic violence" and the now-popular "intimate partner violence" because those terms obfuscate the perpetrator and His purpose: deliberate and pragmatic degradation, abuse, and violence used by men within the complicity and sanction of Androputriarchy to create and maintain male privilege at the expense of women. Intimate Patriarchal Violence is battering, and batterers are the perpetrators of Intimate Patriarchal Violence, whether male or male-identified.

**Ischogyny:** [*ischo*, meaning suppression or restraint; *gyny*, meaning women] the series of interlocking self-created and self-serving myths held, and behaviors, tactics, and actions taken by men/Androputriarchy, that enhance male bonding and male exaltation at the expense of women; the oppression of women. A replacement for "misogyny" which incorrectly concludes oppression of women is based on "hatred" of women, which it is not; so-called hatred is an incidental weapon.

**Jim Crow:** The term originated around 1928 from a white actor named Thomas Rice who performed in "black face" and took the stage-name Jim Crow, portraying an exaggerated, highly stereotypical and degraded black character. He was so successful "Jim Crow" became a stock character in minstrel shows, along with counterparts Jim Dandy and Zip Coon. Rice's subsequent blackface characters were Sambos, Coons, and Dandies. White audiences were receptive to the portrayals of blacks as singing, dancing, grinning fools. By the beginning of 1900, the words Jim Crow referred instead to Amerikkkan segregation laws, rules, and violent actions perpetrated by whites from when Reconstruction ended in 1877 and continued until the mid-1960s. Blacks who violated Jim Crow norms, for example, drinking from the white water fountain or trying to vote, risked their homes, their jobs, even their lives. Whites could and did assault and kill blacks with impunity. Blacks had little legal recourse against these assaults because the Jim Crow criminal justice system was all-white: police, prosecutors, judges, juries, and prison officials. Violence was instrumental for Jim Crow, and its most extreme form was lynching. Lynchings were public, sadistic murders carried out by white mobs. Many blacks resisted the indignities of Jim Crow and paid for their bravery with their lives.

**Maidyn name:** the name or names, created or existing, a boy or man gives himself once or more in his lifetime to honor and identify with his matrilineal lineage or any woman or groups of women he admires. As opposed to one's "surname" [sur meaning "above"] which is almost always patrilineal, or how women are expected to relinquish their name to a man upon marriage. Maidyn name is similar politically to how some African-Americans choose to disavow their "slave" names and embrace an African or other chosen name.

**Male privilege:** [*male*: from the Latin masculus – a male, a man; *privilege*: from the Latin privilegium – an exceptional law made in favor of any individual] a right, immunity, benefit, or advantage granted to a man, groups of men, or all men not enjoyed by women/children and usually detrimental to them.

**Maleism:** the worship, glorification and deification of men, maleness and so-called masculinity; the primary and deciding factor in the course of human affairs so far. Maleism and His entitlement, male privilege, is and has been malevolent, destructive, greedy, parasitic, oppressive, all-powerful, purposeful, successful, self-perpetuating, and diabolically veiled.

**Mastribel:** [*mas* meaning man; *tribus* meaning three; *belua*, meaning beast] the deadly three-headed beast of man/men/Androputriarchy.

**Men's Heritage Foundation:** is about inheritance; men's inheritance from men and Androputriarchy. This inheritance might include money, but always includes exalted status, entitlement, power, economic advantage, political advantage, religious advantage, primary access to opportunity, and admission to the boys club. It is intergenerational male privilege. It is a King's crown handed to all boys at birth. Like a scrotum, it comes with the penis. Men's Heritage Foundation are those undeserved privileges men accumulate over decades and centuries of oppressive entitlement, inequitable accumulation of resources, and unearned advantage that is passed down to male sycophants/mercenaries.

**Misterconception:** the simplistic and ridiculous lies, concoctions, deceptions, decoys, fabrications, falsehoods, fictions, illusions, obfuscations, fakes, frauds, ploys, scams, and Trojan horses created by Androputriarchy to confuse and baffle women, and legitimize abusive, selfish, and criminal behavior by men. For example, a Misterconception under Androputriarchy is that women who wear certain clothes in certain places at certain times want to be, deserve to be, or are to blame for being, raped. This is a misterconception concocted by men to benefit men at women's expense.

**Mistermanaged**: a replacement for "mismanaged" that reveals the completely volitional man-ner in which men purposefully and intentionally rig things for our own purposes and goals. For example, anger Mistermanagement: how men carefully use anger as a weapon and then cover it up as if it were unintentional or beyond our control.

**Mutualism** (biology): A type of symbiosis where two (or more) organisms from different species live in close proximity to one another and rely on one another for nutrients, protection, or other life functions. Both (or all) of the organisms involved benefit from the relationship.

**Necrophilia**: [*necro* meaning the dead, corpse, dead tissue; philia meaning unnatural attraction, tendency]: *"the most fundamental characteristic and first principle of patriarchy: hatred for and envy of Life; the universal message of all patriarchal religion: death worship."

**Parasitism** (biology): A type of symbiosis where two (or more) organisms from different species live in close proximity to one another and one (parasite) organism obtains food and other needs at the expense of the other (host).

**Patriarchy**: I purposely forgo this word in my fulminations. I use my word "Androputriarchy" instead. Although standard dictionary definitions of patriarchy do reveal the "men have authority over women" degeneracy, men have put lipstick on that pig and patriarchy is thought of as a benevolent thing. That's a lot of lipstick. **Patriarchy** (*The American Heritage® Dictionary of the English Language, Fourth Edition copyright ©2000 by Houghton Mifflin Company*): A social system in which the father is the head of the family and men have authority over women and children. A family, community, or society based on this system or governed by men.

**Patrifaction**: the corrosive effect upon anything and everything, especially female human beings, through exposure and vulnerability to Androputriarchy.

**Prepetrator**: the precedent for "perpetrator" and a replacement for "forefather" this word describes the generations of men who established the social environment that now entitles and enables your male perpetrator to abuse you.

**Problemism**: the deception used by Androputriarchy, and ignorantly accepted by the rest of us, to label highly successful strategies for maintaining power and control for men, male privilege, and Androputriarchy as "problems." For example, referring to so-called "domestic violence" as a "problem" couldn't be further from the truth—for Androputriarchy.

**Rapism\***: "the fundamental ideology and practice of patriarchy, characterized by invasion, violation, degradation, objectification, and destruction of women and nature; the fundamental paradigm of racism, classism, and all other oppressive –isms."

**Religionism**: how religion and spiritualism is Mistermanaged under Androputriarchy, regardless of the regional gerrymandering by men, for the establishment, support, and perpetuation of male privilege and male exaltation.

**Survivor**: a woman/child who continues to function or prosper in spite of opposition, hardship, physical/sexual assault, or other setbacks imposed by Androputriarchy.

**Wealthism**: how money is Mistermanaged under Androputriarchy, regardless of the regional gerrymandering by men, for the establishment, support, and perpetuation of male privilege and male exaltation.

**Weave of absence**: all of the purposeful tactics and strategies used by Androputriarchy, and their cumulative results, to make women and/or men invisible when it is in Androputriarchy's interest.

---

\* "Websters' First New Intergalactic Wickedary of the English Language" by (my shero) Mary Daly.

# Speaking of Women

If women speak Standard English, we're unimaginative and stupid. If we don't, we're sluts as well. Male ineptitude becomes, as usual, a virtue.

~ Julia Penelope
(1941–2013)

The issue, simply stated, is power: who has it and who doesn't. Men do the things they do to protect their territory. The boundaries are sometimes shifting and fuzzy, but men will defend to the death every square inch of what they believe they "own." In this conflict, control of language is the crucial weapon white men must keep from their enemies because it is the first and most important method for internalizing oppression in the minds of those they oppress. Language is an intangible, almost invisible weapon. Its messages are implanted in our minds when we are babies and left there to maintain our allegiance to men and their institutions. If the oppressed are convinced that we deserve to be oppressed and can hope for nothing better, the oppressors' work is done with only an occasional show of power.

~ Julia Penelope
(1941–2013)

Give us that grand word "woman" once again,
And let's have done with "lady"; one's a term
Full of fine force, strong, beautiful, and firm,
Fit for the noblest use of tongue or pen:
And one's a word for lackeys.

~ Ella Wheeler Wilcox
(1855-1919)

Woman under patriarchy has faced an inhuman choice: to do without an identity, or to identify with what she is not.

~ Avital Ronell
(1952-)

The first excuse given to the civilized world for the murder of unoffending Negroes was the necessity of the white man to repress and stamp out "race riots."... It was always a remarkable feature in these insurrections and riots that only Negroes were killed during the rioting, and that all the white men escaped unharmed.

~ Ida B. Wells
(1862-1931)

I asked them why... one read in the synagogue service every week the "I thank thee, O Lord, that I was not born a woman... It is not meant in an unfriendly spirit, and it is not intended to degrade or humiliate women." But it does, nevertheless. Suppose the service read, 'I thank thee, O Lord, that I was not born a jackass.' Could that be twisted in any way into a compliment to the jackass?

~ Elizabeth Cady Stanton
(1815-1902)

When we speak we are afraid our words will not be heard or welcomed. But when we are silent, we are still afraid. So it is better to speak.

~ Audre Lorde
(1934-1992)

So what we have in effect, each of us, is miles and miles of underground corridors full of filing cabinets in which we are busily filing mountains of data every day. Somewhere in these endless subterranean storage cabinets, women have a unique file entitled "teaching what it means to be female in a male world."... The miraculous part of an epiphany is that when the file bursts, and all the file data flows into the conscious mind, they are perfectly organized; they present one with conclusions. I knew instantly what the women's movement was all about; I knew it in my very bones.

~ Sonia Johnson
(1936-)

## about the infidel
## michael elizabeth marllynson

### Androputriarchy-approved credentials:

Mike received his Masters of Social Work degree from the University of Michigan; his Bachelors of Social Work degree from Eastern Michigan University (Summa Cum Laude - 3.91); his Associates in General Studies degree from Washtenaw Community College (Summa Cum Laude - 4.00).

He was a member of the Phi Kappa Phi National Honor Society and President of the Student Social Work Organization at Eastern Michigan.

Mike was an Honoree at the Third Statewide Summit of the Michigan Domestic Violence Prevention & Treatment Board and at his state's Third Annual Batterer Intervention Services Coalition Conference. Mike was selected the Distinguished Alumni of the Year by the Eastern Michigan University School of Social Work.

Mike was engaged as a social worker in the following areas and activities: day treatment services for chronically mentally ill adults; jail-based drug and alcohol treatment; inpatient and outpatient drug and alcohol treatment; psychotherapy for individuals and couples; batterer accountability services.

Mike was engaged as a social worker in the following aspects of public education regarding the coordinated community prevention of domestic violence: co-founder of a state batterer intervention services coalition; faculty of a university lifelong learning program; bachelors and masters level student field placement supervisor; twelve presentations on local, statewide and/or national television; three training videotapes for state law enforcement officers; two radio interviews; interviewed by and/or wrote articles for 18 publications; keynote speaker at 18 conferences; presenter in over 50 professional workshops; presented over 75 in-services for his peers; created the kNOw EXCUSES poster and Coordinated Community Action Model posters (both at http://www.csswashtenaw.org/ada/resources/poster.html); guest speaker at over 50 university classes and three high school classes; presented testimony to his state legislature on three occasions.

Mike is a great guy all around, thoroughly indoctrinated in all of the Androputriarchy-approved dogma and propaganda required of him to be an "expert," and behaved himself more or less until he was incurably infected with feminism.

### mike approved credentials:

- I survived my father (dead, thankfully) who was a wife and child batterer.
- I was proclaimed "Honorary Woman" on two separate occasions by my work peers.
- I am a kidney donor.
- I've donated over eight gallons of blood to the Red Cross.
- I initiated bi-monthly family meetings in our home in 2001 and have benefitted from them since: they teach accountability, democracy, and problem solving to all family members.
- I have benefitted from psychotherapy, both by myself and with a partner, over a half dozen times in my life.
- Though not vegan, I have been a non-meat eater for over 35 years.

- I "published" an internet listserve called Speaking of Women from 1996 until 2001 to 200+/- subscribers that offered the words, reflections and experiences of women past and present.
- I participated in the 1994 Gay Games in New York City with the Motor City Blade Runners men's ice hockey team, and the 2006 Gay Games in Chicago with the Philadelphia Phury men's ice hockey team.
- I had the honor of being recognized for my support of the LGBT community at the Triangle Foundation's annual banquet in 1995.
- I have been a supporter, with my money and with my time, of feminist, animal rights, anti-racist, and gay/lesbian/bisexual/transgender rights causes.
- I have changed my legal name twice to reflect my connection to the women in my life.
- I co-founded the Battered Women and Children's Memorial Garden.
- I grieve on Memorial Day, Veterans Day, President's Day, Flag Day, Independence Day, Columbus Day, Penis Day, and all other days, events, ceremonies, and solemn occasions which promote and enforce the worship of men and male privilege.
- I support labor unions. Being sole proprietor of a business and working alone I had, as you can imagine, some difficulty unionizing myself. However, after much searching the Coalition of Labor Union Women generously took me in, and I am a proud dues-paying Associate Member of CLUW.
- I always leave the toilet seat down.
- I seek the company, wisdom, and leadership of women.
- I have no male friends.

## About my name

My name is not legally Michael Elizabeth Marillynson, although I have legally changed my name twice in my adult life. In both instances I did so to reflect my relationship with a woman, and my desire to honor women. For example, I went through the court process to replace my childhood-given middle name with my partner's first name. Hence, Michael Elizabeth.

Given my revulsion of Androputriarchy it is likely I will eventually discard my "surname" which, like most humans on earth, follows the patrilineal pattern of me being branded with my father's lineage. Neither my father nor Patriarchy has done anything to earn that acknowledgement.

If I were to change my surname today I would use my nom de guerre "Marillynson," as I am the son of Marillyn. I would do so to affiliate myself with those who have loved, nurtured, and mentored me. That has been women. This would be my new **maidyn name.**

> **Maidyn name:** the name or names, created or existing, a boy or man gives himself once or more in his lifetime to honor and identify with his matrilineal lineage or any woman or groups of women he admires. As opposed to one's "surname" [sur meaning "above"] which is almost always patrilineal, or how women are expected to relinquish their name to a man upon marriage. Maidyn name is similar politically to how some African-Americans choose to disavow their "slave" names and embrace an African or other chosen name.

# Speaking of Women

The law of grab is the primal law of infancy.

~ Antoinette Brown Blackwell
(1825–1921)

It can be less painful for a woman not to hear the strange, dissatisfied voice stirring within her.

~ Betty Friedan
(1921–)

I remember and I make sure my daughters know, it was old biddies like we are now and young women who brought the King down. We are the Revolution, ladies, and we carry it in our blood to the future.

~ Marge Piercy
(1936–)

Pornography doesn't burn by itself; it needs your help.

~ Nikki Craft
(1949–)

I wanna be part of the problem.

~ Nikki Craft
(1949–)

People get used to anything. The less you think about your oppression, the more your tolerance for it grows. After a while, people just think oppression is the normal state of things. But to become free, you have to be acutely aware of being a slave.

~ Assata Shakur
(1947–)

## men have taught me some things about male privilege

welcome to the penile colony

This is the appetizer before the main course: if the list excites, this book is for you.

**Male:** (Latin: masculus—a male, a man.) Of, characteristic of, or suitable for members of this sex; masculine; virile; strong; vigorous.

**Privilege:** (Latin: privus—separate, peculiar, and lex, a law.) A right, immunity, benefit, or advantage granted to some person, group of persons, or class not enjoyed by others and sometimes detrimental to them.

The deification and worship of males, men, and **Androputriarchy** is the root of all human evil on Earth today.

Batterers, rapists, bullies, stalkers, reproductive rights clinic bombers, heterosexists, racists, child abusers, animal abusers, environment destroyers, religious fanatics, dictators, "honor" killers, sex-traffickers, and torturers are men, only more so.

Male privilege is founded upon, and demands, the worshipping of men and maleness at the expense of women, children, and nature.

Men who batterer, abuse, and rape wives, womenfriends, partners, children, and family are the front-line soldiers in the worldwide war on women and children.

Disloyalty to Androputriarchy is punishable by death, torture, poverty, ridicule, career destruction, forced separation from family, imprisonment, acid attacks, maiming, dismemberment, foot binding, castration, poisoning, burning alive, and aborted female fetuses, among other punishments.

Ongoing resistance to male privilege will change your personal, familial and professional world forever.

Male bonding as it is expressed in the world today, as an act of solidarity between men at the expense of women and children, is far more dangerous, destructive, and significant than any individual man's violence.

Male bonding is a seductive yet resistible force on men, but few men choose to resist.

Men control language, language controls everything, and men use language to subjugate women, children, and nature.

Male privilege is, and has always been, the largest organized religion on Earth. All other patriarchal religions, for example Christianity, Islam, Hinduism, Buddhism, Taoism, Confucianism, Shinto, Sikhism, Judaism, etc. are sub-religions of the one true faith: Androputriarchy.

Under Androputriarchy, girls, boys and women's bodies are mandated to be accessible first and foremost for boys and men's pleasure, control, and/or destruction.

Androputriarchy, as it exists in the world today, is a form of parasitism. That is, men as a herd benefitting from their

**Androputriarchy:** [*andro* meaning male, man; *putrere,* meaning rotten, or proceeding from decay; *archy* meaning ruler] an alternative for "patriarchy" that attempts to make clearer the corruption, malevolence, and destructive blight that male supremacy has been in human history and remains to this day.

close relationship with their "host"—women, while women are mostly harmed by the relationship.

The more any social institution, movement and/or organization, or any individual man enjoys legitimacy under Androputriarchy, the more it/he should be held suspect.

To extract concessions from Androputriarchy we are forced to appeal to men's self-interest—never their empathy or righteousness. If not, then by force.

Under Androputriarchy we all live in and have to devote enormous amounts of our human essence adapting to and surviving a world occupied by a hostile (male) army.

Social workers, psychologists, counselors, psychiatrists and their ilk are willing and destructive tools of Androputriarchy unless they make feminist career-threatening decisions to advocate for and empower women and children, and have proven this with their actions.

Women who do not fear men are a testimonial to male privilege—either to resistance, collusion or submission.

Our school systems, colleges, universities and research institutions are bulwarks of male privilege and Androputriarchy and, at the very least, defend and sustain the status quo.

Male privilege is founded on, among a great many other things, the silencing of women and children's voices.

**Horizontal hostility** is orchestrated by and crucial to the purposefully oppressive and self-interested success of Androputriarchy.

So-called "reverse discrimination" is a mediocre tactic used by whites that is actually white male privilege—doubled. Although mediocre as a notion, it is wildly popular and successful due to the racism, self-interest, and stupidly

brilliant self-delusion of white people, and white males in particular.

Pornography is unconscionable and unforgivable violence perpetrated on women and children by men. If men stopped the production, distribution and use of pornography tomorrow it would take generations before the human race recovered from this scourge.

The term "political correctness" was a tactic invented by powerful white males to silence women who seek justice and it works very well.

All men benefit from men's violence, and all men can and are responsible to make it stop.

Acknowledging we are, in fact, a man-hating world (and rightly so) is far too dangerous, so we direct our rage toward women and children—a safer target—instead.

Men, as a herd and individually, have caused untold anger, hatred, resentment and enmity. Ironically, these emotions are absolutely necessary for women to the resistance and overthrow of Androputriarchy—and of course are vilified as individualistically unhealthy and not suitable for women or children.

Under Androputriarchy a man's physical presence always acts to silence women.

Male privilege allows primary power to men only (mostly heterosexual and white), so women and children must fight over what is left—and are ridiculed for doing so.

Due to the advantages of male privilege, men have gratefully learned to be superficial, impatient, lazy, undisciplined, weak-minded, and demonstrate little interest in courage, benevolence, or endurance.

The use, and threatened use, of violence is necessary in any social system based on inequitable and self-interested lies, like in Androputriarchy. Violence is but one of the many oppressive measures meted out by Androputriarchy to cover up His lies and crimes.

It is indicative of the smooth operation of male privilege and Androputriarchy that women not be aware of, nor desire to be aware of, the depth and fervor with which men disrespect, loathe, and hold them in utter contempt and disdain.

Under Androputriarchy as we know Him today, men gathering in groups for any reason unsupervised by women, is inherently dangerous and ill-advised.

**Horizontal hostility:** people of oppressed groups believing, acting on, or enforcing the dominant system of discrimination and oppression against themselves and others. This "hostility" can occur between members of the same group or between members of different, targeted groups. Basically, the old notion of "let's you and her fight."

"Reasoning" with men and "saying it in a way they can hear it" is a game women have been forced to play that has demonstrated little or no significant or lasting success—other than to the benefit of Androputriarchy.

So-called "prostitution"—actually the serial rape, sexual humiliation, torture and slavery of women—reminds all women they are better off submitting to their male oppressors, especially husbands, than to face the nightmare of the alternative. "Prostitutes" do not exist: prostituted women are, unfortunately, plentiful.

Women and children's mere survival under Androputriarchy is, by definition, successful resistance to its crushing effects. All women resist male privilege.

Resisting male privilege makes you a feminist whether you like it or not.

Men will never, ever willingly capitulate male privilege—it will have to be thrown off by women.

Making male privilege visible is a necessary step for the overthrow of Androputriarchy, and will exact a dear price on those who engage in its actualization.

A man's attitudes, interests and actions regarding sex are probably the single most revealing and useful measure of his (dis)respect for women and children and his male bonding with Androputriarchy.

Not one violent, abusive, or disrespectful thing men and/or Androputriarchy has ever done was a mistake or unintended. The oppressive, parasitic scourge that is Androputriarchy as we know Him is purposeful, planful, goal-oriented, intended, extremely effective, and malevolent to women and children.

Men, as a herd, have no interest in women as human beings with individual identities and interests. What we are interested in is your compliance with the status quo under Androputriarchy.

History has abundantly shown us the absence of men in a geographic, psychic, institutional or any other human location/area has proven to make it more peaceful, safe, just, advanced, intelligent, and a sought-after place to be.

Women and children's centuries of resistance to, and survival of, Androputriarchy are far more inspirational, educational, rich, dynamic, and beneficial to teach our children than any endeavor men have engaged in.

Someone is trafficking, beating, prostituting, raping, renting the mouths, vaginas and anuses of, and murdering millions and millions of women and children in this world. The odds are very high it is one or more of the men in your family.

The "isms"—racism, sexism, heterosexism, religionism, wealthism, etc. are all sub-persecutions to the Father and King of all tyrannies: Androputriarchy.

Violence, abuse, and sexual assault doesn't come in "families" or "relationships" or "marriages" or "households" or "couples" or "homes" or "backgrounds" or "romances:" it is perpetrated by men onto others to further their interests.

Women have been telling us men long enough, even though we have no intention of listening: the personal is political. Men: I hold you personally responsible for your part, and your forefathers part, in Androputriarchy, from the worldwide war on women to how you treat every human being in your life—especially your family members.

Accountability (along with sunlight) is the best disinfectant for Androputriarchy and male privilege. Accept no substitutes.

---

Religionism: how religion and spiritualism is Mistermanaged under Androputriarchy, regardless of the regional gerrymandering by men, for the establishment, support, and perpetuation of male privilege and male exaltation.

# Speaking of Women

The whole history of the progress of human liberty shows that all concessions yet made to her august claims have been born of earnest struggle... If there is no struggle, there is no progress. Those who profess to favor freedom, and yet deprecate agitation, are men who want crops without plowing up the ground, they want rain without thunder and lightning. They want the ocean without the awful roar of its many waters.

~ Frederick Douglass
(1818–1895)

Society, being codified by man, decrees that woman is inferior; she can do away with this inferiority only by destroying the male's superiority. All oppression creates a state of war.

~ Simone De Beauvoir
(1908–1986)

Every religion oppresses women. I talk about the Koran because I know this book best. It allows for torture and other mistreatment, especially for women. And I despise the Sharia laws. They cannot be changed. They must be thrown out, abolished.

~ Taslima Nasrin
(1962–)

If justice were king,
Neither female nor male would lose,
But mostly, I am certain
Custom reigns, rather than justice.

~ Christine de Pisan
(1364–1431)

lessons from running a batterer accountability program

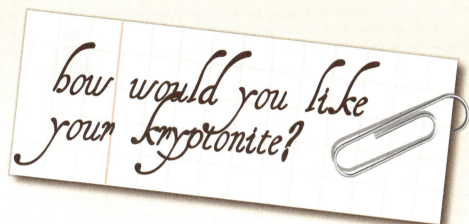
*how would you like your kryptonite?*

### How, indeed

After being utterly immersed in batterer accountability work on the local, regional, state, and national levels for over 11 years, the only good thing I can say for certain that came out of it was my expanded awareness about Androputriarchy and my strengthened commitment to fight for women's rights.

I hope other good things came out of it, but I can't with any certainty say anything did. Given the resources required to enable me to have these experiences, and the certain risk this type of work put battered women in, and all of the women in the affected communities, I can't say it was justified or I am not complicit in yet further antics that obfuscated actual justice for women and children.

I considered myself a feminist before I started in this work in 1988. My immersion into the world of batterers, and the incredibly courageous women engaged in fighting for justice, gave me a victim's-eye-view of reality that indebts my life to remain loyal to the disempowered, lead the discussion, ask questions, challenge gendered assumptions, expose and oppose oppression, apply accountability, honor diversity, practice responsible environmental stewardship, speak truth to power, make privilege visible, and eradicate misogyny.*

I left the work of batterer accountability, and the career of social worker, on January 1, 2000 for the same reasons. Aside from various workplace dramas of no importance, it was clear the support I enjoyed for 11 years to make a nuisance of myself in the service of battered women and children was being systematically eroded and I was faced with a tipping point of compromise I could no longer abide.

Unlike most people engaged in that type of work then, as today, I had a commitment to be accountable to battered women and children and to use myself as a medium for justice. When it became clear I would instead be forced to muzzle myself and my passion so as to engage in politesse, compromise with moronic social workers and probation officers, and have to look battered women in the eyes and know I was with cowardice compromising with their assailants and conspirators to keep my job and get a paycheck, I had a choice to make.

At that point I was being censored by my employer, gagged by my state and national social work organizations, and muzzled by my state batterer intervention coalition. I could no longer advocate for women as a social worker in a way acceptable to me, and I didn't want to do anything else as a social worker—I had been completely captivated by my growing feminist understanding of the world and wouldn't be satisfied playing social work do-gooder in a cubicle somewhere.

That decision, although difficult, was life-saving for me. I have been successfully self-employed for the past 13 years, and free to speak my mind about all things related to Androputriarchy. It doesn't mean I am not still punished for my views, but I say them nonetheless.

To all of the battered women and children, and those courageous women who advocated for them, who may have suffered in some way due to my "career" as a batterer accountability intervener, I apologize to you. If you were or are angry or outraged with me, you have every right to be.

---

* Guiding Principles of the Battered Women and Children's Memorial Garden (www.memgarden.org)

I do not seek so-called "forgiveness" or "forgetting" as it is none of my business how you may feel about me, and these things would not help my accountability for my past, nor my desire to continue getting smarter about demanding justice for women. If I harmed you I am to blame. I continue to educate myself about the tactics of Androputriarchy, male privilege, and what male accountability could look like, including in my own life. I will keep doing so.

After much soul-searching, and the adamant urging of a few cherished women in my life, I decided to write these "field notes." I write it not because I am interesting or noteworthy, because I am not; I write it because I am blessed to have the experiences I have had and hope a lesson or two I learned might be useful to someone somewhere. I write it in solidarity with women, children, animals, and our declining environment.

## Don't take it personally

One of the customs of workshop presenters is to utilize a brief questionnaire for feedback from audience members to be pondered over after all is said and done. I tended to get the extremes of comments: on one end were the women with feminist leanings who loved what I was saying and thought it astounding coming from a man. In the middle were all of the social work-types that wanted to maintain their pretense of "professionalism" and made vanilla, inane comments intended to make them look smarter than me. On the other end were the men and male-identified women who personally wanted to crush a sensitive part of my reproductive anatomy under their heels, or so they intimated.

The "feedback" from the latter group usually included such charming observations as: you have a lot of father issues and you are taking it out on men; you're a man-hater; you should be fired from your job; you have been sold on the feminist agenda; it's not as simple as you say it is; you sound more like a cop than a therapist (actually, that one I liked); you are just giving your political opinions; what's this got to do with patriarchy?; you just complain and don't give any solutions; back off on the subjective opinions—too controversial; you have unresolved anger and resentment issues;

you are too emotional; you are not open minded; you are too radical; why do you have to be so confrontational?; you are a bad role model; why do you hate Alcoholics Anonymous?; you are not professional; you battered us; you treated us like batterers.

I worked by butt off to learn everything I could about battering and batterers. The more I learned, the more outraged and determined I got. I conducted public presentations two to three times per week at times, in addition to my full-time family and job. I made lots of mistakes—oftentimes in large rooms full of people. I am an "errors of commission" type of person instead of "errors of omission." I said what I thought and if I was wrong I allowed myself to be ashamed and embarrassed for about 24 hours. I would then figure out how I was wrong, get it right, and get back to the effort. I challenged my accountability at work and at home.

A couple of years into this work I was brought into a meeting with the three (male) district court judges of my city to be dressed down because I apparently had caused someone's death. The judges had been visited by the wife (victim) of one of the batterers in our program who shot himself (dead) and told them it was our fault because of how we treated him in our batterer accountability program. The holy triumvirate, as punishment (they needed a scapegoat and I knew how to baa-a-a-a-a) for my mysterious ability to kill, insisted, if I wanted the court to continue sending batterers to our program, I take a class on the psychology of suicide and we gather research on the validity and reliability of our program model.

Dutifully, I did as coerced. I went to the local "king of suicide"—a local college professor who was the acknowledged expert on suicide, and he generously allowed me to monitor his class. Result: he laughed at my dilemma and assured me there is no reliable way to predict suicide.

We spent literally a year amassing a sizeable heap of research articles on the relative effectiveness of batterer accountability efforts and how we had integrated them into our program. We then got all dressed up like real purrfeshinnuls and presented our findings to the monthly meeting of our Advisory Council, which included the head of probation of that court (the judges propose; the flunkies dispose). The result? Absolutely none. The court couldn't care less. They didn't spend three minutes going over our documentation. They merely trotted out new cretinous complaints about us and our program.

After a week or two of erupting and ruminating and erupting some more, it finally dawned on me (I'm fast catching on about some things; slow at others) what was happening: it was all a ruse! It was sleight of hand. The court couldn't care less about this guy offing himself or what they asked us for—they just wanted to keep us back on our heels, on the defensive, and compliant.

They knew that to silence the message, they should attack the messenger. This was the moment I learned it wasn't personal. It wasn't about me. There was nothing more or less wrong or deficient about me than the next person (at least not that way). They just didn't want to hear the message I was delivering, and I was the only one who would deliver it.

This realization changed my life. I was astounded at how thick I had been to be hoodwinked this way. For some idiotic reason I thought it was all a reasonable request and our sincere efforts to address the court's "concerns" would result in love flowing all around!

Ha ha ha ha ha ha ha ha! What a happy-go-lucky stooge I had been!

It was liberating now to grasp the tactic I had been laboring under, and it freed up so much more of my passion and energy to do the work. I was twice the pain in their ass once I wasn't wasting so much of my life's blood on the merry-go-round.

## Welcome to the female race

One of the ways I discovered "professionals" in "systems" I worked around tried to control and silence me was by "feminizing" me. That is, social workers, probation officers, judges, and their ilk attempted to discredit me to the public, and shame me personally, by labeling me with so-called "feminine" terms. That is, I was called "gay" and "too emotional" and "not properly detached from your work" and "you act like a victim" and "too sensitive" and, of course, "too submissive to the women at the domestic violence shelter."

This tactic I figured out more quickly, probably because I was flattered.

## Are you sure?

People were usually surprised when I told them batterers are generally very poor arguers. Even the really intelligent ones didn't do so well when their accountability was challenged in group. I learned to see it as their three-step argumentation method; first, they tell their victim to do something; second, if they don't get what they want they tell their victim to do it or else; third, if they are not getting what they want, they hit her. Works far more often than not.

But it doesn't teach how to argue with cogent accountability. So when the men came into the groups and were expected to explain themselves, their excuses and lies and blaming fell apart very quickly.

## Sit down and...

I don't remember when I first started doing it, or why, but long ago I began one of the feminist male-resistance acts which has now become a many times daily re-enactment of stunning bravery: I sit down when I pee.

You might be surprised how many comments this has garnered me over the last 30 years—from men. They all think something is wrong with me. Little do they know.

This is one of those ugly little make-believe man-rituals that men will not violate for fear that their privilege license—penis—might fall off and then where would they be? More importantly, who would they be?

Penises always get me thinking about batterers, and any which way I could figure it, I came to the same place: a foundation of male privilege and hence a solution to the plague of male privilege is about the entitlement of males to get someone else (hmmm... let me think—women?) to clean up their messes for them.

I used to conjecture to audiences that I was such a brilliant behavior modification tactician I devised a plan where I could extinguish, in just one generation of males, the habit of all men standing up when they pee. How? By requiring all men, and only men, to be responsible to keep clean all toilets on Earth.

This requirement would "extinguish" men's groveling interest in standing while peeing in favor of having less mess to clean up come chore day. Not to worry: we'd find some other foul way of demonstrating our "manhood."

The simple imperative that boys and men are responsible to clean up their own messes, without exception, is a profound revelation. It pierces through the gaudy trappings and ostentation that attempt to make male privilege appear appropriate, and gives a simple but brutally effective course of action to save ourselves.

## Say what?

In the past, I was asked to come in to communities—always by long-time feminist activists in those communities—to be a keynote speaker at conferences intended to initiate a coordinated community response to domestic violence. This meant having all of the "key players" in attendance who would be needed to create and maintain such a response: domestic violence shelter staff; judges, prosecutors, and probations officers from the courts; police and sheriff staff; health care professionals; mental health staff; politicians; drug and alcohol treatment people; battered women; batterer intervention people, etc.

I was the "500-pound gorilla" brought in to set off the dynamite of ideas, and then head out of town so the activists could use the tensions left over to get things going. This appeared to be a successful formula as I was asked to do this over and over again. I was happy to be invited and thrilled to speak my mind to such audiences.

The sad part was the fact pointed out to me every time I participated in these meetings by the women who invited me: "We've been telling these male judges (prosecutors, probations officers, cops, physicians, therapists, politicians, etc.) for years what you just told them, but when it comes out of the mouth of a man they all finally hear it for the first time."

I have yet to figure out if my appearance at such events empowered, or disempowered, the women who were trying to make their communities better.

## The alpha to omega

Related to "cleaning up their own mess" above, I learned accountability is everything in dealing with male privilege. Note I didn't say "dealing with batterers"—I found working with the batterers themselves was the part of my job I enjoyed the most. It was dealing with the people around the batterers, the courts, social workers, and addiction counselors in particular, that was at all times a bitter and losing struggle.

Focusing in on a batterer's clumsy attempts to divert attention from his accountability is both simple and doable if they are put into a position where they have to sit still for it. That comes in basically two forms: those men who were court-ordered into our program, and those that were "victim-ordered." There never were, nor will there ever be, any "voluntary" men in a batterer accountability program, no matter how much anyone desires you to think otherwise.

Accountability is a fascinating thing. We had a few men (out of thousands) who stayed on in our program after they completed the 52-week minimum requirement—some for many years—and I think their primary interest in staying on was about the effects accountability can have on one's life and mind. I'm not saying here that any of these men had an interest in accountability to women, or for their own past behavior, necessarily. There is no way to ascertain that from sitting in a group room with them.

It is a completely different beast in dealing with the arrogance, privilege, entitlement, and vicious clinging-to-power that is encountered when dealing with judges, prosecutors, probation officers, cops, physicians, therapists, politicians, etc. These so-called professionals looked absolutely no different than the batterers: they were contaminated with the same corruption that comes from male privilege and entitlement. However, they were far more intractable in their willingness to be accountable because there was nothing forcing them to do so.

If I could work with batterers only, I would probably still be doing it. It was these other people who drove me from the work. I don't say that as a "victim" and I don't say it with pride. I only did this work professionally for about 12 years. There are women activists dealing with us stupid men for half a century and continue on after countless battles lost and lives destroyed. They continue to tirelessly witness for justice and accountability. These are the bravest, most incredible people I've had the honor to know.

## With friends like me, who needs enemies?

If there is someone out there who can tell the world the truth about Androputriarchy, publically demand accountability regarding male privilege, and stand up to the entrenched interests of men—and be universally liked—I'd like to know who that person is.

In the meantime I'd like to warn you, from my personal experience, publicly witnessing for male accountability will make you very unpopular, including among most women.

The latter was not an easy lesson for me. It was difficult for me to coincide my desire to work for women's interests and at the same time be assailed by women. I learned it came with the territory and helped me dig deeper in my understanding of how Androputriarchy works, and the paltry options it leaves women. It was also a constant reminder of my own male privilege and how it clouded my view.

I also found, despite the myriad "professionals" who let me know they were much smarter and slicker than I, when you actually get to the point of holding batterers to account, it is not convenient, comfortable, or non-conflictual no matter how you pretend it is otherwise. I had so many social work-types say stupid stuff like, "you've got to develop a relationship" with the batterers before you hold them accountable, or other variations on the theme of not being so blunt. However, when I observed others waste time on all of the window dressing before actually confronting the batterer with the truth, it just meant it took three months to get to the explosion instead of the 30 minutes I took. Obviously, I preferred the 30-minute version. However, it doesn't do much for one's social life.

## One for all

Another one of the dilemmas I struggled with was being confronted by battered women who were very angry about "mandatory" or "preferred" arrest policies in domestic violence cases.

Mandatory and preferred arrest policies adopted by police agencies means the officers are either required or expected to arrest someone they conclude through their own "information and belief" is a perpetrator of domestic assault and/or battery. This is instead of the age-old policy of doubling the trauma of battered women and only arresting and/or prosecuting batterers if their victims are "willing" to press charges and/or testify "against" him.

What some women objected to with "mandatory" or "preferred" arrest is that the judicial system was disempowering them, individually, by taking the option of prosecution out of their hands. I had to sit with this one for a while to figure out where I stood on it. I concluded, even if it does disempower some women, it is a policy enacted in an attempt to empower women as a group, and hold all men as a group to account for their actions. For that reason I wholeheartedly support the policy for the greater good.

## You might win some, you definitely lose most

"Why do you keep doing this work if you are so negative about it?"

This is one of those questions that reveals more about the asker than the askee. However, I do think it deserves an answer even if the reason for the question is not on the up-and-up.

I can't say my answer sheds a very good light on me. I thought about this a lot and insisted our program talk about it: should we be doing this work at all? For example, there is scant research evidence any of our efforts make a significant change in any of the batterers. Far more important than that, what message does it send battered women and children and to the community? I believe the mere existence of these programs leads women to believe we are going to "fix" him or we are going to make her safe in some way. This couldn't be further from the truth.

If I believe that then why, indeed, would I engage in this work? I don't have a good answer. I really wanted to be part of the solution and this was a part of the work I was good at. The work allowed me to go out in public and have plenty of ears to fill with what I hoped was important insights on men, male privilege, and Androputriarchy. Does any of that justify doing the work? No.

On the same question from the perspective of motivation: holding men accountable for male privilege isn't work to engage in if you are motivated by success. There are few, if any, successes.

Why do it then? I grew up in a home that suffered under a batterer (my father) and I want to make a difference. It is determination that propels me, not success.

Until the day when Androputriarchy is only a memory and male accountability is a fact (I predict I will be 753 years old when that happens), there will be no "win" with batterers; only minimizing the damage.

I would also point out my experience with those various and sundry students, thrill-seekers, and others who came to our program professing an unquenchable desire to be mentored and participate as a facilitator. Due to my experience I would always go through the drill with them: if you come in to this program as a facilitator it will change your life; you will be held mercilessly accountable by staff; you will get drilled by batterers in the group and will have to be accountable in your response to them; you will go home most times angry, upset, or feeling hopeless; you will be expected to hold us accountable and improve our program.

The answer to these warnings was always, "Of course I still want to be facilitator. I am really committed." The average amount of time spent with the program for such volunteers was two weeks. They would inevitably leave angry, feeling abused by everyone and everything.

## When the cat's away, the mice will play

I worked in a program that solicited the mentorship, supervision and critical analysis of women, especially battered women. Due to my feminist perspectives before I ever got involved in this program, I already had an appreciation for collaborating with women. But it was through this purposeful scrutiny of women that I began to learn more deeply the importance of any and all men being openly (regardless of voluntarily) accountable to women.

I tended to be the "brains" behind my program and took ultimate responsibility for our policies, methods, goals, etc. There were times we would talk, analyze, propose and re-think certain topics for hours on end. Sometimes we came up with ideas we thought were spectacular and foolproof. There were times we would then take these beautiful and most perfect ideas to our monitoring committee (made up of staff and (ex)residents of our local domestic violence shelter) and they would patiently listen to them and easily point out fatal flaws within moments. We would be left to shake our heads at how we had missed it. But miss it we did, and I more and more relied on their analysis and advice.

Similarly, I am convinced all men are in dire need of women's mentorship, supervision, and critical analysis. We will know a man can be trusted when we see this as a norm for all men.

## Leaving and a lot to be desired

Toward the end of my tenure speaking with the public about "batterer tactics" it became harder and harder for me to limit the topic of what I had to say to batterers. I had always known audiences really like to hear about batterer's tactics and how we dealt with them: it is titillating and "sexy." But the more I inserted the actual issue—male privilege, male entitlement, and Androputriarchy—the more flack I got, the more I wanted to solely focus on the larger issues, and the fewer invitations I got.

I guess my impending departure from a social work "career" made me less invested in satisfying anybody who wanted to limit the discussion to a "safe" little corner of the problem. As I have detailed more clearly elsewhere, one day I made my decision to stop limiting the target of my public presentations. It also ended any and all invitations for me to speak publically.

## As far as they could throw me

Women have every right to mistrust and marginalize men engaged in feminist work. In case I am not making myself clear, let me say: women have every right to mistrust and marginalize men engaged in feminist work.

Back in the day, this was very much the case with me and the batterer program with which I was involved. The director of our local domestic violence shelter was a powerful woman who took no crap from anyone and had an extremely jaundiced view of our program. I'm glad she did. Most men "involved" in so-called "feminist work" are unreliable flakes who just go about their male privilege in a different, victimy, creepy way.

This doesn't even include the men who don't bother to appear "feminist" and engage in work around the edges of domestic violence engaged in shameful practices like anger management, sweat lodges, weekend programs, couples counseling, etc. A pox on their houses.

It is a fact in the life of feminist activists to have to suffer men of varying "helpfulness"—the "white knight" cops who say they'd just as soon shoot the batterers; the therapists looking for business; the do-gooder volunteers looking for mommies; the sleazy Casanova's trolling for sex. Half of all of the above are actively battering their families in the meantime.

Not to mention how us men are going to swoop in and decide we are the boss and should be in charge or have a larger voice in affairs than we have earned.

The good news was most of these men (98%?) would quickly disappear when they weren't treated like fucking royalty, taking a few pot shots on the way out because of how un- or under-appreciated they were.

I learned to be skeptical of any woman in or around this work who came to me or our program looking for collaboration of some sort who didn't hold us at arm's length and with a healthy dose of suspicion. The more skeptical they were, the longer our relationship seemed to last.

# Speaking of Women

They that think much and are not willing to do such base things [as housework], have little regard of well-doing or knowledge of themselves.

~ Margaret Clitherrow
(1556–1586)

To make a poor Maiden or woman a whore,
They care not how much they spend of their store.
But where is there a man that will anything give
That woman or maiden may with honesty live?

~ Joane Sharp
(fl. 1617)

The entire social order...is arrayed against a woman who wants to rise to a man's reputation.

~ Germaine de Stael
(1766–1817)

We want rights. The flour-merchant, the house-builder, and the postman charge us no less on account of our sex; but when we endeavor to earn money to pay all these, then, indeed, we find the difference.

~ Lucy Stone
(1818–1882)

Profits and prostitution—upon these empires are built and kingdoms stand.

~ Adela Pankhurst
(1885–1961)

Patriarchy is... the prevailing religion of the entire planet, and its essential message is necrophilia.

~ Mary Daly
(1928–2010)

Now the goddesses are back and no one knows what to do with them! And we ask, "Is this what you're so scared of: this moist pussy? Is this the Terrifying Other—the clitoris that has to be excised or chopped off or rendered mute?"

~ Carolee Schneemann
(1939–)

The Vatican is wont to portray feminism as a cultural development that has arisen out of the narrow context of white, liberal, materialistic culture, yet Rome is unable to accept that any of its teachings on women have arisen out of the narrow confines of a white, conservative, seminary-bred male culture.

~ Joanna Manning
(1943–)

I became a feminist as an alternative to becoming a masochist.

~ Sally Kempton
(1943–)

Women of today are still being called upon to stretch across the gap of male ignorance and to educate men as to our existence and our needs. This is an old and primary tool of all oppressors to keep the oppressed occupied with the masters concerns.

~ Audre Lorde
(1943–1992)

Although the connections are not always obvious, personal change is inseparable from social and political change.

~ Harriet Lerner
(1944–)

We live in a world that loves to kill beautiful things.

~ Karen Finley
(1956–)

# Daddy's Little Feminist

How could a phantom semblance
of a loose strand of your DNA helix
weave its way
into the fury of my feminism?

Your ramrod grip
of my nascent being
surely was enough
to stuff me into the masculinity coffin.

So cocksure were you
of your celestial gravity
that no mere speck
dare deviate from your glorious orbit.

But deviant I was
to my utter dismay;
shrinking from the penis jousting
to my inner haven of doubt.

Propelled forward both
by the anti-gravity of your beastliness
and the tender yearnings
of my untrammeled spark.

Into the world I went
gathering the blooms
and releasing the nettles
of my beloved bouquet.

Improbably midwifed
by the strong hands of women
to my rightful place;
Daddy's little feminist.

©2014 Michael Elizabeth Marillynson LLC - from the book "Contrary to the Custom of Men: Field Notes on the Pestilence of Patriarchy from a Disloyal Son." For re-printing permission go to: con2men.info.

35

## it's not dysfunctional or a problem if it's working

## harming you is success; empowering you is failure

**Androputriarchy:** [*andro* meaning male, man; *putrere*, meaning rotten, or proceeding from decay; *archy* meaning ruler] an alternative for "patriarchy" that attempts to make clearer the corruption, malevolence, and destructive blight that male supremacy has been in human history and remains to this day.

**Mastribel:** [*mas* meaning man; *tribus* meaning three; *belua*, meaning beast] the deadly three-headed beast of man/men/Androputriarchy.

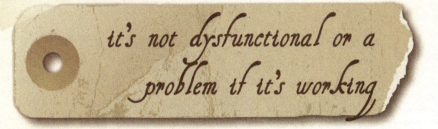

**Problemism**: the deception used by Androputriarchy, and ignorantly accepted by the rest of us, to label highly successful strategies for maintaining power and control for men, male privilege, and Androputriarchy as "problems." For example, referring to so-called "domestic violence" as a "problem" couldn't be further from the truth—for Androputriarchy.

If I were able to pass only one thought on to women from my years of witnessing and studying the ugliness of **Androputriarchy** there is no question what that message would be. Not to mention it is one of the lessons I believe women least understand and/or want to know: speaking for Androputriarchy—we absolutely intend every bit of brutality, tyranny, treachery, and malevolence we perpetrate on or cause to befall you—without exception. Ever.

Like it or not this is our purposely chosen legacy etched with scars on your hearts, minds, bodies, and families. Coming to terms with this nightmare can be both horrifying and liberating. There will be no understanding, identifying, or overthrowing your Androputriarchal oppressors without fully coming to terms with our intentional depravity.

I want to point out some of the ways that constant mistrust and analysis of Androputriarchy's intentions and tactics is necessary, so that the women who choose to do so can hold their eyes open in the presence of the predator **Mastribel**.

## Message One: It's not dysfunctional if it's working

Dysfunctional [noun]: abnormal or impaired functioning of a social group; a breakdown of normal or beneficial relationships between members of the group.

I found the following sentence while researching the gynocide occurring on the Mexico/United States border over the last decade—claiming at least 400 women who were brutally raped, tortured, and murdered. While genuinely attempting to explain what is going on there, the writer claims that it is "difficult to know" who the perpetrators of this woman-slaughter is...

> "...primarily due to the dysfunction of the Mexican justice system as most cases have been inadequately investigated and documented."

When dealing with Androputriarchy who, we should remember, is responsible for the above savagery—we must always keep in mind from whose viewpoint we are concluding that something is "functional" or "dysfunctional." From the viewpoint of a sane person or the victims here, the Mexican justice system should be called dysfunctional—if not worse.

But from the viewpoint of men/Androputriarchy, the Mexican justice system is perfectly functional. It is perfectly serving the functional needs of Androputriarchy by enhancing the privilege of men as a herd at the dear expense of women. It is that simple and ugly.

It is in the interest of the male-privilege-serving Mexican "justice" system to not take these crimes seriously. The Mexican justice system indeed has "adequately" investigated and documented these crimes if the goal of that system is to enforce the male privilege status quo—which it is. Let's be clear, this is not just Mexico we're talking about here; this is the reality of the male-controlled brothel and slaughterhouse known as Earth.

If I want you to shut-the-fuck-up and you don't, I slug you in the face. You then shut-the-fuck-up. This is a perfectly functional and rational method of goal attainment that works from the relationship level and all of the way up to the international level—if you are the perpetrator.

The secondary reason it is important to understand this is so we don't get confused about what we are witnessing in front of our very eyes. When the television says a social institution like the police are "dysfunctional" in how they are ignoring crimes against women, I turn to you and say, "It's not dysfunctional—that is the ingenious and perfect way to handle this situation if you are Androputriarchy. It is and has been working fabulously for centuries." In this way I am witnessing the truth and asking you to consider doing the same.

## Message Two: It's not archaic if it is happening now

Archaic [adjective]: of, relating to, or characteristic of a much earlier, often more primitive period; no longer current or applicable; antiquated; ancient; out of date and not in ordinary use.

To suggest that men's, or men's religion's, or male employer's, or male politician's attitudes or practices are "archaic" is probably always erroneous if, for nothing more, because it is being claimed as such.

When a Republican political operative says in 2012 that the best birth control for a woman is to "hold an aspirin between her knees," this could only be conceived of as "archaic" if it weren't a re-assertion, for the trillionth time this week, of men's legacy of tyranny and arrogance. It is not archaic if it is still actively employed.

While I haven't seen any Glyptodonts (extinct giant South American armadillos) walking down my sidewalk lately, one need only cast a gaze upon the nearest man to see that dinosaurs do still walk the Earth. Manosaurs may have lost some body hair over the millennia, but we haven't changed our interest in oppressing you women one bit—evolution be damned. Maybe this is the real reason the religious knuckleheads don't like the idea of evolution.

37

Again, to understand and challenge your oppressor, you need to see through His tactics and minions, and the notion that an attitude, belief, or method which He is currently using is labeled as "archaic" is a blatant example of burying the truth under an avalanche of lies. It is meant to confuse, confound, and silence you.

## Message Three: all men benefit from any man's violence

To think of men's violence as "detrimental to society" is to not understand how hugely beneficial it is to men. Physical, sexual, and psychological violence are the three horse-men of the Manpocalypse. These are the lubricants upon which Androputriarchy grinds on its merry and privileged way over the bones, ligaments, and blood of women and children. Given that men "own" society and always have, then clearly men's violence is beneficial to men's society.

It is most definitely detrimental to all women and children and, on occasion, a man here and there.

On the individual scale, if I am an arrogant, sexist asshole then I benefit from the oppressive blueprint that Androputriarchy has laid out for me. If I am an accountable, respectful man committed to women's empowerment, then I am considered "special"—again, I benefit from men's violence and depravity.

## Message Four: There are no misconceptions in Androputriarchy

Misconception ~ [noun]: A mistaken thought, idea, or notion; a misunderstanding: a false or mistaken view, opinion, or attitude. For example, a misconception I was taught as a kid is that eating less than an hour before swimming increases the risk of experiencing muscle cramps or drowning.

Misterconception [noun]: the simplistic and ridiculous lies, concoctions, deceptions, decoys, fabrications, falsehoods, fictions, illusions, obfuscations, fakes, frauds, ploys, scams, and Trojan horses created by Androputriarchy to confuse and baffle women, and legitimize abusive, selfish, and criminal behavior by men. For example, a misterconception under Androputriarchy is that women who wear certain clothes in certain places at certain times want to be raped. This is an invention concocted by men to benefit men at women's expense.

In an August, 2013 The World (PRI) story titled "Family Choices—Fertility and Infertility in Africa" by Anders Kelto, he writes:

> "Harun, 30, a Kenyan man interviewed at a bar, has [this] reason for opposing birth control. He says women who use it can't be trusted. 'They will just go out and have sex,' he says, 'because they

know that they cannot give birth.' Health organizations say this is a common belief. And there are other **misconceptions**—for instance, that birth control causes women to lose their sex drive, and that vasectomies leave men impotent."

Despite what you've been told several thousand times in your life, there are no misconceptions in Androputriarchy, although there are plenty of Misterconceptions.

Misterconceptions must be seen and understood on at least two levels: what man/men are using it, and; to what particular end is that man/men using it? In the case of the Kenyan men they gladly accept and promote the Misterconceptions of "they will just go out and have sex" and "birth control causes women to lose their sex drive" and "vasectomies leave men impotent" because it leaves them well-positioned with the patriarchal power and control their culture gifts to them.

Looking at it from the reverse angle, why wouldn't Kenyan men, or any men, "labor" under the "misconception" that "women are smarter and wiser than men so men should turn all of their money over to their wives, and follow all of her decisions about their home life and career." Anyone seen that misconception around lately?

Misconception, under Androputriarchy, is a code word for "I've got just the lie I need to get what I want."

# Message Five: If it ain't broke, it's worse than we thought

I trust you are getting the drift here. I warned you—it takes courageous eyes and much vigilance to keep track of Androputriarchy's mischief.

I wish I could believe that Androputriarchy is just "broken" or "has a problem" or is "dysfunctional" or "has lost its way." That would be a far more hopeful scenario. But hope does not a survival plan make.

Contrary to the fraudulent notion that the world of humans is fraught with intractable "problems," the truth couldn't be more the opposite. The world of humans, as dictated by Androputriarchy, is set up and running perfectly for the benefit of Androputriarchy.

It could be that the establishment and maintenance of male privilege and Androputriarchy (one and the same) is causing **you** or **me** problems, but Androputriarchy is doing just fine, thank you.

I have come to understand that any conversation about the world's so-called problems—their so-called causes and so-called cures—are meaningless hot air unless they first and foremost acknowledge and address the putrid affliction of Androputriarchy and male privilege.

Endless and/or "enlightened" discussion won't fix anything as long as Androputriarchy isn't addressed first and foremost. War and armed aggression won't fix anything as long as Androputriarchy isn't addressed first and foremost. Personal insight and tranquility won't fix anything as long as Androputriarchy isn't addressed first and foremost. Reaching a hand out between historical enemies won't fix anything as long as Androputriarchy isn't addressed first and foremost. Different economic or political systems won't fix anything as long as Androputriarchy isn't addressed first and foremost. Environmental protection efforts won't fix anything as long as Androputriarchy isn't addressed first and foremost. Different religions or atheism won't fix anything as long as Androputriarchy isn't addressed first and foremost. Marching on the government or assassinating the enemy won't fix anything as long as Androputriarchy isn't addressed first and foremost. Forgiveness, love, and nonviolent ethics won't fix anything as long as Androputriarchy isn't addressed first and foremost. A return to traditional values won't fix anything as long as Androputriarchy isn't addressed first and foremost. A healthy balance of heart, mind and body won't fix anything as long as Androputriarchy isn't addressed first and foremost.

I am not invested in the heartfelt lengths most courageous peace and human rights activists go through to help others when their analysis of what is going on is utterly devoid of a feminist perspective. I may love and respect them as courageous persons, but they are shirking their responsibility to be truthful about Androputriarchy. Not to mention that they will never see their efforts come to any lasting fruition unless Androputriarchy is rendered benign.

Androputriarchy isn't broken—it's humming along just fine as it always has. If something is not done about it, one day, probably soon, it will require the bones, ligaments, and blood of your children or your children's children—if they are not already taken.

# Speaking of Women

Keep woman under rule.

~One of seven precepts of Apollo on his temple at Delphi

Women should remain at home, sit still, keep house, and bear and bring up children. If a woman grows weary and, at last, dies from childbearing; it matters not. Let her die from bearing; she is there to do it.

~ Martin Luther
(1483–1546)

Woman is by nature meant to obey.

~ Arthur Schopenhauer
(1788–1860)

What a misfortune to be a woman! And yet, the worst misfortune is not to understand what a misfortune it is.

~ Kierkegaard
(1813–1855)

Are you going to women? Do not forget the whip!

~ Friedrich Nietzsche
(1844–1900)

The conditions of our sex is so deplorable that it is our duty even to break the law in order to call attention to the reasons why we do so.

~ Emma Goldman
(1869–1940)

Women have very little idea of how much men hate them.

~ Germaine Greer
(1939–)

A woman is like a horse: he who can drive her is her master.

~ Argentine proverb

Satisfy a dog with a bone and a woman with a lie.

~ Basque proverb

Beat your wife on the wedding day, and your married life will be happy.

~ Japanese proverb

# THE PERFECTLY MANGINEERED WOMAN

**Suttee** is the Hindu practice of forcing women whose husbands have died to burn themselves to death on his funeral pyre. The alternative to this horrible death, if available, was for the woman to live the rest of her life shunned by her family and community in isolation, poverty, humiliation, and starvation. There were likely hundreds of thousands of such executions carried out.

**Dowry deaths/bride burnings** are the deaths of young women who are murdered or driven to suicide through continuous harassment and torture by husbands and in-laws in an effort to extort an increased dowry. The Indian National Crime Records Bureau reports 8,172 dowry deaths in India in 2008. Project that back over the last century and we have 817,200 murders.

A **hysterectomy** is the surgical removal of the uterus, usually performed by a gynecologist. In 2003, over 600,000 hysterectomies were conducted in the United States alone; these rates are the highest in the industrialized world and are likely being performed for unwarranted and unnecessary reasons.

1,354,858 total **cesarean births** in the United States in 2011. 32.8% of U.S. births in 2010 were by cesarean section. It is conjectured that the high rate is due its profitability by hospitals, relative ease of the procedure by physicians, and lower malpractice claims by women.

The World Health Organization states that sexual violence, including but not limited to **rape, sexual assault, prostitution, child brides, and sexual slavery and trafficking** is perpetrated by men and boys against one-third of women and girls worldwide. That's 1.155 billion women and girls.

**Witch burnings/lynchings** claimed the lives of an estimated 40,000 to 60,000 women.

It is estimated that more than one billion Chinese women suffered **foot binding** from the late 10th century to the mid-20th. Men insisted on this maiming, concluding that it is "erotic."

The punishment of **shaving a woman's head** has biblical origins. In Europe, the practice dates back to the dark ages, and the Visigoths. During the middle ages, this mark of shame, denuding a woman of what was supposed to be her most seductive feature, was commonly a punishment for adultery. Shaving women's heads as a mark of retribution and humiliation was reintroduced in the 20th century. Tens of thousands of French, German, Spanish, Belgian, Italian, and Norwegian women are known to have been shorn by men who accused them of being collaborators with the enemy during war.

According to the Acid Survivors' Foundation, 267 women had **acid** thrown on them in 2005 in Bangladesh alone. This was down from 500 in a previous year.

The **radical mastectomy** procedure was begun in the 1890's. The breast, skin, nipple, areola, pectoral muscles, and all the axillary lymph nodes were surgically removed. Studies published in 1985 concluded that less drastic surgical options had just as good of outcomes as radical mastectomy. From 1895 to the mid-1970's about 90% of the women being treated for breast cancer in the United States underwent radical mastectomy.

Women had 92 percent of **cosmetic procedures** in 2008, or 9.3 million women. The procedures included: breast augmentation (355,671); botox (2,239,024); lipoplasty (309,692); hyaluronic acid skin injections (1,200,420); eyelid surgery (166,426); laser hair removal (1,101,255); abdominoplasty (143,005); chemical peel (554,492); breast reduction (139,926); laser skin resurfacing (532,008).

**Female genital mutilation** is defined by the World Health Organization as "all procedures that involve partial or total removal of the external female genitalia, or other injury to the female genital organs for non-medical reasons." It is usually performed without anesthesia using a knife, razor, shard of glass, or scissors. The WHO estimates that 100–140 million women and girls on Earth today have suffered this maiming.

©2014 Michael Elizabeth Marillynson LLC - This poster is from the book "Contrary to the Custom of Men: Field Notes on the Pestilence of Patriarchy from a Disloyal Son." For re-printing permission go to: con2men.info. Images courtesy of Wikimedia Commons: monica giovannini, carmelo d'atri, quirino piubello and annamaria molino; azoreg; michael s. schwartz; bob k.; goga312; bobjgalindo

# demaletarized zones

### a good thing in our own backyard?

**Demaletarized Zones:** 1. the embarrassing fact that any and all places on Earth are better off in every way without the presence of men and/or Androputriarchy; 2. a replacement for the insanely brilliant term "demilitarized zones" that unveils the truth about what these zones actually are; 3. a hope for the future when these zones are actually created, free of men, and exist for the welfare of women and children.

There is something endlessly fascinating to me about the so-called "demilitarized zones" around the world.

They seem an embarrassing but accurate snapshot of Androputriarchy and we men dressed in our most bizarre vanity, arrogance and pompousness. The emperor has comical, albeit lethal, clothes indeed.

So-called demilitarized zones are a male mental construction insanely top-heavy with flash, pomp, color, pageantry, and make-believe. Let's not forget irony. They practically dare anyone to speak the obvious truth about them.

I am particularly amused with the, what I will call henceforth, demaletarized zone between North and South Korea.

From Wikidpeia.com:

The Korean Demilitarized Zone (DMZ) is a strip of land running across the Korean Peninsula that serves as a buffer zone between North and South Korea which runs along the 38th parallel north. It is 250 kilometers (160 miles) long, approximately 4 km (2.5 mi) wide and is the most heavily militarized border in the world. This natural isolation has created an involuntary park which is now recognized as one of the most well-preserved areas of temperate habitat in the world.

First, how, exactly, could we describe a strip of land which is "the most heavily militarized border in the world" a demilitarized zone? Wouldn't demilitarized mean no military? Or is there some arcane rule the boys made up that if the largest massing of military in the world is 1.25 miles or more away then it is not militarized? Kind of like, "If I close my eyes and put my head under the covers I will be safe from the monster?" Oh, those adorable boys and their darling stories.

Second, how do we explain the tortured irony to our children, especially our male children, that a strip of land no men are allowed to enter is, basically, paradise on Earth? Is there a Grimm's fairy tale to explain this one away? Let's see—in this place it's all men and it is hell on Earth, and in this other place there are no men and it is paradise on Earth. Hmmm...

Third, if I were an explorer from outer space (I wouldn't be an invader—invasion, violation, and domination are male traits only on this suffering rock) and I saw the Korean demaletarized zone I would

42

be filled with grief and sadness that it takes all of this militarization to protect the only 2.5 mile strip of Earth left that is a paradise. That is what the military is there for, isn't it? Surely the Venusians would wonder why we don't turn our guns around the other way and make the neglected 2.5 mile strip the hell on Earth where all of the men are and the other 24,899.05 miles the paradise zone.

Fourth, with that 2.5 mile strip of paradise sitting there mocking us, hasn't someone else besides me noticed this irony? I have to think so.

Assuming I'm not the first to notice it, what horrible brainwashing must we have been subjected to that we don't insist the whole Earth be made a paradise immediately? How we have come to accept it is better for us to live in a maletarized zone than a demaletarized one?

Now, on to what this whole notion of demaletarized zones could be for us.

If there was ever a case for separatism for a people this is it. What would happen if we set up 10 demaletarized zones on every continent to explore what life on Earth could be like? The world would see the largest human migration of women and children ever. Women would risk their lives and defy any hardship or threat to enter these zones. The rest of us men would then be free to rape, pillage, and plunder each other.

And fellas, if you don't like this notion, it is very simple: do what is necessary so women and children would have no reason to want to live in a demaletarized zone.

# Speaking of Women

Then let us [women] have our Liberty again.
And challenge to your selves no Sovereignty;
You came not in the world without our pain,
Make that a bar against your cruelty;
Your fault being greater, why should you disdain
Our being your equals, free from tyranny?
~ Emilia Lanier
(1569–1645)

We are the grief of man, in that we take all the grief from man; we languish when they laugh, we lie sighing when they sit singing, and sit sobbing when they lay slugging and sleeping.
~ Jane Anger
(fl. 1589)

Women instead of being elevated by her union with man, which might be expected from an alliance with a superior being, is in reality lowered. She generally loses her individuality, her independent character, her moral being. She becomes absorbed into him, and henceforth is looked at, and acts through the medium of her husband.
~ Sarah Moore Grimke
(1792–1873)

Male parasitism means that males must have access to women; it is the Patriarchal Imperative. But feminist no-saying is more than a substantial removal (re-direction, re-allocation) of goods and services because access is one of the faces of power. Female denial of male access to females substantially cuts off a flow of benefits but it has also the form and full portent of assumption of power.
~ Marilyn Frye
(1941–)

Girls raped by their fathers and other male relatives, women beaten and raped by their husbands, and Lesbians all know what happens in our minds when our experience contradicts the version of reality presented to us. We can decide that "consensus reality" is still true and label our own experience unique, personal, contrary to fact; we can deny that whatever men did to us didn't happen and suppress the information, or we miraculously, against everything we've been taught, accept the validity of our knowledge. We are either alienated from ourselves or from the society that lies to us. Those of us who refuse to "adjust" to the demands of patriarchy are labeled crazy, misfits, malcontents, freaks.
~ Julia Penelope
(1941–2013)

Romantic love, in pornography as in life, is the mythic celebration of female negation. For a woman, love is defined as her willingness to submit to her own annihilation. The proof of love is that she is willing to be destroyed by the one whom she loves, for his sake. For the woman, love is always self-sacrifice, the sacrifice of identity, will, and bodily integrity, in order to fulfill and redeem the masculinity of her lover.
~ Andrea Dworkin
(1946–2005)

If animals are burdened by gender, by gendered associations, by the oppression that is gender, then they can't be liberated through representations of gender oppression. It isn't helping animals, and it certainly isn't helping men—to continue to believe that privilege is something to hold onto or even to masturbate to.
~ Carol J. Adams
(1951–)

If there were no men in this world, there'd be a bunch of fat, happy women and no crime!
~ Samantha Davis
(dates unknown)

44

45

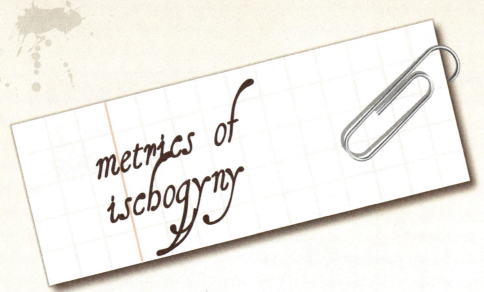

## metrics of ischogyny

### the numbers of oppression are not accidental

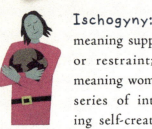

**Ischogyny:** [*ischo*, meaning suppression or restraint; *gyny*, meaning women] the series of interlocking self-created and self-serving myths held, and behaviors, tactics, and actions taken by men/Androputriarchy, that enhance male bonding and male exaltation at the expense of women; the oppression of women. A replacement for "misogyny" which incorrectly concludes oppression of women is based on "hatred" of women, which it is not; hatred is an incidental weapon.

Some numbers come straight from God.

For example, in the United States women, on average, make $0.72 for every dollar men—with comparable skills and education—make.

Or, one of every three girls in the United States will be sexually assaulted by the time she is 18.

At the same time I have always found these types of numbers infuriating and outrageous, I also thought of them as coincidental to, or a random byproduct of, Androputriarchy.

Not anymore.

I now understand these "numbers" as perfect, accurate, and revealing indicators of how Androputriarchy works. Kind of like the gauges on the dashboard of your automobile tell you how all of the systems are running.

In America at this time, the "magic" number of girls to sexually assault to train girls to submit to sexual abuse by men is 33%.

Likewise, the "magic" number necessary to train women to submit to economic abuse by, and economic dependence on, men under Androputriarchy is 28%.

These numbers aren't coincidental, they are revelatory.

It is the same with many things: your automobile engine functions most efficiently at a certain temperature; our bodies function best at a certain percentage of hydration; vegetation grows best in different parts of the world with certain amounts of sunlight.

Androputriarchy's machinations are found in the ugly numbers of the optimal conditions for keeping women oppressed, obedient, and silenced.

It is necessary, as seen by these Metrics of Ischogyny, for Androputriarchy to maintain a certain ratio of raped to not-yet-raped women and girls at all times to maintain unhindered sexual access to all women and girls.

It is necessary for Androputriarchy to maintain a certain ratio of geographic areas where it is "not safe" for women and girls, in contrast to where it is proclaimed to be "safe," so we may properly isolate women.

It is necessary for Androputriarchy to maintain a certain ratio of domestic violence perpetrators attacking women and children in the "home" to non-perpetrators so women will think they must submit to their men, or busy themselves with figuring out how to keep this particular one from abusing them.

It is necessary for Androputriarchy to maintain a certain ratio of men in positions of leadership in the clergy, military, government, business, athletics, health care, criminal justice, media, education, social service, etc. so girls know what limitations they must submit to.

Be aware that these Metrics of Ischogyny work both ways: that is, the "plus" side of the metric is the ways men are allowed to dominate every area of life so women learn to accept their oppression; and the "minus" side where a small piece of the pie is bestowed upon women to benefit from so they still remain invested in and striving to survive the Androputriarchal system.

That sickening sound you hear is the perfect humming of the Metrics of Ischogyny. It's great to be a guy, eh?

The Metrics of Ischogyny are wonderfully flexible as well: they can be and are applied anywhere from the family unit up to nations, and can be different in different families and nations.

For example, in some nations openly raping women with machetes and rifle barrels in front of the community happens to 25% of the women in that region; in another country, that would be unheard of. And while the men of these two different nations "Tut, tut" at the quaintness or barbarity of the other nation, they are similarly enjoying the fruits of Androputriarchy.

Another example of the Metrics of Ischogyny would be cosmetics. $55,000,000,000 (that's 55 BILLION dollars) was spent in 2011 on cosmetics, almost entirely by women. Compare that number with the amount of money spent by women on self-defense classes to protect themselves from the violence of men who apparently want them to "look pretty." The pressure on girls and women to wish to make themselves desired by men, compared to the pressure on girls and women to shun the notion of empowering themselves physically, are revealing statistics—if you are willing to look. They are not random, accidental, or coincidental numbers: they are the Metrics of Ischogyny.

Here's what I suspect about the Metrics of Ischogyny: the difference in the severity of the punishment meted out to women and children by Androputriarchy in any given region/ nation is inversely proportional the amount of resistance women push back with. Where the push-back by women is weakest, out come the machetes. Where the push-back is strongest, women who are prostituted get medical insurance.

Back when I was a social worker I knew many social work-type researchers. I can guarantee you not one of them has done any research or statistical analysis of what I am bringing up here. Why is that? Aren't these supposed to be the smartest, savviest, most highly-educated, do-gooder people amongst us who are dispassionate in where their studies lead them?

Maybe they could start a new research career or center studying the Metrics of Ischogyny amongst, hmmmm, let me think, college faculty!

# Speaking of Women

If a test of civilization be sought, none can be so sure as the condition of that half of society over which the other half has power—from the exercises of the right of the strongest.

~ Harriet Martineau
(1802–1876)

… true emancipation begins neither at the polls nor in courts. It begins in a woman's soul.

~ Emma Goldman
(1869–1940)

Women if you want to realize yourselves—you are on the eve of a devastating psychological upheaval—all your pet illusions must be unmasked—the lies of centuries have got to go—are you prepared for the Wrench? There is no half-measure—NO scratching on the surface of the rubbish heap of tradition, will bring about Reform, the only method is Absolute Demolition.

~ Mina Loy
(born Mina Gertrude Löwry 1882–1966)

Men decided a few centuries ago that any job they found repulsive was women's work.

~ Frances Gabe
(1915–)

A question that has been raised more than once and that gives me no inner peace is why did so many nations in the past, and often still now, treat women as inferior to men? Everyone can agree how unjust this is, but that is not enough for me. I would also like to know the cause of the great injustice… it is stupid enough of women to have borne it all in silence for such a long time, since the more centuries this arrangement lasts, the more deeply rooted it becomes… many people, particularly women, but also men, now realize for how long this state of affairs has been wrong, and modern women demand the right of complete independence! But that's not all, respect for women, that's going to have to come as well!

~ Anne Frank
(1929–1945)

The vote means nothing to women. We should be armed.

~ Edna O'Brien
(1930–)

Women are the only exploited group in history to have been idealized into powerlessness.

~ Erica Jong
(1942–)

By the time we are women, fear is as familiar to us as air. It is our element. We live in it, we inhale it, we exhale it, and most of the time we do not even notice it. Instead of, "I am afraid," we say, "I don't want to," or "I don't know how," or "I can't."

~ Andrea Dworkin
(1946–2005)

48

## my commitment to treason from androputriarchy

**Treason** (noun): Violation of the allegiance owed to one's sovereign or state; any betraying, treachery, breach of faith, or betrayal of trust.

**Androputriarchy:** [*andro* meaning male, man; *putrere,* meaning rotten, or proceeding from decay; *archy* meaning ruler] an alternative for "patriarchy" that attempts to make clearer the corruption, malevolence, and destructive blight that male supremacy has been in human history and remains to this day.

I gleefully and publicly proclaim and verify my premeditated and unalterable commitment to enact ongoing and relentless treason against Androputriarchy in all of His infinitely hideous and malevolent forms and disguises, and against His institutions, agents, customs, traditions, privileges, tactics, strategies, manipulations, directives and coercions.

- I commit to world change, which starts with how I treat my family, friends, etc. Feminist insurrection starts in me, then my home, then the world.

- I commit to continue working diligently on my own accountability as a man and member of Androputriarchy to all women and children, which I estimate will take me another 593 years to fully enact. My credibility, reputation, trustworthiness, integrity, and status in my community and the world must be based first, foremost, and always on how I behave at home with my closest loved ones, companion animals, etc.—not by what I accomplish in, or project out to, the world.

- I commit to personal trustworthiness and safety for women and children. Safety, security, peace, respect, and empowerment starts at home and requires that I protect my family from violence, insecurity, fear, disrespect, and oppression from me.

- I commit to trusting my intellect, observations, analysis, outrage, and growing feminist understanding of the human world.

- I commit to listening to women and children and respecting their voices, languages, wisdoms, ways, and knowledge. I commit to talk less and listen more.

- I commit to ongoing efforts to pull from my eyes, mind and heart the veil of Androputriarchal lies, manipulations, self-interest, destruction, malevolence, obfuscation, victim-blaming, fear mongering and male-worship.

- I commit to manage the money and resources in my care in a manner that accentuates the wellbeing of women, children, and the Earth.

- I commit to questioning everything I think, everything I experience, and everything I am told, through the purifying and clarifying antidote of feminism.

49

- I commit to keep in check my Androputriarchal necrophilic tendencies.

- I commit to clean up my own messes.

- I commit to learning about, knowing, appreciating, and expressing those parts of me strangled by Androputriarchy, particularly those things called "feminine."

- I commit to always value women's, children's, and nature's safety and wellbeing as at least equal in importance as my self-expression or self-gratification.

- I commit to rely on my studied judgment as to who the perpetrators and who the victims really are.

- I commit to doing my best to see the world through women's eyes/experiences.

- I commit to remembering I cannot tell the "good ones" from the "bad ones."

- I commit at all times and in all places to be willing and honored to discuss the unearned privileges bestowed on me by: oppressive social circumstances, being male, being white skinned, enjoying relative financial affluence, my physically ability, my American citizenship, my general heterosexuality, etc. This discussion includes my acknowledgement of the advantages given me, how I use or disavow these advantages, and how I resist the social structure that poisons the Earth with such inequity.

- I commit to identifying with the victims, the disempowered, and the oppressed and not with the aggressors, the privileged and the oppressors.

- I commit to violation of the Androputriarchal fellowship, brotherhood, fraternity, trust, faith, bond, expectations, collusion and conspiracy expected of me from my brothers, fathers, sons, male friends, male colleagues, uncles, nephews, grandfathers, grandsons, male teammates, and their ilk.

- I commit to, at all times, mistrust of Androputriarchy especially when I am told there is no reason to. I commit to always remember that Androputriarchy is worse than I realize, or anyone else realizes.

- I commit to seeking no special recognition because I am a man saying many of the same things women have been saying, and dying for saying, for centuries. I make these commitments because they are life-saving for me. I do not require validation or reward from anyone, particularly not women.

- I commit to always keep in mind oppressed people, whether they are women, children, people of color, LGBT people, sexually and/or economically exploited people, disabled people, etc. must speak in code under the malevolent glare of Androputriarchy, and have every good reason to exclude me from their thoughts, or to withhold the truth from me.

- I commit to learn from women about resistance to, and transcendence of, oppression.

- I commit to remember Androputriarchy's past and how it and the continuing putrefaction of Androputriarchy sickens the world every day.

- I commit to remain loyal to the oppressed and disempowered, especially when I don't want to.

- I commit to the quarantining and remediation of Androputriarchy worldwide as we have known and suffered under Him.

- I commit to making male privilege and His stepson, male bonding at women's expense, visible and shameful.

- I commit to comforting those afflicted by Androputriarchy and afflicting those comfortable with Androputriarchy.

- I commit to asking questions inconvenient to all who strive to protect their privilege under Androputriarchy.

- I commit to exposing and opposing oppression and/or male privilege and demand accountability, including but not limited to, reparations from men and Androputriarchy.

- I commit to spreading seeds of discontent and rebellion against Androputriarchy, and fertilize that garden, knowing full well it will bring me grief.

- I commit to challenging the simple-minded, power-enhancing and catastrophic Androputriarchal dualistic notions of sexism, genderism, heterosexism, racism, classism, ableism, patriotism, ecodestruction, militarism, monoculture, wealthism, rapism, capitalism, profitism, religionism, male bonding, male worship, male privilege, maleism, speciesism, and all such ploys.

- I commit to continue to catalog the crimes, tactics, cover-ups, extortions, goals, intentions, and putrefaction of Androputriarchy.

- I commit to use my knowledge and understanding of Androputriarchy, as a man/male, to fight Androputriarchy. This includes doing my utmost to use Androputriarchy's tactics, strategies, and propaganda against Him. I commit to use my whole life's education as a man to continue to decipher and break the Androputriarchal codes of deception.

- I commit to keep the blame, focus, prosecution, attention, shame, and demand for accountability where it belongs: on men and Androputriarchy.

- I commit to holding each and every man responsible for his own sexist thoughts and actions, all other men's sexist thoughts and actions, and Androputriarchy's sexist thoughts and actions.

To be continued…

In solidarity with all those who "remain loyal to the disempowered, lead the discussion, ask questions, challenge gendered assumptions, expose and oppose oppression, apply accountability, honor diversity, practice responsible environmental stewardship, speak truth to power, make privilege visible, eradicate misogyny…"*

> Religionism: how religion and spiritualism is Mistermanaged under Androputriarchy, regardless of the regional gerrymandering by men, for the establishment, support, and perpetuation of male privilege and male exaltation.

> Maleism: the worship, glorification and deification of men, maleness and so-called masculinity; the primary and deciding factor in the course of human affairs so far. Maleism and His entitlement, male privilege, is and has been malevolent, destructive, greedy, parasitic, oppressive, all-powerful, purposeful, successful, self-perpetuating, and diabolically veiled.

---

*  With gratitude to the Battered Women and Children's Memorial Garden for their eleven organizational Guiding Principles (www.memgarden.org).

# Speaking of Women

Under common law, husbands were empowered to beat their wives but had no right to kill them. When husbands overstepped the legal boundary and did kill their wife or a servant, they were charged with murder. In contrast, the statutes provided that "if any servant kill his Master, any woman kill her husband, or any secular or religious person kill his Prelate to whom he owes Obedience, this is [petty] treason," similar in kind to threat or assault on royal government, which was defined as high treason. One justice of the peace succinctly explained in 1618 that a wife or servant who "maliciously killeth" a husband or master was accused of treason, while a husband or master who "maliciously killeth" a wife or servant was accused of murder, "for that one is in subjection and owe their obedience, and not the other." …for women, both high and petty treason were punished by burning at the stake.

~ Pavla Miller
[Transformations of Patriarchy in the West, 1500–1900]

We [women] are determined to foment a rebellion, and will not hold ourselves bound by any laws in which we have no voice or representation.

~ Abigail Adams to John Adams,
31 March, 1776

Of all the old prejudices that cling to the hem of the woman's garments and persistently impede her progress, none holds faster than this. The idea that she owes service to a man instead of to herself, and that it is her highest duty to aid his development rather than her own, will be the last to die.

~ Susan Brownell Anthony
(1820–1906)

… women have been called queens for a long time, but the kingdom given them isn't worth ruling.

~ Louisa May Alcott
(1832–1888)

When people had slaves, they expected that their pigs, chickens, corn and everything lying loose about the plantation would be stolen. But the planters began by stealing the liberty of their slaves, by stealing their labor, by stealing, in fact, all they had; and the natural result was that the slaves stole back all they could.

~ Tennessee Claflin
(1845–1923)

The happiest excitement in life is to be convinced that one is fighting for all one is worth on behalf of some clearly seen and deeply felt good.

~ Ruth Benedict
(1887–1948)

If you can't raise consciousness, at least raise hell.

~ Rita Mae Brown
(1944–)

**Feminist Carrying Card**

I, _____,

hereby affirm and announce that I am a feminist and advocate feminism in all my affairs.

Coven: _____

Continent: _____

Planet: _____

Galaxy: _____

Reasons for Membership:
_____
_____
_____
_____
_____
_____

Feminist Since: _____ / _____ / _____

---

**Feminist Carrying Card**

I, _____,

hereby affirm and announce that I am a feminist and advocate feminism in all my affairs.

Coven: _____

Continent: _____

Planet: _____

Galaxy: _____

Reasons for Membership:
_____
_____
_____
_____
_____
_____

Feminist Since: _____ / _____ / _____

---

 **Feminist Carrying Card**

I, _____,

hereby affirm and announce that I am a feminist and advocate feminism in all my affairs.

Coven: _____

Continent: _____

Planet: _____

Galaxy: _____

Reasons for Membership:
_____
_____
_____
_____
_____
_____

Feminist Since: _____ / _____ / _____

---

**Feminist Carrying Card**

I, _____,

hereby affirm and announce that I am a feminist and advocate feminism in all my affairs.

Coven: _____

Continent: _____

Planet: _____

Galaxy: _____

Reasons for Membership:
_____
_____
_____
_____
_____
_____

Feminist Since: _____ / _____ / _____

## take a walk on the reviled side

### cast your lot with battered women

"To study psychological trauma is to come face to face both with human vulnerability in the natural world and with the capacity for evil in human nature. To study psychological trauma means bearing witness to horrible events. When the events are natural disasters or "acts of God," those who bear witness sympathize readily with the victim. But when the traumatic events are of human design, those who bear witness are caught in the conflict between victim and perpetrator. It is morally impossible to remain neutral in this conflict. The bystander is forced to take sides… It is very tempting to take the side of the perpetrator. All the perpetrator asks is that the bystander do nothing. He appeals to the universal desire to see, hear, and speak no evil. The victim, on the contrary, asks the bystander to share the burden of pain. The victim demands action, engagement, and remembering."

~ Judith Herman
(1942–)

This quote brings to mind an experience I had driving home with a gay teammate from a queer hockey team I played with for three years. We were talking about the local queer softball league, and how popular it is. I asked him, if he was walking home from a softball game with a softball bat in his hand, would he purposely hold the bat in a less-threatening way—with the fat end of the bat in his hand instead of the skinnier handle—if he was approaching a woman on the sidewalk? "No" he said emphatically, "I am not threatening her and how she takes my holding a bat is not my responsibility." I was not surprised by his answer.

I am a "late bloomer" in aspects of my life, including educationally. I spent far more time drug-seeking in high school than studying, resulting in grades that would barely gain me access to the local community college if I had harbored such a notion—which I didn't. After casting about in shitty jobs for five years I then made the weird choice to get into psychotherapy which, ultimately, doomed me to become a social worker myself.

I worked my biscuits off and four years later had acquired Associates, Bachelors, and Masters Degrees. I was one proud Wolverine, churned out by the University of Michigan School of Social Work. My fanaticism and arrogance were typical of a male alumnus—I'm a Michigan alumnus; I'm badass; I have the bumper sticker to prove it.

Years later I am sitting in male batterer intervention groups willingly letting my brain be re-oriented by these missionaries of Androputriarchy. As I am grasping the privilege and pride and arrogance and—most importantly—the identification with the powerful—of these men, I am pondering how I am privileged and prideful and arrogant and—most importantly—what and whose power I identify with.

You've probably figured out where this is going.

I began to doubt my "loyalty" to my school. I began to wonder why it was so important to me that I have a

"MICHIGAN" sticker on my automobile, but not some other sticker more reflective of what I was telling people was important to me—like women's reproductive rights, women's economic and legal rights, and lesbian and gay rights.

The more I thought about what mattered to me, and bringing my life into alignment with my values, the more my tight bonds and friendships with my university and alumni pals began to reek of the same foul odor I smelled in the presence of batterers—and of most men. These relationships began to fade away.

This is but one example of how I needed to turn my life upside down to figure out who I am, what is important to me, and who I choose to give my allegiance to. There were hundreds more.

To come full circle, I came to understand, although I was working with so-called domestic violence perpetrators, they weren't my primary clients or the persons to whom I owed my allegiance. My primary clients were their victims. It was on their behalf I worked, and I insisted our program adopt that notion as boilerplate policy.

This policy, of course, resulted in much community derision, isolation, and punishment. This punishment came primarily from the criminal justice system and other psycho-related occupations, like social workers, psychologists, and drug and alcohol treatment "professionals."

Our batterer program also solicited the oversight of our local domestic violence shelter, whom we paid to sit in on our staff meetings so as to review our policies, interventions, thinking, and accountability to battered women and children. This oversight was invaluable.

These women furthered my own introspective searching and questioning. They helped me understand everything we did in our program had to be examined through the oppressive reality of Androputriarchal tyranny and, conversely, what this tyranny means in the day-to-day and minute-to-minute reality of women.

All of this eventually led me to a predictable and repeating experience when conducting public presentations when I would be asked, usually by women: What can we do to help battered women?

My two answers were routinely met with howls of derision: "You can help battered women by being willing to put your feet in their shoes and understand the world from their vantage point; and you must get more women elected to the United States Congress."

It was during these types of public discussions I comprehended our community's and nation's interest in the welfare of battered women and children are a mile wide and an inch deep.

Our American way of life, as designed by Androputriarchy, is to pretend to care about a certain subject and to provide one bandage for the entire train wreck and forget about it. It is made clear, in one way or another, not to look deeper into the matter.

You see this, for example, in the "one hit wonders" that are the darlings of the media: the "Megan's Law" type of buffoonery. Some bereaved person or family is victimized by some perpetrator and they get all self-righteous and go on a crusade to get some law passed and Congress stands up and makes self-righteous re-election speeches and names the new law after the "victim" and everyone feels important and effective and then we can all get back to our televisions for tonight's reality TV programming.

Nowhere in this process does anyone dare transcend the specific instance of their "victimhood" to broach the parasitic fraternity of Androputriarchy that has continued to oppress and victimize unabated during all of this back-slapping self-congratulation.

This "Megan's Law" stuff is feel-good window dressing meant to keep us identifying with the aggressor—not the victim. If we really sided with all of the victims all of the time we would instantly know that this perpetrator did not act alone. We would also know this new law does nothing to address the real problem: male privilege and Androputriarchy. The same male privilege and Androputriarchy that got those white males in their thrones to make the laws in the first place. The same male privilege and Androputriarchy that breeds and grooms male predators to sexually and physically assault and murder our families—and Megan's.

So it is very simple: if you want to help battered women—or any women—you have to make the life-changing choice to side with the victims. You have to make the life-changing choice to side with the disempowered, the trampled upon, the weak, the ridiculed, and the oppressed. You have to make the life-changing choice to see clearly how oppression works and how the oppressors want us to collude and that we will be punished for seeing and witnessing otherwise.

This brings to mind the notion of "outing": I wonder if the feminist community can harness this to promote the public revelation of how people and institutions choose the side of the oppressor or the oppressed; the empowered or the disempowered; women or Androputriarchy; victim or perpetrator.

Would we use the word "outing" or a different one? Do we have an equal responsibility to "out" others as we do to "out" ourselves? Should we have national outing month where we insist that powerful people and/or institutions take a position on current events involving the exploitation or oppression of women and/or children?

I suspect, at this point in my investigation, that the key buttress that must go for Androputriarchy to fall (which He must if we are to survive) is women's so-called "horizontal hostility" and women's identifying with the aggressor. I don't say this to blame the victim. It is not women's responsibility, but it will be your burden. We men aren't going to do it. As usual, you will have to clean up our mess, at least initially, if anything good is going to happen.

It's going to take a critical mass of women to midwife this mutiny, and it will then take decades/centuries of careful tending by women to raise this benevolent offspring.

Representation in the 113th United States Congress
82 women, 353 men in the House of Representatives = 19%
20 women, 80 men in the Senate = 20%

Horizontal hostility: people of oppressed groups believing, acting on, or enforcing the dominant system of discrimination and oppression against themselves and others. This "hostility" can occur between members of the same group or between members of different, targeted groups. Basically, the old notion of "let's you and her fight."

# Speaking of Women

There is no country in the world where there is so much boasting of the "chivalrous" treatment she enjoys… In short, indulgence is given her as a substitute for justice.

~ Harriet Martineau
(1802–1876)

…from the earliest dawn of reason I pined for that freedom of thought and action that was then denied to all womankind. I revolted in spirit against the customs of society and the laws of the State that crushed my aspirations and debarred me from the pursuit of almost every object worthy of an intelligent, rational mind.

~ Emily Collins
(1818–1879)

I was a woman before I was an abolitionist. I must speak for the women.

~ Lucy Stone
(1818–1893)

The world enslaves our sex by the mere fear of an epithet; and as long as it can throw any vile term at us, before which we cower, it can maintain our enslavement.

~ Tennessee Claflin
(1845–1923)

We used to say, in the suffrage movement, that we could trust the woman who believed in suffrage, but we could never trust the woman who just wanted to vote.

~ Jeannette Rankin
(1880–1973)

Women cannot serve two masters at once who are urgently beaming antithetical orders… Either we believe in patriarchy—the rule of men over women—or we believe in equality.

~ Sonia Johnson
(1936–)

Once again, the men who head the world's powerful religious hierarchies remain conspicuously silent about uncaring and violent sex—even when it is as extreme as genital mutilation and rape. Instead of pressuring world leaders to hold men fully accountable for rape, they expend their considerable resources on trying to stop women and men from the "sins" of contraception and abortion.

~ Riane Tennenhaus Eisler
(1937–)

We will be ourselves and free, or die in the attempt. Harriet Tubman was not our great-grandmother for nothing.

~ Alice Walker
(1944–)

I truly believe that unless we move into feminine systems of governance we don't have a chance on this planet. I'm someone who's looking for a reason to hope, and for me hope looks like feminine systems of governance being instated in, like, the major religious institutions and throughout corporate and civil life. And it might sound far-fetched, but if you look at your own beliefs, just imagine how quickly you accepted the idea that the ocean is rising and the ecology of our world is collapsing. We can actually imagine that more readily than we can imagine a switch from patriarchal to matriarchal systems of governance—a subtle shift in the way our society works.

~ Antony Hegarty
(1977–)

Yours truly on the Mall in Washington D.C. for the April 25, 1993 March on Washington for Lesbian, Gay and Bi Equal Rights and Liberation. I had my photograph taken with lots of lesbians that day—what a blast! Got a little sunburned, too.

**Extreme heterosexuality is a perversion.**
~ Margaret Mead (1901-1978)

**The most sympathetic men never fully comprehend women's concrete situation.**
~ Simone de Beauvoir (1908-1986)

**If you think you're too small to have an impact, try going to bed with a mosquito in the room.**
~ Anita Roddick (1942-2007)

©2014 Michael Elizabeth Marillynson LLC - This poster is from the book "Contrary to the Custom of Men: Field Notes on the Pestilence of Patriarchy from a Disloyal Son." For re-printing permission go to: con2men.info.

**follow the repellent stream back to its sewage tank**

androputriarchy played backward

Remember the good old days when you could play Beatles records backwards and discover the real fate of Paul McCartney?

Well, for all you guys still living in your parents' basement trying to prove Paul died and was replaced by an impersonator; I've got a new challenge for you.

It's called the "Follow the corpse trail back to **Androputriarchy**" game and it has certain rules by which we all must abide:

*Rule One:* the game starts when you choose an action, intention, or result of any human behavior (Point Z), now or in the past. For example, I have a fence around my yard.

*Rule Two:* You win the game when you work backward from where you are to Androputriarchy (Ground Zero). It's that simple. For example, why do I have a fence around my yard?

7) I put up a fence because it looks so beautiful.

6) I really put up my beautiful fence to keep people out.

5) I want to keep people out so they are less likely to steal my stuff or assault my family.

4) The "people" most likely to steal my stuff or assault my wife are adult men.

3) Men steal and/or assault because male privilege (under Androputriarchy) has taught men they are entitled to possess property and/or women.

2) Men's obsession and striving for private property, even the poorest of men, reinforces the entire system of exploitation through wealthism and Androputriarchy.

1) So-called "private property" is one of the many tenets and foundations of Androputriarchy, so all men strive for it no matter what their economic lot.

**Ground Zero)** Androputriarchy devised the notion of private property, and Androputriarchy is the institution of men's superiority and entitlement at the expense of women. The never-ending and never-examined quest for private property reinforces the overall notion of men's superiority and entitlement at the expense of women.

I got from Point 7 to Ground Zero. I win!

**Androputriarchy:** [*andro* meaning male, man; *putrere*, meaning rotten, or proceeding from decay; *archy* meaning ruler] an alternative for "patriarchy" that attempts to make clearer the corruption, malevolence, and destructive blight that male supremacy has been in human history and remains to this day.

59

> **Weave of absence:** all of the purposeful tactics and strategies used by Androputriarchy, and their cumulative results, to make women and/or men invisible when it is in Androputriarchy's interest.

See how easy this game can be? If you are like most people you will find this game quite addictive and terrifying. The more you do it, the better you get at it, and the more friends you lose.

This process is a touchstone for me: when something is happening in my world or in my mind I can't quite figure out, I remind myself to conduct this analysis. It always helps me find clarity, and I puzzle why I neglected to do it in the first place.

I find this to be the case with a feminist analysis altogether: I taught myself (who else was going to teach me?) to always analyze where women fit into, or are totally absent from, any situation. What is or isn't being done to or for them? Why are they absent? How is the **weave of absence** constructed and by whom? Why are their interests not being mentioned or considered? What does Androputriarchy want in this situation and how is He going about getting it? Who is being silent about what Androputriarchy is doing and how are they covering that up?

This feminist analysis will not make you many friends. And certainly not any male friends.

It reminds me of the inane, idiotic cops and robbers and lawyers television shows to which Americans love to gratify themselves. They are peopled with FBI agents and cops who are world-wise and always suspect the worst in people as they go about their jobs solving crimes. We are meant to appreciate their jaded suspicion/mistrust of everyone's motives because they have seen it all and know not to believe anything that is told them or what seems obvious on the surface.

Yet, when I constantly voice my suspicions of Androputriarchy's every move—even though I have one million times more evidence of Androputriarchy's malevolence, crimes and cover-ups than any of the dopey television shows—I am told there is something wrong with me; that I hate all men; that I think the worst about everything; that I am not positive enough; that I need to be more trusting of human nature; that my "negativity" is not good for me; that I am not "creating a positive space"; that I am indulging a "low vibration"; that I am Chicken Little and "we're tired of hearing you whine about the sky falling," and blah, blah, blah.

Maybe I should join the FBI and have a more fulfilling life. Carry a badge; throw my weight around; have a really big dick.

I considered writing something that examined ways you can confirm the presence of Androputriarchy in your life/experience. However, that would assume there are places in anyone's life/world where Androputriarchy does not reach. Alas, Androputriarchy contaminates all things at all times.

I also want to convey how utterly important this vigilance is on your part. It basically comes down to this: if you are not vigilant for how Androputriarchy's cancerous hand is at work in your life/world, you will not be aware of how you make decisions that are at odds with your own wellbeing, and the wellbeing of all other women, especially disempowered women. Also, if you are not vigilant for Androputriarchy's tactics, you will make the mistake of thinking you are the problem: it is only you that doesn't "get it"; it is only you that is fucked up; it is best to shut up, realize you are wrong, and forget about it.

Androputriarchy never sleeps. He is worse than rust in that way. So, I offer a couple ways I have learned to accept it is not a matter of if or when Androputriarchy is at His corrosive work in our lives, but only how.

You can confirm the presence of Androputriarchy when capitulation to your own oppression, or the oppression of others, is your best option in a given situation. This would also be true when you are observing the behavior of others. This is a fundamental and necessary underpinning of the corrupt despotism of Androputriarchy.

You can confirm the presence of Androputriarchy when you have a nagging feeling something in front you just doesn't seem right. You keep looking at it over and over and try to figure out why it doesn't make sense but you are unable to. You are nervous/confused that no one else seems to notice. Finally, when you remember my sage advice, you apply the "Follow the corpse trail back to Androputriarchy" game and it becomes perfectly clear.

You can confirm the presence of Androputriarchy when you speak your truth about what you have learned about Androputriarchy and the people you thought would be your friends and defenders to the death suddenly, or slowly, begin to creep away from you. You feel isolation and aloneness. You try to address it but the response you get is vague and slippery and you begin to do what I advised against: you begin to conclude it is about you, and not about Androputriarchy.

You can confirm the presence of Androputriarchy when you witness horrible things—in small instances and huge—that happen to disempowered people and you are mostly disturbed not by what happened to them, but to how their community or the world responds, or doesn't respond, to it. You think to yourself, "What is wrong with these people? Don't they get what is going on?" Whether "these people" do or don't get what is going on, Androputriarchy does and His cold, clammy hand is omnipresent.

If you apply vigilance you will find that the "blind spots" and areas of "vulnerability" in your life are distinct from those I personally have, and Androputriarchy teaches the world to focus in on your particular vulnerabilities. This is not a mistake or coincidence. Androputriarchy has damaged you in a way particular to you, and will use your particularities against you to silence you. It's how the beast feeds.

# Speaking of Women

We have moreover, the profound conviction that only by the power of association based on solidarity—by the union of the working classes of both sexes to organize labor—can be acquired completely and pacifically, the civil and political equality of women, and the social right for all.

~ Jeanne-Francoise Deroine
(1805–1894)

All philanthropy—no age has seen more of it than our own—is only a savory fumigation burning at the mouth of a sewer. This incense offering makes the air more endurable to passersby, but it does not hinder the infection in the sewer from spreading.

~ Ellen Key
(1849–1926)

Foremost among the barriers to equality is the system which ignores the mother's service to Society in making a home and rearing children. The mother is still the unchartered servant of the future, who receives from her husband, at his wages. For mothers who must earn, there is indeed no leisure time problem. The long hours of earning are increased by the hours of domestic labor, until no slightest margin for relaxation or change of thought remains.

~ Katharine Anthony
(1877–1965)

Establish democracy at home, based on human rights as superior to property rights.

~ Jeannette Rankin
(1880–1973)

According to patriarchal values, that which is "commonplace" is "of little worth," for in a competitive, hierarchical society scarcity is intrinsic to "worth." Thus gold is more important than fresh air, and consequently we are forced to live in a world in which gold is easier to find than pure air.

~ Mary Daly
(1928–2010)

Schools closed because learning got in the way of patriotism.

~ Karen Finley
(1956–)

Men grow up with a conviction that they are always stronger than somebody.

~ Natalie Angier
(1958–)

Women must understand that it's not another woman who is the enemy, but the power structure that sets it up for very few women to get jobs and makes them fight each other for the few goodies thrown their way. We don't tend to see structural or institutional problems. We focus on the other person.

~ Michelle Faludi
(dates unknown)

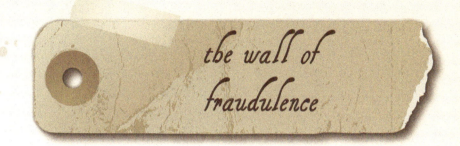

# the wall of fraudulence

Sitting in a batterer accountability group and hearing a man, for the millionth time, offer some lame lie for why he assaulted his victim got me thinking. I suggested to our intervention team that we put large pieces of paper on the wall of the group room, make it a requirement of the group to catch each time a man uses such a fiction, and have him immediately write it on the paper. We adopted the strategy and soon the walls were literally covered with hundreds of such deceptions from the truth.

The truth is men planfully choose who, when, where, and how to assault. Period.

I wasn't **able** to stop there
It was an **accident**
I don't **accept** change
I didn't know how to be more **accountable**
I was still learning **accountability**
**Accountability** didn't stick with me
I didn't get my **act** together
I didn't **adapt** to the way society is now
My **adrenaline** overflowed
We're **Afro-American** and that's how we talk
She was coming **after** me
It was an **afterthought**
I guess I got too **aggressive**
That's what got me **aggressive**
She was the initial **aggressor**
She **agitated** my behavior
Everything was up in the **air**
**Alcohol** came in to play
**Alcohol** brought the violence out of me

**Alcohol** enhanced the problem
**Alcohol** escalates a little bit
The **alcohol** controlled me
**Alcohol** was involved
The **alcohol** started talking
**Alcohol** set me off like a keg of dynamite
I had an **alcohol** problem
I had a little **alcohol**
I'm more susceptible to violence on **alcohol**
The **alcohol** changes my personality
It was an **alcohol** related incident
I was really under the influence of **alcohol**
She wouldn't **allow** me to cool off
She didn't **allow** me to leave
She **allowed** it
It was **a lot** at one time
There was an **altercation** happening
We got into a little **altercation**
I had no **alternatives**
She was **anemic**

I tried to let her know what life is like in **America**
That's how I **am**
I didn't **analyze** the situation
**Anger** comes out of me
The **anger** escalates
I have an **anger** problem
I was venting my **anger**
I couldn't control my **anger**
I had an **anger** problem
I did it out of **anger**
I don't handle **anger** well
I couldn't control my **anger**
**Anger** creates violence
I had an inability to control my **anger**
My **anger** controlled me
I didn't know how to vent my **anger** a different way
I was in to the **anger** thing
My **anger** got the better of my rational thinking
I got **angry** and didn't use patience

63

I didn't have the right **answers**

We kept upping the **ante**

It was an **animal** response to a perceived threat

An **argument** broke out

Before I knew it we got to **arguing**

It's an **arguing** type situation

We had a violent **argument**

The **argument** started in the bedroom and went into the kitchen

I was **avoiding** an argument

We got into an **argument** match

I got into a violent **argument**

The **argument** got out of hand

We had a basic sibling **argument**

We had a normal **argument**

We had a domestic **argument**

We just had an **argument**

We had physical **arguments**

It was an overheated **argument**

We were in a heated **argument**

We both used all of our **artillery**

She **asked** me to hit her

I was half **asleep**

I didn't have an opportunity to be **assertive**

It was a detrimental **atmosphere**

I kind of got an **attitude**

I have an **attitude** problem

I bring a lot of **attitude** home with me from work

My **attitude** overtook my actions

**Attitude** sets me off

My **attitude** got the best of me

It became **automatic**

It's kind of **automatic**

I was **avoiding** the bigger problem

I was **avoiding** hurting her

I was **avoiding** punching her

I didn't get **away** from the situation

I came **back** on her

My **back** was up against the wall

I **backslid**

I was just getting **back** at her in some demented way

I had a physical **background**

If she was a **bad** woman she deserved a pop in the eye

My relationship went **bad**

It got really **bad**

I'm **baffled** about it all

I was **baited** into it

She lost her **balance**

I went **bananas**

She was in the **bar**

Without thinking I **barked**

It was that strong German **beer**

That **behavior** came out

My **behavior** was wrong

My **behavior** repeated itself

It was violent **behavior**

**Being** what I am

Things got the **best** of me

It was the **best** I could do

I let my inner self get the **best** of me

I was **beside** myself watching

I wasn't a **better** man

I just avoided the **bigger** problem

Sometimes I get angry and **blackout**

I **blew** up

The flame **blew**

I just **blew** up

It built up inside until I **blew** up

We both **blew** up

It was a **blight** on our weekend

I was **blind** to what was going on

Sometimes I have **blinders** on

The abuse **blossomed** in our relationship

It's in my **blood**

The **blood** boiled

We **blow** up at each other

We had a **blowout**

I might have **blown** up

It happened out of the **blue**

I **blurted** out

My anger **boiled** over

I got to my **boiling** point

I was **boiling**

I just **boiled** over

I took so much until I get to the **boiling** point

I didn't put it in my **book**

All of a sudden, **boom**, it happens

Then, **boom**, out of nowhere

I was **born** with aggressiveness

I let women **bother** me

I was **boxed** in

I didn't engage my **brain** before my mouth

I don't know how to **break** off

I didn't put on the **brakes**

We had a mutual **breakup**

I was **brewing**

I was pushed to the **brink**

That's when everything **broke** loose

I **broke**

I **broke** there

I was **brought** up that way

I guess things **build** up in me

I **build** and **build** and one day boom

It **builds** up

It was all **built** up inside me

A lot of things **built** up to it

Everything **built** up on me

I was like a **bull** in heat

It was the stress of my **buttons** being pushed all the time

People push my **buttons**

I let a lot of things push my **buttons**

She controlled my **buttons**

She pushed my anger **buttons**

She pushed my hot **buttons**

I had a **buzz** on

Sometimes it just goes right **by**

I **calmed** her down

She destroyed my **calm**

I couldn't **calm** down

I couldn't keep it **calm**

I **calmed** her down

That's the way it **came** out

The abuse **came** up out of me

It **came** out of me before I could stop and think about it

It just **came** out

I **can't** shut up

I wasn't **careful**

I was getting too **carried** away

I got **carried** away

I didn't **catch** myself

I didn't **catch** a key subject that came up

I was **caught** off guard

I got **caught** up in anger

I got **caught** up in my violent behavior

I got **caught** up in this one incident

I got **caught** up in the situation

Something **caused** me to do it

It was **cause** and effect

It takes two to **cause**

I was off **center**

I didn't get a second **chance**

I **changed**

I was going through some **changes**

**Chemicals** altered my way of judgment

My **chemistry** takes over

I was just being **childish**

I did things in a **childish** way

I did it for the **children**

I didn't have a **choice**

I had no **choice**

I made the wrong **choice**

I made a bad **choice**

I made bad **choices**

I made horrible **choices**

I made some real poor **choices**

I don't **choose** to yell and scream

I was in a violent **circle**

The whole **circumstance** came down

I don't know if I'm going to **click**

It wasn't the suit of **clothes** I wanted to put on

**Cocaine** showed the bad side of me

There was physical **combat** between us

The b-word **comes** out

It **comes** out

It just **comes** out that way

This problem kept **coming** up

My anxiety and frustration starts **coming** out

I couldn't **communicate** with her

Our **communication** didn't work

It's the only way I know how to cover up my **communication** skills

I put myself in a **compromising** situation

I couldn't **concentrate**

I jumped to **conclusions**

I had a nervous **condition**

I was **conditioned** to act that way

There was a **confrontation**

I got **confused**

I'm not good at **confusion**

I did not **consciously** do it

I was out of my **context**

We had hostile **contact**

I was **containing** her

I couldn't **control** my temper

I wasn't in **control** enough of what I said

It led on to where I got out of **control**

I couldn't talk without losing **control**

I lost **control** and everything bad

I couldn't **control** myself better than that

It was a situation I couldn't **control**

My efforts to **control** myself failed repeatedly

I was on the verge of losing **control**

I got out of **control**

I lost more **control**

I didn't have enough **control**

I didn't want to, but then I lost **control**

We both lost **control**

I tend to get out of **control**

Things got way out of **control**

I didn't know how to **control** myself

I was being **controlled** by someone else

I felt like she was **controlling** me

I was backed into a **corner**

I was **cornered**

I **couldn't** avoid a confrontation

I **couldn't** take it anymore!

I **couldn't** stop it

We're like a lot of **couples** in that respect

It had to run its **course**

I **cracked**

I went **crazy**

It was **crazy**

I just went **crazy**

My bad attitude **crept** back in

I **crossed** the border

I **crossed** over

I'm on **cruise**

It was the **culmination** of a lot of things

It was a **daily** abusive thing

We did this **dance** together

I had a hard **day**

I brought a bad **day** home with me

I was having a hard **day**

It was a **daily** abusive thing

It's just how I **deal** with things

I couldn't **deal** with it

I couldn't **deal** with the situation

65

I just fucked up and made the wrong
**decision**

I made that bad **decision**

I made the wrong **decision**

I made a very, very bad **decision**

I went off the **deep** end

It's a character **defect**

I reacted to **defend** myself

I was **defending** myself

I automatically take a **defense**

It was a **defensive** reaction

I was brought up on the **defensive**
side

It was a **delusional** thought I acted
on

I was **deranged** with bitterness

I'm not perfect at **diagnosing** people's problems

I **didn't** do it

I was **diffusing** her upset and irrational behavior

I was just **directing** her out

I have never **directly** abused them
from a physical standpoint

I didn't have self-**discipline**

We had some **discrepancies**

It's a **disease**

That's my attention deficit **disorder**

It was a minor **dispute**

It was a **divorce** issue

I was on her like a rabid **dog**

If she just acted like my **dog** everything would have been okay

I **don't** know what I do

It was a domestic **dispute**

I took a **dominant** role

It caused me to go **domestic**

It was a real cheap **door**

She went **down** to the ground

I didn't realize what was going on
until it all went **down**

I get angry when I **drink**

The **drinking** made it physical

**Drinking** had a little bit to
do with it

I was **driven** toward that goal

I was **drunk**

She initiated the whole thing by
being **drunk**

I was half way **drunk**

I go off the **edge**

I was right on the **edge**

She took me over the **edge**

I was set over the **edge**

I'm **elderly** and have been like this
all my life

I get too **emotional**

I get a little bit too **emotional**

I am **emotionally** weak

My **emotions** were at wits end

I should have handled my **emotions**
better

My **emotions** take over

I didn't keep my **emotions** down

My **emotions** erupt

I can't handle my **emotions**

I had angry, violent **emotions**

I **ended** up hurting her shoulder

I **ended** up hitting her

I **ended** the argument

Drinking **enhanced** my problem

It had an **energy** of its own

I couldn't do **enough** for her

I didn't remove myself from the abusive **environment**

I'm not **equipped** to handle things
ahead of time

It **erupted** in me

I finally **erupted**

Violence **erupts**

The argument would **escalate**

Our fight was **escalating**

Everything **escalated**

We **escalated** our voices

It **escalated** to physical abuse

It got **escalated**

The situation really **escalated**

It **escalated** from that

It kept **escalating** on

A small argument **escalated** into a
serious situation

I got **even** with her

It was an abusive **event**

My **evil** side came out that night

I'm not the domestic violator her
**ex-husband** was

We **exchanged** some words

There were words **exchanged**

I got overly **excited**

I didn't see any **exit**

I more or less **expected** her to be
obedient

I **explode**

I hold it in and hold it in and
then **explode**

Things build up and I **explode**

I **exploded** at her

I **exploded** at them

She was irrational and **explosive**

I was just **expressing** my opinion

We got in each other's **face**

I was a **failure**

I took a **fall**

It's easy to **fall** into things

It had gone too **far**

We went **farther** than any time
before

I was going too **fast**

My **father** doesn't have a lot of
patience

It's a **fault** of mine

It's a **fault** that leads to
argumentation

I returned the **favor**

My **fear** came out in abuse

I was **fed** up

I don't **feel** good

I am unable to express my **feelings**

It's what I did with my **feelings**

I **fell** into it

I **fell** back into it

I **fell** off the map

I **fell** back into that old person

It was a situation I **fell** into

It **festered** until it came out into the open

I couldn't **figure** her out

We ended up getting in a **fight**

Our **fight** got extreme

We had a **fight**

We had a fist **fight**

We got in a **fight**

It was because we were **fighting**

The **fights** started to get a little more physical

I **find** myself doing it

My **finger** poked her in the eye

My **fingernails** grow too fast

My **fingernails** were a little longer than they are now

It was the **first** thing that came to me

I did not use **fisticuffs**

I was too **fixated**

I **flew** off the handle

The situation just **flew** by me

It's because of my **flighty** thinking

I **fly** off the handle

It set me off on a bad **foot**

I realized that I used too much **force**

She **forced** me to

I was **forced** to

There were other **forces** at work

We **found** ourselves in conflict

I **found** myself arguing back with her

I **found** myself somewhere I didn't want to be

I **found** myself chasing her

I'd **freak** out

I was in a **frenzy**

I was venting **frustration**

We **fucked** up

I blew a **fuse**

I have a short **fuse**

I had a short **fuse**

I blew a **gasket**

She poured **gasoline** on the fire

I'm a **Gemini**

It was a **generational** cycle

In my **generation** it's the way we spoke

It was a **generational** thing

It's in my **genes**

I was **genetically** born with it

My anger came out like a bad **Genie**

I was on my **gentlemanly** way and she proceeded to hit me

I let her **get** to me

I let it **get** to me

She would **get** me to do it

I **go** off

I could only **go** so far

I let myself **go**

She **got** my goat

I got **going** with what I had to do

I get **going** and shit

I got **going**

I'm not **good** in one-on-one relationships

I thought the violence was going to be **gone**

There was a **gun** involved

It had **gone** too far

I'm not **good** at that

She **got** to me

That's the way I **grew** up

I got real **grim** with her

I got into a **groove** of life

I didn't want to **grow** up

She wasn't **grown** up

I was hanging in the wrong **group**

It caught me off **guard**

That's the kind of **guy** I am

I was that **guy** again

It was because I was out with the **guys**

I have this bad **habit**

I have a very bad **habit**

It's a bad **habit**

Force of **habit**

I picked up her bad **habits**

I **had** to

Things got out of **hand**

Every man should be able to **handle** one woman

It was too much for me to **handle**

I didn't **handle** it well

I used my **hands**

An argument **happened**

What **happened**, **happened**

When that **happened**

The assault **happened**

It **happened** that way

Things **happened** quick one night

The incident **happened**

It **happened** in an argument

It's what **happened** in the past

I **happened** very fast

It **happened** so fast

It just **happened**

It **happened**

Something **happened**

The phone **happened** to be ripped out of the wall

It **happened** to me

We fight and it **happens** again

Sometimes that **happens**

Something bad **happens**

I had a **hard** day

Came to a **head**

I didn't know what was **heading** me
into this

I was **headed** down that road

**Heat** of the moment

It happened in the **heat** of an
argument

Sometimes when the **heat** gets
turned up things come out

It got **heated** up

**Heat** of passion

I got **heated** up

Some **heated** words were exchanged

It just kept **heating** up

I **held** her back from hitting me

I got into it with **her**

All **hell** broke loose

I can't **help** myself

It's **hereditary**

I have a high **history** of violence
in my life

That's a **history** of mine

I was trying to **hold** back

I was **holding** her in my arms

The **honeymoon** wore off

She had a bad **hormonal** imbalance

That's what brought out my **hostility**

It was a **hot** button

It just kept getting **hotter** and
**hotter**

My **house** needs to be designed
differently

It's an abusive **house**

I don't know **how** to stop it

It's because I'm **human**

I get **hung** up

I had no **idea** I would be offensive

I was showing my **ignorance**

An **immature** part of me came out
and took over my body

I became very **immature**

I knew violence was **imminent**

I didn't know how to handle a situation once it reaches an **impasse**

In previous times I have been
**impatient**

I do things **impulsively**

It was **in** me

I was into the battering **incident**

I just wanted to stop the **incident**

It was an isolated **incident**

They were **incidents** I had

This little **incident**

There were **incidents**

There have been **incidents** of
violence

I was **incoherent**

She **initiated** the violence

I dealt with it **inappropriately**

I went **insane**

It was an **insecure** thing

Alcohol was the **instigator**

It's my basic **instinct**

It's my natural **instinct** as a batterer

It's my aggressive male **instinct**

My masculine **integrity** was
devoured

My **intellect** ended

I was not very **intelligent**

I didn't have any **intention** to do that

I had no **intention** to deliberately
say that

I got **into** it with her

I was **intoxicated**

I **introduced** a gun into the
discussion

I was too personally **involved**

I **involved** her in my frustration

I was **irrational**

It was rather **isolated**

It was a wrong **judgment** call

It just **jumped** off

It's our **karma**

I was acting like a little **kid**

It was **knee** jerk

We **knew** each other too well

I acted the only way I **knew** how

Before I **knew** it I was off to jail

Before I **knew** it I was in the county
jail

The next thing I **knew**

The **knife** was thrown in the fire

We **knocked** each other down

I don't **know** what happens to me

I didn't **know** another way to stop
her

I didn't **know** better

I don't **know** what came over me

It's the only thing I **know** how to do

It's the only thing I **know** right now

I didn't **know** whether I was coming
or going

After a while I just—I don't **know**

I didn't **know** what I was doing

I don't **know** how it came up

I was **lacking** in communication

I **lapsed** in to my same pattern

It was too **late** to pause and reflect

I was up **late** that night

I didn't **laugh**, my lip just went up

I didn't **learn** my lesson

One thing **led** to another

It all **led** up to that

I was on the edge of what was **legal**

I was giving her a **lesson**

We didn't **let** it go

I had **license** to be angry

Violence was a part of our **life**

Sometimes **life** is abusive

I'm just **like** that

**Liquor** makes me violent

The **liquor** was controlling me

I've been **living** that lifestyle

I was with her too **long**

There are situations where I really
**lose** control

When I get mad I **lose** something

I was verbally **losing** it

I was **losing** it at that point

I was **losing** it

I **lost** my ability to control myself

I **lost** my cool

I **lost** it when I first walked in the house

I **lost** my ability to negotiate

I **lost** control

I **lost** it

We get **loud** sometimes

I become a **loud** person, too

It was **loud**

We weren't in **love**

What I did was not conducive to a **loving** environment

I was out to **lunch**

I have a problem with **lying**

It **makes** me

I was not being a **man**

I'm not that kind of **man**

I wasn't **man** enough

It **manifested** itself

It was a bad **marriage**

That's not **me**

I didn't **mean** to hurt her

I have a **mean** streak

I said a lot of things I didn't **mean**

I didn't **mean** to do it

I didn't **mean** it

I didn't **mean** to say that

I didn't **mean** it that way

It was a **meeting** of the thing

All the **men** in my family do it

It was a bad **mess**

I was a **messed** up person

She **messed** me up

Your **mind** comes up against a roadblock

I can't know what was in my **mind**

I don't know what was going through my **mind**

My **mind** wasn't on it

I wasn't in my everyday **mind**

I naturally wasn't in my right **mind**

I had too much on my **mind**

I wasn't in my right **mind**

I was **misconstrued**

I was **misinterpreted**

I **missed** it

I **misspoke** myself

I made a stupid **mistake**

It was a **mistake**

It was all a gigantic **mistake**

I made a human **mistake**

I repeated my **mistake**

It was because of how she spent **money**

It was my **mood** change

I was in a **mood**

It was this ornery **mood** I have

I was in a bad **mood**

She was in the arguing **mode**

We have our **moments**

There was still **more** abuse after that

I was going through the **motions**

I engaged my **mouth** without thinking

I let my mouth get me in a lot of **trouble**

It was my bad **mouth**

I didn't know what was coming out of my **mouth**

It was coming out of my **mouth** flowing like water

I **moved** her out of the way

I came back to **myself**

It's a **natural** human response

It comes to me **naturally**

It's just my **nature**

Its second **nature**

It's in all men's **nature** to be abusive and violent

Somebody **needed** to do it

It was a **need** I had

I pulled something **negative** out of the situation

She got on my last **nerve**

I let it get to my **nerves**

I get **nervous**

I was a little **nervous**

I was a **nervous** wreck

I get real **nervous**

I didn't go to a **neutral** place

I intimidated her in a **non-physical** sense

I am a **non-violent** person

It was before **noon**

I wasn't my **normal** self

There was **nothing** I could do about what happened

It came out of **nowhere**

I was still **numb**

Out on the **nut**

The fight **occurred**

The whole situation **occurred**

An affair **occurred**

We move from one **octave** to "what the fuck?"

I went **off**

I just came **off** that way

I **offered** to shoot my wife

I had an **old-fashioned** way of doing things

I'm getting **older**

It was the **only** way I knew

Her purse had **opened** up

I was all out of other **options**

I couldn't let the **opportunity** go by

My abuse got **out** of hand

It just came **out**

I had an **outburst**

I had a little **outburst**

We had a violent **outburst**

I was **over** reacting

I **overreacted** a little bit

I reacted totally **overboard**

I went **overboard**

I **overdid** it

I **over-disciplined** her

I was **over-hyper**

I can't stop being abusive **overnight**

I **overreact**

I **overreacted** to the situation

I **overstepped** myself

I **overstepped** my bounds

I was **overworked**

My **parents** formed my values

It was a **part** of me

I can't get **past** this

It's what I saw in the **past**

I was led down the wrong **path**

I lost my **patience**

**People** let me do it

I wasn't being very **perceptive**

I was another **person**

It's in my **personality**

It was a **part** of my **personality**

I have a "take charge" **personality**

It's just part of my **personality**

What my inside **personality**, Igor, did was very bad

I didn't keep things in **perspective**

It was **petty** behavior

This was a **phantom** incident

It was a **phase** I was going through

The **phone** hit her

The **phone** hit her in the face

Before I knew it was getting **physical**

It wasn't **physical**, just a little head lock

It got **physical** at that point

It got to the point where it was a little **physical**

It got a little **physical** sometimes

When it's about to get **physical**

I'm not a **physical** person

I was **physical** with her

We got **physical**

Things got **physical**

We were on a different **plain**

It went until it **played** itself out

I was less than **pleasant**

I couldn't **please** her

I was just getting my **point** across

I get to the **point** where I get somewhat violent

I reached my breaking **point**

It just **popped** out of me

Something **possessed** me to do it

I was **powerless** and didn't know what to do

She **precipitated** my way of thinking

I can't think as **precise** when I'm ticked off

I can't keep the **pressure** from blowing up and hurting someone

**Pressure** builds up because she goes to school

I can't control the **pressure** inside of me

I threw my **principles** out the window

I turned off my **principles**

I had a big **problem** with that

That's one of my **problems**

I had a little **problem**

I had this little **problem**

I ran into a **problem** and the police were involved

My son had become a **problem**

I have a **problem** with abuse

I was **programmed** to act this way

I was **programmed** to react a certain way

It **progressed** from that point

It was blown out of **proportion**

I tried to **protect** myself and ended up an abuser

I was **protecting** myself

I was **protecting** my son

I was **protecting** my property

I was **protecting** my family

I was **protecting** the car

She **provoked** me

She **provoked** it

She can **provoke** me and get me in trouble

She **pulled** her head away

It was because of the air **pump**

It was a **punctuation**

I didn't do it **purposely**, but methodically

**Push** turned in to shove, shove turned into choking

I get **pushed** over the edge

I got **pushed** along a little bit

It started out as a **pushing** thing

We had a **pushing** match

I'm a **pussy** if I walk away

I just tried to ask a **question**

It all happened **quick**

I have a **quick** temper

Everything happened so **quick**

I went into the **rage**

I let the **rage** get the better of me

It's my **rage**

I would **rage**

I woke up in a **rage** of fighting

I had to express my **rage**

It's how I was **raised**

I was just **rambling**

I kind of **ran** into a little situation

I was not thinking **rationally**

I **react**

I **react** badly

I **reacted** stupidly

I **react** in the same manner

I would **react** violently

I just **reacted**

I **reacted** wrongfully

It automatically caused a **reaction**

It was a non-thinking **reaction**

It was a simultaneous **reaction**

It's my normal **reaction**

It was a **reaction**

I was out of touch with **reality**

It wasn't **reality**

I didn't **realize** I was being abusive

I don't **realize** I'm doing that until
it's pointed out to me

I didn't **realize** I was being
controlling

I didn't **realize** the impact of what
I said

I did it before I **realized** what I was
doing

I didn't **realize** what I did

It took me a long time to **realize**
what was happening

I did it for no **reason**

There was no **reason** to it

It happened for no apparent **reason**

My **reason** went bye-bye

My ability to **reason** was swept away

I **received** domestic violence

It was a **reckless** act

I couldn't **recognize** my bad choices

It wasn't **recoverable**

I was **reflecting** past aggression

It's a **reflex**

I just used it as a **reference**

I didn't **refuse** to do it

I **relapsed**

It was an abusive **relationship**

It was a new **relationship**

It was a broken **relationship**

It wasn't a good, strong **relationship**

Our **relationship** was going to end
anyway

I am guilty of a bad **relationship**

I couldn't **relax**

I had to let it **release** a little

I **released** my anger

I needed to **remove** myself from the
situation

I needed to **remove** the violence
from my system

No **repair** was possible

I was **restraining** her

I didn't **restrain** myself

Things were **repetitive** and hostile

My **resentment** had a lot of
angry energy

I **responded**

It's my normal **response**

She needed physical **restraint**

I was **restraining** her

I **retaliated**

I hit the point of no **return**

I should have got **rid** of her some
other way

I couldn't let it **roll** off of me

Everything **rolled** into one

I go through the **roof**

It was the end of the **rope**

I guess I got too **rough**

My father **rubbed** off on me

She **rubbed** me the wrong way

We were in a **ruckus**

Some things were **said**

I just **said** something back

I didn't **say** that

I didn't know how to **say** it

The **scales** tipped to set me off

It was an intimidating **scenario**

It was a bad **scene**

We got into a little **scuffle**

We were **scuffling**

I didn't **see** what I was doing

I just **seemed** to be doing that

If I had any **sense** I wouldn't have
battered

I had no common **sense**

I was out of my **senses**

She **set** me up

She **set** me off

It **set** me off

I was trying to **settle** her down

I was **settling** her down

I was only **seventeen** and she was
thirty

I was **shooting** from the hip

I **shot** off at the mouth

That comment just **shot** out of my
mouth

A **shouting** match proceeded

There was some **shoving**

We were in a **shuffle**

I don't know to **shut** up

I was **sick** then

It's a **sickness**

That's a **side** of me that doesn't show
up that often

I got on her bad **side**

That **side** of me came back out

It started out as a bad **sink** and
quickly escalated into something else

It was that kind of **situation**

The **situation** just comes along

I couldn't get out of the **situation**

It was a hit or be hit type of
**situation**

I let the **situation** take control of me

The **situation** didn't diffuse itself

The **situation** was destined to get
out of control

The **situation** didn't resolve

I don't have the **skills**

She put me to **sleep**

I wasn't getting enough **sleep**

It was a **sleeping** disorder

Things just kind of **slid** there

**Slip** of the tongue

She **slipped**

It **slipped** out

I **slipped** back into my old habits

I **slipped** in to threats

It was **slipping** in

I **snapped**

I **snapped** fast

It grew like a **snowball**

**Something** was coming

I was never violent when I was **sober**

My relationship went **sour**

She was from the **south**

We **spark** off

**Sparked** a violent streak

I couldn't **speak** in a logical way

I **speak** before I think

Figure of **speech**

It was a **speech** problem

I **spoiled** a romantic evening

Things happened **spontaneously**

I killed the **spontaneity** of our interaction

**Spur** of the moment

It was a **spur** of the moment thing

I was pulled out of my **square**

I couldn't **stand** it anymore

She **started** it

That's when the physical violence **started**

This is the **state** we're in

She **stepped** between us

I **stepped** into intimidation

The **stick** hit her

I got the short end of the **stick**

I went by a bunch of **stop** signs

I just can't seem to **stop** myself

The **storm** had to pass

I didn't **straighten** up

I had a violent **streak**

I got it from the **streets**

It jumps out when I'm under **stress**

My words were **stumbling** out

I just **stung** her

I was **stupid** enough to do it

I do **stupid** shit when I'm mad

I did it out of **stupidity**

Things **succeeded** from there

I **succumbed** to the fact

It was a big **suggestion**

I couldn't **take** it anymore

I didn't **take** myself out of the situation

I didn't have anywhere to go and **talk** about it

I couldn't **talk** it out

I thought I was **talking** nice

I let my **temper** out

I have a quick **temper**

I have a problem with losing my **temper** when we disagree

I didn't know how far my **temper** could go

I lost my **temper**

I have a quick and violent **temper**

I have a problem with my **temper**

I have a bad **temper**

I'm hot **tempered**

I have a **temper** problem

I lose my **temper** on occasion

It was my **temper**

I lost my **temper** enough

I don't know how to hold my **temper**

I have a short **temper**

My **temper** flared to an extreme

My **temper** got the best of me

I lost my **temperature**

My **temper's** got a lot to do with it

I have a **tendency** to yell

I had a **tendency** to overpower people around me

I was just being **tender**

I released my **tension**

**Things** succeeded from there

I didn't give myself time to **think**

I didn't **think** about what I did before I did it

I don't even **think** about it

I couldn't **think**

I didn't **think**

I don't **think** before I talk

I didn't **think** to myself

I don't **think** about it at the time

I didn't **think** enough to walk off

I wasn't **thinking** straight

I had impaired **thinking**

I wasn't **thinking** right

Sometimes I don't realize what I'm **thinking**

There was no **thinking**

Stopping and **thinking** was not always there

I just do it without **thinking**

I was only **thinking** about what I was doing with my hands

I wasn't **thinking** much about her until that point

I wasn't **thoughtful**

It wasn't a **threat**, it was a promise

I slipped into **threats**

She takes **threats** well

I had a lot **thrown** at me

It was part of the **tide** of violence

I'm a **time** bomb

As **time** goes on it gets worse

I didn't have **time** to figure it out

I do it all the **time**

It was because I was so **tired**

I had an increase in chemical **tolerance** and aggressive behavior

I didn't have the right **tools**

It's a **topic** that gets me into trouble

It goes back to my old **traits**

It's a **trait** I have

I got caught up in a **trap**

I couldn't help but get caught up in the **trap**

I was building a **trap** for myself
I **tried** everything I could
She **triggered** my actions
Something **triggered** it
My work **triggered** me off
We had that **trouble**
I didn't **try** hard enough
I wasn't **trying** to do it
It takes **two** for an argument to happen
It takes **two** to fight
Things were **ugly** in the house
I was an **ugly** person then
I was **uncertain** about myself
It was **unconscious**
I was **unconsciously** thinking
My voice became **unconsciously** very strong
I was leading an **uncontrollable** life
It turned into an **uncontrollable** situation
I came **unglued**
I was **unhealthy**
I was **unloading**
I was **up** all night
It was **ugly** in the house
It was my **upbringing**
I got **upset** and mean
I just get **upset**
I'm here for being **upset**
I get **upset** and worked up
I had an irresistible **urge**

She was **used** to it
I **vented** my anger
We used a lot of **verbal** and it turned into physical
It got **verbal**
I'm not **verbal**
I was a **victim** of her abuse
I have **violence** problems
I have domestic **violence**
I got violent with her after she got **violent** with me
I'm not a **violent** person
The excitement of the moment blurred my **vision**
It was a **visitation** thing
I was just a little bit more **vocal** than usual
We had a **volatile** relationship
You can only **walk** away from so much
I couldn't **walk** away from it
I did not **want** to do it
That's just the **way** I am
It was the **way** it went
There was no other **way**
I couldn't see it any other **way**
It was the only **way** I knew
**We** got into it
It was the hot **weather**
Somehow we got **wedged** in the door together
I **went** back to those old ways

She **weighs** a lot
The discussion was not going **well**
It was something we **went** through
I don't know **why** I did it
You don't know my **wife**
Things were kind of **wild**
I tried to **wiggle** it out
I **wiggled** right through them
I had loss of ordinary **willpower**
I **woke** up that way
We had **words**
My **words** came out of my mouth
I didn't leave **work** at **work**
It was a **work** related type of thing
I was too **worked** up
We weren't **working** it out
It came up **worse** than it should have been
We got **worse** and **worse**
I got pretty **wrapped** up in what was going on
We **wrestled** and I won
We ended up **wrestling**
I made **wrong** decisions
It just came out **wrong**
Some people take me the **wrong** way
She took it **wrong**
It took ten **years**
It's been going on for ten **years**
A lot of **yelling** took place
I just **zipped**

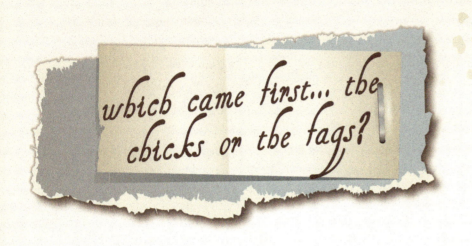

# which came first... the chicks or the fags?

## aren't we supposed to call out bullies?

Being a playground bully is not all peaches and cream; there are important choices to make.

Consider the playground bully's favorite target/victim: the skinny, funny-looking kid with thick glasses who is always good for some flinching, crying, and humiliating. Well, that kid's parents just accepted a job a continent away and we won't see that unhappy face anymore.

What to do? How does the playground bully pick a new punching bag?

It could be that stupid little black nerd who gets all of the attention for her science experiments. Or that faggy long-haired kid who wears tight jeans. Or maybe that quiet zit-faced fat boy who smells funny. Or that tomboy girl who can outrun all the boys. Everybody will get a laugh out of me making them pee their pants in fear.

To help the playground bully make this important choice we need look no further for guidance than Androputriarchy. Androputriarchy has always known how to make these choices, as evidenced by the historical record.

But it's not as simple as just picking a person. Oh no. It is about picking the right group and having believable justifications for why one is doing so. Again, Androputriarchy has always been very good at this.

For example, Androputriarchy has always enjoyed bullying (up to and including possible extermination) those whose gender identity and expression has been identified as not living down to the dualistic man-woman, masculine-feminine tedium.

So we bully them (up to and including possible extermination), thankful there is a vulnerable group available to us for this erotic, masturbatory pleasure.

But where it really starts getting interesting is in the can of worms behind the "faggots-bad-must-kill" label.

For example, Androputriarchy's deceptions for what this is all about and how we should think about it has been a wildly successful propaganda campaign due to His fear-inducing threats and our willful ignorance/blindness. Today, the ongoing bullying (up to and including possible extermination) of the transgendered/bisexual/lesbian/gay community has been surrounded by what discussion points?

Religion (it is a sin, it is against God's plan, blah, blah, blah), nature (it is not natural, it is not nature's plan, it cannot produce spawn, blah, blah, blah), family (it undermines the Androputriarchal family pod, it leads to divorce, it cannot produce spawn, blah, blah, blah), and immorality (it promotes more "irresponsible" sex than straight people have devised, it encourages sex without the purpose of spawning, blah, blah, blah).

What is our response to these insipid, lethal, and self-interested lies? We play right along, arguing over the pestilent propaganda by trying to counter the ridiculous arguments. Hello! That's called "losing" by strategists.

We nervously make sure all of the religious fascists do not get their uniforms and funny hats ruffled when we meekly disagree with their "position" but flagellate ourselves

74

publically to make sure, God-forbid, we do not interfere with their right to clutch onto their murderous and despicable "religious" views.

We argue it isn't a sin; we argue it isn't against God's plan; we argue it is natural; we argue it isn't against nature's plan; we argue it doesn't undermine the cardboard cutout family; we argue it doesn't lead to divorce; we argue gay people can spawn; we argue it doesn't promote irresponsible sex; we argue and argue and keep losing because we are wasting our time on banal diversions to the real issue—which is exactly what Androputriarchy wants us to do.

The issue, as always, is not what the victim does or doesn't do. Didn't women/feminists get us all to understand about rape a long time ago? That it isn't about what she wears, or where she goes, or what time it is, or how much she drank, or who her friends are, but it's ALL ABOUT THE PERPETRATOR!?!

Yet we haven't figured this out yet for other groups that are oppressed by Androputriarchy? This isn't about sin or God's plan or nature or the family platoon or divorce or spawning or irresponsible sex. This is about bullies smartly choosing vulnerable targets and then covering up their purpose for doing so in lies upon malodorous lies.

What is the purpose? The purpose for the playground bully is the same for Androputriarchy and is the same for all tyrants—power, control, domination, and my exaltation at your expense. Of course, there are other ways for a person to exalt themselves, but despotism is time-proven and relatively easy depending on your proximity to power (proximity meaning male privilege).

We should be only talking and arguing with these religions and conservatives and white supremacists about their tactics of tyranny and about the shamefulness of their bullying. We should be publically pointing out their purposes, their tactics, their violence, their enforcement activities, their careful and successful selection of vulnerable populations, the privileges and benefits accruing from their discrimination and bullying, and how they obfuscate their actions and attempt to get us to accept their propaganda.

We should, at the same time, be allying ourselves with any targets/victims of the bully. We should know by now we should be allying ourselves with the targets of the bully if for no other reason than because we know why the bully chooses a target. Because we understand the bully really has no interest or moral issues with his targeted group, he is just glad they are vulnerable to attack and exploit. When we ally with the targeted group, we make them less vulnerable and exploitable. When we ignore the targeted group we make them more vulnerable and exploitable. There is no middle ground for us or them on this matter.

The Androputriarchal perpetrator creates the victim depending on need, not "hate" or any other explanation. Androputriarchy has had a millennial love affair with bullying women, but they have not been His only targets. It's kind of a flavor-of-the-month deal over history—the Jews; the witches; the women; the aboriginal peoples; the homosexuals; the children; the mentally ill; the Armenians.

Androputriarchy nimbly changes His targets as necessary. To get caught up in the blizzard of lies about the particular target is to be forever lost and in tacit agreement to sacrifice them to save ourselves from Androputriarchy's menacing glance.

# Speaking of Women

The political arena leaves one no alternative, one must either be a dunce or a rogue.

~ Emma Goldman
(1869–1940)

If we search the polemic writings of the most militant feminists, we can nowhere find expressions which compared in venom and ruthlessness with the woman-hating sentiments of certain medieval "saints" and modern "philosophers."

~ Katharine Anthony
(1877–1965)

The few who profit from the labor of the masses want to organize the workers into an army which will protect the interests of the capitalists.

~ Helen Keller
(1880–1968)

Man's role is uncertain, undefined, and perhaps unnecessary. By a great effort, man has hit upon a method of compensating himself for his basic inferiority.

~ Margaret Mead
(1901-1977)

I cannot understand anti-abortion arguments that centre on the sanctity of life. As a species we've fairly comprehensively demonstrated that we don't believe in the sanctity of life. The shrugging acceptance of war, famine, epidemic, pain and life-long poverty shows us that, whatever we tell ourselves, we've made only the most feeble of efforts to really treat human life as sacred.

~ Caitlin Moran
(1975–)

The LGBT community is overwhelmingly the group most targeted in violent hate crimes, according to an Intelligence Report analysis of 14 years of federal hate crime data. Gay men, lesbians, bisexuals and transgender people are more than twice as likely to be attacked in a violent hate crime as Jews or blacks; more than four times as likely as Muslims; and 14 times as likely as Latinos.

~ Southern Poverty Law Center,
Intelligence Report, Spring 2012, Issue Number: 145

# hate is overrated
## —by design

Be careful who, what and how you hate or **Androputriarchy** will gladly send you down the rabbit hole, never to be heard from again.

Whatever happened to good, old-fashioned hate? The kind of hate that meant something before Androputriarchy mutilated it?

It concerns me how hate has been man-ipulated to the point those of us who are on to Androputriarchy's tactics are still not careful enough in our thinking about what hate actually is and how so-called hate is used against us.

Just as I have proposed elsewhere in my rants about how men/Androputriarchy manufactures anger to accomplish all sorts of misdeeds, the same is true with so-called hate.

For example: women/feminists have known for a long time, and been telling anyone who would listen, sexual assault is not "about" sex, it's about power and control and degrading women. Sexual assault **uses** sex as a means to an end—the oppression of women—but it is not about sex. Just as hitting a woman over the head with a frying pan is not "**about**" cooking even though it uses an implement of cooking, stabbing a woman against her consent with a penis is not "about" sex even though it uses sex as a weapon.

This leads me to two well-meaning but erroneous words/concepts that obfuscate clarity for women. The first is the term "misogyny."

**misogyny:** [noun – **miso** = hatred, **gyny** = woman]—the hatred of women.

At the same time I understand and sometimes use the word misogyny, it is a concept that is mostly erroneous in its meaning and use.

For example, I have no idea if most men do or do not hate women, but it is irrelevant to this issue. Under Androputriarchy, we men are herd animals. Although we could do otherwise, we basically think and do as we are told. And why not? It works quite well for us altogether. We are told to hold women in contempt and disrespect; men in honor and deification—which we gladly do.

The notion that one need "hate" women to treat them like shit is wholly false and one women need to see through. Men's bonding with one another around disrespect and abuse of women for our own exaltation as a herd is the point. "Hating," or whatever, is just one of the man-ipulative tools handed to us to confuse you with. There are other tools used by us men daily that are equally as effective and destructive, but they don't necessarily carry this official label of "misogyny."

For example, the lie women are "conniving." Claiming women are

**Androputriarchy:** [*andro* meaning male, man; *putrere*, meaning rotten, or proceeding from decay; *archy* meaning ruler] an alternative for "patriarchy" that attempts to make clearer the corruption, malevolence, and destructive blight that male supremacy has been in human history and remains to this day.

conniving is a great tool of oppression as it puts the onus of male-volence on women, and the victim-status label on men. What a great switcheroo. But we have to be clear not to confuse "facts"—that women are or are not conniving—with "tactics." The tactic here being the ability to label women en masse and hence oppress them because "they deserve it."

I hope women/feminists would not tolerate a change to the definition of misogyny as follows because it would be an obvious fabrication with built-in motives:

**misogyny:** [noun]: the conniving nature of women

So-called misogyny is merely one tool of oppression. All of those tools of oppression added together still do not make a legitimate claim that all of women's oppression is due to "hatred of women."

I suspect, by the way, it is much simpler and more obscene than that. It is not about women at all. It is about us men. It isn't about hatred of women, but about hatred and worship of men and Androputriarchy. At the same time we men love or loathe Androputriarchy, we definitely love male bonding above all other things. If it is useful to pretend we share a cult of hatred of women, so much the better. If it is useful to pretend we share a cult of dead-guy-on-a-cross worship, so much the better. If it is useful to pretend we share a cult of hatred of vaginas, so much the better. We must not confuse etiology with tactics.

Here's my attempt at a better starting place: **ischogyny** [**ischo** = to restrain or suppress; **gyny** = woman]:

**ischogyny:** (noun)—the series of interlocking self-created and self-serving myths held by men/Androputriarchy that enhance male bonding and male exaltation at the expense of women. –**ischogynly**, adj. –**ischogynistic**, adj. –**ischogynistically**, adv.

I don't like the so-called "hatred of women" deception for other reasons as well. First, it lends itself to the nauseating lie of men as victims. Men just have this "hatred problem" that women have to help them overcome—if we love and forgive them enough. Those poor haters. They just need a woman's loving and delicate touch.

Second, this whole notion assumes that, if we took this definition on its face, women's oppression would be over the minute we helped all of those poor men stop hating women. Do you really believe that would happen? Really? Do you really think men would give up enjoying the rewards of Androputriarchy regardless of what or who they individually or collectively "hate?"

Do you really give men/Androputriarchy that much credit to think we bother to hate you at all? Do you really think you are that significant to us? We men hate growing old and not being a sexual weapon anymore; we hate other men getting more of the plunder from pillaging women than us; we hate not being Lords of the Fucking Universe; but you are

mistaken if you think hating you is that important, in and of itself.

How do you explain that if one is true then the other should be true: what about women's hate? Doesn't every woman have 100 trillion more reasons to hate men/Androputriarchy with the most scorching and well-deserved fury humankind has ever known?

Yet women, en masse, have not set a multi-millennial agenda of the subjugation of men. If we have concluded "hatred" inexorably causes the multi-millennial agenda of the subjugation of something or someone, then why wouldn't women have one million times more motivation to perpetrate such a thing on men, given women's well-deserved hatred quotient?

While on the subject of women's hate, which apparently doesn't exist in recorded human his-story, we are told by a phalanx of psychotherapists—a barely credible bunch on a good day—that hate is one of those feelings (like resentment, anger, yadda, yadda) that enlightened humans aren't supposed to harbor and if women do so then they are fucked up and unresolved and regressed and blah, blah, blah.

Why is it that, if men's so-called misogyny (hatred of women) has been bestowed its own word, we don't seem to talk about women's hatred at all? What would those conniving women do if they were all of the sudden hating? We certainly try to smother such notions by ridiculing them and calling them "man-haters"—a label women have come to loathe as much as a breast cancer diagnosis.

78

It's all part of the hate conundrum craftily constructed by Androputriarchy.

On another fulmination, I'm sure many women had to work many years to get Congress to enact a "hate" crimes bill. Kudos to them for doing so.

I would ask Congress, with all due respect, to consider renaming this legislation. They could call it "bias" crimes using their own language from the bill. Or "oppression" crimes. Oppression is better language because it acknowledges the institutional, societal, cultural collusion of the fathers of "bias."

The United States Congress defined a **hate crime** as a "criminal offense against a person or property motivated in whole or in part by an offender's bias against a race, religion, disability, ethnic origin or sexual orientation." You'll notice bias against women for being women was left out of that bill. We all know women have never been oppressed or the victims of bias in America, right?

The most I will concede on the matter is the option of calling something a hateful crime, but not a hate crime.

Before examining "love" under Androputriarchy I want to single out one other word/concept: so-called homophobia.

homophobia: (noun)—
intense hatred or fear of homosexuals or homosexuality

My concerns with this concept are the same as with "misogyny," including that we need a new name for it.

For example, there may be some men in America who fear or hate to sit down on the toilet when they pee. Maybe most or all men in America fear or hate to sit down when they pee. But this is not why they stand up to pee. They do that for other reasons, and to slap "hate" on it just plays into the Androputriarchal deception. So here's my contribution to why men pee standing up:

Misoinsideo—[miso- from Greek for hatred and insideo from Latin for sit upon something] - the hatred of sitting upon something

Men stand while peeing to bond with other men, and with Androputriarchy, and to distance ourselves from any risky identification with women. Hatred and fear may, or may not, be the lash used to convince us men to stand up while peeing, but either way the lash is in the hand of Androputriarchy.

The fact remains we men gladly engage in our ever-complementary dance with Androputriarchy: our learned disrespect for women and the actions we take to oppress women reinforces Androputriarchy, and Androputriarchy lends us His muscle whenever we need or want Him—or even if we don't.

Do men who beat their wives, womanfriends, mothers, daughters, sons, or pets hate them? Do they hate women? Some do, some don't. Some may hate **and** love their prey. Again, this is a romp around the mulberry tree we must flee for our own survival.

Finally, the subject of love. Can batterers possibly love the people

they terrorize and brutalize? Some do, some don't. Again, their "love" or "hate" of their quarry is no more relevant or elucidating than the color of pumpkins.

It concerns me even more when I hear—as I have many times in public discussions—women desperately attempt to declare to themselves and anyone within earshot that a man who batters his family cannot possibly love them. I have heard women proclaim this with heartfelt and religious fervor—to the point disagreeing with them (I do disagree, although I would never argue in that public forum with them about this) could lead to open conflict.

But I am convinced such thinking is evidence of how seriously we have collectively brainwashed and traumatized women. How we have put them in such horrible circumstances as to need a simplistic, and untrue, explanation of what has happened, and is happening, to them in this fucked-up man's world.

My father battered my mother, my two sisters, my brother, me, and all of our pets. His friends were afraid of him, and he assaulted neighbors, cops and others. He was a mean, terrifying asshole. But I have no doubt he deeply loved all of us.

He loved us, and he loved his male privilege. I loved, feared, hated, admired, and was ashamed of him.

Finally, we get to the purposeful absurdity Androputriarchy has injected into the notions of love and hate we see in the newspaper headlines practically every day: "HUSBAND KILLS WIFE BECAUSE HE

LOVED HER AND COULDN'T LIVE WITHOUT HER."

If one were to take two seconds to follow this logic to its obvious conclusion it reveals the five-year-old mentality of Andropotriarchy and men: the men who love their wives the most are the most homicidal men.

So women, here is a great dilemma for you: if you want to live a life without violence, you should marry the man who has the absolute least amount of love for you. Women, if you are so fucked up and stupid you want a man who is head-over-heels in love with you then you must be prepared to be murdered by him because true manly love equals homicide.

## Speaking of Women

But standing alone we learned our power; we repudiated man's counsels forevermore; and solemnly vowed that there should never be another season of silence until we had the same rights everywhere on this green earth, as man.

~ Elizabeth Cady Stanton
(1815–1902)

Resolved, that the women of this nation in 1876, have greater cause for discontent, rebellion and revolution than the men of 1776.

~ Susan Brownell Anthony
(1820–1906)

I want to agitate, even as I am agitated.

~ Laura Towne
(1825–1901)

Ah, women, I wish I could fill your hearts with a desire for liberty like that which boils in my heart.

~ Matilda Joslyn Gage
(1826–1898)

Upon women the burden and the horrors of war are heaviest ... When she sees what lies behind the glory and the horror, the boasting and the burden, and gets the vision, the human perspective, she will end war. She will kill war by the +simple process of starving it to death. For she will refuse any longer to produce the human food upon which the monster feeds.

~ Margaret Sanger
(1883–1966)

The tragedy of machismo is that a man is never quite man enough.

~ Germaine Greer
(1939–)

# WELCOME TO EARTH!

 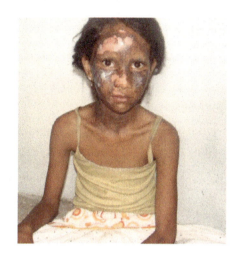

## Too bad you're a girl.

Women perform 66% of the world's work, but receive only 11% of the world's income, and own only 1% of the world's land.

Women make up 66% of the world's illiterate adults: 515 million. Worldwide, more than half the population of women over age 15 cannot read or write.

Women head 83% of single-parent families.

Two-thirds of the world's children who receive less than four years of education are girls.

3 out of 4 fatalities of war are women and children.

Gender-based violence kills one in three women across the world and is the biggest cause of injury and death to women worldwide, causing more deaths and disability among women aged 15 to 44 than cancer, malaria, traffic accident, and war.

Since 2003, only 3.8% of overseas development aid has been allocated to gender equality.

41 million girls worldwide are denied a primary education.

Approximately 80% of human trafficking victims are women and girls and up to 50% are minors. The average age of entry for children victimized by the rape trade industry is 12 years. Approximately one million adult women are trafficked across international borders annually, and two million girls between ages 5 and 15 are abducted into the commercial rape market.

600,000 women—one every minute—die each year from pregnancy-related causes. Most of these deaths are preventable.

There is no country in the world where women's wages are equal to those of men.

Around the world, at least one in every three women has been beaten, coerced into sex, or abused in some other way—most often by someone she knows; one woman in four has been abused during pregnancy.

Nowhere in the world except Sweden are women represented in government proportionally to their percentage in the population.

Female genital mutilation is common in 28 countries. An estimated 130 million women worldwide have undergone this maiming.

An estimated 4 million women and girls are bought and sold worldwide, either into marriage, prostitution or slavery.

At least 60 million girls who would otherwise be expected to be alive are "missing" from various populations, as a result of sex-selective abortions, infanticide or neglect.

For women aged 15 to 44 years, violence is a major cause of death and disability worldwide. In no country on Earth are women safe from this type of violence.

Worldwide, half of the women who die from homicides are killed by their current or former husbands or partners.

Worldwide, one in five women will become a victim of rape or attempted rape in her lifetime.

The majority of the world's women cannot own, inherit, or control property, land, and wealth on an equal basis with men.

**To assess the damage is a dangerous act. ~ Cherrie Moraga** (1952-)

©2014 Michael Elizabeth Marillynson LLC - This poster is from the book "Contrary to the Custom of Men: Field Notes on the Pestilence of Patriarchy from a Disloyal Son." For re-printing permission go to: con2men.info. Images courtesy of Wikimedia Commons: all india christian council; nasa

# keepsakes

### (after a dream, age 42)

In a box I keep the Matchbox car you brought me from England
one wheel missing
a shiny red diversion
instead of safety.

In my sleep I keep the nightmares
of you tormenting mom
she's gripping a gun over her head
with both hands
catatonic
fear petrifying her into a rubber mannequin.

In my gut I keep your bullying
paralysis surrendering movement
a safe distance
the reward of vigilance.

In my marriage I keep your discord
confusion, guilt and uncertainty
keep the monster close
not so bad.

In my mirror I keep your face
sneering at me
jaw set tight
eyes too open.

In my heart I keep the fury
stoked in your furnace
scorching hot steel
hammered thin.

©2014 Michael Elizabeth Marillynson LLC - from the book "Contrary to the Custom of Men: Field Notes on the Pestilence of Patriarchy from a Disloyal Son." For re-printing permission go to: con2men.info.

**intoxicated batterers are marvels of intention and tenacity**

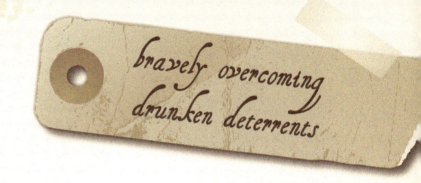

I've spent a lot of my time thinking about drunks and batterers. Good times, indeed.

When I worked in the batterer programs, it was my job to "treat" the alcoholics and addicts who also had the charming inclination to wreak violence on their so-called families.

I dutifully toed the party line about addiction treatment (you'd better in that sick field—or else) for years but as I sat in rooms with these men, the more I knew I was missing something important. All of the "disease concept" substance abuse treatment dogma, and the "we were powerless over people, places, and things" Alcoholics Anonymous dogma I was funnel-fed just didn't make sense with what I was coming to understand about the tactics of batterers.

I remember the day a man was describing how he wanted to scare his wife who—surprise, surprise—was leaving him. He claimed he had never been violent towards her before, or even abusive, and he didn't drink. That night, however, he drank a lot of liquor, got his handgun, and went to a party and threatened her with death if she left him.

Women can always be won over with romance.

In his "therapy" group, he continued to cling to his Heritage Foundation, handed down to him from time immemorial by Androputriarchy, that this wasn't something he would "ordinarily" do and the alcohol was the culprit.

I was struggling with my burgeoning understanding that so-called domestic violence is all about power and control over women, and there is no "lack of control" at any time or in any aspect of this behavior. Yet everything I had been taught about alcoholism treatment ran headlong at odds with what I knew to be true from my experience with these guys.

That was the day the lies melted away before my eyes. That was the day my brain neurons short-circuited and had to be re-routed around the truth I was clumsily falling around.

This led me to conduct the following exercise during public presentations: I would ask a member of the audience to do something once I gave him the instructions. (I liked asking men to do this exercise.)

The instructions were to stand up, pick up the piece of paper on his desktop, walk it across the lecture hall, and hand it to a person sitting in a particular seat and then stand there. I asked him if he understood the instructions, and then asked the audience to watch him very carefully. He would then walk the piece of paper over to the person and hand it to her. (I liked having women be the recipient.)

I would tell the audience this was "exhibit **A**."

Now, for "exhibit **B**" I ask the man to do basically the same thing in reverse—get the piece of paper from the woman and walk it over to his chair and sit down with it. However, this time he was to do the task while acting like he was so drunk he could barely accomplish the task, but still do it. I would also tell him he had to do this in a way he didn't hurt himself or anyone else.

He would then, in whatever acting skills he possessed, stagger and stumble back to his chair with the piece of paper, maybe dropping it a couple of times or giving it to someone he wasn't supposed to.

I would then ask the audience: under which condition, exhibit **A** (sober) or exhibit **B** (drunk), did the man have to use more of his physical strength and effort to complete the task given him? More of his focus and attention? More of his time? More determination to complete the task? More things he had to overcome?

This would usually get a surprised and nervous whispering started in the room.

I would then pick on alcohol a little more. I would ask the audience to give me examples, which I would write on the chalkboard, of the ways in which alcohol "impairs" a person who is drinking it, and assume the more one drinks, the more extreme the impairment becomes. Here is a typical list:

### Alcohol Consumption

impairs reasoning
impairs memory
impairs physical balance
impairs perception, comprehension
impairs visual acuity and peripheral vision
impairs eyes ability to recover
from bright, glaring light
impairs perception of color, form,
motion and dimensions
impairs reaction time
impairs hearing
impairs fine motor movements
impairs gross motor control
impairs concentration
causes drowsiness
causes dizziness
causes confusion
causes blurred, double vision
causes slurring and impairment of speech
causes anxiety
causes restlessness
causes emotional instability
causes nausea
causes staggering gait
causes difficulty sitting upright in a chair
causes memory loss
causes vomiting
causes stuporousness
causes incontinence
causes irregular breathing
causes loss of consciousness

Now let's try that list again with a new heading (you may want to sit down before you read the rest of this).

### Impairments I Will Need All of My Strength, Focus, and Determination to Overcome So I Can Still Slap That Bitch Around

impaired reasoning
impaired memory
impaired physical balance
impaired perception, comprehension
impairs visual acuity and peripheral vision
impairs eyes ability to recover
from bright, glaring light
impaired perception of color, form,
motion and dimensions
impaired reaction time
impaired hearing
impaired fine motor movements
impaired gross motor control
impaired reaction time
impaired concentration
drowsiness
dizziness
confusion
blurred, double vision
slurring and impairment of speech
anxiety
restlessness
emotionally instability
nausea
staggering gait
difficulty sitting upright in a chair
memory loss
vomiting
stuporousness
incontinence
irregular breathing
loss of consciousness

Wait a doggone minute—I thought intoxication made it easier, more likely, to "lose control" and assault people!

Intoxicated batterers remind me of Houdini—they can still manage to physically assault someone even while they are being hung upside down by their chained legs in a tank of water, while wearing a straightjacket. That's impressive!

Yet, we don't give batterers their due credit for being such incredible examples of willfulness, determination, and fortitude. How could we have ever gotten this so wrong?

How indeed.

The "I was drunk" artifice is the gift that keeps on giving for Androputriarchy and men. It's like frequent flyer miles—the more I use it the more I get to use it with less cost to me.

The lies of being "drunk and out of control" and that men have diminished responsibility for what they do while intoxicated have served the mayhem and cruelty of Androputriarchy since fermented wheat malt and barley were first combined.

Now on to the question I always enjoyed asking audiences to whom I was solemnly presenting "batterer tactics." That is, how drunk do you have to be to cut off both of your feet with an axe? Or if you prefer, how drunk do you have to be to sexually abuse your children?

The answer I always got was, "I couldn't be that drunk." Really?

Well, if you couldn't be that drunk, what does this tell us about batterers who use intoxication as their excuse to assault the people who love them?

If you couldn't be that drunk, what does this tell us about what a batterer has already given himself permission, while sober, to do while intoxicated?

Why wouldn't "beat my wife" be on the list of things you would never do along with "cut off both of my feet with an axe" or "sexually abuse my children"?

If it is not on your "would never do" list, why isn't it?

# Speaking of Women

I am at a boiling point! If I do not find some day the use of my tongue on this question I shall die of an intellectual repression, a woman's rights convulsion.

~ Elizabeth Cady Stanton
(1815–1902)

The male is completely egocentric, trapped inside himself, incapable of empathizing or identifying with others, or love, friendship, affection or tenderness. He is a completely isolated unit, incapable of rapport with anyone. His responses are entirely visceral, not cerebral; his intelligence is a mere tool in the services of his drives and needs; he is incapable of mental passion, mental interaction; he can't relate to anything other than his own physical sensations. He is a half-dead, unresponsive lump, incapable of giving or receiving pleasure or happiness; consequently, he is at best an utter bore, an inoffensive blob, since only those capable of absorption in others can be charming. He is trapped in a twilight zone halfway between humans and apes, and is far worse off than the apes because, unlike the apes, he is capable of a large array of negative feelings—hate, jealousy, contempt, disgust, guilt, shame, doubt—and moreover, he is aware of what he is and what he isn't.

~ Valerie Solanas
(1936–1988)

If women abdicate violence without being capable of it anyhow, it makes less of an impact than if that abdication were a real choice. Self-defense enables women to internalize a different kind of bodily knowledge. As such, self-defense is feminism in the flesh.

~ Martha McCaughey
(1966–)

# INSTANT ASSHOLES.
## ...just add Patriarchy

War, poverty, discrimination, racism, rape, genocide, torture, murder, imprisonment, homelessness, slavery, abuse, addiction, inequality, corruption, tyranny, harassment, illiteracy, crime, heterosexism, persecution, cruelty, lawlessness, bullying, gang violence, sexism, environmental destruction, mindless consumerism: these are the inventions and distractions of Patriarchy. Patriarchy is the King of Oppressions from which these human miseries flow. Our boys will be turned into monsters unless we reckon with Patriarchy.

©2014 Michael Elizabeth Marillynson LLC - This poster is from the book "Contrary to the Custom of Men: Field Notes on the Pestilence of Patriarchy from a Disloyal Son." For re-printing permission go to: con2men.info. Images courtesy of Wikimedia Commons: paul la porte; tim & annette gulick fr; christopher; james gordon; mckay savage; hamed saber; mark knobil; adam jones; steve evans; dvidshub

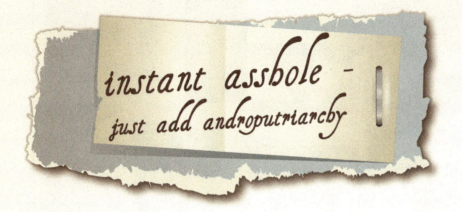

# instant asshole – just add androputriarchy

**exposure to androputriarchy is the leading cause of premature death worldwide**

When I drink coffee, I can expect to begin running to the bathroom in the next hour. When I touch my cat's front toes, I can expect to get bit. When I don't pay my credit card bill, I can expect to get socked with exorbitant interest fees.

When I talk to men about the deleterious effects of Androputriarchy on women, I can expect to hear, "But what about its effects on men?" Feel free to repeat that question aloud with all the whininess and self-pity you can muster for proper effect.

Well fellas, here's a moment where I think we can agree the case should have a thorough airing.

From my decades of exploration on the subject of Androputriarchy one thing I find is the alluring "casino" effect on them. That is, Androputriarchy long ago assassinated any benevolent communion of "fellowship" among men and replaced it with a reeking, corpse-like caricature dressed in macho drag and soaked with aftershave to hide the putrescence. The promise of "making it big" and "being Mr. Big" and "having the Biggest One" draws boys and men to the Masculinity Casino to gamble away their humanity for a one-in-a-billion shot at "making it." The fact that it grinds the other 999,999,999 into such things as the fodder of war, the drones of commerce, and the brutes of family, is the tradeoff for that insatiable man-dream. So, even though Androputriarchy basically mows down anything or anyone that stands in its path, it is driven by and for boys/men.

If boys/men had ever bothered to bond together to make the slightest effort to dethrone the stinking carcass of Androputriarchy over the millennium, I might have an interest in this aspect of the question. Alas, we have not, and I do not.

What I am looking for is different than that: I want to understand how Androputriarchy privileges boys/men; how Androputriarchy arms boys/men; how Androputriarchy enables boys/men; how Androputriarchy drives boys/men like dim-witted cattle on a stampede to carnage.

As I will one day tire of this ridiculous interest, this is where I recommend researchers begin their investigations:

## 1) Consider Instant Asshole—Just Add Androputriarchy:

### Ingestion of alcohol in Men

- excitability and euphoria
- increased pain threshold
- loss of shyness
- feeling of well-being
- lower inhibitions
- lowering of caution
- increased self-confidence
- increased sociability
- overall improvement in mood
- self-confident or daring
- altered reasoning and memory
- shortened attention span
- risk taking
- happiness
- exaggerated behaviors
- verbally argumentative
- emotionally labile
- exaggerated emotions
- sexual disinhibition

### Ingestion of male-bonding, male privilege, and male-entitlement in Men

- excitability and euphoria
- increased pain threshold
- loss of shyness
- feeling of well-being
- lower inhibitions
- lowering of caution
- increased self-confidence
- increased sociability
- overall improvement in mood
- self-confident or daring
- altered reasoning and memory
- shortened attention span
- risk taking
- happiness
- exaggerated behaviors
- verbally argumentative
- emotionally labile
- exaggerated emotions
- sexual disinhibition

You'd have to admit you've seen Androputriarchy have that effect on boys/men. The imperious influence of Androputriarchy on males can be seen in the tiniest of interactions between children and the hugest disasters between nations. This is not a causal relationship: that is, one causes the other. This is a convenience relationship. Men choose to take advantage of their intoxicant, and could just as well choose not to.

## 2) Next, Consider King Baby—
## The Making of Men Under Androputriarchy:

As I was one day facilitating a batterer intervention group and thinking about the awesome and revolting display of male privilege, I got to thinking about how that sense of entitlement comes about. That night, I launched an email to many of my womenfriends and asked them:

What words would you pick to describe the likely characteristics of a child raised with no discipline, no limits, and who never hears the word "No"? Here is what I got:

| | | | |
|---|---|---|---|
| above the rules | dependent | me first | special |
| acting out | dangerous | mean | tyrant |
| attention-seeking | doesn't think of others | narcissistic | temperamental |
| aggressive | entitled | needy | undisciplined |
| arrogant | greedy | non-empathetic | unhappy |
| bossy | hollow | obnoxious | unyielding |
| bully | hateful | outrageous | unruly |
| conceited | inconsiderate | reckless | unsubstantial |
| careless | insecure | rude | uncontrollable |
| debased | inattentive to others | sullen | vindictive |
| dictatorial | lazy | self-centered | whiny |
| demanding | loud | selfish | |
| disrespectful | manipulative | spoiled | |

Hmmm... Now, from my experience, how would I describe the 1,000 or so batterers I've worked with over the years? Let me think...

| | | | |
|---|---|---|---|
| above the rules | dependent | me first | special |
| acting out | dangerous | mean | tyrant |
| attention-seeking | doesn't think of others | narcissistic | temperamental |
| aggressive | entitled | needy | undisciplined |
| arrogant | greedy | non-empathetic | unhappy |
| bossy | hollow | obnoxious | unyielding |
| bully | hateful | outrageous | unruly |
| conceited | inconsiderate | reckless | unsubstantial |
| careless | insecure | rude | uncontrollable |
| debased | inattentive to others | sullen | vindictive |
| dictatorial | lazy | self-centered | whiny |
| demanding | loud | selfish | |
| disrespectful | manipulative | spoiled | |

Taking King Baby to one of His putrid ends: the notion that war is the exceptional circumstance that "brings out the worst in men." War, like alcohol/drugs and male privilege, is merely another male social fabrication that happily removes the "normal" restrictions imposed on men so that they may do the things they wish to do in the first place.

## 3) Finally, Male bonding:

The usual suspects for the excuses of men's vileness—woman-hating; low self-esteem; not enough Jesus; drunkenness; over-sexed, etc. just don't hold up. It seems we give male bonding too little credit. As I have claimed elsewhere, male-bonding may be the most powerful force and motivation for boys/men in Androputriarchy.

I'm convinced that to choke the Androputriarchal weed off at the root, we will have to find the herbicide for male-privileged bonding.

There has been plenty of research done on the subject of how "people" make choices differently when they act alone or in groups/crowds. I suspect this research has all been conducted on/with men without identifying it as such. This would demonstrate the best of both worlds: not blame men for gang rape, etc. and hand off half of the blame for crowd-related mayhem to women.

Again, if we ever get around to looking closely at the everyday—all the way up to the spectacular—examples of men's depravity, we will see men focusing not on women but on how their behavior positions them with other men.

How well they are doing in the casino. Dare I say there is something downright homoerotic in all men's interests?

For example, is violent and degrading pornography depicting the suffering of women, children and/or animals about sexual obsession, or is it about male bonding and identification?

Another example would be so-called "gang rape" or more accurately "male gang rape." In 1994, 10.6% of rapes and sexual assaults were committed by multiple [male] assailants (United States Department of Justice, 1994). The point of male-perpetrated gang rape is bonding with other men. The victim is a token; coincidental. If it weren't a woman, it would be someone/something else to humiliate and bond around.

The other side of male-bonding that offers promise is men's proclivity to obediently herd together. As Yoda said, "the force has a strong influence on the weak-minded." We men are in fact weak-minded due to our King Baby privileges. So if that time ever comes when men have no choice but to be herded in a better direction, just get out the bullhorns.

# Speaking of Women

Better far that my body should suffer outrage than my soul.

~ Hroswitha of Gandersheim
(c.935–1000)

All goes awry and lawless in the land,
Where power takes the place of justice.

~ Margaret of Austria
(1480–1530)

Women, like toys, are sought after, and trifled with, and then thrown by with every varying caprice.

~ Caroline Lamb
(1785–1828)

You never knew what it is to be a slave; to be entirely unprotected by law or custom; to have the laws reduce you to the condition of a chattel, entirely subject to the will of another. You never exhausted your ingenuity in avoiding the snares, and eluding the power of a hated tyrant; you never shuddered at the sound of his footsteps, and trembled within hearing of his voice.

~ Harriet Brent Jacobs
(1818–1896)

Pray for the dead and fight like hell for the living.

~ Mother Jones
(1830–1930)

I comforted her [Mother Cobb] by telling her that while it was disagreeable and unreasonable to have our wearing apparel described in the newspapers, it was inevitable in this stage of woman's progress, editors and reporters being much more able to judge of our clothes than they were of our arguments.

~ Olympia Brown
(1835–1900)

The ability however, to collect facts, and the power to generalize and draw conclusions from them, avail little, when brought into direct opposition to deeply rooted prejudices.

~ Eliza Burt Gamble
(1841–1920)

Culture, as we know it, is patriarchy's self-image.

~ Susanne Kappeler
(1949–)

We keep our victims ready.

~ Karen Finley
(1956–)

the enthusiastic promotion of unknowable motives

*man robs bank— motive unknown*

This one still has me a bit stumped—I think. We'll begin the investigation with a massacre perpetrated in my neck of the woods on July 7th, 2011 in Grand Rapids, Michigan: Rodrick Shonte Dantzler shot to death two female ex-partners, two children—including his own daughter—and three other adult relatives of these women. He eventually shot himself in the head after much man-drama and, thankfully, died. All of the following quotes in the news accounts were attributed to the Grand Rapids Police Chief:

> "What happened is so uncharacteristic it boggles the mind."
>
> "For some reason… he went out hunting down ex-girlfriends."
>
> "There was 'no question' the killing spree was premeditated, but what, if anything, provoked it, may never be known."
>
> "The motive behind the shooting spree may never be known."

Having worked in the batterer intervention industry for many years, I always cringe when I read "MOTIVE UNKNOWN" in the news because I know it is such a complete prevarication and highly effective propaganda. But how I wanted to expose and oppose it in my writing was the problem. My original intention was to lay out the statistics that begin to reveal how genocidally ridiculous the fabrication of "we don't know what motivates this" is:

- Each year, an estimated 3.3 million children are exposed to violence by family members against their mothers or female caretakers.*

- 40-60% of men who abuse women also abuse children.*

- 1-4 million American women experience a serious assault by an intimate partner during an average 12-month period.*

- Nearly 1 in 3 adult women experience at least one physical assault by a partner during adulthood.*

- 70% of intimate homicide victims are female.**

- 90-95% of domestic violence victims are women.**

- As many as 95% of domestic violence perpetrators are male.***

- 47% of men who beat their wives do so at least 3 times per year.****

---

\* American Psychological Association; Violence and the Family: Report of the American Psychological Association Presidential Task Force on Violence and the Family
\*\* Bureau of Justice Statistics Selected Findings: Violence Between Intimates (NCJ-149259), November 1994.
\*\*\* A Report of the Violence against Women Research Strategic Planning Workshop sponsored by the National Institute of Justice in cooperation with the U.S. Department of Health and Human Services, 1995.
\*\*\*\* AMA Diagnostic & Treatment Guidelines on Domestic Violence, SEC: 94-677:3M:9/94 (1994).

- Approximately one-seventh of all domestic assaults come to the attention of the police. *****

- More than 17% of domestic homicide victims had a protection order against the perpetrator at the time of the killing. *****

- 65% of intimate homicide victims physically separated from the perpetrator prior to their death. *****

- In 1994, 38% of domestic homicides were multiple-victim, usually combining a spouse homicide and suicide, or child homicide. *****

- Where there are multiple victims in a domestic homicide, 89% of perpetrators are male. *****

- In 2009 there were 1,579 women murdered in domestic homicides (that have been officially recorded) in the United States. ******

- 22 million American women will be raped by American men at some time in their lives. ******

Please allow me some assumptions: 1) effective police/detective work is based on scientific, logical methods refined over the ages from experience, research, and education, 2) most, if not all, police/detective agencies in the United States of America have access to adequate training, education, and methods to diagnose and process common crimes, 3) domestic assaults/murders are one of the most common crimes police/detective agencies encounter, hence 4) there would be no excuse for police/detective agencies and/or individuals to be unable to speak knowledgeably and accurately about such crimes.

How on Earth, then, could police departments all over this great Fatherland of ours be so wholly and consistently clueless and half-witted about the motives of domestic violence perpetrators?

Clearly, they either 1) aren't clueless and half-witted but pretend to be so for some reason, or 2) are clueless,

***** Florida Governor's Task Force on Domestic and Sexual Violence, Florida Mortality Review Project, 1997
****** Violence Policy Center—http://www.vpc.org/press/1109dv.htm

half-witted, or couldn't investigate their way out of a wet paper bag. More on that later...

The next clue in my investigation was the news industry's lack of motive attribution in other crimes. For example, when you read your newspaper, don't you want to know the motive for why George robbed the bank? Don't you want to know the motive for why Bill was burglarizing an apartment? Don't you want to know the motive for why Dan was driving drunk? Don't you want to know the motive for why Larry was jaywalking? Don't you want to know the motive for why Dale was shoplifting?

What the hell is wrong with our newspapers today that we don't get big splashy headlines like:

# MAN CAUGHT SHOPLIFTING— MOTIVE UNKOWN

But wait just one damn minute—maybe it's not the newspaper's fault at all. Maybe the police are telling them, "Yeh, this guy was brazenly stealing toothbrushes, video games, and cigarettes and we don't have a fucking clue as to why." I mean, the newspaper can't write what they don't know (unless they are owned by Rupert Murdoch).

But we still have our investigative hats on here, and can't we reasonably take the leap that the motive for a man to shoplift is because he didn't want to pay for the items he was taking?

Can't we reasonably assume Bill was burglarizing the apartment to take something of value that belonged to someone else? Can't we reasonably expect Dan was driving drunk because he wanted to drive himself from point A to point B and figured he could do so without getting caught? Can't we reasonably imagine George robbed a bank to acquire more money than he already had? Can't we reasonably calculate Dale shoplifted because he wanted items without paying for them? Can't we reasonably anticipate Larry was jaywalking because he didn't want to walk a little bit further to cross the road legally at the corner?

Yet the crimes of domestic violence and domestic homicide are older than all of those other crimes by centuries and we still haven't figured out the motive?

Now I do want to give blame where blame is due—to those times when the police and/or newspapers **do** ascribe motive. It does happen. Favorite bogus concoctions include "money problems" and "love triangles" and "substance abuse" and "unemployment" and "mental illness" and "family problems" and "love gone awry, and "jealousy" and blah, blah, and blah.

But these excuses are—you guessed it—the same old bullshit that any police department would be wise to if they had taken their fingers out of their ears for even five minutes over the last 50 years and learned from feminist scholars and activists. Women have been telling police departments for at least that long that domestic violence/homicide is about male privilege, male entitlement, male-bonding, and men's insatiable quest for power and control at the expense of women. All the other excuses are purposefully, and obviously successful, distracting noise.

Maybe police departments and journalists should be burning incense, getting out their Ouija boards, and reading tea leaves when they get a domestic violence report—that would be a more productive strategy at investigating crimes than what they are doing now.

So here we are back in Grand Rapids at square one about this "motive" thing. You remember what the Grand Rapids Police Chief said, right?

"What happened is so uncharacteristic it boggles the mind."—1,579 women murdered by their male partners in 2009, between 1-4 million women physically assaulted by their male partners annually, and 22 American million raped by American men in their lifetimes—what is uncharacteristic about this particular crime?

"There was 'no question' the killing spree was premeditated... he went out hunting down ex-girlfriends... for some reason..., but what, if anything, provoked it may never be known."

Huh?

Grand Rapids guy is not doing well here—he needs to go to finishing school or marketing school or Junior Republicans or whoever can help him polish up his Androputriarchy and stay on script.

So, although I like my logic so far I still feel unsatisfied—like a Catholic priest pedophile who isn't allowed to hang out at Sunday school anymore.

Then it dawns on me—it's all hiding in plain sight—I've been looking under the rug too hard and it was the rug all the time.

There is something hypnotizing about putting "MOTIVE UNKOWN" in the news headlines over and over and over and over and over and over and over and over and over and over and over and over and over and over (repeat 1,579 times) again that is the trick. I overlooked my own rules about investigating Androputriarchy—every inexplicable thing leads back to Androputriarchy—and got myself lost in the labyrinth toilet of deception.

Like I said: hiding in plain sight. It isn't a mistake "MOTIVE UNKOWN" is always linked to this crime, and not to others. There is a shrewd, intended, and fantastically successful method to it all.

One of the reasons I can know it works is because Androputriarchy is behind it. Duh—who else would be? And like the stupid, vanilla, false tripe of "God made me and God doesn't make mistakes," I know Androputriarchy pretty much comes "pre-mistaked" at this point. Women: just look at history. We've been experimenting on you for millennia and we know how to dominate and suck your life blood by now, even if we do spill a little too much now and then.

"MOTIVE UNKOWN" is the ultimate example of Orwell's doublethink and Newspeak from his novel "1984." If you put it in capital letters big enough, repeat it often enough, keep its significance just below consciousness, and link it to the correct target—voila—you get the desired result.

I suspect one of those results is to get women and men to "not know" what they obviously could and should know. It is also to strike fear in women's hearts that violence and death are unpredictable, random, and hence unpreventable and no collective action need be contemplated, let alone taken.

This same messaging to boys and men would have the alternate, and successful, effect of making violence and death perpetrated on women mysterious, powerful, and even romantic.

# Speaking of Women

... militarism... is one of the chief bulwarks of capitalism, and the day that militarism is undermined, capitalism will fail.

~ Helen Keller
(1880–1968)

Since women have been outside the system for so many centuries, it would be odd if they had not worked out an inner language that permitted them to puncture the pomposities.

~ Colette
(born Sidonie-Gabrielle Colette, 1873–1954)

The emotional, sexual, and psychological stereotyping of females begins when the doctor says, "It's a girl."

~ Shirley Chisholm
(1924–2005)

We both want to believe in male change, and have little reason to do so.

~ Gloria Steinem
(1934–)

Women do not believe that men believe what pornography says about women. But they do. From the worst to the best of them, they do.

~ Andrea Dworkin
(1946–2005)

The purpose of domination is to keep an unequal social order in place—providing privileges to one group at the expense of another. This is not a natural state and can only be kept in place by violence and/or the constant threat of it. Wealth is amassed through a system of exploitation and forced dependency. Those in power take a disproportionate amount of resources and labor, which, in turn, strips the exploited of having sufficient means to provide for themselves. Consequently, their survival depends on those who are the cause of their problems in the first place. This is not what one calls a balanced state. Without a worldview that justified violence, hierarchy would be in sorry shape.

~ Margo Adair
(1950–2010)

I think women should have an "ideal": the only people you treat as equals are other women. And when you want subordinates, you can fuck a man in the ass! That is basically the future. So you [men] should feel lucky that you at least have this service you can offer me.

~ Diamanda Galas
(1955–)

Ministry for the Promotion of Patriarchy and Prevention of Treason

SEDITION TO PATRIARCHY; INFIDEL; SISSY; WHITE RACE TRAITOR; FEMINIST; UN-AMERICAN ACTIVITIES; DOESN'T SUPPORT THE TROOPS; VEGETARIAN; MANGINA

# WANTED BY M.P.P.P.T.

## MICHAEL ELIZABETH MARILLYNSON

**ALIASES**: Big Sissy, Man Hater, Feminazi, Man Traitor, Disloyal Son, Pussy Whipped, Judas

**PRINTS**

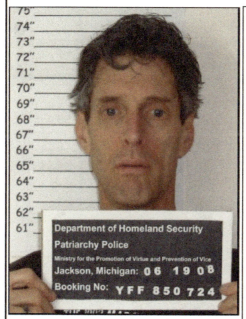

**DESCRIPTION**
AGE: 56, born July 21, 1956, Jackson, Michigan
HEIGHT: 6' 3"  EYES: yes
WEIGHT: 162 pounds  COMPLEXION: white
BUILD: skinny  RACE: White
HAIR: black, graying  NATIONALITY: American
OCCUPATIONS: lawn mower, veterinary assistant, nurses assistant, fence builder, anesthesia technician, shipping and receiving clerk, house cleaner, group home attendant, social worker, yellow pages salesperson, handyperson, bookkeeper, custodian
SCARS AND MARKS: scar on right thumb, scar on left sole, scar through navel, scar on right heel
REMARKS: atheist infidel

**CAUTION**
JACKSON HAS BEEN KNOWN TO BE A PERSUASIVE SPEAKER AND IS EXTREMELY COMMITTED TO THE CAUSE OF TREASON TO PATRIARCHY AND TREASON TO WHITE SUPREMACY.

Warrants were issued December 31, 1999, at Ann Arbor, Michigan, charging Jackson with treason to patriarchy and treason to the White race; disrespect to patriarchal institutions, including all patriarchal religions, the military, meat eating, NASCAR, the Elks, the NRA, the Ku Klux Klan, sexism, woman beaters, heterosexists, pornographers, pimps, rapists, child beaters, etc.
IF YOU HAVE INFORMATION CONCERNING THIS PERSON, PLEASE CONTACT YOUR LOCAL **M**INISTRY FOR THE **P**ROMOTION OF **P**ATRIARCHY AND **P**REVENTION OF **T**REASON.

©2014 Michael Elizabeth Marillynson LLC - This poster is from the book "Contrary to the Custom of Men: Field Notes on the Pestilence of Patriarchy from a Disloyal Son." For re-printing permission go to: con2men.info. Images courtesy of Wikimedia Commons: jomegat; annafoxlover; lucyin mahin; jim thomas

# gender oppression: full speed ahead

## of mobs and men

I suspect that when a person such as me is infected with the feminism bug, it can be surprising what captures ones attention.

Mob violence, for instance. It was probably the images I saw on television of a destructive and violent mob that contained only—you guessed it—men. So that got me thinking: why is it only men? What does this mean about men? What does it mean about women? What does it mean about Androputriarchy?

What I saw in this male-mob behavior was identical to what I see in everyday male-bonding behavior, just at a different "speed."

Mob violence is merely Androputriarchal oppression, corrosiveness, and self-absorbed arrogance occurring at a faster pace than the slow, steady, inexorable pace of everyday Androputriarchy. A flash floods destruction compared to a steady glaciers grinding down.

In a mob, men are shoulder to shoulder carrying weapons, attacking people, and destroying property with sometimes angry, sometimes happy, sometimes intoxicated faces (look at the lynching photos in "Without Sanctuary: Lynching Photography in America" by James Allen). There is a sense of brotherhood and bonding among the men, along with a sense of solidarity, power, a lust for "control over," and the excitement of destruction and humiliation of those who are weak.

This is the definition of male bonding under Androputriarchy. Men's mob violence is the same "male privilege and male bonding" that occurs on a daily, grinding, and for most people who aren't looking, imperceptible way under Androputriarchy. It's just that, with mob violence, it is more easily seen and recognized for what it is.

I find it helpful to keep this in mind when news sources and Androputriarchal hirelings attempt to obfuscate by describing either version of male bonding as something other than what it is.

# Speaking of Women

Wife and servant are the same
but only differ in the name,
for when that fatal knot is tied,
which nothing, nothing can divide,
when she the word obey has said,
and man by law supreme has made,
then all that's kind is laid aside,
and nothing left but state and pride.
> ~ Mary Lee
> (1656–1710)

...the wantonness of tyranny that induces men to exercise power merely because they have it...
> ~ Charlotte Smith
> (1749–1806)

...a man never looks so ridiculous as when he is caught in his own snare.
> ~ Elizabeth Inchbald
> (1753–1821)

It was rapidly becoming clear to my mind that men regarded women as a servant class in the community, and that women were going to remain in the servant class until they lifted themselves out of it.
> ~ Emmeline Pankhurst
> (1858–1928)

Many women find female solidarity hard to reconcile with almost any other of the many competing pulls on them; ethnic, racial, religious—and male. Perhaps especially male. Men seem better able to 'gang up' against women than vice versa.
> ~ Jessie Shirley Bernard
> (1903–)

Some may think that woman suffrage just happened, that it was 'in the air,' but we know...changes...are the result of ceaseless, unremitting toil.
> ~ Theodora Winton Youmans
> (1863–1932)

I would trust a men's movement that made rape the most shameful, disgusting, unmanly thing a male human being could do.
> ~ Starhawk
> (1951–)

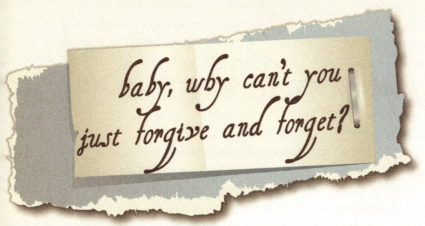

## the forgive and forget tactics

One of the favorite refrains of batterers I "worked" with in batterer intervention programs was, "I'm trying to put that in the past."

This self-important declaration was delivered, of course, with self-righteous drama and gnashing of teeth for optimal effect.

I would then ask the man what his profession or favorite hobby is.

I would then ask if he has an interest in being good at his profession or hobby ("Yes, of course!").

I would then ask if he ever made any big mistakes when he was first learning his profession or hobby ("Yes, of course!").

I would then ask if it is better, assuming he wanted to be good at his profession or hobby, to remember his mistakes as he learned, or to forget everything about his mistakes ("Yes, to remember my mistakes, of course!").

I then would ask if it is a good strategy now to put his abusive and battering behavior "behind him and forget the past" if he sincerely wants to stop being an abuser.

As you would suspect, he would rather wet his pants than answer this question. Some may have for all I know.

The fundamental, moment-to-moment workings of how this man, like all men, benefits under the male privilege brotherhood of Androputriarchy is usually hidden and secret, and it is inconvenient when pointed out. It is an unusual experience for men in Androputriarchy to have to squirm under the exposed naked ugliness of their tactics—a thing they have had very little experience dealing with before.

"Forgetting" is what Holocaust deniers want us to do. "Forgetting" is what White supremacists want us White Americans to do about slavery and Jim Crow. "Forgetting" is what White Americans forced Native Americans to do about their customs and heritage. "Forgetting" is a fundamental tactic the oppressor uses to keep His advantages over the oppressed.

"Forgetting" is yet another male prerogative canonized by the usual cretins of male entitlement psychobabble: mental health professionals, clergy, etc. This prerogative is not extended to women and children, who will be punished for past "sins" as needed.

The "forgetting" imperative has the usual effect of increasing men's license to be King Baby, and to force women and children to doubt their own eyes, ears, minds, and hearts.

As always, sunlight is the best disinfectant.

Forgiveness is the incestuous kissing cousin of forgetting in Androputriarchy.

Again, the learned morons of Androputriarchy like mental health professionals and clergy insist it is somehow good for us to "forgive" the collective and individual ways men harm us, which is the exact opposite of what is required for our collective and individual wellbeing.

Our wellbeing is improved by rage against our oppressors, and "forgiveness" of ourselves for the untold ways we have been forced to collude with them. Forgiveness that we are the victims of Androputriarchy; forgiveness that we were not responsible for abuse heaped on us; forgiveness that we are not dirty or bad or at fault.

What maintains our health, power in the world, and ability to love and be happy is by remaining in solidarity with ourselves instead of capitulating to our tormenters.

The top-secret key men use to unlock the treasure of "forgiveness" is apology. Apology in Androputriarchy is the "get out of jail free" card; the "sleight-of-hand" magic act; the hustler's scam.

In Androputriarchy apology is not only the opposite of accountability, contrition, self-reproach, or responsibility—it is an active tactic* of coercion and intimidation.

"Apology" was invented by men as an active agent within, and complimentary to, the oppressive cloak of male privilege to gain sympathy and release from responsibility from those oppressed and harmed, and avoid self-reflection and memory.

In the batterer program I co-facilitated we had a poster on the wall which read something like:

1) No apologies.
2) Acknowledge what I did, including the tactics I used.*
3) List the consequences I have given myself for my actions.
4) Explain how I will make sure I won't do this again.

Apologies are antithetical to accountability. An apology does absolutely nothing to aid in my own self-awareness or self-improvement as a decent human being.

Apology asks for attention and consideration from the person I have harmed who owes me no such attention or consideration. It puts the person I have harmed in the position of having to accept or refuse my apology, which is yet another burden beyond my abuse of them.

The person I have harmed has no reason or duty to listen to nor accept my apology, especially since apologizing is 99.9% of the time it is a tactic I have used on them before, and they know it is a tactic and nothing more, and I am once again attempting to escape responsibility.

It is an elemental ingredient of Androputriarchy to teach you, and enforce, what is His version of true, what is His version of real, what you are supposed to accept as normal and right, and what will happen to you if you do not comply.

Behind the bloated and protective shield of Androputriarchy, we men want and expect you women to forgive and forget what we have done, and continue to do, to you. We want and expect you women to forgive and forget history. We want and expect you women to forgive and forget what we've done to you for millennia. We want and expect you women to forgive and forget anything that interferes with our unfettered male privilege.

On a related subject, I have this challenge for men: I'll forget the past—if you will. Before you go slapping me on the back and performing the Boy's Club Moose Call you should know what you are going to be forgetting so we can all just get along: you'll have to "forget" all of your privileges, your **Men's Heritage Foundation**: you'll no longer earn $1.00 for each $0.72 women earn; you'll no longer be able to escape parenting duties for your children; you will only sit in 10 of the Fortune 500 executive seats; you will be sexually assaulted by the time you turn 18; you will be beaten, and maybe murdered, by one or more of your wives or womanfriends; you will be thrust into poverty by divorce; you will not control any leadership positions in the clergy, military, government, business, athletics, health care, criminal justice, media, education, social service, etc. So if you're cool with burying that past and a whole lot more, I'm in a forgetting mood.

---

* Tactics refers to the Duluth Model Power and Control Wheel which clearly explains the tactics that batterers (men) use to abuse (http://www.theduluthmodel.org/pdf/PowerandControl.pdf).

---

**Men's Heritage Foundation**: is about inheritance; men's inheritance from men and Androputriarchy. This inheritance might include money, but always includes exalted status, entitlement, power, economic advantage, political advantage, religious advantage, primary access to opportunity, and admission to the boys club. It is intergenerational male privilege. It is a King's crown handed to all boys at birth. Like a scrotum, it comes with the penis. Men's Heritage Foundation are those undeserved privileges men accumulate over decades and centuries of oppressive entitlement, inequitable accumulation of resources, and unearned advantage that is passed down to male sycophants/mercenaries.

# Speaking of Women

Conventionality is the tacit agreement to set appearance before reality, form before content, subordination before principle.

~ Ellen Key
(1849–1926)

When a man can't explain a woman's actions, the first thing he thinks about is the condition of her uterus.

~ Clare Booth Luce
(1903–1987)

Anger is protest.

~ Lillian Hellman
(1905–1984)

Think wrongly, if you please, but in all cases think for yourself.

~ Doris May Lessing
(1919–)

Anger is loaded with information and energy.

~ Audre Lorde
(1934–1992)

I have a right to my anger, and I don't want anybody telling me I shouldn't be, that it's not nice to be, and that something's wrong with me because I get angry.

~ Maxine Waters
(1938–)

Anger is a signal, and one worth listening to.

~ Harriet Lerner
(1944–)

The first step in claiming yourself is anger.

~ Jamaica Kincaid
(1949–)

At least if I can stay angry I can stay alive.

~ Magdalena Gomez
(1953–)

## of pants and pads

Ever think about where the phrase "Who wears the pants in your family?" came from or what, exactly, it means?

Why isn't it "Who wears the dress in your family?"

It's "pants" because it refers to men having the decision-making authority in the family. And why? Has the evidence proven men have amply demonstrated their judicious and humane ability to make decisions for their families?

Of course not; completely the opposite.

It means, as usual, men get to have power over as an unearned privilege of Androputriarchy that is bequeathed, unquestionable, and unearned.

I suggest we change this malevolent saying to "Who wears the pad in your family?"

The pad I am referring to is the menstrual pad, usually worn by women. The monthly cycle of menstrual blood being symbolic of life, birth, growth, nurturance, safety and inter-generational well-being.

So, "Who wears the pad in your family?" is the question that asks who most exemplifies respect for and protection of life, birth, growth, nurturance, safety and inter-generational well-being, regardless of gender or unearned privilege.

This is the person who demonstrates devoted nurturance of the family; demonstrates hands-on involvement in the well-being of the family; the person who has chosen to fulfill that role for a family.

# Speaking of Women

If men could menstruate... clearly, menstruation would become an enviable, boast-worthy, masculine event: Men would brag about how long and how much... Sanitary supplies would be federally funded and free. Of course, some men would still pay for the prestige of such commercial brands as Paul Newman Tampons, Muhammed Ali's Rope-a-Dope Pads, John Wayne Maxi Pads, and Joe Namath Jock Shields--"For Those Light Bachelor Days."

~ Gloria Steinem
(1934–)

Without menstruation and the sciences of measurement women developed from watching first the moon and then the stars, there would be no clocks or watches, no astronomers, no mathematicians or physicists, no astronauts, none of the architecture and engineering which have been born from exact measurement and proportion.

~ Judy Grahn
(1940–)

Each month
The blood sheets down
Like good red rain.
I am the gardener.
Nothing grows without me.

~ Erica Jong
(1942–)

Suppose that society is a lie, and the period is a moment of truth which will not sustain lies.

~ Penelope Shuttle
(1947–)

If blood is thicker than water, then menstruation is thicker than brotherhood.

~ Sandra Cisneros
(1954–)

Men like war: they do not hold much sway over birth, so they make up for it with death. Unlike women, men menstruate by shedding other people's blood.

~ Lucy Ellmann
(1956–)

How might your life have been different for you if, on your first menstrual day, your mother had given you a bouquet of flowers and taken you to lunch, and then the two of you had gone to meet your father at the jeweler, where your ears were pierced...and then you went, for the very first time, to the Women's Lodge, to learn the wisdom of the women? How might your life be different?

~ Judith Duerk
(dates unknown)

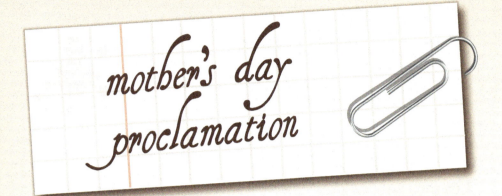

# mother's day proclamation

by Julia Ward Howe, 1870

Arise, then, women of this day!

Arise, all women who have hearts, whether your baptism be that of water or tears!

Say firmly: "We will not have great questions decided by irrelevant agencies. Our husbands shall not come to us, reeking with carnage, for caresses and applause. Our sons shall not be taken from us to unlearn all that we have taught them of charity, mercy and patience. We women of one country will be too tender of those of another to allow our sons to be trained to injure theirs."

From the bosom of the devastated earth, a voice goes up with our own. It says, "Disarm, Disarm!"

The sword of murder is not the balance of justice. Blood does not wipe out dishonor, nor violence indicate possession. As men have often forsaken the plow and the anvil at the summons of war, let women now leave all that may be left of home for a great and earnest day of counsel. Let them meet first, as women, to bewail & commemorate the dead. Let them solemnly take counsel with each other as to the means whereby the great human family can live in peace, each bearing after his own time the sacred impress, not of Caesars but of God.

In the name of womanhood and of humanity, I earnestly ask that a general congress of women without limit of nationality may be appointed and held at some place deemed most convenient and at the earliest period consistent with its objects, to promote the alliance of the different nationalities, the amicable settlement of international questions, the great and general interests of peace.

American feminist, reformer, and abolitionist writer Julia Ward Howe was born May 27, 1819 in New York City. After the Civil War, she campaigned for women's rights, equality, and world peace. She published several volumes of poetry, travel books, and a play. She became the first woman to be elected to the American Academy of Arts and Letters in 1908. She was an ardent antislavery activist who wrote the Battle Hymn of the Republic in 1862, sung to the tune of John Brown's Body. She wrote a biography in 1883 of Margaret Fuller, who was a female pioneer in journalistic review, a feminist, abolitionist, prison reformer, and influence on such women's rights activists as Susan Brownell Anthony. Ms. Ward Howe died in 1910.

# Speaking of Women

Let not oppression shake your fortitude, nor the hope of a gentler treatment cause you for a moment to swerve from strict duty.

~ Anna Elliott
(fl. 1770s)

Better that we should die fighting than be outraged and dishonored... Better to die than to live in slavery.

~ Emmeline Pankhurst
(1858–1928)

You can no more win a war than you can win an earthquake.

~ Jeannette Rankin
(1880–1973)

Shamed, dishonored, wading in blood and dripping with filth, thus capitalist society stands.

~ Rosa Luxemburg
(1870–1919)

I have noticed that as soon as you have soldiers the story is called history. Before their arrival it is called myth, folktale, legend, fairy tale, oral poetry, ethnography. After the soldiers arrive, it is called history...

~ Paula Gunn Allen
(1982–)

# my abusive relationship was sent to prison

## abusive relationships and other lies

"You knowingly stayed in a violent relationship, Mrs. Jones…" the judge drones on; "so I am going to sentence your relationship to four years in the penitentiary."

We hear it all the time: a violent relationship; a violent family; a violent household; a violent marriage; a violent home; a violent situation; a violent couple; a violent background; a violent romance; a violent union; a violent environment; a violent partnership. The prisons must be full of them.

It seems there is a lot of violence going on, but no human beings perpetrating it. Just houses, marriages and romances.

Can a relationship be convicted to prison for perpetrating criminal violence? If not, why not? Just what is a violent relationship anyway?

It is yet another complete and total fabrication and utterly effective tactic perpetrated by Androputriarchy to subjugate women and children and keep the public in a blissfully confused coma. It is an intelligent trick that works to hide the agency of the perpetrator and the brotherhood he—and all of us men—work for.

It allows us to look the other way—any way other than directly at the perpetrator. Looking at the perpetrator is akin to having the misfortune of walking up on a man that has just shot someone in the street. He then turns, gun in hand, and looks you in the eye. You are involved now. You have seen the violence and the violence perpetrator; what are you going to do now? Are you going to hold him accountable or make excuses for him? What is at stake for you at this moment?

We hide accountability out of fear, convenience, and self-interest.

To continue hiding, let's re-name the perpetrator an "abusive family" and then everyone is responsible, more or less, or maybe no one is responsible, more or less. That's even better. No one is responsible. Whew! Now I can get the hell out of here.

Then we can take the "family problem" to the stupid "professionals"—the social workers, psychologists, psychiatrists, ministers, priests, mullahs, counselors and their ilk who should know better if they cared to—and they can bury the victims in the latest psychobabble, preaching, and one-size-fits-all pet theories.

Of course, journalists and pseudo-reporters are more than happy to pass these clownish and deadly deceptions along to the public, who in turn are eager to have a comfortable explanation of events.

Taken to its deadly conclusion, "abusive relationship" always ends up in the coffin of the victim(s). "Why did she stay in an abusive relationship?"

Perfect.

# Speaking of Women

The progression or emancipation of any class usually, if not always, takes place through the efforts of individuals of that class...

~ Harriet Martineau
(1802–1876)

I'm not one of those as can see the cat in the dairy and wonder what she's come after.

~ George Eliot
(1819–1880)

Sit down and read. Educate yourself for the coming conflicts.

~ Mother Jones
(1830–1930)

Let us start a world-encircling revolt, a revolt which shall make a junk heap out of the civilization of Kaisers and Kings and all the things that make of man a brute and of God a monster.

~ Helen Keller
(1880–1968)

The rack and stake were replaced in the 18th century and 19th centuries by more subtle abuses, aimed at suppressing women legally, politically, economically, and psychologically.

~ Barbara G. Walker
(1930–)

To name oneself is the first act of both the poet and the revolutionary. When we take away the right to an individual name, we symbolically take away the right to be an individual. Immigration officials did this to refugees; husbands routinely do it to wives.

~ Erica Jong
(1942–)

What civilization has done to women's bodies is no different than what it's done to the earth, to children, to the sick, to the proletariat; in short, to everything that isn't supposed to "talk," and in general to whatever the knowledge-powers of government and management don't want to hear, which is thus relegated to exclusion from all recognized activity, relegated to the role of a witness.

~ Tiqqun
(French philosophical journal, founded in 1999 and dissolved in 2001)

for the correct answers to this Poppa Quiz, please consult yourself

1) **Bank Robbers rob banks because** (*please choose one*):
    a. they are mentally ill.
    b. they love too much.
    c. they are intoxicated.
    d. they lost control.
    e. they are unemployed.
    f. they have anger management problems.
    g. that's where the money is.

2) **Whites lynch Blacks because** (*please choose one*):
    a. they were mentally ill.
    b. they loved too much.
    c. they were intoxicated.
    d. they lost control.
    e. they were unemployed.
    f. they had anger management problems.
    g. they want to terrorize Black people.

3) **Corporations destroy the environment because** (*please choose one*):
    a. they are mentally ill.
    b. they love too much.
    c. they are intoxicated.
    d. they lose control.
    e. they are unemployed.
    f. they have anger management problems.
    g. it is very profitable to do so.

4) **People drive above the speed limit because** (*please choose one*):
    a. they are mentally ill.
    b. they love too much.
    c. they are intoxicated.
    d. they lose control.
    e. they are unemployed.
    f. they have anger management problems.
    g. they are in a hurry.

5) **Men batter their wives/partners because** (*please choose one*):
    a. they are mentally ill.
    b. they love too much.
    c. they are intoxicated.
    d. they lose control.
    e. they are unemployed.
    f. they have anger management problems.
    g. they enjoy having power and control over their wives/partners.

the "men are victims of patriarchy" con, hustle, and scam

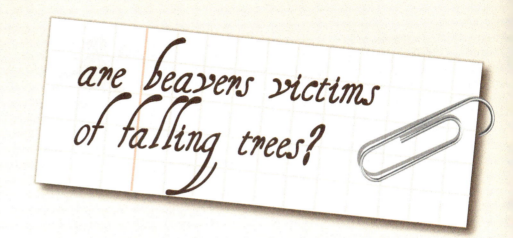
are beavers victims of falling trees?

**Myth:** an ill-founded belief held uncritically, especially by an interested group.

Are millionaires victims of capitalism?

Are White Supremacists victims of racism?

Are white male heterosexual Americans victims of gender discrimination protection laws?

And, of course, (yawn) are men victims of **patriarchy**?

Who would ask such an insipid thing—let alone believe it—and why? What kind of culture or community would insist that this drivel be listened to, let alone taken seriously?

King Baby, if you are such a seeker of truth, justice and the American Way and think men are victims of patriarchy, I assume you have concluded patriarchy is oppressing you, hence patriarchy is an oppressor.

If patriarchy is oppressive and your oppressor, what are you doing to challenge patriarchy? No, not just your personal situation, but the problem of patriarchal discrimination and oppression altogether?

I have yet to get an answer to that question from a man.

I assume that I have not gotten an answer because men are not seekers of justice for gender discrimination and oppression. Instead, men prove the point about male privilege by claiming they are "victims" and want attention or validation or pity or sex or something—anything but actual justice as that would work against their interest.

This is not exactly the way to start a gender revolution guys—Hello!

Instead, the men who trot out this tired, ridiculous, and time-honored "complaint" know patriarchy "has their back" and they are in line to get some goodies from their pitiable whining. Goodies such as continuing to benefit from patriarchy's suffocating grip by getting it both ways—as a member of the patriarchal special class and a so-called victim of it. What a racket!

Let's be clear: all men benefit from patriarchy. All men benefit from men's violence. All men benefit from the systematic, purposeful, and organized oppression of women and children. All men benefit from women's and children's second-class status. All men benefit from patriarchy's sexual, economic, intellectual, spiritual, and social captivity, occupation, and enslavement of women and children.

No exceptions. Anywhere. Ever.

**Patriarchy:** I purposely forgo this word in my fulminations. I use my word "Androputriarchy" instead. Although standard dictionary definitions of patriarchy do reveal the "men have authority over women" degeneracy, men have put lipstick on that pig and patriarchy is thought of as a benevolent thing. That's a lot of lipstick. Patriarchy (*The American Heritage® Dictionary of the English Language, Fourth Edition* copyright ©2000 by *Houghton Mifflin Company*): A social system in which the father is the head of the family and men have authority over women and children. A family, community, or society based on this system or governed by men.

111

Does patriarchy also hurt particular men, or some groups of men? Of course. At His putrid heart, patriarchy only cares about His advantage and exultation right now, this minute, and with no care about anything but doing what is necessary to maintain the advantage and exultation. But that advantage and exultation comes from the systematic, purposeful, centuries-old construction and maintenance of a social system built on the bloody and broken bodies and souls of women and children. It is an obscenely efficient nightmare based on one necessary fact: men's power and control over women and children.

If any man anywhere had a serious interest in justice for himself or for anyone else he would, by definition and necessity, have to be prepared to take on patriarchy—the powerful and ugly beast with 4 billion heads. That is a tall order and basically suicidal—for men or women.

Instead of being courageous and taking those risks, He settles for whining and throwing a Big Pity Party for Himself, and in the process, showing you His true colors.

Men-as-victims is a cottage industry in America.

It is one of the few brotherhoods open to women, as long as her analysis blames women for the "oppression" of men.

This pretense goes from one extreme of vitriolic attacks on "feminazi's" by men, all the way to the other extreme of angst-ridden worry by Androputriarchy-steeped women who fret about "excluding the men" from our women's gatherings/efforts.

Included in this willfully ignorant bunch is the "reverse discrimination" cartel: the "women have more rights than men" mob; the "don't speak angrily/violently about men because it lowers your vibration" society; the "men have feelings, too" league; the "does empowering women dehumanize men?" coterie.

For men this is simply blunt and useful armament with which to bash women about the head in our successful desire to maintain compliance with Androputriarchy.

For women it is a calculated bargain for favorable treatment with the undead demonic walking corpse that is Androputriarchy.

Back when the internet was young, I sent out a daily email to a couple hundred women called "Speaking of Women." I would include quotes by women and/or stories by or about women.

Sometimes I hosted guest writers, or shared comments/feedback I had received. It wasn't unusual for me to receive anguished feedback about how one of the readers didn't like how one my guest writers (always women—I excluded men) had used "violent" language or expressed "hatred" for men, etc.

At the same time I respected the responders' feelings and arguments, I was and continue to be unmoved by such arguments. I guess it strikes me as akin to being concerned about firefighters seeing my messy living room while they are hosing down my home engulfed in flames.

I am in favor of women expressing their anger/rage. I am not the least bit concerned with women using violent words when expressing their blunt opinion about the imperious infestation of Androputriarchy. In fact, I find myself drawn to such women. I find them more trustworthy. I find them refreshingly truthful. I find them to be, generally, full of vigor, humor, and passion for justice.

Androputriarchy: [*andro* meaning male, man; *putrere*, meaning rotten, or proceeding from decay; *archy* meaning ruler] an alternative for "patriarchy" that attempts to make clearer the corruption, malevolence, and destructive blight that male supremacy has been in human history and remains to this day.

# Speaking of Women

All revolutions are treason until they are accomplished.

~ Amelia Barr
(1831–1919)

Evolution when blocked and suppressed becomes revolution.

~ Nellie McClung
(1873–1951)

Give me then the man who is not a Christian, and who has no religion, for if the man who loves his wife and children, who gives to them the strength of his arm, the thought of his brain, the warmth of his head, has not religion, the world is better off without it, for these are the highest and holiest things which man can do.

~ Marilla Marks (Young) Ricker
(1840–1920)

No one who understands the feminist movement, or who knows the soul of a real new woman would make the mistake of supposing that the modern woman is fighting for the vote, for education, and for economic freedom, because she wants to be a man. That idea is the invention of masculine intelligence. Woman is fighting today, as she has all the way up through the ages, for freedom to be a woman.

~ Anne B. Hamman
(1914–)

…with respect to the individual oppressor as a person. Discovering himself to be an oppressor may cause considerable anguish, but it does not necessarily lead to solidarity with the oppressed. Rationalizing his guilt through paternalistic treatment of the oppressed, all the while holding them fast in a position of dependence, will not do. Solidarity requires that one enter into the situation of those with whom one is solidary; it is a radical posture. The oppressor is solidary with the oppressed only when he stops regarding the oppressed as an abstract category and sees them as persons who have been unjustly dealt with, deprived of their voice, cheated in the sale of their labor—when he stops making pious, sentimental, and individualistic gestures and risks an act of love.

~ Paulo Freire
(1921–1997)

You can stand tall without standing on someone. You can be a victor without having victims.

~ Harriet Woods
(1927–2007)

However possessed males may be within patriarchy, it is their order; it is they who feed on women's stolen energy. It is a trap to imagine that women should save men from the dynamics of demonic possession; and to attempt this is to fall deeper into the pit of patriarchal possession. It is women ourselves who will have to expel the Father from ourselves, becoming our own exorcists. Breaking through the Male Maze is both exorcism and ecstasy.

~ Mary Daly
(1928–2010)

And let's put one lie to rest for all time: the lie that men are oppressed, too, by sexism—the lie that there can be such a thing as 'men's liberation groups.' Oppression is something that one group of people commits against another group, specifically because of a 'threatening' characteristic shared by the latter group--skin color, sex or age, etc. The oppressors are indeed FUCKED UP by being masters, but those masters are not OPPRESSED. Any master has the alternative of divesting himself of sexism or racism—the oppressed have no alternative—for they have no power—but to fight. In the long run, Women's Liberation will of course free men—but in the short run it's going to cost men a lot of privilege, which no one gives up willingly or easily. Sexism is NOT the fault of women--kill your fathers, not your mothers.

~ Robin Morgan
(1941–)

Throughout all history, books were written with sperm, not menstrual blood.

~ Erica Jong
(1942–)

# i feel your pain

### empathy and other deceptions

On their first date he made mention of her "lovely brown eyes," but she did not seem impressed so he didn't say more.

On their second date he made mention of her "beautiful, long dark hair" and she lit up and sparkled like a midnight star.

Over the next six months of their courtship, he often mentioned her beautiful hair and how much it pleased him "how you wear it."

In the seventh month she said she was thinking about getting her hair cut, and he voiced his displeasure she would "do something like that, knowing how much I like your hair as it is."

In the tenth month—two weeks after he proposed marriage to her and she accepted—she had her hair trimmed and surprised him with a new style at the same restaurant where they first met.

When they returned to her apartment, he immediately began berating her. "I guess the wedding is off now, what with you whoring around with your new haircut, huh?" he barked.

Totally confused, she asked him what he meant.

"You know what I mean. You know I liked your hair the way it was before. I guess you've had enough of me and found yourself a new boyfriend who likes your new haircut. He must fuck you better than I do, huh?"

Her hair always being a source of pride and positive self-image, she was now devastated.

With this story, you've just learned everything you need to know about men and empathy, even though Androputriarchy and the mental health imbeciles will insist otherwise.

The notion that men do "bad" things because they lack empathy is an insidious and purposeful decoy on the order of the Trojan horse—besides being wholly false.

In fact, abusers and batterers, like the one in the story above, can teach us all about empathy skills because they are masters of the skill.

When I spoke with audiences about "batterer tactics," one of the exercises I conducted was titled "I Love Your Hair, Baby."

I began by asking them to generate a definition of the word/concept "empathy" and I wrote their definition on the chalkboard. It generally ended with something like "the ability to feel or identify with the circumstances of others."

I then asked them what a man's empathy skills, or lack thereof, has to do with domestic violence perpetration. I typically heard all the common fiction we've had to gag down over the years:

## Lack of Empathy Skills Causes Domestic Violence Because...

- communication breakdown in intimate relationships
- adversarial attitudes
- keeps you locked inside a self-centered world
- breeds emotional isolation, disconnection and polarization
- don't understand who that person is or what they need
- misinterpret how others think or feel about you

- don't grasp that others can be right about what they think or feel
- make judgments about others that may not be true
- consider honest actions taken by others as menacing
- think you have nothing in common
- healing can't begin unless you open up and let the other person open up

- can't share emotional wounds, leaving their loneliness and injury intact
- can't listen to another's pain, or share their own
- stuck in their own domestic abuse injury and can't move beyond the pain

This is a typical list, I kid you not. Obviously, my audiences were highly weighted with mental health "professionals."

I would then begin asking the questions that betray this subterfuge.

1 Can a batterer possibly be successful in his battering if he does not monitor the relative effectiveness of his controlling behaviors on his victim(s)?

2 How, exactly, would a batterer know whether his control tactics were working or not?

3 Is the answer to #2 above "empathy skills"—by your own definition?

I would point out, by their own previously agreed-upon definition, they have just ascertained batterers have excellent empathy skills, and in fact must be competent enough in empathizing to batter successfully.

I would then ask them why on earth social workers, psychologists, psychiatrists, and their ilk would claim "empathy training skills" are a necessary service needed by batterers, and why those "professionals" would want to make a living offering that "service." Needless to say, they didn't have a ready answer for me.

I also remarked that this audience now had a better understanding of batterer tactics than 99% of all the therapists in the world. Most were insulted; a few were not. I repeated that battering is simple and it has been made convoluted by interested parties—including batterers and therapists.

Androputriarchy teaches us men to use our victim's interests, attachments, fears, aspirations, desires, hopes, and whatever you deem important against you to further our control of you. This is not rocket science; it is Androputriarchy 101, which we are spoon-fed starting in the crib.

Now that we've established the evil-doers are just as talented, if not more so, in empathy than the rest of us commoners, where does this leave the issue of the "other side" of empathy—that is, it's role in changing things for the better?

Nowhere.

Our empathic abilities are no different than our hands in this regard—we men use them based on our interests, whether for safety and compassion or for degradation and violence. When we use them for violence, you see our interests and skill in satisfying our interests—there is no deficiency or lack of ability involved. In fact, quite the opposite.

After working with some 2,500 batterers over 11 years, I conclude that self-interest, never empathy, is the only avenue for changing men's battering behavior and thinking. That self-interest would have to be taught from birth and populated with self-respect flowing from when I provide safety and compassion to those around me, and shame when I perpetrate degradation and violence.

Period.

The human race is presently drowning in the rank toilet of Androputriarchy which teaches boys and men it is honorable and praiseworthy to be selfish, arrogant, spoiled bullies and we act accordingly. Our empathy skills help us excel in this.

It need not be so.

# Speaking of Women

I beseech your Majesty, let me have Justice, and I will then trust the law.

~ Elizabeth Hoby Russell
(1528–1609)

Men are taught to apologize for their weaknesses, women for their strengths.

~ Lois Wyse
(1926–2007)

Responsibility to yourself means refusing to let others do your thinking, talking, and naming for you… it means that you do not treat your body as a commodity with which to purchase superficial intimacy or economic security; for our bodies to be treated as objects, our minds are in mortal danger. It means that you refuse to sell your talents and aspirations short… and this, in turn, means resisting the forces in society which say that women should be nice, play safe, have low professional expectations, drown in love and forget about work, live through others, and stay in the places assigned to us.

~ Adrienne Rich
(1929–2012)

We have a double standard, which is to say, a man can show how much he cares by being violent—see, he's jealous, he cares—a woman shows how much she cares by how much she's willing to be hurt; by how much she will take; how much she will endure.

~ Andrea Dworkin
(1946–2005)

The reason there are so few female politicians is that it is too much trouble to put makeup on two faces.

~ Maureen Murphy
(1952–2008)

If you're not their mother, you're their wife. If you're not their wife, you're their secretary. But it's all the same job.

~ Erin Roberts
(dates unknown)

Unfortunately, all men were created equal.

~ Unknown

# Take Your Son to Brothel Day

Take Your Son to Brothel Day was conceived out of two very important concerns: one, that women shouldn't be the only ones to get recognition for doing something that appears to be good and, two, we men must always seek ways to be different from women. Below are suggestions that promote male-bonding with our sons, teach them not to be like girls, and give us the opportunity to go places we would normally have to lie about.

**Take your son to the brothel!** It's your responsibility to teach your boys how to "handle" women, if you know what I mean! And hey, if you've got the money, why not take him to Thailand where he can buy a girl younger than he is! Yeehaw!

**Take your son to the tavern!** Drinkin', carousin', fightin'—this is what a man lives for. Women don't go for the wine-sipping sissies! It's a big responsibility—but whom better to teach him what to do with vomit-covered clothes, an empty wallet, syphilis-teeming organs, and strange phone hang-ups?

**Take your son to the slaughter house!** The smell of viscera on the floor, a sharp bloody knife in the hands of a man who knows how to use it—these are things your boy must learn. When he goes back to the playground tomorrow the girls—and boys—will know who's boss!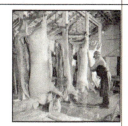

**Take your son to the toilet stall!** There may be nothing more important for your son to learn than how boys are different from girls: spitting, belching, farting, and playing with themselves in public. Remember—boys and average men pee standing up; real men shit standing up!

**Take your son hunting!** Shooting, killing, gutting: there are some things that prepare a boy for adulthood like nothing else can. Once your boy wraps his adorable little fingers around that cold, blue steel and witnesses bullets rend flesh he will know his rightful place in the community—and the world.

**Take your son to construction site!** There is a time in a boy's life when he must learn to speak at women the way men do. That time is, well, whenever you feel like it. Take him to the site and proudly listen as your boy screams "Whatsa matter bitch, on the rag?" and "C'mon, smile for us lezzy!" Just try holding back the tears.

**Take your son to college!** He's going to get hazed: if he's lucky, like you were! Give him a jump on the other pledges by practicing running the gauntlet, gang-rape, wearing feces shirts, sleep deprivation, bondage submission, hypothermia, branding, beatings, and forced masturbating! These are the good times you'll always remember!

**Take your son to the gun and ammo store!** A boy who is afraid of guns might as well be a girl! Watch his eyes light up when he sees the 1,250 rounds-per-minute Uzi, or the .338 Lapua Magnum that can take out an ex-wife at just under one mile.

**Take your son to the gentleman's club!** You will find many gentlemen here who can be a positive role model. He can save his allowance for a lap dance. You can talk about why Mommy left Daddy, and why sis is learning to pole dance. You can talk about boners and next year's trip to the brothel.

**Take your son to the boxing match!** Playing with Barbie dolls won't teach your boy how to take a left hook to the beak. Men's world is a contact sport where the mean and pitiless survive. Watching men beat each other senseless teaches the essence of manhood.

©2014 Michael Elizabeth Marillynson LLC - This poster is from the book "Contrary to the Custom of Men: Field Notes on the Pestilence of Patriarchy from a Disloyal Son." For re-printing permission go to: con2men.info. Images courtesy of Wikimedia Commons: kay chernush; hikaru iwasaki; mjcdetroit; margaret maloney; thomas hawk; shubert ciencia; fishcop; alexandr frolov; crosa; joppo kelin

token gestures

 Sometime in 1997, I commenced sending out a daily group email called "Speaking of Women" in which I featured the stories, news, and words of women. I sent it out every day for five years, and at its height, I had about 200 women on the distribution list.

One day during that time a woman responded to something I sent out about sexual harassment in the workplace. I was working in a "batterer intervention program" at the time. We had a couple of email responses back and forth on the subject and I include them below. Her name has been changed.

Dear Mike,

I was struck with your comments about the harassment issue at Ford, and your comparison with the population [batterers] that you work with.

When I worked for an automaker 6 or 7 years ago, one of my co-workers got a bad case of the dumbs and said some stuff to me in front of a supervisor that the supervisor had an issue with. The issue got to be a major big deal.

I had a lot more trouble with the way the issue was handled, rather than the unwanted sexual comments. It took me a long time to get past the emotional fallout and put the incident behind me. By that I mean put it into a perspective that I could learn and grow from rather than just react emotionally.

How do you allow your population [batterers] to work through the guilt and shame and move to a place where they can also "get past" or "put it behind them" so that they can start unlearning negative behavior and replacing it with new?

I guess my deepest motivation for writing is that I felt a gut level understanding of the seemingly contradictory statements of the auto plant people. Since the mess we had, my work group has had diversity training and a lot of my co-workers have changed their attitudes. I am still their token woman, and am treated with respect because I earned it. (I also am VERY STUBBORN and refuse to go away. January will make 16 years.)

~ Janet

Hi Janet,

It is nice to hear from you and get your perspective on something I included in Speaking of Women.

I'll respond to some of your thoughts and questions. Be warned I have strong opinions on these matters and it has been known to upset people.

You stated "one of my co-workers got a bad case of the dumbs." I'm going to assume two things you did not clarify: first, you were speaking about sexual harassment, and second, it was a man.

Sexual harassment has absolutely nothing to do with "dumb"-ness, intelligence, or education. In fact, what your co-worker did was quite smart, given his goal. His goal was to humiliate and control you—as is all sexual harassment—and it certainly isn't a dumb thing to do when that is his goal.

It is always in the interest of the perpetrator/oppressor to utilize his victim's cloudy thinking to his advantage, and when a sexual harasser hears from his victim—"one of my co-workers got a bad case of the dumbs"—he is already establishing the obfuscation for his behavior he desires.

You said, "I had a lot more trouble with the way the issue was handled, rather than the unwanted sexual comments."

Of course you did. We live in a patriarchal, sexist society where victims are almost always victimized at least twice. First, when they are initially harassed and, second, when the patriarchy makes sure the person who objects is taught it is better not to.

Again, it is music to the ears of your harasser that the way the issue was handled caused you more trouble than the abusive behavior in the first place: more obfuscation, which sexually abusive men gladly use to continue their controlling behavior.

"How do you allow your population to work through the guilt and shame… "

The last time you wanted to work through your guilt or shame about something, what did YOU do? Let's assume it was, "I did x, y and z" and that x, y and z are productive, respectful solutions.

Out of the 2,000 batterers I have worked with, how many do you think did x, y and z like you did? I'd guess maybe 10, if that. Why so few, you ask? Is it because it is so difficult? Because guilt and shame are such powerful emotions? Because they were abused as children?

No.

Because they didn't care to. They didn't give a shit. And why didn't they give a shit? Simple. Because they didn't have to. They had an investment in their partner's fear of them and the control it afforded them. Just like your abuser had an investment in frightening and controlling you.

This stuff is very simple. The only reason it seems complex or difficult is because abusers make it that way to cover their tracks. We are in a collective coma when it comes to holding men accountable for their behavior.

"How do you allow your population to move to a place where they can also 'get past' or 'put it behind them' so they can start unlearning negative behavior and replacing it with new?"

Janet, they could do this before they darkened my door. They were expert at putting it "behind them" and insisting "the bitch" do so also. Or else.

What makes you think batterers, or any human being, can't "start unlearning negative behavior and replacing it with new" at any instant in their lives they choose to?

Let me ask you this: If you want to move your sofa 4 feet over so you can vacuum under it, what do you do? Let's assume you push it with 10 pounds of force. But that only moves it 2 feet. What do you do then? How about using 20 pounds of force? Let's assume you use 20 pounds of force and that moves it the needed 4 feet.

Does that mean you are using "negative behavior?"

What I just described is what a batterer or abuser does. I want you to sweep under the sofa. I say "Janet, sweep under the sofa."

You don't.

I then say, "Godammit, Janet, sweep under the fucking sofa."

You still don't.

I then walk over and slap your face and say, "What the fuck is wrong with you? Sweep under the sofa now!"

And you do it.

Is that "negative" behavior?

Not to the abuser.

It is "positive" behavior because it gets him what he wants. It is also immoral, abusive, cruel, and in some places in the world, illegal.

What is there to feel guilty or ashamed about? I've known a shitload of abusers who felt guilt and shame—when the police arrived, or when they were in front of the judge, or when their victims served them with divorce papers. Is that guilt—or manipulation?

"How do you allow your population to start unlearning negative behavior and replacing it with new?"

I want you to you vacuum under the sofa. I say, "Bitch, vacuum under the sofa."

You don't do it.

I then say, "Bitch, if you don't sweep under the sofa I'm going to cut out the dog's heart while you watch."

You then sweep under the sofa.

Do you really think I, as an abuser, didn't just "unlearn negative behavior and replace it with new"? Abusers are learning machines. They are learning, testing, and modifying their behavior all the time.

However, what YOU want them to do is modify it in a way which satisfies YOU. They, of course, are modifying it in a way which satisfies THEM.

If they want to stop being abusive they can and will. IT IS THAT EASY. PERIOD!

But why would abusive men give up all the benefits that come with controlling people? This is why abusers choose not to change their behavior. It has absolutely nothing to do with guilt, shame, ability, morality, instruction sheets, or anything else.

"I felt a gut level understanding of the seemingly contradictive statement of the auto plant people."

I'm not surprised, Janet. We live, I believe, in a world occupied by a hostile, "foreign" army. And that army's flag is patriarchy.

To survive, we all must, to some extent, come to terms with our oppressors. As a loving, caring, compassionate person you identify even with a person who abuses you. That is great because it means you are still a loving, caring human.

The down side is you, and I, are easily manipulated and exploited by men. You and I have grown up breathing and drinking patriarchy—our ability to or willingness to see it and challenge it is impaired.

Abuse is simply about weighing the benefits against the costs of controlling people. If your male co-workers concluded 2 minutes from now it is to their benefit to treat you like shit, because you are a woman, and it would cost them nothing, they will likely do so.

I hope to hear what you think of my response, and wonder whether you would be interested in sharing our conversation with the Speaking of Women readership.

In solidarity, mikee

Hi Mike,

I think that perhaps you paint with a broad brush when you paint all women as victims, and all men as harassers. I do not see myself as a victim, now. I was involved in a relationship where my partner was an alcoholic. In five years I had never seen her drunk. One night she got drunk and used my face as a punching bag. I was so shocked and surprised that I forgot to defend myself until she drew back for the third punch.

I had to get every filling in my mouth repaired or replaced. I was smart enough to get out without any more violent behavior on either of our parts.

I do not accept the role of victim. I believe that it is entirely possible that someone may choose to try to make

me a victim. As a lesbian I feel threatened by society and the hatred that the white male religious right spews out.

I also believe, much to the chagrin of many of my friends, that women and gays and lesbians should be arming themselves and educating themselves in self defense. I believe that another holocaust could happen. I think that women, gays, and lesbians and other marginalized groups will be the victims. I will not go peacefully into that long night.

I did not grow up in an abusive household. I did grow up in a very poor household, and I lived on the wrong side of the tracks and went to inner-city schools. I learned a lot in the school of hard knocks. I will never stand by and let any human being abuse another human or animal. I have also had to work very hard to be aware and control my responses to situations.

I understand that the world is controlled by the patriarchy. Since I don't want to end up in jail I do not pursue my vigilante fantasies. I guess my point is I have to be beyond seeing red and reacting in order to gain control of my emotions and violent feelings before I can change my behavior.

What I hear you saying is that men are all abusers and will always be. They can learn any time they want to but choose not to. Women are all victims and can't do anything about it. What am I misunderstanding?

~ Janet

Hi Janet,

Thanks so much for writing to me.

"I think that perhaps you paint with a broad brush when you paint all women as victims, and all men as harassers. I do not see myself as a victim, now."

Janet, I do not consider all women victims, nor do I consider all men harassers. Nor do I believe I said that in my communication to you.

My perspective on the labels "victim" or "survivor" are the same as all the alcoholics I've ever worked with (as a social worker I've worked with drug addicts and alcoholics for 15 years): people use whatever labels suit them—either for good or for ill.

As a therapist, I didn't toe the standard line that an alcoholic has to call him or herself alcoholic or else they were in denial. If someone preferred to call themselves Tweety Bird because it helped their sober lifestyle, then that was okay by me. I was always for whatever worked.

Some women refer to themselves as victims, while others insist on survivor. It is not up to me to decide how a woman uses words to define her reality. Yet, I also think it can be revealing when she does so. Some women, and this sounds like it might describe you, very brashly and with bravado, claim for all to hear they are not victims, and never will be. It's not my business or my interest to suggest how you see or label yourself. But how you label, or don't label, yourself doesn't change the realities of patriarchy.

Janet, who decides whether you are a victim? Who decides whether you are a survivor? Who decides whether you are a battered woman? Your writings would indicate you think you do.

When your ex-partner knocked your fillings out, SHE decided you were a battered woman. You became a statistic that day, whether you liked it or not, whether you consider yourself a victim or not, regardless of what you tell yourself. SHE DECIDED THIS, not you.

Patriarchy decided a millennium ago you have less value than a man. Patriarchy decided a millennium ago as a lesbian, you have less value than a devalued straight woman. Patriarchy decided a millennium ago we would be debating the term "victim" over the Internet.

"I hear you saying that men are all abusers and will always be."

Am I saying all women are victims, and all men perpetrators? No. Regardless, the majority of women will experience sexual and physical violence and/or disrespect at the hands of men—most likely heterosexual men—sometime in their lives. Regardless, the majority of men will perpetrate sexual or physical violence and/or disrespect towards women sometime in their lives.

"Women are all victims and can't do anything about it."

Women, everywhere in the world, can "do" something about their abuse at the hands of men. But they will pay a price. Just as you describe in your case, the aftershocks were possibly more damaging than the initial assault.

A woman trapped in prostitution certainly has the right as a human being to rebel against her pimp, but if she does so, she will very likely be beaten for it, and very possibly killed.

And who is going to rescue her—her next "customer?"

Janet, if I were to say sexual harassment was rampant at your auto plant, would I be "paint[ing] with a broad brush"?

If so, then I am painting with a broad brush. If I say it is likely the sun will come up tomorrow morning, and that means I am painting with a broad brush, then so be it.

These perspectives have been taught to me by the malest of males—domestic violence perpetrators.

~ mikee

# Speaking of Women

The women's movement has not acknowledged the debt it owes to the unorthodox, freethinking women in its ranks. Their non-religious views often have been suppressed, as if shameful, when in fact repudiation of patriarchal religion is an essential step in freeing women… the status of women and the history of the women's rights movement cannot be understood except in the context of women's fight to be free from religion… if there was one cause which had a logical and consistent affinity with free thought, it was feminism.

~ Anne Nicole Gaylor
(1926–)

We're not asking for superiority [for women] for we have always had that; all we ask is equality.

~ Nancy Witcher Langhorne Astor
(1879–1964)

Marched into Russia: murdered the Jews; strangled the women; killed the children; everyone knows what we bring.

~ Willy Peter Reese
(1921–1944), German Infantryman, eastern front

# WOMEN TRAPPED IN BROTHEL RESCUED AFTER 1,873 DAYS

OCTOBER 13, 2010, DETROIT, MI—Each time the red, white and blue-draped woman exited out of the hellhole on Wednesday to applause and the waiting arms of her family, the scene replayed all around the world with a joy that never seemed tired.

By late afternoon, the precarious operation to remove 33 women and girls who were trapped in this pit of suffering for more than five years was moving along so efficiently that officials expected the job to be completed by the end of the day, far ahead of schedule.

"All okay!" 48-year-old Cassandra Thomas, the 20th rescued woman, shouted to her rescuers right before they shuttled her off to the hospital. Once freed from the cage-like pit, she thanked God and walked to hug her mother. Workers then wrapped her in a blanket and took her to triage for medical treatment.

After routine preparation, the rescuers went back into the brothel to fetch the next woman—olanda Barrios, 50, who became the group's medic in the bordello. She arrived to hearty handshakes and hugs from the doctors outside.

When the 17th woman, Ordena Sebastian, 16, was released from the place of misery, she got down on her knees, then held her hands in the air and waved the blue, green and white flag of women's suffrage.

For more than 15 hours, the women have been emerging at regular intervals in a pageant that has moved a worldwide audience—watching on television, on computers, even on mobile phones—to tears and laughter.

The second woman to reach freedom, Maria Rice, left the trap of women's sexual exploitation in a kind of victory dance, hugging family members and officials. She embraced the American president, Barak Obama, three times and presented people with gifts: objects given to her from other women who had been trapped in, and mysteriously disappeared from, the brothel. She punched fists with the crowd and led a cheer: "Virago! Virago!" they shouted. "Strong, courageous woman!" The refrain echoed as subsequent women reached the clean outside air.

"I've been near God, but I've also been near the devil," Ms. Rice said. "God won."

The 12th woman—Emily Johnson, 24, known for doing exercise every day in the house of anguish—stepped from the patriarchal sewer to rapturous cheers and the embrace of her girlfriend, and then another from Mr. Obama.

"Thank God we're alive," Ms. Rice said. "I know now why we're alive."

Lorraine Golborne, the National Organization for Women minister, praised the rescue operation at an afternoon briefing on Wednesday, saying that officials were able to reduce the time between women rescued from an hour to 45 minutes.

"We hope to finish this successfully by the end of this day," she said.

Ms. Golborne did note two small problems, however. She said that some of the male police were identified as "customers" of the brothel.

As of early afternoon, there were five rescue workers currently in the brothel, and a sixth rescue worker would go in "in a few hours" to replace some of the other workers.

Thus far, Ms. Golborne said, the most difficult rescue was that of Marie Clarondon, 63, the oldest woman in the group, who had struggled with a lung condition. "We took additional precautions in this case, but she's fine."

Janie Miller, the health minister, said one patient was suffering from acute pneumonia and two others had dental infections requiring surgery, but that 17 of the first 20 women rescued were in conditions that were "more than satisfactory." To respect the privacy of the women, she said she would not reveal the identity of the sick.

Ms. Miller said that two medical rescue workers were sent into the prison of women, one to focus exclusively on the patient with pneumonia and to start her on a course of antibiotics. "She is now better than she was a couple of days ago," she said. "If all goes well, at the very maximum, she should stay at the hospital through this weekend."

Cameras inside the brothel showed the women sending off an evacuee with cheers, and another camera positioned on the top of the door carried images of a pathway cleared through the squalor of this place of imprisonment.

The race to save the women has thrust America into a spotlight it has often sought but rarely experienced. While lauded for its economic management and austerity, the nation has often found the world's attention trained more on its human rights violations than on uplifting moments.

The women had to withstand over five years of waiting for this day, hanging firm to discipline and collaboration in the pitiless, dank place. Their perseverance has transfixed the globe with a universal story of human struggle and the enormously complex operation to rescue them.

President Obama staked his presidency on the effort. It has involved untold millions of dollars, specialists from NASA and rescue experts from a dozen or so countries. Some here at the brothel have compared the rescue

effort to the Apollo 13 space mission, for the emotional tension it has caused and the expectation of a collective sigh of relief at the end.

The ordeal has also riveted Mexico, home to one of the women, 24-year-old Carlita Mamani, who kissed her husband, Vernon, and shouted: "Thank you, America!" The Mexican president, Felipe Calderon, joined Mr. Obama in welcoming Ms. Mamani, and chatting with the ever-growing rescued group in the makeshift hospital. It was a rare moment of rapprochement for the two leaders, whose nations have strained relations.

"I would like to thank the American people. Thank you very much for rescuing our sister, Carlita Mamami," Mr. Calderon said. "Mexico will never forget. This is a historical moment, and this unites us more every day. These events are fostering greater trust between Mexico and America."

Deep in the brothel, the remaining women waited for their turn, along with a rescue worker who descended to their putrid place of enslavement, which was painted in the black and blue of the patriarchal flag.

Despite high expectations, officials here warned two months ago the operation was still in a precarious phase. The rescue door is barely wider than a woman's body.

After the Aug. 5 discovery of the predicament of the women and girls, their fate was uncertain at best. Advisers to Mr. Obama counseled him not to raise expectations that the women would be found alive. Ms.

Golborne, the minister, said publicly that their chances of having survived were slim, comments that bothered many Americans.

Mr. Obama set in motion an intense rescue effort, sparing no expense. Workers drilled a skinny borehole, and on August 22 a drilling hammer came up with two notes: a love letter from Ms. Gómez, the oldest woman of the group, to her girlfirend, and another in red ink. "We are well in the dungeon. The 33," it read.

Suddenly the name of the makeshift vigil at the brothel—Camp Hope—took on new meaning. Mr. Obama flew here right after his father-in-law's wake to celebrate with the women's families.

But the Americans were in uncharted territory. To their knowledge, no one had tried a rescue so far into the heart of patriarchy. Keeping the women alive and in good spirits, much less getting them out, would be an enormous challenge.

Doctors from NASA and American Navy officers with experience in submarines were consulted on the strains of prolonged confinement. The women had lost considerable weight and were living off emergency rations.

Medical officials consulted frequently with the women over a modified telephone pushed in through the skinny borehole.

This is my adaptation of an article describing the
rescue of 33 (male) miners from a Chilean mine in October of 2010.
Photo courtesy of Wikimedia Commons: joe tordiff;

clarity is only
a change of
clothes away

**Malevolent:** having or exhibiting ill will; wishing harm to others; having an evil or harmful influence, intent, or effect.

Are you one of those sincere, thoughtful men who really love women and want what is best for them, but can't wrap your mind around the ridiculous things written in this book or the concept of patriarchy being a bad thing? I have a solution for you.

It is an itty bitty assignment—one any man can do in his spare time (one hour maximum) at very little or no cost, depending primarily on your wardrobe.

It is guaranteed to help you make up your mind, one way or the other, and works every time (not applicable in the Castro in San Francisco).

Here's all you'll need:
- Women's clothes that more or less fit you
- Uncomfortable women's shoes you can walk/run in for one hour
- Facial makeup and some help getting it on right, more or less
- Transportation to downtown (walking or riding a bike is best)

Once you are dressed up as your notion of a fabulous woman and looking snazzy you will spend a maximum of one hour being seen by as many neighbors and community members as possible. You can enjoy typical tasks you would do while downtown: shopping, meeting with friends, etc. Mostly, it is important that you walk around and be seen a lot.

While doing this simple exercise take mental notes of how it feels to fully express yourself as a woman. How does it feel to have men's eyes look you over? What kind of tone do you experience in people's voices and actions? Does it feel liberating or constricting to you as you wholeheartedly express yourself as a woman in a patriarchal society?

Then, if you survive, you can go home and discuss your experience with your family, your neighbors, your buddies, your co-workers, and your hockey team. Listen intently to their comments.

Add up your experiences and comments and decide whether you think patriarchy is an intolerant, violent, abusive, controlling and male-dominated disease; or a kind, affectionate, merciful, tolerant and equitable human organization.

# Speaking of Women

Women want mediocre men, and men are working to be as mediocre as possible.

~ Margaret Mead
(1901–1977)

Why do people say "grow some balls"? Balls are weak and sensitive. If you wanna be tough, grow a vagina. Those things can take a pounding.

~ Betty White
(1922–)

… we will no longer be led only by that half of the population whose socialization, through toys, games, values and expectations, sanctions violence as the final assertion of manhood, synonymous with nationhood.

~ Wilma Scott Heide
(1926–)

Although a rigidly hierarchical social structure like androcracy, which imprisons both halves of humanity in inflexible and circumscribed roles, is quite appropriate for species of very limited capacity like social insects, it is truly inappropriate for humans. And at this juncture in our technological evolution, it may also be fatal.

~ Riane Tennenhaus Eisler
(1937–)

Of all the nasty outcomes predicted for women's liberation… none was more alarming than the suggestion that women would eventually become just like men.

~ Barbara Ehrenreich
(1941–)

In spite of hopes to the contrary, pornography and mass culture are working to collapse sexuality with rape, reinforcing the patterns of male dominance and female submission so that many young people believe this is simply the way sex is. This means that many of the rapists of the future will believe they are behaving within socially accepted norms.

~ Susan G. Cole
(1952–)

If the bird does like its cage, and does like its sugar, and will not leave it, why keep the door so very carefully shut?

~ Olive Schreiner
(1855–1920)

You have to make more noise than anybody else, you have to make yourself more obtrusive than anybody else, you have to fill all the newspapers more than anybody else, in fact you have to be there all the time and see that they do not snow you under, if you are really going to get your reform realized.

~ Emmeline Pankhurst
(1858–1928)

When they were going to be flagrantly, brutally selfish, how men did love to talk of being fair!

~ Kathleen Norris
(1880–1966)

# Burqa's    or    Bikini's

# WHAT MATTERS IS...

...we'll decide what you wear.

©2014 Michael Elizabeth Marillynson LLC - This poster is from the book "Contrary to the Custom of Men: Field Notes on the Pestilence of Patriarchy from a Disloyal Son." For re-printing permission go to: con2men.info. Images courtesy of Wikipedia Commons jorge mejía peralta; trjames; toglenn; نامعلوم

'cause you'll never win  don't let him under your skin*

I wish I better understood how Androputriarchy infects and parasitizes women individually and as a population. It is an evil, cunning, and wholly effective colonization of women's minds and allegiances. Of course, Androputriarchy also infects and putrefies men individually and as a herd, and I better understand this dynamic.

I remember the first brush I had with this contamination that really threw me for a loop.

I was presenting a workshop on "batterer tactics" to a group of around 50 drug and alcohol treatment therapists in Lansing, Michigan. About 2/3 of the way into our allotted time, we were talking about male batterers' power and control tactics flowing from their male privilege and male entitlement under Androputriarchy (back then I used the word patriarchy). It had been a generally "receptive" audience up to that point. Of course, "generally receptive" doesn't mean one human being in that room, outside of me, agreed with anything I was presenting. It only means they hadn't gotten out their pitchforks and torches yet.

Then it happened. A very well-dressed (this woman obviously, even to a fashion-dunce like me, had some serious money invested in her clothes, jewelry, makeup, etc.), "attractive," 30-ish, white, thin, power-house-of-a-woman stood up and began to excoriate me. She told me, and the audience, what I was saying was all wrong, women are just as "bad" and "violent" as men, what I was saying was just "feminist propaganda," I was being disrespectful of women and men by how I was talking, I was over-simplifying things, I was basically a cretin and a lackey, and was wasting her time. Upon conclusion of her indictment she picked up her expensive-looking briefcase and gracefully strutted out of the room.

Suffice it to say, I was shocked, embarrassed, and scrambling to figure out how to proceed. I don't remember exactly how things ended up with that group, but I didn't know how to respond productively to what she said/did.

Believe me, I thought very deeply about what she had to say and what had happened in that room. Like most of us would, I first felt embarrassed and ashamed and assumed she was right and figured I had a lot of explaining to do to myself. I also had a commitment to accountability and to hearing the truth and if she was right, I needed to come to terms with it.

My analysis centered not on what she had to say so much, but on what I had been presenting. Was what I was presenting right or not? Did it hold up to scrutiny or not? Did it play out down to the last detail or not?

I had the good fortune of having the best crucible in the world to test the validity of what I was presenting—batterer intervention groups. There was no place on Earth filled with men who had more of a personal stake in proving me wrong. As I already had a commitment to accountability long before I conducted the Lansing workshop, I already knew how to test my theories, perspectives, and conclusions. I could plug this new experience into that mechanism.

Our batterer intervention program was based solely on an accountability model so, if we as program staff were not accountable in our thinking and actions, it would gladly be

---

* Sweet Talkin' Guy, by The Chiffons; written by Doug Morris

pointed out at the worst possible moment in intervention groups (as it was over and over).

I quickly concluded what I was presenting was accountable, defendable, and accurate. For details on this process, please see, "Why, Mommy?"

What I still hadn't figured out was this woman. Why did what she say, and how she appeared to me, throw me? Was I more threatened by a woman who appeared to enjoy such social and economic privilege, than if it had been by a woman who didn't have that appearance?

In general, this is the question I wonder about to this very day.

First my assumptions:

1. Androputriarchy has colonized all human beings' minds, women and men, and the only questions are how so and how do we deal with it?

2. This colonization purposefully and successfully impairs individuals' willingness/skill to think critically about the fact we are, in all places on Earth today, living as an occupied population under the oppression of a hostile army—that army being Androputriarchy.

3. Although we all live under the hostile occupation of Androputriarchy, we attempt at all times and in all things to pretend as if we are not, with varying success. This would be similar to the denial of stepping into an automobile where 32,788 Americans were mangled to death in 2010, but pretending as if there is no risk of imminent death.

4. Under the oppressive, hostile occupation of Androputriarchy men attempt to believe they are not oppressors and predators of women, while women attempt to believe they are not the prey of men, or oppressed by men, and are "safe."

5. To survive psychologically and emotionally, women then apply Jedi mind tricks to themselves so they can establish make-believe ways they are insulated from men's predation.

I wish we knew more about how Androputriarchy infests women in this way. What are the major factors that influence a particular woman's relative allegiance to her oppressor? Are they the obvious things like the economic, social, occupational, sexual, safety, religious, and/

or other status markers that women can gain from aligning themselves with men? And how do these "external" markers then mix with women's internal psychological and emotional dynamics? What about the history of the individual woman and how she was or wasn't treated and raised as a child?

If we were to come up with the most influential factors that predict a strong allegiance by a woman to Androputriarchy, how would that explain the random and rare rebel who risks it all and becomes a flaming, radical feminist?

One of the ways I used to experience this was with women who publicly and emphatically asserted "I would never let that happen to me" when I was educating about batterer tactics. It was always with sadness I heard women speak this way. First, I am a man so I am not in a position to criticize how women choose to cope. However, I felt sad because I heard this as literally whistling past the graveyard.

To crow "I would never let this happen to me" is, in my mind, identifying with the aggressor. It is the assumption that safety from oppressive violence and threats is to be found in being stronger and more invincible than any assailant.

Second, it shames and distances the woman from her sisters, especially those who have already been battered, abused, raped, and killed. She is, in effect, not calling out the assailants but calling out the victims for their "weakness" and vulnerability. It is quintessentially blaming the victim.

Last, and I think the most painful aspect for this type of woman to contemplate: it is absolutely and completely false for **ANY** woman to conclude she is the arbiter of whether she will be battered, abused, raped, or killed.

Just as for all other strategies employed by women to attempt to remain "safe" under Androputriarchy, you do not decide whether you get battered, abused, raped, or killed; a man and/or Androputriarchy does.

You may be rich, but if I snatch you off of the street and into my car and take you somewhere and rape you, you are a rape victim. You may be tough, but if I drug you and lead you into the alley behind the restaurant and bash your head in, you are an assault victim. You may be politically well-connected, but if I am charming and woo you and marry you and we have three kids and seven years later I beat your ass, you are a domestic violence victim. You may be the best parent in the world, and chief of police, but if I "groom" your daughter just enough and get her into an isolated room just long enough, she is going to become a pedophile victim. And you are going to become the mother of a pedophile victim.

As I have said elsewhere, we do not solve the pestilence of Androputriarchy on an individual basis, or a household basis, or by arming ourselves to the teeth, or by taking self-defense lessons, or by being richer than anyone else, or by having a bigger fence or driveway, or by lying to ourselves.

Safety comes in communities, regions, countries, Earths.

I have been on the receiving end of angry and outraged arguments from women when I have said publicly that you do not choose if you become a victim—men do. I have been told I am sexist for saying this, I am disempowering women, and I am concluding women are weak and cannot protect themselves.

I hope I am wrong about this; though I doubt it.

I have also come to the conclusion most women do not have more of an issue with the prostitution of women and children because they innately sense that these most vulnerable of females take the punishment and, in doing so, offer a layer of "protection" for "normal" women. Cross my fingers and hope they don't do it to me.

Women, girls, and boys who are sexually prostituted are the most vulnerable of the vulnerable. They are the ones most tortured, maimed and killed. Are we sacrificing them for our own "protection?" If so, who else are we sacrificing? What other ways do we think we are building layers of protections for ourselves?

Why is it that baptism of children, especially girls, in the Catholic Church and similar patriarchal religious boys clubs, seems like kissing the ring of a mafia "godfather"? Is for hope of protection in the future? As long as you do as the godfather asks, and as long as there are no arbitrary rulings against you, you will be safe; safe from the Church and the godfather. Maybe.

Now that you are either enraged with me, or utterly depressed, may I offer another stinking charm of Androputriarchy?

We love to pretend to ask questions of women that aren't really questions. They are insults. They are mocking. They are "piling on" as we used to call it on the playground.

So-called questions like, "why do those women just jump from one relationship with a violent man to another?"

By definition, the person who asks this question, whether it be male or female, is not on a quest for enlightenment. They are making a statement about how they are enjoying their distance from vulnerable and victimized women; that they are not so stupid.

Not to mention the fact we are steered by Androputriarchy to talk about victims, but not about aggressors. So in this so-called question we are "addressing" the victims (why do they stay with him) and not the aggressors (why do men do that). If you find yourself neglecting to question, or insisting on accountability from, the aggressors you are doing the aggressor's (Androputriarchy) bidding.

Even if this question was legitimate, which it is not, let's consider how the person asking the question would fare in "picking the right man."

Let's assume you are a heterosexual woman looking for a heterosexual male partner. What is the probability, statistically, if you picked blindfolded from 20 men, you would pick one who will batter you? Do you know these numbers? Do you know where to get these numbers? Does anyone have these numbers?**

Next, let's assume it is half of these men. Which half? How do you figure out which ones are dangerous and which ones are safe? What are the characteristics of these men that you believe you are better at picking out than some other woman could? How did you come up with these characteristics? Are they the result of research on the matter you boiled down? Or did someone tell you what to look for? Did you just come up with the characteristics yourself? Do they just look the most like you racially, socioeconomically, age-wise, etc.?

How many women (millions) in America who are being battered do you think had a list of characteristics they thought was just as good as yours? How many of the characteristics on their list are also on your list?

What if batterers are like serial killers; they hunt mainly in "their own group"? That is, women of their own race, socioeconomic status, education, etc. and it's not about their own characteristics. What if batterers can't be identified

---

** If you know these numbers I'd like to see them. We seem to have compiled a lot of statistical information about victims of men's violence, but we don't, oddly enough, seem to know much of anything about the perpetrators. Why do you think that might be?

by characteristics, but by victim-type preferences? Some men like women who are easily intimidated; some like a challenge.

How are we doing so far? Have we picked out the perfect man yet? Now that you've picked him and you know he is the right one for you, do you know if you are more likely to be assaulted by him now, in the first year of your love affair, or in the fifth year? When would he have more control over you, now or when you have two children together? Would the characteristics you are so certain about be applicable when you are first picking or do they relate to the fifth year of marriage?

Are we still enjoying mocking "those women" who "go from one batterer to the next?"

When you have escaped in the middle of the night with the crying kids from this husband who battered you, are you going to use the same or different criteria for the next man? Will you be better at "picking them" or worse?

## Batterer Manipulation Susceptibility Inventory

| YES | NO | |
|---|---|---|
| | | Do you have charitable feelings towards both men and women? |
| | | Do you wish that couples and families who are experiencing problems could work out their conflicts? |
| | | Have you ever felt love for someone? |
| | | Have you ever had a relationship, with anyone, which lasted longer than one year? |
| | | Do you like to help others? |
| | | Do you have problem solving skills? |
| | | Have you ever felt very sad, or very happy, or very angry? |
| | | Have you ever wanted to feel safe from any sort of physical harm? |
| | | Have you ever wanted someone else's approval? |
| | | Have you ever invested a good amount of your energy in a project which you hoped would be successful? |
| | | Have you ever wanted to protect someone? |
| | | Have you ever felt sad about someone else's situation or problems? |
| | | Have you ever wanted to believe something, even though you suspected or knew it wasn't true? |
| | | Have you ever offered counsel or advice to someone? |
| | | Have you ever tried to be a sympathetic listener to someone? |

**Legend:** your total amount of "yes" answers

**0 – 5** You appear to be relatively devoid of human attachment tendencies and empathy and should, with some vigilance and luck, remain safely detached from a batterer's manipulation. The down side is you are a sociopath.

**6 – 10** You have significant and dangerous tendencies toward human attachment and empathy and are likely to be vulnerable to a batterer's tactics. Beware.

**11 – 15** Unfortunately for you, you are an average person with a "normal" desire for human attachments and empathy and are highly susceptible to a batterer's manipulation. You are hosed. You might as well have "punch me" tattooed on your forehead. Sorry.

# Speaking of Women

I have no sympathy for those who, under any pressure of circumstances, sacrifice their heart's-love for legal prostitution.

~ Harriet Martineau
(1802–1876)

Womanhood is the great fact in her life; wifehood and motherhood are but incidental relations.

~ Elizabeth Cady Stanton
(1815–1902)

It is delightful to be a woman; but every man thanks the Lord devoutly that he isn't one.

~ Olive Schreiner
(1855–1920)

In the greater part of the world woman is a slave and a beast of burden… In most cases she is overworked, exploited, and (even when living in luxury) the oppressed sex… These conditions are opposed by the woman's rights movement… Most men do not understand this ideal; they oppose it with unconscious egotism.

~ Kathe Schirmacher
(1865–1930)

Behind us lies the patriarchal system; the private house, with its nullity, its immorality, its hypocrisy, its servility. Before us lies the public world, the professional system, with its possessiveness, its jealousy, its pugnacity, its greed. The one shuts us up like slaves in a harem; the other forces us to circle, like caterpillars head to tail, round and round the mulberry tree, the sacred tree, of property. It is a choice of evils. Each is bad.

~ Virginia Woolf
(1882–1941)

I myself have never been able to figure out precisely what feminism is: I only know that people call me a feminist whenever I express sentiments that differentiate me from a doormat or a prostitute.

~ Rebecca West
(1892–1983)

One cannot argue that the domesticated animal chose slaughter any more than one could argue that women chose patriarchy.

~ Sunaura Taylor
(1982–)

There is nothing to be gained from women wasting their time trying to change organizations that don't get it now and never will.

~ Kathleen Kelley Reardon
(dates unknown)

What's important now is to mobilize hysteria as a quasi-revolutionary force. It intervenes, breaks up continuities, produces gaps and creates horror—refusing conformity with what is. Feminism could benefit from an affirmation of hysteria; hysteria as a response to what is unacceptable and intolerable in life… as a response to emergency. Women have internalized the censorship of hysteria as though it were an unwelcome disease… whereas it should be welcomed.

~ Avital Ronell
(1952–)

# operation peeved pencil

If you had any doubt that the United States military amply demonstrates the relative immaturity of most men in our country, check out the names of these military operations:

| | | |
|---|---|---|
| Eagle Claw (1980) | Commando Hunt (1968–72) | Rolling Thunder (1967–68) |
| Earnest Will (1987–88) | Enhance Plus (1972) | Sealords (1968) |
| Team Spirit (1976–1993) | Flaming Dart (1965) | Sharp Edge (1990–91) |
| Power Pack (1965) | Ballistic Charge (1965) | Tomahawk (1951) |
| Urgent Fury (1983) | Bear Bite (1965) | Dragon Fire (1965) |
| Just Cause (1989) | Bold Mariner (1965) | Sea Tiger (1965) |
| Steel Tiger (1965–68) | Daring Rebel (1965) | Linebacker (1972) |

You can't argue with the explosive success of our military: we have massacred and oppressed our enemies unabated since 1775. We must be doing something right.

So I suggest we come up with some feminist operation names to drum up esprit de corps among the women-folk. This will give them something to aspire to as we further our top-secret plans for feminist world domination.

Here's my contribution:

**Operation Humpty Bombardment:** this cleverly canine campaign to turn all dogs (man's best friend, after all) homosexual and get a first four-foothold on the American family has already seen limited success: don't tell me you haven't seen some torrid male-on-male and female-on-female dog action in your neighborhood—or even in your own home.

**Strike Force Potent Poontang:** all girls, at around age four, will begin implementing Double-Top-Secret Feminist Agenda Imperative #817-1h, which initiates the indoctrination of their brothers with preconscious vagina envy. We'll know it's working because the boys will want to be the tunnel, not the train, eh comrades?

**Mission Indomitable Amazon:** legions of girls will infiltrate high school and then university science departments in a diabolical mission to genetically turn tomorrow's women into hirsute harpies whose hairy armpits and bodies, as well as fierce demeanors, will so repulse men that the guys will be reduced to sniveling, anxious milquetoasts.

**Offensive Menses Fury:** girls excitedly anticipate the first day of their menstrual blood so they may become initiates in the Church of Flowing Life. All other male religions (war, sadism, prostitution, torture, violence, necrophilia, weapons) quickly become obsolete as men finally figure out where babies come from.

**Sortie Booming Banshee:** objective #1 in overthrowing Androputriarchy and destroying the family unit is to plunder male virility. This should take about a week. All we have to do is train our girls in the martial arts of belching, farting, spitting, and grabbing their crotches. It helps if they can master the menacing growl, "What are you looking at?" but not necessary.

**Excursion Baleful Boodle Besmirch:** you knew, as true feminists, we'd have to get around to destroying capitalism and stealing individuals' incentive to prosper. We'll have our girls and boys draw crude representations of cherished children's toys like Barbie and G.I. Joe in sex-inappropriate clothing (or just any Teletubby) on all of the legal tender we can get our hands on. Women have all of the advantages nowadays, so that's a lot of money! This will throw the financial markets into turmoil, cause decent God-fearing Americans to shun touching money, and cause a feminazisocialist revolution.

**Deployment Homegirl Hammer:** girls will be covertly taught the treasonous language of cow whispering so that, at the appointed hour, they will ride the former feedlot inmates down Main Street to trample meat-eaters into submission to The New Worldwide Order. The fur won't fly as girls institute people before profits, making the personal political, institute compulsory vegetarianism, and go on a chocolate tofu ice cream strike until television becomes relevant.

**Operation Ballbuster Battleaxe:** girls will unobtrusively play with their new toys having clandestine names like Easy Bay Covens (witchcraft "kitchens" involving baying at the moon) and Bar Be Dollz (girls learn the tricks of hooking up with lesbians at the local tavern) in preparation for a titillating adult life of practicing witchcraft and annihilating motherhood. Other fun toys will teach girls gladiatorial skills and techniques, homeopathic medicine, advanced man-hating, nymphomania and birth control, and applying makeup for extended space exploration.

## Speaking of Women

Life in this society being, at best, an utter bore and no aspect of society being at all relevant to women, there remains to civic-minded, responsible, thrill-seeking females only to overthrow the government, eliminate the money system, institute complete automation and destroy the male sex.

~ From the S.C.U.M. (Society for Cutting Up Men) Manifesto by Valerie Solanas
(1936–1988)

I have honorable intentions towards no man.

~ Maxine Elliott
(1911–)

Me care for the laws when the laws care for me.

~ Anne Yearsly
(1760–1806)

If the world were a logical place, men would ride side saddle.

~ Rita Mae Brown
(1944–)

My goal is to be accused of being strident.

~ Susan Faludi
(1959–)

# girls, boys, coons and bitches

"woman is the nigger of the world."*

I was born in 1956.

That year, Dr. Thomas Brewer, an African-American, was lynched in Columbus, Georgia on February 18th.

A month later, on April 22nd, the Reverend L. C. Baldwin, an African-American, was lynched in Huntsville, Alabama.

In June of 1956, nine members of the African-American Taplin family were lynched in Centerville, Mississippi.

That fall, on October 6th to be exact, African-American Mrs. M. A. Rigdon was lynched in Newton, Georgia.

To round out the year and ring in Christmas, African-American Maybelle Mahone was lynched in Zebulon, Georgia on December 7th.

I grew up under the fist of my abusive, racist father Arthur Manning Jackson, Junior. His father was Arthur Manning Jackson, Senior (go figure). The rotten apple doesn't fall far from the diseased tree, and my father's father (I would call him grandfather, but there was nothing grand nor fatherly about him) was even more of a vile cracker** than my father.

They both enjoyed referring to African-Americans with such lovely terms as "jigaboos; niggers; spooks; jungle bunnies; spades."

They also enjoyed calling African-Americans "coons."

Just as we white people have enjoyed our white privilege for centuries here in Amerikkka, we men continue to enjoy our male privilege. However, it would seem we whites have done at least something progressive regarding racism: at least, for the most part, we don't generally use the above terms in public discourse any more. That's good.

This could be a sign of progress, or more likely an indication we conceal our racism more cunningly. Either way, as a society we have taken steps regarding racism we haven't, and apparently won't, with regard to our sexism.

When I worked in batterer intervention groups, I never heard any white man say "nigger" or any of the other slurs listed above. Ever. But I did hear them refer to women as "bitch" quite often, not to mention other invective. Interestingly, I heard men in the batterer groups use the term "bitch" less often than I did from men and women outside of those groups.

I suspect one reason the men didn't use that term so much in the groups is because, when they did, they discovered it resulted in the whole group getting a homework assignment to be handed in at the next meeting.

That homework lesson? Answer the following question: How is calling a woman a "bitch" different than calling an African-American a "coon?" I might add this assignment, and even the mention of the assignment, was loathed by white and non-white men alike.

The conversation the following week on homework night was always a lively one. Inevitably it led to the dumbstruck look on the faces of men having to acknowledge—for the first time in their entitled lives—the

---

** **Cracker:** a term for poor, racist Southern whites. One theory for the origin of the term "cracker" comes from the white Amerikkkan slave plantation and His use of the bullwhip. The bullwhip has a small string or leather strap at the end called a "cracker" and white plantation overseers, among others, would "crack" the whip on slaves as punishment, sadistic pleasure, or general enforcement of white superiority and rule.

---

\* Yoko Ono, 1969

134

everyday, ingrained and invisible disrespect and contempt of women that passes for acceptable and "normal" dialogue.

Of course, the homework assignment is one of those that the more one attempts to claim there is no meaningful similarity in intent and effect between the two, the more they disprove their own argument.

Note also the use of animals in both cases ("bitch" and "coon") to degrade the targeted scapegoat.

The ploy of referring to African-American men as "boy" perhaps puts our acceptance of woman-disrespecting in even more relief.

It was common and generally unquestioned for white people, particularly white men, to refer to a black man as "boy" for well over two centuries in Amerikkka, as this was an ingenious and effective tactic in the arsenal of racism and institutionalized oppression of black children, women and men. To not only take away an adult's name, give him an insulting name he must accept upon pain of

death, and the name equates him to the maturity and capacity of a child is indeed ingenious, if your goal is the oppression and humiliation of a large group of targeted victims.

We might want to call what we have today "Jane Crow****" in that we happily refer to adult women as "girls" at every turn and for the same reason—to humiliate, disrespect, and disempower them.

I ask you the same question: given Amerikkka's obvious history of oppression and disenfranchisement of racial minorities and women, how is calling an adult black man a "boy" any different than calling any adult woman a "girl"?

―――――――――

*** Jane Crow: My take-off of the term "Jim Crow"
Jim Crow ~ The term originated around 1928 from a white actor named Thomas Rice who performed in "black face" and took the stage-name Jim Crow, portraying an exaggerated, highly stereotypical and degraded black character. He was so successful "Jim Crow" became a stock character in minstrel shows, along with counterparts Jim Dandy and Zip Coon. Rice's subsequent blackface characters were Sambos, Coons, and Dandies. White audiences were receptive to the portrayals of blacks as singing, dancing, grinning fools. By the beginning of 1900, the words Jim Crow referred instead to Amerikkkan segregation laws, rules, and violent actions perpetrated by whites from when Reconstruction ended in 1877 and continued until the mid-1960s. Blacks who violated Jim Crow norms, for example, drinking from the white water fountain or trying to vote, risked their homes, their jobs, even their lives. Whites could physically beat blacks with impunity. Blacks had little legal recourse against these assaults because the Jim Crow criminal justice system was all-white: police, prosecutors, judges, juries, and prison officials. Violence was instrumental for Jim Crow, and its most extreme form was lynching. Lynchings were public, sadistic murders carried out by white mobs. Many blacks resisted the indignities of Jim Crow and paid for their bravery with their lives.

Yet, referring to adult women as girls is ubiquitous.

Try this exercise: listen for every time the word "girl" is used to describe a woman 18 years old or older. This includes any media you use or are subject to, like television, radio, and the internet. **And especially what comes out of your own mouth.**

If you listen with this filter, you will be amazed at the ordinariness of Androputriarchy's disrespect of women. Is this the "banality of evil" Hannah Arendt (1906–1975) referred to?

Is this the rapist culture we men have established that purposely confuses the line between women and girls so we can have the sexual access to—and rape of—women and girls we desire?

It is no coincidence we men, supposedly obsessed with accuracy and precision, are purposefully imprecise about labeling women as girls. It is diabolically purposeful.

135

# Speaking of Women

There is a great stir about colored men getting their rights, but not a word about the colored women and if colored men get their rights, and not colored women theirs, you see the colored men will be masters over the women, and it will be just as bad as it was before. So I am for keeping the thing going while things are stirring; because if we wait till it is still, it will take a great while to get it going again.

~ Sojourner Truth
(c. 1797–1883)

I have very serious objections... to being called Henry. There is a great deal in a name... The custom of calling women Mrs. John This and Mrs. Tim That, and colored men Sambo and Zip Coon, is founded on the principle that white men are lords of all. I cannot acknowledge this principle as just; therefore, I cannot bear the name of another.

~ Elizabeth Cady Stanton
(1815–1902)

Every argument for the emancipation of the colored man was equally one for that of women; and I was surprised that all Abolitionists did not see the similarity in the condition of the two classes.

~ Emily Collins
(1818–1879)

What I really feel is necessary is that the black people in this country will have to upset this applecart. We can no longer ignore the fact that America is NOT the "...land of the free and the home of the brave." I used to question this for years—what did our kids actually fight for? They would go in the (military) service and go through all of that and come right out to be drowned in the river in Mississippi.

~ Fannie Lou Hamer
(1917–1977)

I am a feminist, and what that means to me is much the same as the meaning of the fact that I am Black: it means that I must undertake to love myself and to respect myself as though my very life depends upon self-love and self-respect.

~ June Millicent Jordan
(1936–2002)

I am ever mindful of the fact that the groups I belong to—African American people, women people--are still in the process of pulling the gags out of our mouths; that in speaking freely and publicly, in expressing our thoughts and feelings, we do as much for our ancestors and foremothers as we do for ourselves.

~ Marcia Ann Gillespie
(dates unknown)

# PLAYING MY R-ACE CARDS

Today, like all of the 20,436 days of my life, I am going to play cards. It doesn't matter that I'm a lousy card player because the game is rigged. People who look like me: male, white, financially privileged, heterosexual, like to cry about our so-called disadvantages. It's a clever strategy. "So-and-so dark-skinned person is oppressing me by playing the race card! Wah-wah!" Let's put our cards on the table...

### ACE OF COCK

My secret (wink, wink) fellowship card bequeathed by my forefathers, bless their haughty and amoral hearts. My ace-in-the-hole entitles me to see my testosterone soaked likeness in all of the best places: premiers of state, commanders of military, clergy of religion, bigwigs of medicine, lawmakers; captains of industry and business; action heroes; authors of history books; pornography ejaculators; psychology gurus; media magnates; education overseers! Women perform 66% of the world's work: we men get 89% of the income, and own 99% of the land! My Ace of Cock rewards are endless, completely invisible, and no men ever accuse me of using it! Thank you Y chromosome!

### ACE OF CRACKER

I play this card when I want a job reserved for white people; when I want to live in a white neighborhood; to see white people like me on television; to see white people at the bank when I want a loan; when I don't want to deal with black people except on vacation. I get to make-believe that the good things in my life are because I am a good person and hard worker and has nothing to do with my skin color. I get to whine that black people should just forget the American legacy of slavery, lynching, assassination, discrimination, and white supremacy while I enjoy the inheritance of all that it has entitled me to. I don't leave home without it. Thanks founding (all-white) fathers!

### ACE OF GENTRY

I play my wealth card so I can live in nice neighborhoods with white people, attend safe schools that prepare me to attend a good college, which entitles me to acquire a good job, which in turn affords me the accumulation of wealth that I can pass down to my darling white children (like the inheritance my darling white parents gave to me!). This card allows me to, with no shame, complain about those "welfare mothers" and lazy dark-skinned people who make me pay taxes. I pretend that 300 years of white economic advantages have nothing to do with me, while hatching effective deceptions like "reverse discrimination." Thank you free-market (white crony) capitalism!

### ACE OF HETRO

This is my "Great to be Straight!" card. We hetro's pretend that it's about religion and family, but gay-bashing just gives us all sorts of fantastic perks, which is exactly what oppression of queers by heterosexual people is meant to do. I get to openly talk about who I love or am intimate with. I get to hold positions of great power and influence regardless of my sexual identity being known. I get to be thought of as "normal" and "decent" and "virtuous" even though it's well known that, as a heterosexual man, I am the world's primary sexual predator, rapist, woman/child abuser, harasser, and pornographer. At least I'm not a fag! Double-down thanks Y chromosome!!

©2014 Michael Elizabeth Marillynson LLC - This poster is from the book "Contrary to the Custom of Men: Field Notes on the Pestilence of Patriarchy from a Disloyal Son." For re-printing permission go to: con2men.info. Images courtesy of Wikimedia Commons: cburnett; matt; presid. press & info. ofc.

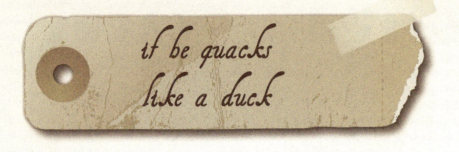

# if he quacks like a duck

## why shouldn't i blame patriarchy for the actions of some or all men?

Think back to those times when you've accidentally caught someone in the midst of doing something wrong. You are confused by what you are witnessing and say, "What are you doing?" They practically jump out of their skin and shout "**NOTHING!?!**" You realize they were doing something wrong because of their wild reaction.

That reaction is basically what we get when White Amerikkans are asked to be accountable for racism in Amerikkka; the same performance we get when straight people are asked to be accountable for heterosexism in America; the drama we get when National Rifle Association members are asked to be accountable for gun violence in America; the spectacle we get when men are asked to be accountable for sexism in America.

It's one of those issues where the reactions of the person(s) being asked the question tell you much more about their beliefs and attitudes than their arguments attempting to justify themselves.

In this case, my question is: why shouldn't each and every man on Earth this minute be accountable for the entire historical record of men's violence, discrimination, degradation, and oppression of women?

I have only been able to come up with one reason any man could logically argue we shouldn't be accountable for all men's violence: we just don't want to. It is simply that self-interested.

To start my observations on the matter, let me take you on a short trip to the west side of my town where the sewage treatment plant is located. I insist.

My home town is in the planning stages of the most expensive municipal project ever undertaken here—a modern public sewage treatment facility that will process human waste into clean water under anything but the worst possible flooding conditions. One of the reasons this is happening now—like practically all other municipalities in America—is that no one was willing to pay the money necessary to take care of the aging facilities for decades. Our purposeful procrastination has ostensibly left us with no other choice than for our good citizens to go out and squat on our front lawns.

Just as all of the fair citizens of the community have agreed for the last 50 years what a shame it is we have a crumbling sewage treatment plant, no one will take responsibility for why it got in this shape or wants to raise one finger (or penny) to do something about it now.

It is not my intention here to compare sewage to Androputriarchy; that would be an insult to sewage.

It is my intention to point out that although a few of us men might "tut, tut" here and there about what a shame it is women are treated so poorly, that's where the personal responsibility ends. It is a "bad thing" that has happened to women, but we are not responsible. How could we be?

Putting aside for the moment our Ruling Overlord Patriarchs will never allow reparations or even acknowledgement or responsibility, let's look at what is possible.

When the city sends a flyer to my door requesting I vote for the millage necessary to build the sewage treatment facility, do I throw it away and say, "That's not my problem; that's never been my problem; I am not responsible for the last 50 years of neglect!" Well, I can do that. And my neighbor can do that. And a majority of the voters can do that. Then what?

Eventually, we flush our toilets and shit flows out of it and onto our floor. What do we do then? We rant and rave and say it's all the city's fault and why are they such are a bunch of incompetent boneheads. And our toilets still overflow.

Well, there is a happy ending to this dirty story. Men apparently reckon feces as more important, or maybe more dangerous, to their lives than women's wellbeing so they eventually hand over money to do what must be done so they can stop squatting on their front lawn. They only take responsibility because they will benefit from that sewage treatment facility.

The story doesn't end so well for women. Never has.

It would appear the benefits of millennial male privilege include either distancing from things that stink, or putting aftershave on it. The stink here is from the never-ending suffering of women at the fists of men and Androputriarchy. So why would men want to bother with this legacy if He doesn't have to?

To answer that, I will speak for myself: I am responsible and accountable to all women for what all men have done and continue to do to women, children, other men, and to all living things on this Earth.

One of the reasons I must be, and am, accountable for what men have done is because I have and do benefit from the ages-old legacy of male privilege, as much as I might attempt to reign in those privileges and advocate for the empowerment of women.

I am a White, upper-middle class heterosexual, well-educated, physically-abled male. I live in a safe neighborhood, have enough money to have a mortgage on a house, and own my own automobile. Although I have always been a hard worker and a self-disciplined person, I know that much of what I enjoy in my life comes to me from my White male privilege. This is a fact.

This is the same fact men and Androputriarchy won't admit to because it undoes their entire argument, if not Androputriarchy Himself. I refer to this male privilege as "Men's Heritage Foundation," wherein we enjoy all of the bountiful benefits handed down to us of the male privilege we have beaten into women.

If we men hadn't enjoyed this male privilege, I would consider hearing the argument for why men might not be responsible for our history of sexist oppression. But we do, so I won't.

Even if it weren't an absolute fact I must be accountable, the reason I choose to be accountable for the wreckage of male privilege is because there is no other way for me to throw myself fully into the fray of trying to make things better for women and children. I choose to align myself with women, with people of color, with lesbian/gay/bi/trans people, with anti-war resisters, with women trapped in prostitution, and I can't see a way to do that part-time or half-assed. From working with batterers for over a decade, I always found this to be true: if it's part-time, delayed, half-assed, convenient, or easy it's never accountability.

Finally, and this is obviously completely selfish, I choose to acknowledge and grapple with my accountability for men's violence and disrespect because it is what is best for me personally as a human being and a man.

I grew up in a household with a violent man/father. I learned from him how to take full advantage of my male privilege and be a King Baby asshole. I am 57 years old now and still have to rescue myself from that tyrant's shadow. I am still trying to figure out who I am and who I might have been had I not been deformed by Androputriarchy. I've worked hard to be accountable to myself. I've worked hard to be the adult male I desperately hoped I would be. It isn't easy and it doesn't end. But accountability to women has been a necessary blessing in my life.

---

**Men's Heritage Foundation:** is about inheritance; men's inheritance from men and Androputriarchy. This inheritance might include money, but always includes exalted status, entitlement, power, economic advantage, political advantage, religious advantage, primary access to opportunity, and admission to the boys club. It is intergenerational male privilege. It is a King's crown handed to all boys at birth. Like a scrotum, it comes with the penis. Men's Heritage Foundation are those undeserved privileges men accumulate over decades and centuries of oppressive entitlement, inequitable accumulation of resources, and unearned advantage that is passed down to male sycophants/mercenaries.

139

# Speaking of Women

I, John Brown, am now quite certain that the crimes of this guilty land will never be purged away but with blood.

~ John Brown
(1800–1859)

The only true happiness comes from squandering ourselves for a purpose.

~ John Brown
(1800–1859)

The limits of tyrants are prescribed by the endurance of those whom they oppress… If we ever get free from the oppressions and wrongs heaped upon us, we must pay for their removal. We must do this by labor, by suffering, by sacrifice, and if needs be, by our lives and the lives of others.

~ Frederick Douglass
(1818–1895)

Whenever man has thought it necessary to create a memory for himself, his effort has been attended with torture, blood, sacrifice.

~ Friedrich Nietzsche
(1844–1900)

My vegetarianism is a great protest. And I dream that there may be a whole religion based on protest… against everything which is not just: about the fact that there is so much sickness, so much death, so much cruelty. My vegetarianism is my religion, and it's part of my protest against the conduct of the world. I did not become a vegetarian for my health; I did it for the health of the chickens.

~ Isaac Bashevis Singer
(1902–1991)

A racial twist has… been given to what is basically an economic phenomenon. Slavery was not born of racism; rather, racism was the consequence of slavery.

~ Eric Williams
(1911–1981)

Courage means standing with your values, principles, convictions, and ideals under all circumstances—no matter what. If you stick to your principles, you will often have to confront powerful interests.

~ Oscar Arias Sanchez
(1940–)

No matter who he is or what he does, he is a man first.

~ Rick Liska
(1955–)

140

# WHAT DO YOU GET WHEN YOU FALL IN LOVE?

 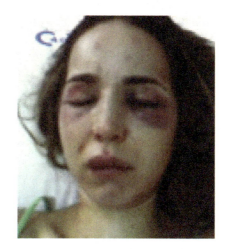

## Suffering under Patriarchy in America.

4 million American women experience a serious assault by an intimate partner during an average 12-month period.

1,200+ women are murdered each year by their husband/partner, most often with a handgun.

Nearly 1 in 3 adult women experience at least one physical assault by a partner during adulthood.

90-95% of domestic violence victims are female. 95-98% of domestic violence perpetrators are male.

47% of men who beat their wives do so at least 3 times per year.

Each year, an estimated 3.3 million children are exposed to violence by family members against their mothers or female caretakers.

50% of male batterers abuse children either physically or sexually.

87% of rape victims are women.

Violence against women/girls occurs in 20-28% of dating couples.

26% of pregnant teens report being physically abused by their boyfriends: about half of them say the battering began or intensified after he learned of her pregnancy.

33-50% of this nation's police responses are to "*domestic disturbance*" calls.

Only one out of seven of all domestic assaults come to the attention of the police. 7% of police responses to "*domestic disturbance*" result in arrest.

#1 cause of homelessness for women is domestic violence.

In cases of marital or dating violence, which accounted for 82% of all protection order cases, 90% of the perpetrators are male.

More than 17% of domestic homicide victims have a protection order against the perpetrator at the time of the killing.

65% of intimate homicide victims physically separate from the perpetrator prior to their death.

More than 1 million women are stalked by an (ex)husband/(ex)partner each year.

Nearly 25% of women are raped by a husband/partner at some point in their lives.

84% of women do not report their rapes to police.

1 in 4.5 college women experience completed or attempted rape during their college years.

54% of all rapes of women occur before age 18; 22% before age 12.

30% rise in woman-battering while she is pregnant. 40% of woman battering begins during pregnancy.

52% increased risk of woman partner being murdered by her batterer after she leaves the relationship.

90% of hostage taking in America is a domestic violence episode perpetrated by a man.

Battering is the single most frequent reason why women seek attention at hospital emergency departments and is the single major cause of injury to women.

**I ask no favors for my sex... All I ask of our brethren is that they will take their feet from off our necks. ~ Sarah Moore Grimké (1792–1873)**

©2014 Michael Elizabeth Marillynson LLC - This poster is from the book "Contrary to the Custom of Men: Field Notes on the Pestilence of Patriarchy from a Disloyal Son." For re-printing permission go to: con2men.info. Images courtesy of Wikimedia Commons: f3rn4nd0; seanmack

# bride burning

## individuating, herding and male collusion

**Individuate:** to form into a separate, distinct entity; to distinguish from others of the same species or group.

**Herd:** a large number of people; a crowd; the multitude of common people regarded as a mass; to unite or associate, keep, or drive as a herd; to conduct or drive a group of people to a destination.

When American soldiers serve their masters by killing on order, it's "one for all and all for one"—we are a team, a squad, a unit, a "band of brothers." We serve each other, we've got each other's back, and we're only as good as our weakest link.

When a squad member doesn't like killing anymore, suffers from PTSD, grows weary of the herd, or for some other reason voluntary or not becomes detached from the herd, he is then the "bad apple in the barrel," or "the malingerer," or "the isolated example," and is left to twist alone in the wind. His former herd abandons, isolates, and individuates him to promote their common interest.

One minute it's in Androputriarchy's interest to herd, the next to individuate. Two sides of the same corrupt coin. It is one of the fundamental foundations of Androputriarchy to keep women, and men for that matter, blind to the truth of His nefarious onslaught by keeping the blame on individuals so we don't pick up our torches and pitchforks and storm the well-oiled conspiracy of Androputriarchy altogether.

Another example of Androputriarchy's application of this herding/individuating **weave of absence** is revealed in the following exercise I conducted with audiences—I first asked:

**Weave of absence:** all of the purposeful tactics and strategies used by Androputriarchy, and their cumulative results, to make women and/or men invisible when it is in Androputriarchy's interest.

## Why Do American Men Kill Their Adult Partners?

- anger management problem
- lack of empathy
- drug/alcohol intoxication/addiction
- emotional expression problem
- low self esteem
- feelings of powerlessness and inadequacy
- low educational attainment
- impulse disorder
- poor personal boundaries
- loss of control
- abandonment issues
- mental illness
- low educational attainment
- poor communication skills
- stress
- family history of violence
- unemployment
- easily provoked
- low educational attainment

Unless there were courageous feminists in the audience, the answers described the "individual pathology" of a man.

I then ask the audience (*In 2010, around 8,391 dowry deaths [bride burnings] were reported to the Indian National Crime Record Bureau*):

## Why Do Men In India (Pakistan, Bangladesh) Burn Their Brides?

- cultural expectation
- economic necessity
- religion
- sexism
- the wealthy preying on the poor
- tradition
- national customs
- equalizing social status with material objects
- societal attitudes
- convention
- marriage institution
- pressure from society to accumulate wealth
- societal expectations on family loyalty and honor
- inferior status of women
- consumerism
- no legal or social sanctions against it

Their answers describing the motivations of men in some faraway nation were sociological and political in nature— not about individual pathology. Why the difference?

This exercise reveals many things, perhaps the most embarrassing is how well we have been indoctrinated by Androputriarchy to herd/individuate as we have been told.

Don't you dare say American men's violence against women is but one purposeful, systematic collusion and conspiracy by men to oppress women for men's gratification and benefit. We're not like those dark-skinned savages and their quaint cultures on the other side of the Earth. Be thankful you live in America, and remember not to provoke your husband into losing control and killing you.

# Speaking of Women

My own sex, I hope, will excuse me, if I treat them like rational creatures, instead of flattering their fascinating graces, and viewing them as if they were in a state of perpetual childhood, unable to stand alone.

~ Mary Wollstonecraft
(1759–1797)

It is organized violence on top which creates individual violence at the bottom.

~ Emma Goldman
(1869–1940)

When men are oppressed, it's a tragedy. When women are oppressed, it's tradition.

~ Letty Cottin Pogrebin
(1939–)

The parasitism of males on females is, as I see it, demonstrated by the panic, rage and hysteria generated in so many of them by the thought of being abandoned by women.

~ Marilyn Frye
(1941–)

Feminist effort to end patriarchal domination should be of primary concern precisely because it insists on the eradication of exploitation and oppression in the family context and in all other intimate relationships. It is that political movement which most radically addresses the person—the personal—citing the need for the transformation of self, of relationships, so that we might be better able to act in a revolutionary manner, challenging and resisting domination, transforming the world outside the self.

~ bell hooks
(1952–)

What's the worst possible thing you can call a woman? Don't hold back, now. You're probably thinking of words like slut, whore, bitch, cunt (I told you not to hold back!), skank. Okay, now, what are the worst things you can call a guy? Fag, girl, bitch, pussy. I've even heard the term "mangina." Notice anything? The worst thing you can call a girl is a girl. The worst thing you can call a guy is a girl. Being a woman is the ultimate insult. Now tell me that's not royally fucked up.

~ Jessica Valenti
(1978–)

# the family history fetish of stoopid therapists

## love and marriage

A "family history" of this-and-that is always a favorite haven of murky and idiotic assumptions and assertions by psychotherapists to and on their clients.

This incompetence and incoherence generally—and especially when the women and children they are supposedly serving are the punching bags of a man—only serve to fatten the therapist's wallet while exposing the women and children to more abuse, isolation, fear and victim-blaming.

If so-called "family history" really is relevant to a man's decision to tyrannize his family, then why wouldn't Androputriarchy's colonization of the family for all of recorded history be as or more relevant to therapy? How many therapists who sacrifice women and children on the altar of their "family history" fetish as an important focus of therapy would put equal or more attention to the deleterious effects of Androputriarchy on that same family?

How many psychotherapists or psychoanalysts have bothered to examine their muddled assumptions about Androputriarchy in their own lives? I assume every hour not spent grappling with how the male-privilege monster has expressed Himself in their lives—not to mention every aspect of the human world——is one more piece of their personal integrity bequeathed to the Androputriarchy Monster-God **Mastribel** for the benefits and privileges they have learned to anticipate from their ass-kissing.

I grew up in the late 1950's and early 1960's. These were times when World War II still reverberated in our lives and consciousness. I was made aware of the occupation of many lands by hostile German forces. I read about what life was like under siege.

What would "family therapy" have looked like in occupied France in 1943? There is Mom and Dad and sister and brother all talking about their "family" problems as the German Occupation Forces soldier, Oberleutnant Schröder, who happens to live in their home, is sitting there listening. Of course, the "family therapist" never mentions the soldier because he is not a member of the family and this type of outside "influence" has nothing to do with family dysfunction or well-being. And it certainly doesn't fit into whatever hocus-pocus theory that is all of this month's rage in "clinical" circles.

Is it any different when the omnipresent, oppressive and occupying fraternity of Androputriarchy is "in the room" with Mom, Dad, sister and brother?

How would it be any different if an African-American family in Alabama in 1955 gets into "family therapy" to "deal with grief" after their grandmother is lynched by the White Knights of the Ku Klux Klan in their front yard? Is racism not mentioned because it is not relevant?

Mastribel: [*mas* meaning man; *tribus* meaning three; *belua*, meaning beast] the deadly three-headed beast of man/men/Androputriarchy.

And just how is "family therapy" supposed to make anything better under these circumstances? Is family therapy a cure for Nazism? Nazi occupation? Is family therapy a cure for Racism? For Jim Crow segregation and lynching? Is family therapy a cure for misogyny?

No, but this doesn't stop the learned and wise therapist from scolding her client because she "loves too much" or is "codependent" or is in some way at fault for the dodging she must do to survive. We all agree it has nothing to do with Androputriarchy.

## Speaking of Women

Would man but generously snap our chains, and be content with rational fellowship instead of slavish obedience, they would find us more observant daughters, more affectionate sisters, more faithful wives, more reasonable mothers—in a word, better citizens. We should then love them with true affection, because we should learn to respect ourselves.

~ Mary Wollstonecraft
(1759–1797)

...Put it down in capital letters: SELF-DEVELOPMENT IS A HIGHER DUTY THAN SELF-SACRIFICE. The thing which most retards and militates against women's self-development is self-sacrifice.

~ Elizabeth Cady Stanton
(1815–1902)

The problem of birth control has arisen directly from the effort of the feminine spirit to free itself from bondage.

~ Margaret Sanger
(1883–1966)

Most women instinctively know the importance of "talking things over" with other women, but the force of this instinct/intuition is diminished by the inaccessibility of living words to express such things. Imprisoned by patriarchal usage, words are forced into taking on the usual habits of prisoners. They become isolated and unimaginative, unable to bond with each other in creative ways. They appear and sound untrustworthy, hopeless, depressing. Women, then, are baffled/bamboozled in their victimization by the concomitant confinement of words under patriarchal rule.

~ Mary Daly
(1928–2010)

Ultimately, to get equality, it's women who will have to lead the way. It's not going to be handed to us.

~ Eleanor Smeal
(1939–)

I'm going to ask you to remember the prostituted, the homeless, the battered, the raped, the tortured, the murdered, the raped-then-murdered, the murdered-then-raped; and I am going to ask you to remember the photographed, the ones that any or all of the above happened to and it was photographed and now the photographs are for sale in our free countries. I want you to think about those who have been hurt for the fun, the entertainment, the so-called speech of others; those who have been hurt for profit, for the financial benefit of pimps and entrepreneurs. I want you to remember the perpetrator and I am going to ask you to remember the victims: not just tonight but tomorrow and the next day. I want you to find a way to include them—the perpetrators and the victims—in what you do, how you think, how you act, what you care about, what your life means to you.

~ Andrea Dworkin
(1946–2005)

**Tired of leaving bloody scab trails?**

**Embarrassed by women *whispering* behind your back?**

**Ready to show the world you are today's MAN?**

...then

- are for you!

These fashionable, high-quality leather gloves come with detachable wheels so that your knuckles won't **ever** have to drag on the sidewalk again.

**Think of it:** *no more festering sores; no more ruined pants; and lots of secret winks from the Ladies!*

*Roller Dukes* – only $49.99/pair
Exclusively at www.con2men.info

©2014 Michael Elizabeth Marillynson LLC – This poster is from the book "Contrary to the Custom of Men: Field Notes on the Pestilence of Patriarchy from a Disloyal Son." For re-printing permission go to: con2men.info. Image courtesy of Wikimedia Commons: eugene de blaas; コーベレータの自作; thermos;

# i know how you feel, man

### anger, guilt, and other male prevarications

Why are we so obsessed with how men feel? Why are men's emotions so important? Why are certain emotions sanctioned for men, while others are verboten?

Let's start with anger—men's favorite emotion.

We've gotten a lot of mileage out of this one, eh fellas? Angry is a great way to strike fear in women, as we have seen over the millennia. We've even made it sexy and avante garde.

Guys, when power and control over others is your goal, anger is the weapon to use. Stock up today!

I can get all angry and self-righteous and victimy and use anger as my excuse for abusing, terrorizing, and assaulting you. Of course, I can get away with it because I am a "brooding" man, or a "wounded warrior" or in some way a romantic victim and avenger.

Who can blame the veteran, returning from war, defending our nation, being all he can be, an army of one, the few, the proud, the blah, blah, blah, for being angry? The epitome of angry manliness. He has the right to be angry because he is a real man, battle tested by war, blah, blah, blah.

So when he drinks too much, is abusive and aggressive too much, and terrorizes and beats his family too much, we understand. He's just a man going through some man stuff and being manly. Men get angry, right?

Take it a step further and we get a whiff of the "angry" man in all action movies, books, stories, myths, etc. The man who is done wrong and wreaks vengeance on those that done him wrong. We all admire him and want him to vanquish the bad ones, right? He has been done an injustice and has every right to be angry. Right?

Well, let's think about that.

If anger comes from being oppressed and victimized and having every right to seek retribution on one's abusers, who do you think should be at the front of that angry line—women or men?

Which group has been humiliated by centuries of unjust rules, customs and laws that disenfranchise one sex to the other—women or men?

Which group continues to suffer outrageous economic discrimination and oppression at the hands of the other sex—women or men?

Which group is kept out of positions of power and influence in all occupations, religions, military, political office, etc. by collusion, brutality, thuggery—women or men?

Who suffers catastrophic sexual and physical violence at the hands of the other sex—women or men?

Yet we all collude together to claim men deserve to be the sacred emissaries of anger? Why?

As you might imagine, while working with batterers for 11 years, I genuinely wanted to understand the role of anger in domestic violence. The more I immersed myself in this world, the more I knew there was something stinky in how men wield anger as a weapon, and how our world justifies, and even deifies, this disgraceful hornswoggle.

So if, as I was speculating, men's so-called anger was really just a convenient tool of control and abuse, was there even such a thing as anger? I concluded there is, and I concluded where it comes from.

"Pure" or "perfect" anger or rage comes from "pure" or "perfect" injustice. And not men's cooked-up, pity-party "injustice."

Men know pity-party injustice. "Poor me" injustice. Wah-wah, I'm a big victim injustice. Men know the "injustice" where I don't get to get away with what Fred across town

148

gets away with, or what Jianguo across the globe gets away with. The "I only pushed her—you can't arrest me for that!" injustice.

The injustice of being a perpetual 14-year-old who deals with women like they are ignorant semen-receptacles to be manipulated and used until they have the audacity to file for divorce from us. How unjust! I'm going to kill her or take the kids from her or ruin her for doing that to me. I'm really enraged and you know what can happen when a man is righteously furious.

Women, on the other hand, are not allowed to feel or express anger because it would be so very dangerous. Men know women's anger is dangerous, but not the way men's manufactured anger is dangerous. Men's anger is a tool invented to accomplish something.

Women's anger is about primal injustice, and this anger is actually about something. It has a core of actual truth in the world about what has been, and is being, done to women and girls worldwide. It is a "perfect" rage in response to mind-boggling injustice and men know that.

We can't let you women scratch the surface of rage because it will blow the human world sky-high and we probably won't be the masters anymore when the dust settles. You can kiss your scrotums goodbye, fellas.

So we'll stick with the very functional plan we have now: men get to be real angry and lionized for it, and women should be docile and smile and appreciate men's great suffering. It's better for everyone—right?

Men also get away with murder, literally, with our contrived "jealousy." It's always useful as a woman control tactic because we get to make up the most ridiculous accusations and then watch our victims squirm while they try to disprove the artifice. The squirming itself is testimony to the delights of male privilege. And what male judge isn't going to feel empathy for the prideful man "forced" to strangle his wife to death because of her "infidelity?"

Jealousy, like anger, is perfect for us men because it casts us as victims—hence, we are righteous in the punishment we mete out. Jealousy also brings along with it a façade of us men actually caring for the target (woman) involved, further positioning ourselves as martyrs to Androputriarchy.

Lastly, it is a widely-held invention us men will somehow be damaged by our guilt if we dwell too long on the wreckage we have wrought through our male privilege.

Honorable mention has to be given to social workers and psychologists for this doozy. While we men are out there, road-testing new and sickening ways to rape girls, boys and women— social workers and psychologists are busy hatching new and improved reasons for why all men shouldn't feel shame or guilt for our collusion in male privilege and Androputriarchy. A shout out to the brotherhood for that doozy.

We wouldn't want men walking around contemplating their rapacious behavior, feeling all ashamed and guilty, now would we? Why, the world might stop turning if men stopped pulling the levers of industry, guarding the boarders, and testing themselves in hand-to-hand combat.

Not to mention thinking the unthinkable—maybe we are responsible for every bad human condition there is or ever has been. No, this is too much for the fragile male psyche. We must shield that delightful male spirit from such a crushing responsibility. Ho.

# Speaking of Women

Taught from infancy that beauty is woman's sceptre, the mind shapes itself to the body, and roaming round its gilt cage, only seeks to adorn its prison.

~ Mary Wollstonecraft
(1759–1797)

Intellect does not attain its full force unless it attacks power.

~ Germaine de Stael
(1766–1817)

The scornful nostril and the high head gather not the odors that lie on the track of truth.

~ George Eliot
(1819–1880)

Guilt is not a response to anger; it is a response to one's own actions or lack of action. If it leads to change then it can be useful, since it is then no longer guilt but the beginning of knowledge. Yet all too often, guilt is just another name for impotence, for defensiveness destructive of communication; it becomes a device to protect ignorance and the continuation of things the way they are, the ultimate protection for changelessness.

~ Audre Lord
(1934–1992)

When I dare to be powerful— to use my strength in the service of my vision, then it becomes less and less important whether I am afraid.

~ Audre Lorde
(1934–1992)

Murder is the apex of megalomania, the ultimate in control.

~ Jessica Lucy Freeman-Mitford
(1917–1996)

The same people who rail against unforgiveness inadvertently promote imitation forgiveness, which does as much damage and is more insidious. Permanent self-estrangement is the price of both.

~ Jeanne Safer
(1947–)

## today in the news
## blah, blah, blah

### unsinkable titanic

My growing understanding of feminism and what it means for my worldview has turned practically everything in my life upside down. For example, whereas I was once very interested in politics on the local, national and world stage, I now find it not only irrelevant but tedious and pointless. I used to be a blissfully happy "political junkie." Not anymore.

As a species we have established a worldwide "news" industry over the last century that includes the far right and the far left; "media" totally controlled by despotic governments and/or totally uncensored by pornographers; golf 24 hours per day; ranting Christians, etc.

I challenge you to find news that is not the servant and tool of Androputriarchy. It all ignores the fact Androputriarchy is invisibly embedded in everything that occurs, and even when the "news" presents the oppression of women, it does so without identifying Androputriarchy and men as the colluding and benefitting perpetrators. It just goes unexplained, or is described as having unknown origins, or blames "human nature," or idiotically blames everyone/no one.

Why would I put an ounce of my energy into keeping track of "what is happening in the news" when it is, essentially, a re-cycling loop of the rearranging of deck chairs on the Titanic?

Let's not talk about this fucked-up vessel men built and told us is beautiful, invincible, and a steel testimony to the power and grandeur of Androputriarchy. Let's talk instead about who gets the best cabins on the upper decks, who is wearing the finest designer clothes from Italy, and who tips the (all-male) cabin crew the most.

All the while, the Titanic warehouses the "under classes" down in "steerage" on a collision course with an iceberg called "reality." That the Titanic carried lifeboats for only 1,178 of the 2,223 people on board seems a pretty good snapshot of Androputriarchy. It is always in Androputriarchy's interest to have everyone fight for and argue over the "possession" of one of the lifeboat seats, which keeps us distracted from the insane fact there is no humane reason why there wouldn't be enough for everyone.

I have come to understand the only question necessary on hearing any "news," or the "consumption" of any "media" is: what about the women and children? Regardless of what is being presented or hidden, regardless of how the story is being packaged, and regardless of who we are being told the players in the drama supposedly are: where are the women and children in the story? How were they involved? How were they excluded? How were they treated? What is their opinion? What do they want? What do they need? How were they disrespected? Why are they invisible? Why are they to blame? How and why are they identified as stupid, irrelevant, masochistic, and/or passive backdrops for men?

I have my own rule for listening to any conversation at any time, whether it is in my family, my workplace, and particularly in the "news" media: if it doesn't devote at least half of its time to addressing, specifically, girls and women's interests, oppression, stake, participation, welfare, or future then it is of no consequence and will lead nowhere. If it doesn't acknowledge the oppression of women and children and animals and our environment by men then it is of no consequence and will lead nowhere.

It is not enough that it discusses "people's" interests, stake, participation, welfare, and future. It is not enough if the speakers are all women. It is not enough if the participants have peace, equality, benevolence, and righteousness as their goal. If the conversation does not specifically and purposefully address and women's and children's interests, oppression, stake, participation, welfare, and future then it is of no consequence and will lead nowhere. The conversation, by my definition, at the very best betrays women and children.

Someday, many generations from now, "news" might be relevant to anything that genuinely matters. Today it does not. Today it is Androputriarchal insult slathered on top of injury. It is listening to the insipid propaganda of happily ignorant and/or willing mouthpieces of Androputriarchy.

## Speaking of Women

We cannot push Abolitionism forward until we take up the stumbling block [women's rights] out of the road.

~ Sarah Moore Grimke
(1792–1873)

Persecution for opinion, punishment for all manifestations of intellectual and moral strength, are still as common as women who have opinions and who manifest strength.

~ Harriet Martineau
(1802–1876)

I shall come out of prison, dead or alive, at the earliest possible moment; and once again, as soon as I am physically fit I shall enter into this fight again. Life is very dear to all of us. I am not seeking, as was said by the Home Secretary, to commit suicide. I do not want to commit suicide. I want to see the women of this country enfranchised, and I want to live until that is done.

~ Emmeline Pankhurst
(1858–1928)

Too often the great decisions are originated and given form in bodies made up wholly of men, or so completely dominated by them that whatever of special value women have to offer is shunted aside without expression.

~ Eleanor Roosevelt
(1884–1962)

Developing countries may have slightly different concepts of human rights than the West, but it is not cultural imperialism to suggest that women should not be mutilated, enslaved, or condemned to die in childbirth.

~ Nana Agyeman-Rawlings,
the first lady of Ghana.
(April, 1999)

We see it where men gather.

~ Rhonda James,
Director of Community Violence Solutions Rape and Crisis Center, regarding the Richmond, California brutal attack on a teenage girl who was gang-raped at her high school. At least 20 people saw the October, 2009 crime but did not intervene.

# PATRIARCHY

## It doesn't get any better than this.

©2014 Michael Elizabeth Marillynson LLC - This poster is from the book "Contrary to the Custom of Men: Field Notes on the Pestilence of Patriarchy from a Disloyal Son." For re-printing permission go to: con2men.info. Images courtesy of Wikimedia Commons: freedomhouse2; d. myles cullen; tourbillion; ria novosti; michael j. macleod; cherie cullen; adam m. stum; russ pollanen

# freeze frame

men may lose control of their prostates, but never, ever, of their behavior

When I worked in batterer intervention programs, there were standard exercises we conducted either in group with the batterers or in public presentations to deal with convenient community myths and outright lies that support Androputriarchy and male privilege.

One of the exercises was called "Freeze Frame" and dealt with the lie men "lose control" of themselves and are then abusive/assaultive/homicidal.

I begin this exercise by asking for a volunteer from the audience, always a male, and ask him to come up front with me.

I immediately begin talking to him as if we have both been in a batterer intervention group the last few weeks, and he and I are now standing up in front of that group.

"Now, George, I know the last few weeks in group have been tough for you. The group hasn't agreed with you that you lost control when you slapped Betty. I thought today we could give you some extra time and an opportunity to resolve this disagreement once and for all. If you really did 'lose control' then it will be of the utmost importance we find the microsecond it happened and analyze it thoroughly so this will never happen again. You've repeatedly said you love Betty and don't want this to ever happen again, right? So what I am going to ask you to do, George, is to position you and me physically, with me as Betty, into the exact positions you and Betty were in that microsecond you believe you lost control. This will be a snapshot, or freeze frame, of that moment."

I then set up the whole thing for him.

"George, you told us you were coming home from work with some colleagues, and you called Betty earlier in the day to ask Betty* to have a meal on the table at 6 p.m. If I remember correctly you said you got home at 5:45

---

\* We had a rule in our batterer intervention groups no one was allowed to refer to women in any way that would objectify them. For example, on one end of the continuum of objectifying women, or making them objects, is calling them "cunts" or "bitches" or "whores." On the other "end" would be to not call them by their name—instead always referring to "her" or "she." So there was the standing joke that our intervention groups sounded like a nest of owls always saying, "Who? Who?" when men were objectifying. By the way, the "facilitators" were responsible and accountable to the same rules as were the assailants.

and the house was a mess, there was no food cooking, Betty said something smart to you, and then you slapped Betty—is that basically it?"

George or Bill or Luther or whoever the man is is going to hem and haw and resist this exercise, just as any man who uses the "I lost control" falsehood would. The "I lost control" fable is probably the most popular invention, along with "I was drunk," men utilize to continue their controlling and abusive tactics, and escape negative consequences.

So I clarify with George, for the audience, this particular thing happened, and then this particular thing was said, and then he did that particular thing, until we get to the point immediately preceding his assault on Betty. This is where we attempt to capture the "Freeze Frame" moment. By this time George has described himself as a big victim of an uncaring partner who has pushed him to the brink and he is only doing the next thing any reasonable red-blooded man would do.

I then ask a question which takes the "loss of control" hoax to it's ridiculous but logical end, like, "So we've found the 'loss of control' moment:

154

this is the microsecond where you ran out in the front yard, put your underwear on your head and began clucking like a chicken?"

George will look surprised or irritated and say, "What? Of course not."

I then say, with complete sincerity and confusion, "But I thought you said you lost control at that moment!?"

George will say he did.

"Well, if you lost control how did Betty get hit?"

"I don't know. I thought you were supposed to know!"

I will then offer, "I'm trying George. Let's try to get to that loss-of-control moment this way: right before you hit Betty what did you want from Betty?"

"I wanted her to shut the fuck up!"

"And did you think hitting Betty would get her to shut the fuck up?"

"It probably would."

"Well, George, I'm concerned about our progress here. I'm working very hard to help you find that moment where you 'lost control' but you seem to be going in the opposite direction. For example, your behavior sounds very deliberate, planful, and goal-oriented. You didn't like it Betty hadn't prepared dinner for you and your friends like you asked her to. You then didn't like how she spoke to you. You asked her to shut up and she wouldn't. You then threatened her if she didn't shut up. When she wouldn't, you hit her across to face to get her to shut up. You had a goal—to shut Betty the fuck up—and you tried increasingly abusive methods to get to that goal. By the way, did Betty shut the fuck up after you slapped her?"

"Yes."

"George, I am more and more in agreement with the group that you never lost control of your behavior. However, let's keep at it. When you told Betty to shut the fuck up and you slapped the toaster, what did Betty do?"

"What? I didn't slap the toaster!"

"Oh. So George, what did you mean to slap?"

"I meant to slap Betty."

"Oh. So you meant to slap Betty to get her to shut the fuck up, you did slap Betty, and she did shut the fuck up. Very thoughtful, goal-oriented and—in this case—successful. It sounds like you were in total control. Where in there did you lose control, George?"

George is really squirming now, and the audience is either thoroughly enjoying his comeuppance (probably most of the women in the room) or bitterly lamenting his comeuppance (probably most of the men in the room).

He's frantically looking for tactics he's used before to keep accountability off of his trail, which he is very skilled at, but he also has not had someone drill him like I am so he hasn't been in this position before. He is also dealing, I suspect, with a momentary loss of faith in Androputriarchy and the Circle of Brothers** that the male privilege tools he has been given aren't working all of a sudden.

There are other questions I might ask "George" or "Bill" or "Luther" depending on how much he either responds aggressively or acts like a big

_____

** well what a surprise this is: wouldn't you know it that Ku Klux Klan is Greek for "circle of brothers"

victim (the usual ends of the continuum for us men in our male privilege), like:

"When was Betty's funeral?"

"What do you mean? Betty's not dead!"

"Oh, well, when you say you lost control I assumed you beat Betty to death! Well, it's good she isn't dead. By the way, how many times did you hit Betty?"

"Twice."

"Just twice, huh? Why only twice? Why didn't you hit Betty thirty times?"

"That's ridiculous! I would never do anything like that to Betty!"

"Hmmmmm. So you lost control but you know you would never hit Betty thirty times, and you only wanted to hit Betty twice and you did hit Betty twice…"

More hemming and hawing, more attacking or playing the victim, more trying to get the group to turn on me, more trying to buy time to figure a way out of this horrid accountability nightmare.

Consider what is happening here: what I am doing to George is akin to spoiling the God-given "truth" of racial superiority to a Ku Klux Klansman; violating the God-given "truth" of assault weapons to a NRA fanatics; ravaging the God-given "truth" of free-market capitalism to a Republican. I am spoiling a world view; confiscating his "get out of jail free" birthright card against his will; defiling the best friend a boy could ever have. In front of an audience. At his expense.

"So you wanted to hit Betty more than once, but significantly less than

155

30? You sound certain that you have enough control to never hit Betty 30 times. It sounds like two was the correct number. But again, George, it sounds like what you did was very calculated and thought out. You hit Betty just the amount of times you thought was right. It sounds like you were in perfect control."

George would like nothing more at this point than to sit down and be left alone so he can think of ways to plant an improvised explosive device in my automobile.

"George, where did you slap Betty on Betty's body—the knee?

"No (laughing)."

"Where then?"

"On her face."

"Why didn't you slap Betty on her knee?"

"I don't know!"

"Well, we've got to know if you want to solve this loss-of-control thing! How hard are you willing to work here today to protect Betty?"

"I'll do anything to protect Betty."

"Great! So why didn't you slap Betty on the knee?"

"Her face was closest to me (I kid you not, this is one of the most popular responses I've gotten)."

"George, you said you had Betty backed up to a wall. What was closer, her face or the wall?"

"The wall."

"So if it's just a matter of what's closest, you would have hit the wall."

"I guess."

"We can't guess and make any progress in this exercise, George. Why did you hit Betty in the face instead of her knee?"

She wouldn't take me seriously if I hit her there."

"So you didn't want to slap Betty on the knee because she wouldn't take you seriously; you wanted to slap Betty on the face because that would work and get her to shut the fuck up, and you did slap Betty twice, but not more, on the face. I still can't seem to find where you lost control."

On and on it goes, merrily we go around the Mulberry tree. In fact, one of the things George or Bill or Luther will eventually say is "You're just going around in circles with these stupid questions!" I make it a point to agree with him, pleading I am doing my best to follow his story, thinking, and explanations and I am getting dizzy following him in his in circles.

There are many sad things to note about this exercise, the first of which is this exercise **ALWAYS ENDS UP IN THE SAME IDENTICAL PLACE**. It doesn't matter who conducts the exercise, as long as one rule is followed—utter and merciless accountability must be pursued to its bitter end. If so, this exercise **ALWAYS ENDS UP IN THE SAME IDENTICAL PLACE**. What is that place? The laying bare of this Androputriarchal prevarication and the cover-up required to maintain it.

Another sad fact of what this exercise betrays: this is the first time in this man's lifetime—and more likely than not, the first time in every person in that room's lifetime—that this sacrosanct lie has been challenged and laid bare. He doesn't know what to do when this handy tool is taken from him because no one has ever taken it from him before.

The metastatic brother to this hide-and-seek is "I lost my temper." Again, we have been force-fed this rancid gruel for so long it tastes oddly palatable.

## Pop quiz — multiple choice

You are a batterer. Your victim is seated across the room with a table between you and her. There are three tools on the table for your use: **rage**, **remorse**, and **ridicule**. These are your "instruments" for the following questions:

1   1) You want to make your victim **fear** you so you go to the table and use _____.

2   You want to make your victim **feel sorry** for you so you go to the table and use _____.

3   You want to make your victim feel **humiliated** so you go to the table and use _____.

a.) rage b.) remorse c.) ridicule

Let us suppose you chose "rage" for question 1).

That must be a good choice, as it is used 437,000,000 times per minute, each day, by men worldwide against women, and the men you idolize most could testify to its effectiveness.

So if all of this is true so far, would it be more accurate to say you "lost" your rage when you wanted to cause fear in someone, or you "found" your rage?

Would it be more accurate to say a batterer "finds" or "loses" his "temper" when he intends to instill fear into his victim(s)?

What would it mean if a batterer said "I lost my knife and stabbed my wife?" Wouldn't a batterer have to find his knife if he wanted to stab his wife? Wouldn't it be more accurate to say "I found my knife and stabbed my wife?"

Isn't Androputriarchal hide-and-seek fun?

## Speaking of Women

We cannot push Abolitionism forward until we take up the stumbling block [women's rights] out of the road.

~ Sarah Moore Grimke
(1792–1873)

In losing a husband one loses a master who is often an obstacle to the enjoyment of many things.

~ Madeleine de Scudery
(1607–1701)

Immodest creature, you do not want a woman who will accept your faults, you want one who pretends that you are faultless—one who will caress the hand that strikes her and kiss the lips that lie to her.

~ George Sand [born Amandine Aurore Lucile Dudevant]
(1804–1876)

Women are too much inclined to follow in the footsteps of men, to try to think as men think, to try to solve the general problems of life as men solve them…

The woman is not needed to do man's work. She is not needed to think man's thoughts… Her mission is not to enhance the masculine spirit, but to express the feminine; hers is not to preserve a man-made world, but to create a human world by the infusion of the feminine element into all of its activities.

~ Margaret Sanger
(1883–1966)

We must not allow other people's limited perceptions to define us.

~ Virginia Satir
(1916–1988)

Since the totality of the Patriarchal lie is not integrity, since it lacks the complexity of real integrity, it tends to fall apart quickly once we see its pattern, once we dare to face "the whole thing."

~ Mary Daly
(1928–2010)

## 10 pretty good explanations*

# domestic homicide

Domestic homicide—that is, husbands killing their wives, manfriends killing their womanfriends, ex-husbands killing their ex-wives, etc.—has been around longer than bank robbery, malicious destruction of property, cattle rustling, arson, misdemeanor drawing on cave walls, spitting on the sidewalk, and all sorts of mischief. Yet our criminal justice professionals and newspaper journalists remain dumb as stumps about the cause and say insipid things like "police baffled as to motive," or "killer's intentions unknown."

Women, feminists, and battered women's shelter staff have known the reason since forever, and have been trying to tell the rest of us for quite some time, but we don't care to get it. As a public service, I'd like to help clueless cops and hack reporters write their reports with at least a little more flair. If you're going to be stupid, you might as well be interesting. Don't worry; the public doesn't care either, so they'll swallow this stuff.

Pretty Good Explanation Number One for Domestic Homicide: **alien experimentation**.

We all know aliens have been abducting people without high school diplomas from the Plains States for years. As much as they may try, it is hard to put women back to together once you have conducted brutal experiments on them and then dumped their bodies in rivers, behind dumpsters, and select areas of Mexico. It's better than the "we don't have a fucking clue" explanation anyway.

Pretty Good Explanation Number Two for Domestic Homicide: **love**.

Headline (seriously): "December 21, 2009: MAN BEHEADS CLASSMATE AT VIRGINIA TECH BECAUSE HE LOVED HER TOO MUCH." Some men just have a lot more love than others. Some men are incredible volcanoes of love—ticking time bombs of love—and aren't afraid to express it to their soon-to-be dear, departed partners. I think it is safe to say any man who ever married a woman and didn't end up killing her must not have loved her very much. You know who you are.

Pretty Good Explanation Number Three for Domestic Homicide: **horses**.

I don't trust horses. I loaned a horse my car once and there was horse crap all over the seats when I got it back. What was he doing in there? And what do those horses do together in the barn when no one is around? When was the last time the police checked the crime scene for hoof prints, eh? Enough said.

Pretty Good Explanation Number Four for Domestic Homicide: **lawn mowers**.

Lawn mowers are loud, fuel guzzling, stinky, and dangerous. Like husbands. The wounds from being run over, say, seven or eight times by a lawnmower could look kind of like a domestic homicide. Sort of. Sometimes. And then men are mistakenly blamed for it. It's enough to make a man hire a lawn mowing service just to get gender justice in America.

Pretty Good Explanation Number Five for Domestic Homicide: **clumsiness**.

Let's face it fellas—you know it and I know it—women are clumsy. You take a pretend swing at her head and she

---

* Not all of the reasons on this list have been officially sanctioned by the National Association of Social Workers. They tend to disapprove of really stupid ideas they didn't think of themselves.

falls down nine flights of stairs. I mean, come on. You pretend there's one bullet in the chamber of the pistol and point it at her face and start pulling the trigger and the next thing you know, she's charging around the house like a lunatic running into things. The cops know what I'm talking about—what do we have to do to get reporters to understand this?

Pretty Good Explanation Number Six for Domestic Homicide: **feminism**.

We've already documented all the other problems feminism causes: lesbianism, Satanism, divorce, acne, lightning, automobile recalls, flatulence, Communism, inflation, hairy legs, and electromagnetism. Once women are exposed to feminism there is nothing but trouble, and we all know where that kind of trouble leads—death.

Pretty Good Explanation Number Seven for Domestic Homicide: **terrorists**.

I mean those guys with the scraggly beards and funny names—not the ones who look like you and me. What better way to destabilize America and turn us all into gay Communist welfare cheats than to sneak into our homes and kill our wives? Think about it. Then the boyfriend gets blamed and an American goes to prison. Wake up America—why do you think Dick Cheney was waterboarding us?

Pretty Good Explanation Number Eight for Domestic Homicide: **gun twirling**.

Listen, we all know women are not good with firearms. So when they start to play with them, anything can happen. The police show up at the shooting and the husband says, "She was twirling that darned gun and I begged her to stop but she just laughed in my face." The next thing you know, some sissy politician blames him, the lesbians jump on board, they railroad him and he's doing 20–45 in prison. When are we going to wise up and start teaching our Polly Purebreds to twirl batons while cheerleading at the football game—and leave the handguns to the men?

Pretty Good Explanation Number Nine for Domestic Homicide: **bad luck**.

I mean, sometimes you leave her in the chokehold as long as usual and—feh!—she's dead! You left your gun with the safety on, someone changed it, and when you go click-click at her it goes boom-boom! You chase after her and she recklessly runs right into traffic. She leans toward you right at the time you punch her in the face. It's not fair—just bad luck. But try to get a reporter to understand that.

Pretty Good Explanation Number Ten for Domestic Homicide: **patriarchal conspiracy**.

I know—this one is pretty hard for a journalist to spell, and for the cops to say. Four syllables each! We're probably better off sticking with the other nine.

## Speaking of Women

That's how deep sexism goes; it's so seamlessly blended into the foundations of our culture that we don't even notice when it's walking around in the nude pointing at its neon dong.

~ Lindy West
(dates unknown)

No woman can afford to be indifferent to anything that degrades women.

~ Marilla Marks (Young) Ricker
(1840–1920)

no, wait, he's a rapist—no, wait...

he's a pedophile

There is no Santa Claus.
Easter Bunny, Tooth Fairy?
Nope, uh-uh.
I don't recall being traumatized upon learning of the worldwide deception being perpetrated upon me at the age of four but, knowing me, I probably was.

Maybe it was a harbinger of things to come for me, as I seem to be a glutton for disappointing truthfulness and accountability. I would dare say my desire for this is slightly above average as indicated by the slightly above average punishment I have realized from Androputriarchy for sticking my nose where it doesn't belong.

I have chosen a life that is a never-ending autopsy on the vital organs, rickety bones and foul fluids coursing through Androputriarchy. In doing so, I repeatedly undergo the paradoxical reality: at the same time I am stumbling into yet another grotesque, sickening and disheartening calamity of Androputriarchy, I am also becoming empowered by clearer thinking, vision, and understanding of what the truth is and what our reality could be if...

It is with the many details, large and small, within the reach of my life I find myself at this happy moment thinking about Androputriarchy, Santa Claus, and sex offenders.

As an oh-so-helpful-and-nice-and-very-professional social worker, I worked with male perpetrators of so-called domestic violence, which of course meant I was also working with murderers, rapists, pedophiles, sexual harassers, etc. I didn't know which ones were the murderers, rapists, pedophiles, or sexual harassers because the batterers were reluctant to disclose that to me. Go figure.

But all of that rubbing elbows with the few, the proud, the batterers, put me in proximity to even more dangerous and toxic people like oh-so-helpful-and-nice-and-very-professional social workers, psychologists, psychiatrists, probation officers, FBI profilers, judges, and college researchers.

Oh-so-helpful-and-nice-and-very-professional social workers, psychologists, psychiatrists, probation officers, FBI profilers, judges, and college researchers are kind of like the vultures or ambulance-chasers of Androputriarchy—they can be found feeding near the train wrecks and putrefying meat. These so-called "professionals" have a vested personal and pecuniary interest in such carnage being thought of in "scientific" ways instead of what I naively call the "actual" way—that is, the result of women's oppression under Androputriarchy.

So to maintain a secure income stream, live a middle class lifestyle, remain unnoticed by Androputriarchy, be thought of highly by whomever they wish to be thought of highly, and avoid open warfare in the streets, they make up little lies for the rest of us to believe in, especially since Santa just isn't doing it for us anymore.

One of their favorite ways to help us avoid looking into the face of the gorgon Mastribel—which, as we all know, would turn us to stone—is to do funny things like make categories and "types" for all sorts of things. It's kind of like what Ben & Jerry's does in naming their ice cream flavors,

Mastribel: [*mas* meaning man; *tribus* meaning three; *belua*, meaning beast] the deadly three-headed beast of man/men/Androputriarchy.

161

except in this case it has homicidal implications. Lucky Ben & Jerry's.

Instead of naming men's enjoyment of sexually, physically, emotionally, spiritually, and intellectually brutalizing and destroying women for what it is—a bonus of male privilege—they line up the perpetrators in little made-up columns and give them little made-up names and invent little made-up activities for everyone involved, much like children playing with their dolls.

For example, here are some of the little made-up "types" oh-so-helpful-and-nice-and-very-professional social workers, psychologists, psychiatrists, probation officers, FBI profilers, judges, and college researchers like to impress us with, instead of taking on the Androputriarchal despot:

## Little Made-up Male Pedophile So-called Types

- fixated pedophiles
- regressed pedophiles
- sex-pressure offender
- sex-force offenders
- preferential child
- seductive subtype
- introverted subtype
- sadistic subtype
- regressed subtype
- morally indiscriminate
- sexually indiscriminate
- inadequate subtype
- clergy

## Little Made-up Male Serial Killer So-called Types

- act-focused
- process-focused
- visionary
- missionary
- lust hedonists
- thrill hedonists
- gain hedonists
- power-seeking

## Little Made-up Male Rapist So-called Types

- unselfish
- selfish
- opportunistic
- power reassurance (compensatory)
- power-assertive (exploitative)
- anger-retaliatory (displaced)
- anger-excitation (sadistic)

## Little Made-up Male Batterer So-called Types

- generally violent
- emotionally volatile
- dysphoric/borderline
- generally violent/antisocial
- cobras
- pit bulls
- common couple violence
- intimate terrorism
- violent resistance
- mutual violent control
- schizoid/borderline
- narcissistic/anti-social
- dependent/compulsive
- sociopathic
- typical
- family-only
- generalized

## Little Made-up Male Sexual Harasser So-called Types

- mr. macho
- one-of-the-boys
- great gallant
- opportunist
- power-player
- serial
- situational
- public
- private
- predatory
- dominant
- strategic or territorial

And then, instead of having the courage to call out Androputriarchy, the Oppressor-of-all-oppressors, the oh-so-helpful-and-nice-and-very-professional social workers, psychologists, psychiatrists, probation officers, FBI profilers, judges, and college researchers put their heads together and gnash their teeth and pour their data into the research test tubes and—voila—they know how to fix everything for us!

Yay!

Consider a social issue our oh-so-helpful-and-nice-and-very-professional social workers, psychologists, psychiatrists, probation officers, FBI profilers, and college researchers could bring their "professional competence" to that is at least as important as all of this mayhem—spitting by male athletes. There is a virtual epidemic of spitting going on—and much of the time you have to watch it up close and in slow-motion replay on television. Gross.

Our fearless-and-dispassionate-and-unbiased-and-oh-so-helpful-and-nice-and-very-professional social workers, psychologists, psychiatrists, probation officers, FBI profilers, judges, and college researchers could invent a plethora of categories and phylums and types and subtypes of spitters. Baseball's categories would most certainly involve chewing tobacco and secret hand signals from the third-base coach. Football's categories would differentiate between spitting with grass in your mouth as opposed to chalk dust. Hockey's categories must take into account how many front teeth the spitter has left, and whether it's Canadian-style spitting or that sissy European-style.

We can't forget how to categorize basketball spitters because they... hey, wait a minute. Have you ever seen a basketball player spit on the court? Basketball players don't spit. Hmmm... Now what do we do with our fucking theories?

I thought male athlete spitters were just like violent men—they do bad things because they are in certain psychological categories and knowing those psychological categories helps us help them. Instead, it would appear they do what is expected of them or what they can get away with given the environment that has been constructed for them by all of the rest of us.

Let's make a secret agreement just between us—let's not tell the oh-so-helpful-and-nice-and-very-professional social workers, psychologists, psychiatrists, probation officers, FBI profilers, judges, and college researchers about this because it will ruin their whole day. And if word got out, there could be a lot of unemployed oh-so-helpful-and-nice-and-very-professional social workers, psychologists, psychiatrists, probation officers, FBI profilers, judges, and college researchers, and who wants that? Think of the trouble they'd get in to then!

In the meantime, I'm thinking one day the oh-so-helpful-and-nice-and-very-professional social workers, psychologists, psychiatrists, probation officers, FBI profilers, judges, and college researchers could put their heads together and gnash their teeth and pour their data into the research test tubes and—voila—come up with helpful categories and types and sub-types of social workers, psychologists, psychiatrists, probation officers, FBI profilers, judges, and college researchers so we could all know how to help them. They clearly need the help, and fair is fair.

I feel a quiver come over me as I contemplate the names I, personally, would give to those categories and types and sub-types of oh-so-helpful-and-nice-and-very-professional social workers, psychologists, psychiatrists, probation officers, FBI profilers, judges, and college researchers. But I digress.

Alas, this daydreaming on my part will not stop the suffering of women around the world. It will not change the need for courageous women to stand up to the daily horror of men's violence while their hands are tied behind their backs by the oh-so-helpful-and-nice-and-very-professional social workers, psychologists, psychiatrists, probation officers, FBI profilers, judges, and college researchers. I'm afraid I must leave this comfy oasis and dive back into the river of tears.

# Speaking of Women

You have put me in here [jail] a cub, but I will come out roaring like a lion, and I will make all hell howl!

~ Carry Nation
(1846–1911)

The real goddesses of Liberty in this country do not spend a large amount of time standing on pedestals in public places; they use their torches to startle the bats in political cellars.

~ Ella S. Stewart
(1871–?)

Any woman who chooses to behave like a full human being should be warned that the armies of the status quo will treat her as something of a dirty joke... She will need her sisterhood.

~ Gloria Steinem
(1934–)

Freud is the father of psychoanalysis. It has no mother.

~ Germaine Greer
(1939–)

Men define intelligence, men define usefulness, men tell us what is beautiful, men even tell us what is womanly.

~ Sally Kempton
(1943–)

He gets off on the illusion [a "john" using a "prostitute"] that she has chosen this freely, when he is taking more than can ever be paid for.

~ Catharine MacKinnon
(1946–)

For me, feminism, as a perturbing intervention into what is, has to very suspicious of anything that coincides with American ideology. For example, this propaganda about "sincerity" and "honesty" which the Right propagates is always in the service of the greatest servility to the law, and docility.

~ Avital Ronell
(1952–)

We, insects, have learned how to see in the dark. We have committed to memory the palace of despair...

~ Diamanda Galas
(1955–)

This teardrop is from the sea of sorrows.

~ Karen Finley
(1956–)

In the face of stigma, irrational regulations, peril to children, and a woman's despair, a researcher's neutrality is known only as collusive silence.

~ Lisa Dodson
(1990–)

"BOYS, TAKE $700,000,000,000 AND CALL ME IN THE MORNING."

- DR. PENTAGON

Could manhood be measured in mercies instead of massacres?

©2014 Michael Elizabeth Marillynson LLC - This poster is from the book "Contrary to the Custom of Men: Field Notes on the Pestilence of Patriarchy from a Disloyal Son." For re-printing permission go to: con2men.info. Images courtesy of Wikimedia Commons: dod; nasa; usn

# sitting at the mall

## what you see is what she gets

You are sitting at the mall, taking a rest from your tiring outing, and giving the kids a chance to let off some steam. As you think about what's left on your list to accomplish today and what is actually going to get done, you hear an unpleasant sound.

At first, the sound goes in your ear and makes you feel uncomfortable before you have any awareness you are even hearing it. Then, you hear it again and you look in the direction of the source. It is the sound of someone arguing angrily and loudly.

As you look to see where the arguing is coming from you see a man and a woman walking towards you from 100 feet away. The man is walking with a very determined and purposeful stride, all the while looking straight ahead. The woman is gesturing frantically and making agitated motions toward the man and is making loud threatening statements.

Your mind begins to race with what your options are to avoid being harmed by this conflict. You think about where your children are and whether or you should move towards them or have them move towards you. You wonder if you can pretend to ignore the conflict and it might pass you by. You wonder what the argument is about and whether anyone will get hurt.

As all of these thoughts go through your mind you feel that sick, fearful sense in your belly. The couple has moved close enough now you can hear what the woman is saying.

"That's my money, godammit! You had no right to take that money. Give it back!"

The man continues to ignore the woman, looking straight ahead.

At the same time you don't want to make eye contact with either of them, it's hard to take your eyes off of them. "What is she doing? Why is she being so belligerent with him? What's he going to do?" you think to yourself.

Then she begins to push him as they are walking, and grab hold of his clothes, and continues to loudly berate him. For the first time, you hear him respond to her, with a quiet and measured tone. "Keep your hands off me. You better keep your hands off me. I'm warning you."

Now you begin to feel panic. "What the hell is she doing? What's going to happen? Why does she keep provoking him?" you think to yourself.

By this time your only hope is they will get past you before something really bad happens. Sure enough, this struggle continues as they walk past you. The woman is so loud everybody is watching her. Less than one minute later, the man shoves her onto the floor and keeps right on walking.

Later that night, after you've put the kids to bed, you talk with your partner about what happened. He responds with the same comments people at the mall made. At the same time the comments make sense, there is also something about them that is disturbing. "What was she thinking? What the hell did she expect to happen? Why do women do stupid shit like that?"

We're taught by Andromputriarchy to see her actions as stupid, foolish, extreme, and she is deserving of that which she "provokes." But, as usual, if you choose to identify with the victim instead of the perpetrator, you will see a different story unfold.

This is a woman who has been battered by this man, and by other men. This is a woman who had her money stolen by this man, and by other men.

166

This is a woman who has financial responsibilities, children, a job, and a desire to have and provide a decent life for her family.

She knows what it's like to confront a man about money at home or another isolated, risky place. She knows what it's like to say no to a man at home or another isolated, risky place. She knows what it's like to stand up for herself when he's drunk and at home or another isolated, risky place. She knows what he's capable of doing if there's no one else around to come to her aid, like there may be out in public. She knows what it's like to have her children beaten in front of her because she had the nerve to ask for her own money.

As usual, if you challenge Androputriarchy because you have a desire to identify with the disempowered, and not collude with the perpetrators, you have the chance to understand the wisdom and necessity of her actions. We see she is, in fact, very smart to do what she's doing. She really is, in fact, the person who is most expert on how to keep safe from this man. We see she is most likely to get her money, and limit the physical punishment she will endure, if she can take the risks in a public place.

It can take a lifetime to undo what Androputriarchy has done to our ability to think clearly. If we are serious about being courageous and standing shoulder to shoulder with disempowered women, it requires of us to look through the lens Androputriarchy will certainly punish us for using.

I used to ask audiences I was presenting to, "What is the smartest thing a woman can do when the police arrive in the middle of her partner assaulting her?"

I would then write their answers on the chalkboard, which were usually along the lines of: tell the police what happened; press charges against him; take that opportunity to get out; cooperate with the police; give the police as much information as possible so they can press charges, etc."

I would then say to the audience I disagreed with this advice; I thought the smartest thing she could do at that moment was attack the police.

Then I would ask them: "In the township/city/county you live in, how long will the assailant be taken away from the home, if at all?"

Most people have no idea what the domestic violence arrest, detention, or prosecution laws are where they live. The answer I would get was usually "a few hours?"

I would then say, "Given that he is probably going to be back in less than 24 hours, and even more pissed off that you didn't do more to protect him from the police, what do you think in hindsight was the smartest thing to do?"

The audience would then agree attacking the police was the smartest thing to do.

Well, what would you guess police officers love to complain about to anyone who will listen—especially to staff of battered women's shelters? "Those battered women won't cooperate with us, and usually attack us!" of course.

# Speaking of Women

She who would be free must defy the enemy, and must be ultra enough to exhaust the possibilities of the enemy's assault; and it will not be until women can contemplate and accept unconcernedly whatsoever imputation and ignorant, bitter, lying and persecuting world may heap on them that they will be really free.

~ Tennessee Claflin
(1845–1923)

It is not alone the fact that women have generally had to spend most of their strength in caring for others that has handicapped them in individual effort; but also that they have almost universally had to care wholly for themselves.

~ Anna Garlin Spencer
(1851–1931)

However sugar-coated and ambiguous, every form of authoritarianism must start with a belief in some group's greater right to power, whether that right is justified by sex, race, class, religion, or all four. However far it may expand, the progression inevitably rests on unequal power and airtight roles within the family.

~ Gloria Steinem
(1934–)

We do not deride the fears of prospering white America. A nation of violence and private property has every reason to dread the violated and the deprived.

~ June Jordan
(1936–)

... anyone with an ounce of political analysis should know that freedom before equality, freedom before justice, will only further liberate the power of the powerful and will never free what is most in need of expression.

~ Catherine A. MacKinnon
(1946–)

## battering is hyper-masculinity

### batterers are men, only more so

Domestic violence perpetrators are the front-line soldiers in the war on women. Research conclusively shows that in the United States of America, at least 95%—and most likely more—of batterers are men. This fact cannot be overemphasized. This is no mistake or coincidence.

Androputriarchy as we know Him is the entitlement program of all time for men that is administered by men for the exclusive benefit of men, and men gladly serve for mutual benefit.

The control of the household and family through brute force and utter contempt of women and children is a fundamental linchpin of men's oppression of women and a crucial foundation of Androputriarchy.

So-called domestic violence is an indispensable arm of the despotic octopus known as Androputriarchy. Independently and collectively, these arms have the purposeful, strategic, systematic, and deliberate goal of enslaving women and children—and they work ceaselessly and magnificently.

Androputriarchy being the primary and sacrosanct religion of men, then the family is the church where our children are preached to about the disrespect and systematic subjugation of women. So-called "domestic violence" is the most powerful, effective, and universal method of that education.

It is the favored method used by the Taliban, the Catholics, the Hindus, the Mormons, the Atheists, the Republicans, the Capitalists, the Democrats, the Educated, the Poor, the Wealthy, the Healthy, the Sick, the Militarists, the Pacifists, the Industrialists, the Unionists, the Racists, the Heterosexuals, the Homosexuals, the Tyrants, the Insurgents, the Protestants, the Muslims, the Buddhists, the Shintos, the Sikhs, the Jews, the Rastafarians, the Unitarians—the Men.

Under Androputriarchy men are told to exhibit certain traits they are spoon-fed, or whip-fed, as "masculine." These include control over others, willingness to perpetrate violence, blind patriotism, unchecked competitiveness, acquisition and control for acquisition and control's sake alone, so-called independence/rebelliousness, lack of mercy, non-emotionality, so-called strength, selfishness, and sexual aggressiveness and abuse.

Men who batter their families display these "masculine traits" better than all other men. They are not only men, they are super-men. They are the best at being men. They are the Gestapo of men. They are the Navy Seals of men. They are men, only more so.

In the service of Androputriarchy, battering, violence and disrespect of women and children are the tactics and traits of hyper-masculinity. The more extreme the tactics, the more successful the man in and for Androputriarchy.

What does this hyper-masculinity get us men and Androputriarchy? Everything! In particular, we get to be Junior Gods in our homes. We get to "Lord" our power and privilege over our families. After all, a man's home is his castle.

Batterers are men, only more so.

Rapists are men, only more so; stalkers are men, only more so; abortion clinic bombers are men, only more so; heterosexists are men, only more so; racists are men, only more so; child abusers are men, only more so; animal

169

abusers are men, only more so; environment destroyers are men, only more so; religious fanatics are men, only more so; white supremacists are men, only more so; wife-killers are men, only more so; so-called "honor" killers are men, only more so; sex-traffickers are men, only more so; torturers are men, only more so; bullies are men, only more so; college hazers are men, only more so.

## Speaking of Women

Why is it that men's blood-shedding militancy is applauded and women's symbolic militancy punished with a prison-cell and the forcible feeding horror?

~ Emmeline Pankhurst
(1858–1928)

If you do not tell the truth about yourself you cannot tell it about other people.

~ Virginia Woolf
(1882–1941)

Women's chains have been forged by men, not by anatomy.

~ Estelle R. Ramey
(1917–2006)

There is a hidden fear that somehow, if they are only given a chance, women will suddenly do as they have been done by.

~ Eva Figes
(1932–2012)

It's only when we have nothing else to hold onto that we're willing to try something very audacious and scary; only when we're free of the allure, the enticements, the familiar and comfortable lies of the patriarchy will we be able to alter our perspective enough, change our feelings enough, gather enough courage to see and grab the next rope and continue our journey home.

~ Sonia Johnson
(1936–)

In my experience men would rather tear a relationship apart than adjust, adapt and change what needs to be changed in their psyche. They prefer the "heroics" of evasion.

~ Carolee Schneemann
(1939–)

If the professional rapist is to be separated from the average dominant heterosexual [male], it may be mainly a quantitative difference.

~ Susan Griffin
(1943–)

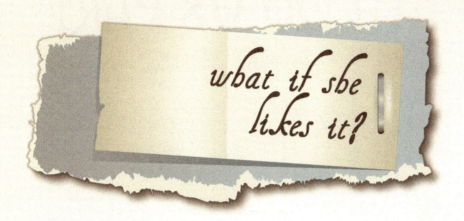

# what if she likes it?

## oops...

One of the men in my batterer intervention program thought he had me one winter night. The group was discussing their tactics of sexual abuse of women. As we were defining what the definition of sexual abuse is, one sub-genius piped up that his wife/womanfriend liked him to hit her during sex. How could that be abuse if she asks for it?

All eyes were on me as the room went eerily silent with the expectation I would be stumped and they would find yet another safe place in their brain pans, and in the male community, where they may go on being unchallenged sadists.

I asked the man whether he would, if asked by his wife/womanfriend, shoot her in the head with a handgun if she liked to be shot during sex.

"No, of course not" was his quick reply.

I asked him if he would shoot himself in the left eye during sex if his wife/womanfriend liked that during sex. No again.

Well, who, exactly, I wondered aloud, is making the decisions here—you or your wife/womanfriend?

"I guess I am," he sputtered.

"Don't guess," I said, "who?"

"I am."

"So, are you doing whatever she asks or tells you to do and blaming it on her, or are you making your own judgment about what is right and wrong?"

"I don't know."

The rest of the guys are squirming now.

"You're in a batterer intervention program, you have to know. We don't accept 'I don't know' here—which is it?"

"I am making my decisions."

"Well, if you are making your decisions about what type of physical assault you will commit, and you are in a court-mandated program for assaulting your wife/womanfriend, do you think it is a good idea for you to be assaulting women even if they ask you to do it?"

The attention he was getting at this point was not what he anticipated when he cheerily made his first comment. No longer was he enjoying his usual advantage of being class clown and top dog amongst his admiring male peers. He was caught up in his own ugly snare—a snare no man in his world had ever contemplated, let alone set.

172

# Speaking of Women

Women's degradation is man's idea of his sexual rights.

~ Elizabeth Cady Stanton
(1815–1902)

Prostitution is named a choice, a job, work, a victimless crime, and on Craigslist it's called "a wide range of personal meeting and relationship opportunities." These pimp-messaged slogans are good for business but there's not much truth to them. What's wrong with prostitution is the renting out of a woman's mouth, vagina, or anus, and what it does to her, psychologically.

~ Melissa Farley
(1942–)

I see my body as an instrument, rather than an ornament.

~ Alanis Morissette
(1974–)

…Pornography is the theory and rape is the practice.

~ Cheris Dramarae
(1985–)

These wealthy middle aged white men tell us what to do with our bodies while they wage wars and kill other people's babies.

~ Sonya Renee Taylor
(dates unknown)

I see rape as representing the reality of women's lives. It is at the end of a continuum which includes all levels of our oppression. The fear of rape constantly reminds all women of our second-class status. That fear has been the most useful tool that men have created to keep us 'in line.' So, even though all men don't rape, all men benefit from its reality. We once believed, naively, that awareness was the key and that once men realized how many women and children were being abused, steps would be taken to correct the problem. In developing an analysis of why our oppression was continuing and even escalating, it became clear that the male-controlled systems which regulate our society had no interest in changing anything! Government, organized religion, the legal system, medicine, education, the media and the economy all feed and flourish on women's oppression. For this reason, I have no choice but to be a radical feminist. No woman does.

~ Diane Duggan
(dates unknown)

The only difference between rape and prostitution is time; one ends, the other doesn't.

~ Kathleen Barry
(dates unknown)

173

# PIMP

## The World's OLDEST, Oldest Profession

*The asswipes change, but the raping goes on.*

©2014 Michael Elizabeth Marillynson LLC - This poster is from the book "Contrary to the Custom of Men: Field Notes on the Pestilence of Patriarchy from a Disloyal Son." For re-printing permission go to: con2men.info. All photos of men convicted of "pandering"—pimping.

androputriarchy formally invites you to what a conspiracy is not

# a most isolated incident

John goes to his estranged wife Sarah's home to "have visitation time" with their four children. He has the "right" to do so because the court has ordered it as in the best interests of the children, even though he has been convicted on prior occasions of domestic violence, stalking, making threats and probation violation. He then proceeds, during this "family time," to execute his ex-wife and all four children by shooting each in the face, and then killing himself.

He is completely successful in his plan for that day. His message is sent.

Through use of the newspaper, radio and television stations, and with a stated wish to reassure the public they are "safe," the police call this an "isolated incident of family violence" and not terrorism.

In America alone this "isolated incident" happens, on average, four times per day (according to the FBI). Over the last ten years that would be 15,000 "isolated incidents" of women killed by their husband/boyfriend/lover/partner in this country alone.

Elsewhere in the United States on the same day, 19 men carry out a coordinated plan to fly aircraft into carefully-selected buildings.

They meet with mixed success: two direct hits, one glancing hit, and one nosedive into a corn field. Their message is sent nonetheless.

The police, sheriff, Secret Service, FBI, NSA, CIA, military, VFW, Republicans, Democrats, state and federal legislatures, the Knights of Columbus, the Knights of the Ku Klux Klan, the White House, the Elks, and the rest of the boys, through use of the newspaper, radio, television stations, internet, and every other conceivable media, and with a stated wish to reassure the public they are "safe," call this a "terrorist plot and conspiracy carried out by cowards."

Let's be generous and say men have purposely flown aircraft into buildings to kill people 500 times in the history of the human race.

So, which one really is the "isolated incident" and which one is the "terrorist plot and conspiracy," and why?

The United States of America's Federal Bureau of Investigation defines Terrorism thus:

> "Terrorism is the unlawful use of force or violence against persons or property to intimidate or coerce... any segment... of the civilian population in furtherance of political or social objectives."

Okay, so let's see:

175

| Criteria | Apply to wife/family executioners? | Apply to building destroyers? |
|---|---|---|
| unlawful use of force or violence | 👍 | 👍 |
| against persons or property | 👍 | 👍 |
| to intimidate or coerce | 👍 | 👍 |
| any segment of the civilian population | 👍 | 👍 |
| in furtherance of political or social objectives | 👍 | 👍 |

Why don't we refer to men who execute their families as "terrorists" colluding with all other men in a conspiracy? Why don't we refer to men who fly aircraft into buildings as "loners" or "lone wolves" engaged in "isolated incidents" to which the public is statistically far more "safe?"

We don't because we are told not to. If you think or speak otherwise you will be punished. This is how Androputriarchy works. That the facts are totally twisted around to be backwards is not a coincidence. It is not an accident or a fluke any more than hazing in fraternities, humiliation in military boot camp, or barring women from positions of power in churches and mosques.

This switcheroo is specifically **about** the purposeful, planful and goal-oriented concealment of the worldwide assault on women and their rights, and their ability to fully express themselves as they choose as human beings.

This is specifically **about** the concealment of the worldwide tactic of Androputriarchy to create a boogeyman to distract our attention away from what Androputriarchy is doing to all of us; women and men.

Consider: who are you more concerned of being harmed by, on any given day or night—a so-called "terrorist" setting off a bomb in your workplace or flying an aircraft into your city hall, or your father or husband or brother or son physically or sexually assaulting you? Which of these people **should** you be more concerned about?

Why don't we refer to fathers or husbands or lovers or boyfriends or uncles or brothers or sons who physically or sexually assault us as "terrorists" or "assassins" or "cowardly?"

Conversely, to untwist the purposeful and effective Androputriarchal lie yet one more turn, if there was ever a truthful example of an "isolated" incident, it would be the rare instance of male accountability.

Male accountability to women and women's rights is so rare as to be non-existent, and would truly be "isolated" not only because it would occur in a standing Androputriarchal quasi-military colonization of the Earth which utterly crushes such treasonous behavior.

If you want to test the truth of this you might, at your own peril, ask anyone you know, especially any man, what they think of this idea. You will be accorded the full benefit of the Androputriarchy mind-correction apparatus.

As has been amply proven over the millennia, we men are determined to suppress and oppress you women. It is our political and social objective and expectation. One of the most time-tested and proven ways to do so is to terrorize and oppress women in their homes. Violence and degradation are the gifts handed down to us from our proud fathers, grandfathers, churches, governments, economies, schools, militaries, hospitals, libraries, courts, and families. It is Men's Heritage Foundation.

It is anything but isolated.

---

Men's Heritage Foundation: is about inheritance; men's inheritance from men and Androputriarchy. This inheritance might include money, but always includes exalted status, entitlement, power, economic advantage, political advantage, religious advantage, primary access to opportunity, and admission to the boys club. It is intergenerational male privilege. It is a King's crown handed to all boys at birth. Like a scrotum, it comes with the penis. Men's Heritage Foundation are those undeserved privileges men accumulate over decades and centuries of oppressive entitlement, inequitable accumulation of resources, and unearned advantage that is passed down to male sycophants/mercenaries.

# Speaking of Women

We are contrary to men because they are contrary to that which is good.

~ Jane Anger
(c.1589)

Being a woman is a terribly difficult task, since it consists principally in dealing with men.

~ Joseph Conrad
(1857–1924)

The vampire I play is the vengeance of my sex upon its exploiters. You see, I have the face of a vampire, perhaps, but the heart of a feministe.

~ Theda Bara [Theodosia Burr Goodman]
(1885–1955)

Under phallocracy, grammar is an instrument of social control. Consequently it must be controlled by the sadosociety's linguistic overseers.

~ Mary Daly
(1928–2010)

I had no feelings in carrying out these things because I had received an order to kill the eighty inmates in the way I already told you. That, by the way, was the way I was trained.

~ Nazi S.S. Captain Josef Kramer,
known as "The Beast of Belsen," discussing how he personally carried out the gassings of 80 Jewish men and women, part of a group of 87 selected at Auschwitz to become anatomical specimens in a proposed Jewish Skeleton Display.

You must learn to say no when something is not right for you.

~ Leontyne Price
(1927–)

Benevolent patriarchy is still patriarchy.

~ Elizabeth A. Johnson
(1941–)

To assess the damage is a dangerous act.

~ Cherríe Moraga
(1952–)

# fathers

## (in love and solidarity with jill on the death of her father)

What collective subterfuge
has allowed us to name and think of
our fathers as "fathers?"

We would be equally justified
to call malaria or stab wounds
"father."

Where does this leave us
through our lives
and at his death?

Without words or concepts
to tell the truth.

Without words or concepts
to know who he is,
who we are
and what happened to us.

Denied entry
into the loving human family
we sought
and hope exists.

Instead, buried up to our chins
in the suffocating deceit,
excuses and stinging reproaches
of collusion and conformity.

Left to twist in the wind alone.

Left to our doubts, fears and confusion.

How long do we hold on
to our desire
to seek or know the truth
about these men?

The lines on our faces
and the weakness in our muscles
slowly, imperceptibly,
leading us to reassuring indifference.

©2014 Michael Elizabeth Marillynson LLC - from the book "Contrary to the Custom of Men: Field Notes on the Pestilence of Patriarchy from a Disloyal Son." For re-printing permission go to: con2men.info.

the outrageous notion of "therapy" for batterers

wall street billionaire therapy group

An agent for the Federal Bureau of Investigation walks into the lobby of a high-powered stock trading company just after the door is opened for business in the morning. She identifies herself and asks the receptionist for the location of Phil T. Luker's office. She proceeds to Mr. Luker's office and promptly arrests him for suspicion of securities fraud. The FBI's investigation reveals in his position as Vice President of Dewey, Cheatham, and Howe, Mr. Luker has swindled over 3,000 middle-income families out of their life savings to support his lavish lifestyle.

A few hundred miles to the south, Red "Nick" Krakkur, the small town police chief of a racially-segregated Mississippi town, is arrested by a Federal Bureau of Investigation officer. Evidence has amply demonstrated he is also the local Grand Wizard of the Ku Klux Klan whose actions have included burning crosses on the lawns of African-American families, poisoning the livestock of a local and very successful African-American farmer, and anti-Semitic graffiti on the home of a Jewish family.

In both cases the defendants are told the cases against them are solid and air-tight. They are both given the same two options: go to court and take what sentence is meted out, or successfully fulfill certain pre-sentence requirements and have the charges dropped.

What are the pre-sentence requirements you ask? I will tell you.

You have to successfully complete group therapy with the people you harmed, or a court-mandated program that teaches you what you did was wrong.

The Wall Street tycoon decides to go with the court-mandated program. Why? Because it's cheaper.

The man attends the classes with the other magnates and is lectured about how he should have more empathy for the poor and if he did he wouldn't steal their money and use it to pay for prostituted women and solid gold toilet seats. He is taught he has money management issues and if he just learns to control his money he wouldn't need to construct Ponzi schemes.

While he is being lectured, he daydreams about whether his private jet is stocked with enough cases of Domaine de la Romanée-Conti wine to show off to a colleague, who drives a Bugatti Veyron Super Sports coupe. He also thinks about how he is going to make the person who turned him in to the feds pay for this outrageous travesty of justice.

Is Mr. Luker's "problem" that he is enjoying the results of his privilege as a white, heterosexist, greed-driven male in a capitalist economic system? Or does he just have a money management "problem?"

On the other side of the Mason-Dixon Line, Sheriff Krakkur—who doesn't have the money of Mr. Luker but does have the admiration of his white neighbors—has chosen to attend group therapy with four of the African-American families who still have scorch marks on their lawns.

At these "healing" sessions he has a chance to learn how to communicate better with other people who are "not like you" and can "get in touch" with his feelings about race relations in America and the legacy of an unhappy childhood.

Oddly enough, while sitting in these interminable sessions, Sheriff Krakkur is also thinking about prostituted women. He is thinking about how he'll make sure and patrol the seedy hotel district downtown tonight and arrest a couple of hookers so they can pay their "alternative bail" if they don't want to spend the night in jail. That's the least he is owed for having to listen to this whiney, faggot therapist drone on about his "inner child."

Hey, maybe when this court-mandated bullshit is completed he can set the therapist on fire in a black family's front yard!

Is Mr. Krakkur's "problem" that he is enjoying the results of his white privilege in a white racist social system? Or does he just have an "empathy problem?"

Which brings me to other questions: Do we really have therapy groups for Wall Street robber barons? For White Supremacist terrorists? If so, why? If not, why not?

Why can't barons who successfully complete finance management groups as a jail diversion program be allowed to have their charges dropped?

Why don't we allow racists who commit hate crimes to attend group counseling so they can work out their White Supremacy issues?

If it is odd, or outrageous, to think of offering "therapy" to financial barons and racists instead of incarceration, then what about the other side of this Androputriarchal coin— inventing the notion "therapy" is an appropriate response to men who perpetrate violence against their family members?

Why are there "batterer intervention programs" in this country? Why are there "anger management" programs in this country?

Why do we play the same, exact "treatment" games outlined above with men who are committing the most heinous and devastating crimes on the fabric of America—destroying our families from within with violence, degradation, sexual assault, stalking, terrorism, and—with impunity?

Working as a "therapist" in a "batterer intervention program," and always trying to challenge myself to think about whether what I was engaged in was proper or accountable, and how this "effort" fit in to the Androputriarchal goal of oppression of women and children, I came to think of these programs as dumpsters.

Ever notice how businesses always park their dumpsters out by the back door, never by the front door? Why is that? We all know businesses produce garbage—in service to us. We all know they put it in dumpsters. We all know big stinking trucks periodically come and empty the dumpsters and take the garbage—where?—to the landfill, way out in the country.

This is all done in a way that we can pretend together there is no garbage around us, the garbage does not stink, and it is being "taken care of" so we don't need to think about it anymore than that. Ah, Androputriarchy in a nutshell. Garbage is good because it means capitalist free-market growth, which means profit, which means wealth, which means...

Androputriarchy and certainly His Androputriarchal "organ," (pun intended) the criminal just-us system, similarly has no interest whatsoever in dealing with the oppression of women brought about by male privilege and sexist tyranny. The minions of Androputriarchy only have an interest in keeping their jobs, looking professional and exercising power.

One of the ways they do this is to construct asinine, but extremely popular and Androputriarchy-supporting and supported, court-mandated programs where they can dispose of our stinking garbage and keep it out of sight.

Any "batterer program" like the one I was involved with that doesn't "successfully graduate" most of their garbage for "successful completion" of probation requirements doesn't get any more referrals from the court. The court wants to tell the public their programs are successful and they have nothing to worry about because the garbage problem is being taken care of.

Instead, the court sends the batterers to "weekend programs" and "anger management programs" and "couples counseling" and other disgraceful hocus-pocus so they can go home at night and blissfully shine their prominently-placed college diplomas. Or maybe visit the prostituted women.

Androputriarchy should erect a statue to the psychologist or other evil genius who came up with this whole thing—he concocted a brilliant and diabolical punishment to women and children everywhere.

By the way, in case you are interested, where does the garbage go?

It goes home, of course. The garbage goes home to continue to tear into, dominate and control his family like the God He deserves to be under Androputriarchy, as facilitated by His brothers, the lackeys of Androputriarchy.

## Speaking of Women

As things are, they [women] are ill-used. They are forced to live a life of imbecility, and are blamed for doing so. If they are ignorant, they are despised, and if learned, mocked. In love they are reduced to the status of courtesans. As wives they are treated more as servants than as companions. Men do not love them: they make use of them, they exploit them, and expect, in that way, to make them subject to the law of fidelity.

~ George Sand
(1804–1876)

I began to ask each time: "What's the worst that could happen to me if I tell this truth?" Unlike women in other countries, our breaking silence is unlikely to have us jailed, "disappeared" or run off the road at night. Our speaking out will irritate some people, get us called bitchy or hypersensitive and disrupt some dinner parties. And then our speaking out will permit other women to speak, until laws are changed and lives are saved and the world is altered forever. Next time, ask: What's the worst that will happen? Then push yourself a little further than you dare. Once you start to speak, people will yell at you. They will interrupt you, put you down and suggest it's personal. And the world won't end.

~ Audre Lorde
(1934–1992)

It is hard for us to imagine an art where scenes of men killing are virtually absent, where the act of giving birth is depicted as sacred in sculptures and paintings of the Goddess herself, and where... the act of coitus is a religious rite. It is also not easy for us to imagine menstrual blood as a divine gift, as we are not used to thinking of the human body, much less sex, as spiritual. And it is particularly hard for us to see woman's sexuality, her vagina, her pregnancy, her birth giving—as associated with a deity rather than as something shameful, unfit for polite discussion, much less religious art.

~ Riane Tennenhaus Eisler
(1937–)

If sex and creativity are often seen by dictators as subversive activity, it's because they lead to the knowledge that you own your own body (and with it your own voice), and that's the most revolutionary insight of all.

~ Erica Jong
(1942–)

Women are natural guerrillas. Scheming, we nestle into the enemy's bed, avoiding open warfare, watching the options, playing the odds.

~ Sally Kempton
(1943–)

# anger Mistermanagement

**a precisely-parceled privilege ploy**

...when there's too much of nothing,
it just makes a fella mean.
~ Too Much of Nothing, by Bob Dylan

**Mistermanaged:** a replacement for "mismanaged" that reveals the completely volitional man-ner in which men purposefully and intentionally rig things for our own purposes and goals. For example, anger Mistermanagement: how men carefully use anger as a weapon and then cover it up as if it were unintentional or beyond our control.

**Male privilege:** [male: from the Latin masculus—a male, a man; privilege: from the Latin privilegium—an exceptional law made in favor of any individual] a right, immunity, benefit, or advantage granted to a man, groups of men, or all men not enjoyed by women/children and usually detrimental to them.

In these lean times, let's talk about something important: money, of course.

To be precise, it's about inheritance; specifically men's inheritance. This might be an inheritance that includes money, but it is always an inheritance that includes superior status, entitlement, power, economic advantage, political advantage, religious advantage, inter-generational advantage, and reputational advantage. I call it a Men's Heritage Foundation. That is, **male privilege**.

Male privilege is a crown handed to all boys at birth. Like the scrotum, it usually comes with the penis.

So it is basically the drama of each boy and man's life to see how he either squanders or makes good on his inheritance.

If he chooses to be adept at using the tools of his inheritance, he may see his male privilege grow to untold heights, which he can then hand down to his male heirs. Or, like me, he can squander* or ignore his Men's Heritage Foundation and benefit little from his birthright. Isn't there a Bible story about this?

One of those wonderful privilege tools inherited by all men is anger. In Androputriarchy, anger gives so much to men for so little investment—the gift that keeps on giving.

---

\* Squander: I don't really like the brotherhood, so I have done self-destructive things like forfeit my Men's Heritage Foundation, which means I have lost a lot of friends and money since I started thinking this way. Oy.

182

You have probably noticed anger is a very special prize men hold on to dearly. You have also noticed how we don't really like to share anger with women—it's best if we keep it.

Anger is so useful—it scares the hell out of women and children and pretty much gets them to do whatever we want them to do. We can combine our anger with other blessings, like violence or rape, and can get other men to put psycho-babble terms on it that make us look like victims. Awesome.

Anger makes us look so masculine and brooding and wounded that the ladies flock to us! And when we get caught going overboard with the violence stuff, we can go to "anger management" classes where we all get to rub our scrotums together and make man sounds. In case you wondered, man sounds are kind of like "Wah, wah, poooor me! What about myyyyyyy Men's Heritage Foundation!?!"

So contrary to what we've got you ladies believing, we men have been taught how to micro-manage our "assets," like anger, since our fore-father-cavemen first discovered snot.

Men's anger is like duct tape: there's always plenty of it around, it's useful for all sorts of stuff, and if you make a mistake by under- or over-using it, you learn and do it even better next time.

Some men are better than others at anger management, just like in all things. The best example is probably batterers. All men can learn from batterers how to wield anger effectively.

Batterers know if a little anger doesn't get them what they want, a little more probably will. If a lot is needed, then they take a lot out of their Men's Heritage Foundation knapsack and use it—there's plenty more where that came from. Or they might just use an overwhelming amount towards the beginning of a relationship and it can then pay dividends for years to come… like the stock market. See? I told you we would talk about money.

You can think of how we men manage our male privilege "portfolios" like how one could manage sewer water. We turn the sewage valve on and let it flow depending on how much is called for. We can let it out one drop at a time, or we can blast away with the fire hose. Isn't that great!?

It's the same with all of our other power tools (as in power and control).

Take it another step further: how does Androputriarchy then maneuver the sacrosanct male archetype of rage to His advantage? Duh—by controlling the concept of in/justice.

Hence, men's obsession with so-called "justice." Us men who batter and/or kill our family members do so with a completely self-assured sense of "rage" born of "injustice." What you ("my" woman/child) is doing is wrong/unfair/unjust and I am not only right but "just" in meting out your punishment. The more Androputriarchal my culture, the more severe and rudimentary the concepts and enactment of my "justice."

To be clear, to possess the weapon of "rage" the privileged group (men) must establish the platform of in/justice. Hence, controlling both the "justice" and "rage" apparatus is man-datory. The survival of Androputriarchy, as we know Him, rests on this Men's Heritage Foundation.

Do you see why we don't like the ladies to get too much of it? It's pretty special to us. I'm getting choked up just thinking about it.

Back to Bob Dylan: Why is it too much of nothing for men is sung about, glorified, romanticized, and warned against by nations? Why is it "too much time on men's hands" is a matter of national security and urgency, resulting in changes in priorities to national budgets and programs?

Better yet, why is it not a problem when women have too much of nothing? Men know "anger" and "rage" and violence get results. Androputriarchy knows convincing all of us to pretend men's anger is special and deserving of such attention is a "good" thing.

If this were truly so, why shouldn't it lead all women to conclude they would be much better off individually and collectively if they revolted with raging violence in the streets? I highly recommend they think carefully about this option. It would certainly focus a nation's attention.

# Speaking of Women

Money does not change men, it only unmasks them.

~ Marie-Jeanne Riccoboni
(1714–1792)

Let come what will come; no man, be he priest, minister or judge, shall sit upon the throne of my mind, and decide for me what is right, true, or good.

~ Marilla Marks (Young) Ricker
(1840–1920)

Above all other prohibitions, what has been forbidden to women is anger, together with the open admission of the desire for power and control over one's own life.

~ Carolyn Heilbrun
(1926–2003)

To call a man an animal is to flatter him; he's a machine, a walking dildo.

~ Valerie Solanas
(1936–1988)

While it may be laudable for a pope to denounce male violence, it is disturbing that he cannot acknowledge that it is precisely within his kind of thinking on the nature of women that is at the roots of violence against women are found.

~ Joanna Manning
(1943–)

Emotional neglect lays the groundwork for the emotional numbing that helps boys feel better about being cut off. Eruptions of rage in boys are most often deemed normal, explained by the age-old justification for adolescent patriarchal misbehavior, "Boys will be boys." Patriarchy both creates the rage in boys and then contains it for later use, making it a resource to exploit later on as boys become men. As a national product, this rage can be garnered to further imperialism, hatred and oppression of women and men globally. This rage is needed if boys are to become men willing to travel around the world to fight wars without ever demanding that other ways of solving conflict can be found.

~ bell hooks
(1952–)

# ANGER MANAGEMENT

## FOR MEN

Can birds manage their flying?
Can fish manage their swimming?
Can spiders manage their webs?

Men with so-called "anger management problems" have us all bamboozled. Men who abuse are expert at skillfully and purposefully using anger as a tool to control, intimidate, and confuse. Men never "lose their temper"—on the contrary, we always keep it close at hand (in our abuse toolbox alongside jealousy, drunkenness, stress, work problems, family problems—you name it, we use it) so we can find it and deploy it at the right time, the right amount, and against the right person(s). Abusive men are better anger managers than anyone. Always. Without exception.

©2014 Michael Elizabeth Marillynson LLC - This poster is from the book "Contrary to the Custom of Men: Field Notes on the Pestilence of Patriarchy from a Disloyal Son." For re-printing permission go to: con2men.info. Image courtesy of Wikimedia Commons: jacqueline godany

## which men should i trust?

**no homework = no credibility**

It took me decades and countless failures to figure out what I need from any particular man to risk investing my trust in him. It shouldn't have taken so long. When one has only his (her) bare hands to dig out from under the Androputriarchal shit pile it is not an endeavor characterized by speed—at least not for me.

To get clarity I had to come to grips with those so-called "good men" who do things that are worthy of much praise for their selfless efforts on behalf of humanity. For example, those men who put their safety and/or lives in harm's way in resistance to despots, racists, heterosexists, right-wing gun nuts, environment despoilers, militarists, Republicans, religious fanatics—the usual cretins.

I admire and laud their courage, conviction, and sacrifice. I have even joined forces with them in their efforts. But these things in themselves are not and cannot be enough to gain my trust as a human being.

Men: One thing and one thing only will prompt my trusting you: have you and are you acknowledging, examining and working to be accountable for your male privilege, and are you working to expose and destroy Androputriarchy? If not, then you don't "get it" and you are not trustworthy.

Men's accountability is not optional, situational, accidental, a "favor" to women, or a "right" to not choose. There is no point in a man's life where he has achieved accountability and then gets a free pass.

It is the same regardless of whether it is a man, a group of men, a corporation of men, an army of men, a nation of men, a planet of men. It is the same regardless of whether that man is your father, your husband, your lover, your son, your physician, your minister, or your male deity.

A man's "credibility" portfolio must begin with, and be saturated in, male privilege accountability. All other considerations are secondary, regardless of how important, sacrificial, or noteworthy.

The poisoned and corrupt root of Androputriarchy is the trunk of the tree of all oppressions, not an insignificant or occasional branch. All socially constructed plagues are born of Androputriarchy; hence, it requires the most concerted effort of all to remediate—especially by men.

Here in America, we hate the British one week and the next week we're their good friends; we hate the Cubans one week and the next week we're their good friends; we hate the Iranians one week and the next week we're their good friends; round and round the mulberry tree we men go.

This Androputriarchal construction is not American made. All Androputriarchal nations, which means all nations, which means all men, employ and enforce this purposeful stratagem.

What remains constant across all nations and over all times is male privilege at women's expense. We men are not fickle or capricious on this imperative and benefit—ever.

Every minute of every month of every millennium we men disrespect, degrade, torture, and cause suffering to women. We do so across all borders, all religions, all ideologies, and all other "straw men" we prop in place to continue our grotesque and self-involved charade. We men are a unified and harmonious fellowship when it comes to this. For he's a jolly good fellow!

If I cannot clearly and obviously see your male privilege accountability homework then you have no credibility with me. The rest of your homework is wasted.

Is it fair for black Americans to fear and mistrust a white male American who is a member of a white supremacy group? Is it fair for labor union members in America to fear and mistrust what the Chamber of Commerce is doing behind closed doors in our legislative capitals? Is it fair for Catholic mothers to fear and mistrust a male priest's overly-friendly behavior toward her children?

Is it "fair" to make such statements about men? Absolutely, and we men have only ourselves to blame. Is it fair to assume any man or group of men is untrustworthy until proven otherwise to you, personally? Absolutely.

We'd have to be wholly brainwashed, controlled, man-ipulated, and beaten down by Androputriarchy not to fear and mistrust every single man—starting with me.

When a woman has the audacity to walk down the streets of her community and is raped we whine "Why did she go down that street?!" When a woman says "I'm not going down that street—some man is going to rape me!" we say "How can you make such illogical, unfounded, and unfair accusations against all men? Wah, wah, wah, poor us, you conniving bitch!"

As Alice Walker declares in her poem "Democratic Womanism" regarding how long it is going to take to dig ourselves out of the sewer of Androputriarchy: "What will we need? A hundred years at least to plan (five hundred will be handed us gladly when the planet is scared enough)..."

What do I have to offer to women about what to look for in the "homework" I am requiring? Not much. I forward two reasons for this: first, given the Earth has virtually never seen male accountability before who knows what it truly looks like? Second, there is no "standard" of behavior or thinking men have not been able to subvert and use as a lure to capture, enslave, and recapture women.

I do think women will have to give themselves permission to mistrust men in every way and at all times. From this mistrust would come the best vantage point to inoculate oneself to the myriad tactics of men, male privilege, and Androputriarchy.

Put another way, I have absolute trust in men: I always trust men to bond with other men against women, children, and nature. I always trust men to use their male privilege to affect their own short- and long-term interests regardless of the cost to their families, communities, and Earth. I always trust men to indulge in the corruption of Androputriarchy and lie about it as necessary. Men are trustworthy in this way.

# Speaking of Women

I would rather be a beggar and single, than a Queen and married. . . . I should call the wedding ring the yoke ring.

~ Queen Elizabeth I of England
(1533–1603)

When not one man, in the million, shall I say? No, not in the hundred million, can rise above the belief that Woman was made for Man, —when such traits as these are daily forced upon the attention, can we feel that Man will always do justice to the interests of Woman? Can we think that he takes a sufficiently discerning and religious view of her office and destiny ever to do her justice, except when prompted by sentiment—accidentally or transiently?

~ Margaret Fuller
(1810–1850)

Modern society is not a society of people; it is merely a society of males. When liberal-minded men want to bring about some improvement in the position of women in society, they first inquire whether public opinions—men—will approve. It is the same as asking wolves whether they favor new measures for the protection of sheep.

~ Henrik Ibsen
(1828–1906)

Either of my parents would have done anything in the world for me—except tell me the truth.

~ Daisy, Princess of Pless
(1873–1943)

But when you remember the suffering, which you have not deserved, do not think of vengeance, as the small man does. Remember, rather, as the great remember, that which they have unjustly suffered, and determine only that such suffering shall not be possible again for any human being anywhere.

~ Pearl S. Buck
(1892–1973)

My father was often angry when I was most like him.

~ Lillian Hellman
(1905–1984)

When I started working on women's history about thirty years ago, the field did not exist. People didn't think that women had a history worth knowing.

~ Gerda Lerner
(1920–)

We must all recognize, at last, that misogyny is cultural and institutional, and that it acts insidiously on the brain and behaviour of every man and woman on this planet. Patriarchal cultures are ALL violent towards women, a violence not isolated, not accidental and not the work of madness but a systematic, daily violence, both physical and mental. Down through the centuries, in all ages and in every social climate, humanity has taken part in this bloody quadrille which divides human beings into two categories—the men on one side, the women on the other—to identify clearly those whom one can crush, massacre, mutilate, beat to death and annihilate with impunity.

~ Louky Bersianik
(1930–2011)

Being alone and liking it is, for a woman, an act of treachery, an infidelity far more threatening than adultery.

~ Molly Haskell
(1939–)

No means no, my brother.
Are you deaf in your ear, motherfucker?

~ Bitches With Problems
(song lyric from "No Means NO")

# THIS IS WHAT A FEMINIST LOOKS LIKE

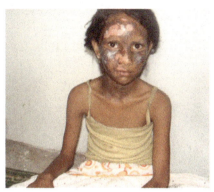

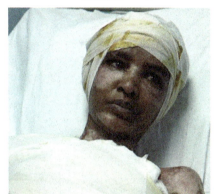
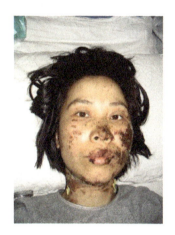
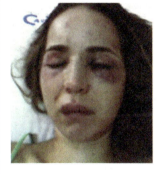

## ...WHICH MEANS SHE LOOKS LIKE ANY OTHER WOMAN UNDER PATRIARCHY.

©2014 Michael Elizabeth Marillynson LLC - This poster is from the book "Contrary to the Custom of Men: Field Notes on the Pestilence of Patriarchy from a Disloyal Son." For re-printing permission go to: con2men.info. Images courtesy of Wikimedia Commons: all india christian council; sand paper; voice of america; rawa; f3rn4nd0

# i have a communication problem, bitch

## somebody call a social worker right away

**Communicate:** to convey information about; make known; to reveal clearly; to express oneself in such a way that one is readily and clearly understood; the exchange of thoughts, messages, or information, as by speech, signals, writing, or behavior.

In 1966 I'm sitting at the dinner table with my parents, two sisters, one brother, and my friend. I am 10 years old.

After dinner, my friend asks me, "That was weird. Why did everybody get so quiet in the middle of dinner?"

"Didn't you see what my dad was doing?" I ask with dismay.

"No."

"Didn't you see how he was looking at my sister?" I ask.

"No."

My friend, luckily for him, was not familiar with how my father communicated.

But if he lives a lucky and wholesome life he might grow up to become an oh-so-helpful-and-nice-and-very-professional social worker or psychologist and will understand how my father communicated, because oh-so-helpful-and-nice-and-very-professional social workers and psychologists possess all kinds of nifty insights and theories about stuff.

One of their self-interested, ignorant, obviously-stupid-if-only-examined-for-five-minutes but nifty nonetheless theories is men assault, batter, humiliate, rape, torment, degrade, and maim (and oftentimes marry) the women in their lives because they suffer a condition called dysfunctional communication skills. Poor babies.

And who better to help these poor, pitiful men heal from the dysfunctional communication skills, all the while making a living wage, than oh-so-helpful-and-nice-and-very-professional social workers and psychologists.

Oh-so-helpful-and-nice-and-very-professional social workers and psychologists know better than you or I that when my father looked at my sister a certain way, it couldn't be as simple as, "You'd better shut the fuck up, or else!"

No, those oh-so-helpful-and-nice-and-very-professional social workers and psychologists know it is much more complicated than that and only they have the skills necessary to make everything right.

It involves all sorts of sloppy stuff like how everybody is feeling, and how everybody really loves each other, and this is a dysfunctional family, and it takes two to tango, and, well, blah, blah, blah.

Call me an ignoramus (I was an oh-so-helpful-and-nice-and-very-professional social worker, after all) but I thought my dad was communicating very effectively. I knew what he was telling us.

In fact, I thought my dad communicated better than anyone else in my family. Not only that, he required (with that great and fully-functional communication tool—the back of his hand) that you be a very good listener and pay close attention to his communications. More intently than anyone else in the family! Or else. And we certainly did.

I don't know where you are going to find better communicators than batterers and tyrants. From households to nations, from husbands to despots (but I repeat myself), the purposeful and effective fiction of poor communication skills lives and breathes under the rank employ and malevolence of Androputriarchy.

Keep in mind men in Androputriarchy are not only extremely excellent communicators, they are also expert in monitoring the success of their communications. How could a successful batterer or dictator calculate whether the tactics of control and intimidation they are using are working if they don't know their effect on the target? The answer: they do know the effects because they monitor them.

If I tell her to shut up and if she doesn't, I will tell her to shut the fuck up. If she still doesn't shut the fuck up I'll slap her face. On and on it goes—communicate—listen for the result—communicate again—listen for the result. Doesn't that fit our dictionary definition from above?

Male tyrants and Androputriarchal institutions and nations do it the same way.

Oh-so-helpful-and-nice-and-very-professional social workers and psychologists are the boot-lickers and toadies of Androputriarchy in this regard. Dressing up in the costume of "professionalism" like children wearing a physician's lab coat, they concoct all sorts of insipid contraptions to entertain the beast **Mastribel**.

Keep in mind, as well, that Androputriarchy will use "communication" in the opposite manner to accomplish His purposes. That is, when His communications are confusing to you, they are purposefully delivered in that man-ner to confuse you.

The next time you visit your therapist would you do me a favor? Ask them just exactly how many communication skills are necessary to not beat your wife? Also, can an extremely dysfunctional person such as myself be in a relationship with a woman and not beat her? Is that possible? Or am I doomed by my dysfunctional communication skills, as amply demonstrated in this book?

> **Mastribel:** [*mas* meaning man; *tribus* meaning three; *belua*, meaning beast] the deadly three-headed beast of man/men/Androputriarchy.

## Speaking of Women

The state of matrimony is a dangerous disease: far better to take drink in my opinion.

~ Madame de Sevigne
(1626–1696)

Though woman needs the protection of one man against his whole sex, in pioneer life, in threading her way through a lonely forest, on the highway, or in the streets of the metropolis on a dark night, she sometimes needs, too, the protection of all men against this one.

~ Elizabeth Cady Stanton
(1815–1902)

Why are women... so much more interesting to men than men are to women?

~ Virginia Woolf
(1882–1941)

Women are confronted virtually with the problem of reinventing the world of knowledge, of thought, of symbols and images. Not of course by repudiating everything that has been done, but by subjecting it to exacting scrutiny and criticism from the position of women as subject... or knower.

~ Dorothy E. Smith
(1926–)

Putrefaction: the process by which a boy becomes a man in patriarchy.

~ Elizabeth M. Shadigian
(1964–)

# seeing is believing

women should be believed—regardless of whether they are telling the truth

On a distant planet where women matter and male accountability is revered especially by men, believing women, girls, and boys when they tell us they have been or are being abused, harmed, insulted, and/or taken advantage of is common sense and mandatory—regardless if they are telling the truth or not.

Believing or not believing women, girls, and boys is not legitimately a debate about their honesty or credibility at all; it is a litmus test about ours.

On Planet Earth, no matter what mountain of statistical information you reference, women and children are being abused, incested, tortured, raped, kidnapped, illegally imprisoned, mutilated, and slaughtered by men in staggering numbers. We have every valid reason to be on guard for this behavior, and to know with certainty it is males perpetrating it. To not do so demonstrates disingenuousness at best and outright collusion with men and the pestilence of Androputriarchy at worst.

If African-Americans in the American Deep South claim they are being racially discriminated against by whites we have every obligation to take their claim seriously first. If itinerant farm workers in America claim they are being economically discriminated against by wealthy farm corporations we have every obligation to take their claim seriously first. If poor people living in slums near pollution-belching factories claim they are being made sick by wealthy corporations we have every obligation to take their claim seriously first. If children who attend Catholic churches claim they are being sexually abused by the clergy we have every obligation to take their claim seriously first.

Yet, Androputriarchy has taught us to come to women's claims they are being abused, disrespected, raped, beaten, harassed, economically cheated, degraded, excluded from opportunities, forced to do things against their will, denied accountable recourse to their grievances, threatened, etc. with the perspective of "she's lying until proven truthful" or "she has no credibility, just look at her" or "she's just a gold-digger" or "why did she get herself in that position?" or "she has as much opportunity as anybody" or "she should just say no" or "why didn't she put a stop to it?" and other equally arrogant, obnoxious, haughty side-with-the-perpetrators bullshit.

This spewing of sexist propaganda is the opposite of truthfulness, sanity, and accountability. Yet it is exactly where puppeteer Androputriarchy has shamefully positioned us today.

If we are courageous enough to see through the ugliness of this male entitlement and privilege, we will know it is right and necessary to take her statements seriously always. To not do so reveals not the facts, but only our agenda.

# Speaking of Women

Every woman should be overwhelmed with shame at the thought that she is a woman.

~ **St. Clement of Alexandria**
in 96 CE

As long as she thinks of a man, nobody objects to a woman thinking.

~ **Virginia Woolf**
(1882–1941)

Women should wear purdah [head to toe covering] to ensure that innocent men do not get unnecessarily excited by women's bodies and are not unconsciously forced into becoming rapists. If women do not want to fall prey to such men, they should take the necessary precautions instead of forever blaming the men.

~ **Malaysia Parliamentarian,**
during floor debates on rape reform

The boys never meant any harm to the girls. They just wanted to rape.

~ **Deputy Principal,**
St. Kizito's boarding school in Kenya after 71 girls were raped and 19 others died when the boys attacked them

The child was sexually aggressive.

~ **Canadian Judge,**
who suspended a 33-year-old man for sexually assaulting a 3-year-old girl

Are you a virgin? If you are not a virgin, why do you complain? This is normal.

~ **Assistant to Public Prosecutor in Peru,**
when nursing student Betty Fernandez reported being sexually molested by police officers while in custody

Abandoning the search for an empowering past—the search for matriarchy—is one step in the right direction. The creation of compensatory myths of the distant past of women will not emancipate women in the present and the future.

~ **Gerda Lerner**
(1920–)

193

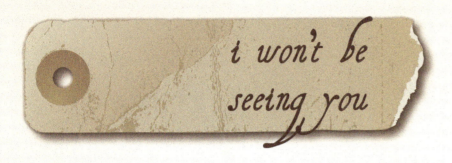

seeing is believing—

isn't it?

**Weave of Absence:** all the purposeful tactics and strategies used by Androputriarchy, and their cumulative results, to make women and/or men invisible when it is in Androputriarchy's interest.

Eyeballs matter.

For those of us gifted with the blessing of sight, we have had the ironic misfortune of witnessing the ugliness of Androputriarchy on our journey. Alas, Androputriarchy has made it His business to blind us in select ways as well.

What we see, what we don't see, and what we think we see is important—just ask marketers.

The biggest marketer of all—The Ministry of Androputriarchal Propaganda—works in mysterious ways. Like the Wizard of Oz, however, it is not quite so inexplicable when the curtain is pulled back.

Much, if not all, of what I have observed and written about has to do with the intricacies of how men and Androputriarchy obfuscate the truth. In this case I want to reflect on the whole enchilada: instead of how things are partially obscured, I want to witness how and why things are made completely visible or invisible.

Consider these photos and their captions:

Muslims observe a moment of silence...

Women protesting for their rights in Jawahar Maharashtra India.

Images courtesy of Wikipedia Commons: Lajpat Dhingra; Al Jazeera English

194

What I've taught myself to watch for and see is women and men's visibility or invisibility, and to ponder why they are being presented to me in that way. I always assume Androputriarchy has malevolent purposes behind it. The closer I look, the more I see I am being spoon-fed in a way that empowers men at women's expense.

When I look at "news" photos like the one on the left above that show nothing but boys/men, the caption describing the men typically depicts them by their religion, or their region, or their nationality, or their gathering purpose without mentioning the obvious—there are no women in the photograph. Why does it not say "Muslim **men**…" observe a moment of silence? Why is it not mentioned there are no girls/women in the photo? Come to think of it, why are there no women in the event photographed?

This is an example of where women's invisibility—non-existence—is demonstrated, taught, made normal, and reinforced. And it is done in a way that when some nutcase like me complains about it, I can be easily dismissed as extreme, histrionic, and needlessly wanting to "whip up" controversy.

Men are considered worthy of being representatives of their group—whatever that group is. Men are a religion. Men are a region. Men are a nation. Men speak for religion. Men speak for a region. Men speak for a nation.

Women being invisible in the photo—and in the caption—is an intentional and powerful method of teaching us not to notice women's absence (and hence potential importance or power), and to defer to men's authority. It is a powerful and continually repeated way of teaching us not to look and see with awareness and discernment. In this case, men's ubiquitous agency is assumed.

Conversely, the right photo above is populated exclusively by women and is captioned to note just that—it is all women. Why? Why not "Workers…" protesting for their rights? And why the difference?

When women are most or all of the people in a photo, it is captioned specifically to say so. Androputriarchy insists on noting it because we couldn't allow anyone to think lowly women are representative of anything important, let alone a religion, a region, or a nation. We are being brainwashed to conclude women, at best, are only qualified to speak for themselves, not for men or anything important. We don't really have to worry when women speak anyway, because we know how women are, right? In this case women's incapacity, incompetence, and self-interest are assumed.

On the other fist of the Androputriarchal in/visibility two-punch, I witness how men's invisibility is constructed in His favor. This is primarily about making men's perpetrator of oppression status invisible.

For example, the following is taken from the National Organization for Women's website on April 8, 2012: (http://www.now.org/issues/global/juarez/femicide.html)

> *For more than a decade, the city of Juarez, near the US-Mexico border, has been a killing field for young women, the site of nearly 400 unsolved murders and many more abductions. Despite the horrific nature of these crimes, authorities at all levels exhibit indifference, and there is strong evidence that some officials may be involved in the crimes. Impunity and corruption has permitted the criminals, **whoever they are**, to continue committing these acts, knowing there will be no consequences.*

Who is invisible in this description of the butchering of women? Who is invisible is the perpetrators—men—as usual.

Of all the organizations one would think would be knowledgeable about in/visibility of perpetrators, understands the importance of naming perpetrators, and would be brave enough to name them, isn't it be the National Organization for Women?

What happens to our tiny little overworked brains when we see something like this? Do we notice, first thing, the perpetrators are not named or are somehow described as not knowable? Of course not.

Given that we've been trained not to notice the invisible perpetrators, I assume many things are going on in our murky minds. For example:

1   It must not be important the perpetrators go unnamed. Even if I have some vague notion it might be important, no one else does, so I must be wrong/faulty.

2   I shouldn't conclude who the perpetrators are, if I don't factually know, because assuming they are men would be un-ladylike and people wouldn't

like me. Not only that, I would have all the liberal male college professors appearing on television telling me how very wrong I am to make such "assumptions."

3  I shouldn't conclude who the perpetrators are, if I do factually know, because stating they are men over and over and over again (which would be warranted) would be man-hating and hurt men's feelings. Then some "men's rights" guy would get on Fox News and talk about how unfair I am because he unearthed facts that prove a group of women hurt a man's feelings 938 years ago and I shouldn't generalize.

4  I would be vaguely aware that no one else is naming the perpetrators and there must be some good reason why they don't and I want to be liked and blah, blah, blah. I would also get this inexplicable bad feeling in my stomach that if I spoke out loud about this, something bad would happen to me. Men's perpetrator status is kept invisible because to name it is to risk incurring the fury of Mastribel.

**Mastribel:** [*mas* meaning man; *tribus* meaning three; *belua*, meaning beast] the deadly three-headed beast of man/men/Androputriarchy.

Where does this leave our eyeballs? We hear of gynocidal atrocities the world over, and throughout history, and the perpetrators of these crimes are consistently invisible by their not-naming. We go on our merry way thinking this is right and proper because that's the way it's always been.

# Speaking of Women

That man over there says that women need to be helped into carriages, and lifted over ditches, and to the best place everywhere. Nobody ever helps me into carriages, or over mud puddles, or gives me any best place! And ain't I a woman? Look at me! Look at my arm! I have ploughed, and planted, and gathered into barns, and no man could head me! And ain't I a woman? I could work as much and eat as much as a man—when I could get it—and bear de lash as well! And ain't I a woman? I have borne thirteen children, and seen them mostly all sold off to slavery, and when I cried out with my mother's grief, none but Jesus heard me! And ain't I a woman?

~ Sojourner Truth
(1797–1883)

O, ye daughters of Africa, awake! Awake! Awake! Arise! No longer sleep nor slumber, but distinguish yourselves. Show forth to the world that ye are endowed with noble and exalted faculties... How long shall the fair daughters of Africa be compelled to bury their minds and talents beneath a load of iron pots and kettles?

~ Maria W. Stewart
(1803–1879)

... woman's discontent increases in exact proportion to her development.

~ Elizabeth Cady Stanton
(1815–1902)

Woman must not accept; she must challenge. She must not be awed by that which has been built up around her; she must reverence that woman in her which struggles for expression.

~ Margaret Sanger
(1879–1966)

Women have served all these centuries as looking-glasses possessing the magic and delicious power of reflecting the figure of man at twice its natural size.

~ Virginia Woolf
(1882–1941)

Language, journalism, food, sex, all is politics. Even innocent love stories are political. When you have two people in a bedroom, that is political—who is above, who is below. There is no such thing as neutrality.

~ Nawal el Saadawi
(1931–)

Lesbian is the word, the label, the condition that holds women in line. When a woman hears this word tossed her way, she knows she is stepping out of line.

~ The Woman
Identified Woman by
RADICALESBIANS,
1970

# This is your brain.

# This is your brain on Patriarchy.

## Any questions?

©2014 Michael Elizabeth Marillynson LLC - This poster is from the book "Contrary to the Custom of Men: Field Notes on the Pestilence of Patriarchy from a Disloyal Son." For re-printing permission go to: con2men.info. Images courtesy of Wikimedia Commons: df5kx; dr. swapna patker damien halleux radermecker; eddie van 3000; angela sevin; steve evans; trialsanderrors; shaun metcalfe; emo fernanda; jorge royan; frances voon; ferdinand reus; hilary rosen

# therapists know better

## red cross

Of all the educational presentations I conducted over the years, there were few as insightful and powerful as the role play "Red Cross." The purpose of the role play was to demonstrate what is really going on when "therapists" offer "couples counseling" or "marital counseling" to a woman or family with the batterer present in the sessions. My hope was to get a few therapists to stop doing couples counseling with batterers, either by appealing to the therapist's intelligence or shame, or to get the general public to put pressure on therapists to cease this dangerous and self-interested practice.

I would begin the role play by naming it, and asking for three volunteer "actors" from the audience, with at least one male. A male plays the part of the "jailer" and the other two actors play the parts of the "inmate" and the "Red Cross worker."

I always tried to finagle it so the Red Cross worker was an actual proponent of couples counseling with batterers, but had little luck with this. I think those therapists sensed they were about to be bushwhacked and so made themselves scarce.

I would set three chairs up in the front of the room with one chair facing the other two, the two being side-by-side. The two chairs side-by-side faced the audience. The "inmate" and "jailer" sat in the side-by-side chairs.

All three actors would be asked to play their roles according to how they think their actual counterparts would.

When the actors were in their chairs I would say, "A Red Cross worker has been called in to this internationally notorious prison for a fact-finding mission. The worker is to meet with an inmate to explore allegations of serious human rights abuses, including extreme uses of torture and deprivation. The prison has agreed to the interview, but only on the condition a jailer is present at all times to "ensure the safety of the Red Cross worker." The Red Cross worker is to get as much information about what is going on while minimizing the risk to any inmates."

I would usually run the role-play for 10-15 minutes. However, on some occasions, when I had a woman with a feminist understanding as the Red Cross worker, she would take about two minutes of silent pondering before she would refuse to participate. In that case, I would ask someone else and inevitably get a volunteer. Sometimes the Red Cross worker would try for a few minutes and then turn to me and ask if they could stop. I would look at the floor and not respond. Almost always they would continue.

You can imagine how this role play goes. The Red Cross worker attempts to ask questions of the inmate that don't put the inmate at risk with the jailer. The inmate answers questions in a way that won't get them in trouble with the jailer. The jailer, if asked questions, denies all reports of abuses and acts kindly to the inmate. The Red Cross worker becomes more and more exasperated as she sees it is a fool's errand, she is not getting any truthful information, and she cannot possibly fulfill her responsibilities and protect the inmate.

Sometimes the actors did things in the role play that were shocking, creepy, and hair-raising. On more than one occasion the inmate, when the jailer turned away, silently mouthed "HELP ME!" to the Red Cross worker. On another occasion, the jailer got out of his chair, got behind the inmate, and stood there with his hands on the inmates' shoulders.

The Red Cross worker's role was a fool's errand indeed. We saw that actor try everything you can imagine. Some refused to do the role play. Some yelled at or threatened the jailor. Some mocked the inmate and scolded them for not giving truthful answers. Some asked the jailer to leave (he always refused). All asked questions that obviously put the inmate at risk, no matter how hard they tried to ask in a covert or protective manner.

Oftentimes, while the role play was going on, there were audible gasps from the audience about things being said. Sometimes audience members would ask that the role play end.

After 10-15 minutes, either I or the Red Cross worker would end the role play. Before the actors went back to sit with the audience, I asked them if they would share their thoughts/feelings about what it was like to be in their role. I would also ask them if they would take questions from the audience.

The jailers would reflect on how much power they had, how easy it was to stymie the Red Cross worker, and how easy it was to silence and intimidate the inmate. They would sometimes say how uncomfortable it was being the jailer, and how they didn't really have to do anything to "win."

The Red Cross workers would say how much they wanted to stop the role play but thought they should try to go on and help the inmate by doing their job. Most became more and more convinced as time went on they could not possibly get useful information nor do anything with the inmate that wouldn't put them at more risk. Interestingly, the Red Cross workers that seemed to show the least insight into what happened in the role play afterwards were the ones who were the most aggressive and threatening towards either the inmate or the jailer. Regardless, they all agreed there was no way they could have a meeting with the inmate, with the jailer present, and get any useful information without putting the inmate at risk.

The only inmate actors who said the experience didn't put them, as inmates, at serious further risk were the ones where the Red Cross worker refused to do the role play altogether.

Otherwise, the inmates said no matter what the Red Cross actor did, whether they were passive, assertive, or aggressive, they were going be punished by the jailer afterwards for their participation. Many said they began to feel frantic; they tried to nonverbally communicate to the Red Cross actor to stop asking them things, and that they felt trapped. Many said that they appreciated that the Red Cross worker was trying to help, but wanted them to stop.

I would then ask the audience a series of questions based on witnessing the role play:

1) Did the jailer's interest in inmate-control benefit or suffer from this meeting? (It always benefitted the jailer.)

2) Did the inmate's interest in personal safety benefit or suffer from this meeting? (The inmate's safety always suffered.)

3) Was there anything the Red Cross worker said or did, or could have said or done, which decreased the jailer's control of the inmate? (No.)

4) Was there anything the Red Cross worker said or did, or could have said or done, which put the inmate at less risk? (No, everything they said increased the inmate's risk.)

5) Was there anything the inmate said or did which put her/him at more risk? (The fact that there was a meeting at all put the inmate at risk. Anything they said put them at risk, and the more they were required to say, the more risk they incurred.)

6) Is there any way possible for this type of meeting to occur which wouldn't benefit the control interests of the jailer? (No.)

7) I asked the audience to list the ways the jailer was in control of the meeting, how the jailer used the Red Cross worker against his inmate, and how he got the inmate to frustrate the Red Cross worker.

8) I asked the audience the jailer's purpose for being involved in the session.

We would then go on to discuss my purpose for this role play: specifically, whether this role-play applies to conducting so-called couples or marital counseling with batterers present.

I facilitated this exercise over the years so at least a thousand audience members have seen it. Therapist-types were usually the majority of people at my presentations. People were usually stunned to have gained the perspective this role play offers on this "practice," and said so.

I had one or two therapists in all of that time argue, although they agreed this role play was representative of the batterer/victim dynamic, they could still conduct such "therapeutic" sessions successfully. Their assertions were met with guffaws of incredulity and heartfelt argument from the other audience members.

I took that to mean the role play was persuasive in revealing the real dynamics of so-called couples counseling with assailants and hostages. Sadly, I never had one therapist ever approach me after a presentation or at any other time and say they would stop conducting so-called couples counseling with batterers because of

this new-found awareness. It would be my studied guess none altered their practices. What might be a good idea for battered women, or other therapists, is not so lucrative to one's own career, cherished notions of personal power, or professional competence.

What does it mean about a therapist's understanding of the dynamics of domestic violence she/he would conduct couples/marital counseling with batterers? About their ethics?

What does it mean about a therapist's understanding of the dynamics of domestic violence she/he would not carefully and routinely screen each individual separately for domestic violence prior to agreeing to couples counseling? About their ethics?

Does this role-play apply to medical examinations with women, especially for trauma, especially in the emergency room, with their batterer present?

What other settings should professionals be thinking about and taking accountable and ethical action on for this issue?

Do organizations like the National Association of Social Workers, or the American Psychological Association, or the American Medical Association have policies in place for accountable and proper practices? If so, what are their policies? If not, why not? And if they do have such policies, do they know if their practitioners are following their policies? If not, why not?

If this role play is shocking to so many therapists, why? I am not that smart. It didn't take me long to think it up as a way to demonstrate these issues. Why haven't a thousand therapists before me come up with this?

I once had a woman who was a battered woman's advocate at the local domestic violence shelter come up to me after this role play and ask, "Do you know of any battered women's shelter that offers couple counseling?"

I said, "No, I assume no shelter would offer that service."

She said, "That's right, they wouldn't."

Ask your local therapists why that is so.

# Speaking of Women

To promote a woman to bear rule, superiority, dominion, or empire above any realm, nation, or city is repugnant to nature; an insult to God, a thing most contrary to his revealed will and approved ordinance; and finally, it is the subversion of good order, of all equity and justice. Nature, I say, does paint women forth to be weak, frail, impatient, feeble, and foolish; and experience has declared them to be inconstant, variable, cruel, lacking the spirit of counsel and regiment. Woman in her greatest perfection was made to serve and obey man, not to rule and command him. So I say, that in her greatest perfection, woman was created to be subject to man.

~ John Knox
(1514–1572 Scottish clergyman and leader of the Protestant Reformation)

When a woman inclines to learning, there is usually something wrong with her sex apparatus.

~ Frederick Nietzsche
(1844–1900 German philosopher, poet, composer and classical philologist)

Chivalry is a poor substitute for justice, if one cannot have both. It is something like the icing on the cake, sweet but not nourishing.

~ Nellie L. McClung
(1873–1951)

No woman can call herself free who does not own and control her own body.

~ Margaret Sanger
(1879–1966)

As children, imbeciles and criminals would be justly prevented from taking any part in public affairs even if they were numerically equal or in the majority; woman must in the same way be kept from having a share in anything which concerns the public welfare.

~ Otto Weininger
(1880–1903 Austrian philosopher)

A pedestal is as much a prison as any other small space.

~ Gloria Steinem
(1934–)

Wife beating is an accepted custom... we are wasting our time debating the issue.

~ Comments made by a parliamentarian during floor debates on wife battering in Papua New Guinea,
1987

Water and women go as men direct them.

~ Bulgarian proverb

When an ass climbeth a ladder you may find wisdom in women.

~ English proverb

As both a good horse and a bad horse heed the spur, so both a good woman and a bad woman need the stick.

~ Italian proverb

Let a woman learn in silence with all submissiveness. I permit no woman to teach or to have authority over men, she is to keep silent.

~ 1 Timothy 2:11-12

There is still the tendency to say it doesn't matter, man or woman, the world is the same. They're denying if you leave home in the morning and you're a woman, life is different.

~ Georgina Ashworth
(dates unknown)

### what will the boys think up next?

### androputriarchal semen-encrusted bliss

Is it just me?

It reminds me of the stupid word tricks we used to play against each other when I was a boy, of the "heads I win, tails you lose" variety.

Here's basically how it works: I'm a 41-year-old Afghan man, I have HIV, and I want to play a game with my brothers where I dream up a cure for myself.

Check.

Next, let's combine that cure with something I can put my dick in.

Check.

Okay, let's see… how about I put my dick in the camp fire and it cures me of HIV?

Booooo! What kind of idiot are you?

Okay, let me think, how about… how about I put my dick in a hornet's nest and it cures me of HIV?

You are such a dope! Your family is so stupid your sisters wear their burqa's inside out!

Ha, ha, ha. Laughter all around.

Fine. Then… how about I put my dick in an 11-year-old girl's evil hole and it cures me of HIV!

Yaaaaaaayyy! You got it—you are not such a Jackal's anus after all!

Sorry to interrupt the frivolity but does this sound eerily familiar to you?

Let's go to parts of India where the men's parlor game is also in earnest.

Fathers there get to "protect" their girl children by marrying them off at age eight! Of course, those same fathers can be on the receiving end of this sweet deal as well, so Oooh La La!

How are these loving fathers "protecting" their girl children? A family debt can be cleared in exchange for an 8-year-old "bride." A family feud can be resolved by the delivery of a 12-year-old "virgin." Getting their girl children the Naraka (hell) out of their homes before some other male predator rapes them means they can deliver the virginal goods while they still have value on the marriage market and are not "ruined."

This definitely beats putting my dick in a hornet's nest.

In Afghanistan they have the charming variation of abducting girl children as part of a "traditional" form of justice known as "baad," and the girl is the payment. This "tradition" was obviously concocted by men. Baad gives men the awesome privilege of "giving away" girls into slavery and forced marriage. In return, those same men can wipe away a "stain" on their "family's honor" they perpetrated, like murder or rape. It can also do cool stuff like tie two warring families together or settle a blood feud.

Are you gals catching on to how fun this game is?

Not to be outdone by those infidels, in Morocco they have "Article 475" of the Moroccan penal code that allows for the rapist of a minor girl to marry his victim to escape prosecution for both the rapist and his victim. Why could the victim be prosecuted? Does it really matter in this game? You have to give it to those Moroccan men— they probably dreamed this doozy up without the slightest use of alcohol. Just to make the deal sweeter for the males all around, the marriage helps "preserve" the honor of the woman's family and avoids scandal.

Ladies, doesn't it make you wonder why it is Article number "475"? Maybe the boys concluded the first 474 laws weren't quite enough to crush the fight and spirit out of you.

> **Patrifaction**: the corrosive effect upon anything and everything, especially female human beings, through exposure and vulnerability to Androputriarchy.

And, of course, there is the sub-Saharan African game where raping a "female virgin" will cure AIDS. It's not slamming your dick between two large stones. It's not tying a rope around your scrotum until your testicles are the size of a camel's heart. It's not raping your grandfather and all of his uncles. It's raping a female virgin.

Did you think these "traditions" were cooked up in some other, more honorable or holy, way? Naaaaah. This is **Patrifaction** in action. This is how we men roll in Africa, Antarctica, Asia, Australia, Europe, North America, and South America. On the high seas and on the moon.

What will those clever boys think of next?

## Speaking of Women

When woman first claimed admission to the privileges of higher education, men pointed out that a female who studied in botany that plants had sex-organs, would be unfit to associate with their respectable sisters. When she knocked at the gates of medicine, men declared that a woman who could listen to a lecture in anatomy was unworthy of honorable wifehood. When she asked for chloroform to assuage the pangs of childbirth, men quickly informed her that if women bear their children without pain, they will be unable to love them. When the married woman demanded the right to own property, men swore that such a radical step would totally annihilate woman's influence, explode a volcano under the foundations of family union, and destroy the true felicity of wedded life, and they assured us they opposed the change, not because they loved justice less, but because they loved woman more. During the many years that woman fought for citizenship, men gathered in gambling-dives and barrooms and sadly commiserated with each other on the fact that woman was breaking up the home. Now woman demands the control of her own body, and there are men who reply that if women learn how to prevent pregnancy, they will abolish maternity. It seems there are always some men who are haunted by the fear that women are planning the extinction of the race. To attempt to reason with such men is folly, and we can only hope that a general knowledge of contraceptive methods, judiciously applied, will eliminate this type.

~ Victor Robinson
(1886–1947)

# Speaking of Women

Our problems stem from our acceptance of this filthy, rotten system.

~ Dorothy Day
(1897–1980)

Women's virtue is man's greatest invention.

~ Cornelia Otis Skinner
(1901–1979)

For the first time in human history the mother kneels before her son: she freely accepts her inferiority. This is the supreme masculine victory, consummated in the cult of the Virgin.

~ Simone de Beauvoir
(1908–1986)

Maybe I couldn't make it. Maybe I don't have a pretty smile, good teeth, nice tits, long legs, a cheeky arse, a sexy voice. Maybe I don't know how to handle men and increase my market value, so that the rewards due to the feminine will accrue to me. Then again, maybe I'm sick of the masquerade. I'm sick of pretending eternal youth. I'm sick of belying my own intelligence, my own will, my own sex. I'm sick of peering at the world through false eyelashes, so everything I see is mixed with a shadow of bought hairs; I'm sick of weighting my head with a dead mane, unable to move my neck freely, terrified of rain, of wind, of dancing too vigorously in case I sweat into my lacquered curls. I'm sick of the Powder Room. I'm sick of pretending that some fatuous male's self-important pronouncements are the objects of my undivided attention, I'm sick of going to films and plays when someone else wants to, and sick of having no opinions of my own about either. I'm sick of being a transvestite. I refuse to be a female impersonator. I am a woman, not a castrate.

~ Germaine Greer
(1939–)

Seduction is often difficult to distinguish from rape. In seduction, the rapist often bothers to buy a bottle of wine.

~ Andrea Dworkin
(1946–2005)

Just call me Lucifer 'cause I'm in need of some restraint.

~ Sympathy for the Devil,
Rolling Stones
(1984)

Luckily I haven't had a drink
'Cause I'll down your ass
Then I'll clown your ass
'Cause the niggas I hang with ain't rich
We're all saying 'Fuck you bitch!'
Now, what I can do with a hoe like you
Bend your ass over then I'm thru'

~ "A Bitch is a Bitch" by N.W.A.
(1988)

205

# BECAUSE I HAVE A SCROTUM...
## THE ANATOMY OF MALE PRIVILEGE

**Colosseum Spermrace** ~ all men know right down to our DNA that the first lesson in toughness and victory is learned as we wriggle our way through the gauntlet of the Colosseum Spermrace! As microscopic mini-men we battle our way to the prize as we undulate past the grandstands of manly gonadery! You are that winner and must take your rightful place in society.

**Sanctified Bonersilium** ~ turgidity is next to Godliness as they say in patriarchal religions! The ability of men's penis' to point up to His Holiness in Heaven unquestionably demonstrates why all pious clergy must be males. The sacred engorgement of the Bonersilium vessels is bloody proof of His divine plan for all of us.

**Glans Ancillary Cerebrum** ~ it was discovered during the heyday of the Malleus Maleficarum that men have a secondary brain which can override the other one when necessary. This makes men smarter than women and better able to tell them how run their lives—for their own good, of course.

**Trophleece** ~ all important things have their protective containers: astronauts had their lunar lander; Fortune 500 CEO's have their Lamborghini's, and the Titanic had its unsinkable hull. Similarly, the wellspring of Earth's rulers has the Trophleece (Greek for "Trophy Fleece" or in Pig Latin: ophy-tray eece-flay) which is the anatomical overcoat for our hormone-given dominion of the Earth.

**Vast Indeferens Duct** ~ the "necrophilia" duct enables men to make important decisions without the burden of human empathy or pity. Thus men may righteously construct large edifices using slave labor; enact various genocides and purging of undesirable human flotsam, produce "snuff" pornography, and attend NASCAR races.

**Sanguineous Alluvion** ~ it is a little known fact that men's gonads, when stimulated by thoughts of telephone poles and the like, can hold up to 73 gallons of blood! Men's innate superiority is partly due to their disregard of pain, fear, and emotion; they have no nerve endings anywhere in their bodies except in this region—where there are plenty, believe me!

**Indolent Coagulum** ~ this is the undefined lump of stuff that just sits on top of the Incubadora Conquista freeloading all day long. It is the part of our male anatomy that signals one of our brains to rightfully expect women and children to do filthy and odious stuff for us that we don't care to do ourselves. Although Indolent Coagulum means "lazy lump" it is also referred to as the "King" gland.

**Incubadora Conquista** ~ the nexus of intelligent design in the universe, the Incubadora Conquista (Spanish for Incubator of Conquest) is the factory of tomorrow's Soldiers of Supremacy. If you don't have a set of these babies you won't win the rat race, you won't come out on top, and you won't die with the most scalps.

©2014 Michael Elizabeth Marillynson LLC - This poster is from the book "Contrary to the Custom of Men: Field Notes on the Pestilence of Patriarchy from a Disloyal Son." For re-printing permission go to: con2men.info. Image courtesy of Wikimedia Commons: buzmattel

out of the mouths of babes...

goddam those fucking children

I am not the guy to advise you on parenting. I was an active step-parent to three under-18 children for about 10 years, and did an adequate job in my role. I offer the following three issues regarding children because they relate to Androputriarchy and how He expresses Himself in the contamination of families.

## Assaulting Children

*"...surveys show that two-thirds of Americans still approve of parents spanking their kids."*

The case against spanking, by Brendan L. Smith, American Psychological Association, April 2012, Vol 43, No. 4

The fact that Americans would be debating the propriety of assaulting their children at all (just as we "debate" other forms of oppressive cruelty, like prostituting women, depriving access to universal health care, depriving access to birth control for women, having a constitutional right to publish violent pornography, wholesale cruelty to animals we eat, etc.) is de facto proof of the impregnation of our collective psyches by rapacious Androputriarchy.

I grew up with a batterer. My father battered my mother, he battered my sisters, he battered my brother, and he battered me. He taught me that children were first and foremost to obey their father, work hard, be racist and sexist, do what they were told without question or mistake, not cry when assaulted, and to obey immediately. He taught me to be a man who is a self-centered, oppressive, violent, mean, raging, feared asshole of the first order.

I am thrilled to share with you that I bitterly disappointed my father.

In 10 years of step-parenting, I never once thought of hitting anyone. I cannot truthfully tell you why. Maybe it is because I found my father so loathsome I couldn't bear to be like him. Maybe I trained myself to be different because I emulated a different kind of adult male. Maybe it is because I would hate myself if I hit them. But does it matter why? What matters is I didn't, and wouldn't. And what matters is hitting/assaulting children is never, ever, ever necessary or justified. Period.

To be clear, this isn't about my impending sainthood. It shouldn't be noteworthy or exceptional to do the right thing. Unfortunately, under the thumbscrews of Androputriarchy, it is.

Anyone who debates or suggests the appropriateness of or actually assaults children is:

1. Lazy. Hitting is about quick fixes now. Assault is about easy. It takes effort, effort, effort, patience, resolve, thought, reflection, perspective, planning, and strategy to be a good parent.

2. Siding with the oppressor, acting as and for the oppressor, and is part of the problem and not part of the solution. There are, unfortunately, many women who assault children because they are being forced to by men, in one way or another. This is one of those places where the accountability becomes difficult to assign. Leaving this factor out of the

discussion for the moment, assaulting children is doing the malefactor's (male-factor's) work.

3 A co-conspirator against children, the oppressed and disempowered, and is teaching children to do likewise. When you affirm violence and assault children, especially ones you have a responsibility to parent, you are teaching them to side with, and act with and for, the perpetrators, the abusers, the aggressors, the assailants, the molesters, the pimps, the rapists, the thugs, and Androputriarchy.

4 Yet another willing tool of Androputriarchy. You are willing to obfuscate this deplorable notion with inane arguments about its appropriateness; like your forefathers arguing slavery was good for black people. Showing off your willingness and pride in assaulting children is shameful and despicable in itself, but in the larger context it makes you a contributor to the pandemic of Androputriarchy. This is but one place, albeit maybe the most important place, you can instead stand up and make a difference if you chose to do so. Even if you have hit children in the past, you can decide today to never do it again and accomplish this. You can become accountable to your victims; tell them what you did was wrong, and that you will never do it again.

Here is a list of words/obfuscations I accumulated while working with batterers who assaulted their children. It makes one wonder: if assaulting children is okay, why do we expend so much effort hiding it with our words?

| | | | |
|---|---|---|---|
| bang | fluff the diaper | not sparing the rod | swat |
| bash | give it to her | "O.J." her (him) | swipe |
| bean | give it the way my old | paddle | switch them |
| beat his butt | man gave it | pat on the butt | take a switch to |
| belt | get their attention | pat | tan his hide |
| blast | give a lickin' | plug | tap |
| blister | got the switch | poke | taught a thing or two |
| bop | handle the situation | pop | teach a lesson |
| brain | instruct the child | pound | they need to cry so I know |
| can't feel it unless they take | jab | put in place | they understood their |
| their clothes off | knock you out | rap | punishment |
| clip | lay into him | remind her who's boss (or | thump |
| clobber | lay him out | "in charge") | thrash |
| clock | let them have it | restrain | tighten up |
| conk | let them know what time | rough her up | wallop |
| correct | it is | safety lesson | whack |
| crack | lick | smack | whup |
| cuff | lit into them | snap 'em | whup |
| deck | make her think twice | spank | whuppin' |
| discipline | needed a lickin' for his own | straighten out | worked over |
| flick | good | stroke | |

# Profanity

One day 20 years ago I was thinking about chivalry. It's not surprising because I worked in a batterer intervention program at the time and was immersed in the squalid world of male privilege, entitlement, and worship. All the things lurching through my brain were being filtered through this scrim. I couldn't quite figure out why I didn't like or trust so-called "chivalry" and then the light bulb went on.

So-called male "chivalry" was supposed to demonstrate honorable, gallant, and high-minded politeness by men towards women. However, it is clearly a poisonous ruse in many ways, primarily as a demarcation of the "no gurlz allowed" boys club. Although it is supposed to look like good works on men's parts, it is instead yet one more way men pretend to respect women, and actually keep their "gentleman's club" doors tightly shut to women (except as rape and sexual degradation targets).

One example of this boy's club is profanity: men are allowed to use it but women are not supposed to. Although it is concocted this way as a supposed chivalrous "protection" of the "weaker sex," the fact is swear words are powerful words and men don't want to share any power with women, particularly powerful words or language.

As my brain percolated, it occurred to me there was another population that was not supposed to use profanity, and I wondered what this meant for them. That group: children.

So I started thinking about why it is we don't allow children to use profanity. I compiled a list of the reasons I could think of adults would likely come up with and I couldn't defend those reasons. So I began asking colleagues (I was so desperate I even asked my social worker friends) and friends if they thought children should be allowed to use profanity and, if not, why not? The fallout was startling to me.

First of all, practically every adult I asked thought children shouldn't be allowed to use profanity. When I asked why, the answers were as I had predicted: inane, indefensible, and there was an agenda behind the excuses they didn't want to think or talk about. Most of them proudly proclaimed they were not going to think or talk about it.

The reason most given, and most defended, was children don't know what these swear words mean and would be reckless in using them. In this recklessness they would get in trouble with teachers at school and offend classmates.

I asked these adults if they themselves used profanity. They affirmed they did. I asked them if they had learned the meanings of these words, and when and where to use them. They affirmed they had.

I asked if they thought their children would learn the meanings of profanity if they used them at school, getting whatever consequences come from it they might, and when and where to use them. For example, your kids have hands, they use their hands in acceptable ways most of the time, but when they put their hands on things or people in ways they shouldn't, didn't they get consequences and learn when, where, and how they should use their hands?

Yep.

That's when the inevitable would happen, and I'd begin hearing the stupid reasons. "Well, I just don't like them using profanity."

Really? Well, you told me you use profanity. Why shouldn't they be allowed the choice to use it? And, by the way, where did they learn profanity? Was it possibly from you?

All of these conversations, if the person was willing to go that far with me, which most wouldn't, finally ended up with me offering the following: we don't want children using profanity because profanity is powerful language and we don't want to share our power with children that way.

A few of my feminist women friends would think about it and say, "Yep, I never really thought about it, but that's right."

My non-feminist friends would "Tut, tut." and mutter and say they didn't want to talk about it anymore because it was stupid (the unspoken message was I was stupid for bringing it up). But not one of them could show me how it was wrong—and I asked incessantly.

My life was revolving around how men and Androputriarchy parasitizes and oppresses women. This one experience really got me thinking about how Androputriarchy also predates children, and disempowers them as well. I should have been thinking about children, but I wasn't (my own male privilege, no doubt).

So I talked this over with my partner Elizabeth and we then talked about it at family meeting (next section) with the kids and made it clear profanity was everyone's choice. I would note I am extremely profane in my conversation, no matter who I am with, including the children. Although the kids know they may use profanity in our household whenever they choose, they almost never do. I don't know why, but I suspect it is because when I use profanity it makes me sound stupid and they don't want to sound stupid like me. Maybe they are embarrassed by it.

I am absolutely convinced profanity, and all other things children have every right to possess and use, is a civic and moral empowerment issue in our world. We must do all we can to empower children, and disempower oppressive Androputriarchy and male privilege.

While I'm on the subject, another lie wrapped in the bloody wrapper of "chivalry" is the so-called "women and children first" notion, as if we cared about them more than men. I do know of plenty of places where women and children come first: raped in brothels, assaulted and sewn up in emergency rooms, populating the lowest paying jobs, sex-trafficked, responsible for child care, etc.

## Family meeting

Last, but not least, I want to offer a form of family "government" we use in our home. 10 years ago, when my step-children were six, eight, and 14 we began holding weekly family meetings. Everything that was possible to be handled democratically in our household, and especially in family meetings, was. For example, the rules and roles we had in family meeting were all voted on and adopted by majority vote. Here are a few:

1 **Shepherd**: title for the family member who facilitates the meeting. All roles rotated through the family, and everyone had to take their turn and fulfill each role. There was no "gender" attached to any role.

2 **Jotter**: title for the person who took notes of important discussions and/or decision votes.

3 **Solutioner**: title for the person who kept track of the agenda items placed on the list of topics.

4 **Speaker**: title for the person who read over the notes from our last family meeting.

5 **Voting**: everyone had one vote, and all votes were of equal power. Generally, a vote was affirmed with a majority method. However, some votes had to be unanimous, like if a family member wanted to invite someone to family meeting.

6 **Agenda**: anyone could add an item to the agenda to be discussed.

7 **Proposal**: anyone could make a proposal to be discussed and voted on.

8 **Emergency family meeting**: we held family meeting usually once per week on Sunday at 5 p.m. However, anyone could call an "emergency family meeting" if they felt there was an important issue that needed to be attended to right now. This probably happened five times or less in 10 years.

9 **Consequences**: if anyone, adults included, exhibited unacceptable behavior they would be responsible to discuss their behavior and come up with consequences for themselves that would be voted on at family meeting. Both children and adults brought up examples of unacceptable behavior. If we failed to come up with appropriate consequences, consequences would be assigned to us.

10 **Reward Ribbons**: we made reward "tickets" on slips of paper that anyone could fill in and give out at family meeting in recognition of anyone who had done something praiseworthy. They were always for someone else; never for oneself. The person who received the ribbon would be asked to read it aloud to all of us, whereupon they would be cheered and would get to "spin the wheel."

11 **Reward Ribbon Wheel**: we made a prize wheel that anyone with a reward ribbon would spin at family meeting and receive a reward. The rewards included: one dollar; ice cream cone; no chores that week; things that both adults and kids would feel rewarded by.

At first the kids loathed the idea of family meetings and made sure we knew it. But after a year or so when they saw we were not going to stop the meetings, and they began to realize family meeting was a place they had a voice and could get things changed or started that they had an interest in. They began to take ownership of how we did things in family meetings. They also got better at coming prepared to make proposals and convincing arguments for their case so they could win votes.

It is very empowering for a seven-year-old to get to say who speaks next, and who must wait. Not to mention all of the other responsibilities and authority the Shepherd has in our family meetings. I have told many people about our family meetings and how they function. Many of them have told me how a seven-year-old can't handle that kind or responsibility or role, and I have invited them to, with everyone in my family's permission, attend one of our family meetings and see for them self. They all declined.

Some of the empowerment happens in small ways, like not being interrupted while adults and children take their turns, with everyone's turn equally important. When everyone was working hard we came up with novel solutions to problems that wouldn't have occurred without adults and children's input. Everyone's opinion is respected regardless of age, and age-appropriate expectations are discussed and agreed to.

I include this aspect of my life in this examination of children's issues to show how we tried to take empowerment of children seriously, and to make our home one with appropriate and just use of power. It is not enough for me as a man to talk about Androputriarchy and male privilege and not to make my personal accountability a priority in my life.

homemade reward spinning wheel

211

# Speaking of Children

from "Beyond Silence: The United Nations Secretary General's Study on Violence against Children"
—http://www.violencestudy.org/r25

And they all say that we, the children, are the future of this country, but this does not mean that we are not the present also; and no child can be the future if the child is being ill-treated and abused in the present.

(13-year-old girl)

That [violence against children] is a big problem in our country, but very few people are interested in solving it.

(17-year-old boy)

Do something for the sake of all of us! Please!

(17-year-old girl)

If violence against a child is committed, make it 40 years imprisonment. This is how it should be!

(9-year-old girl)

Violence is when someone wants to beat a child—just like that.

(9-year-old boy)

Violence against children has for a long time been viewed as taboo. It was not spoken about and was not supposed to be spoken about. Beating and maltreating a child was normal.

(12-year-old girl)

Physical violence is terrible, but one doesn't know which one is worse—physical or psychological. But the psychological one hurts more than the physical because if your parents beat you up you'll get over it, but if they give you a hard word, it'll stay till the end of your life.

(12-year-old boy)

'You shut up. You know nothing, you're a child!' If all children said how much some of them experience such things, it would change.

(13-year-old boy)

We live in a dangerous society!

(9-year-old boy)

There is no protection when he [the perpetrator] is so powerful.

(16-year-old boy)

Children are ashamed to say that their parents ill-treat them. As much as they are ashamed, they are afraid. And so it is not talked about…

(13-year-old girl)

I think that there are no reasons to hit a child.

(10-year-old boy)

Be quiet and suffer!

(9-year-old boy)

It is terrible when there is nobody to protect a child!

(15-year-old boy)

Many children are afraid to ask for help because of fear that their parents might hurt them even more. And most of them are silent. Because more violence is hidden than known about, children are afraid to tell.

(17-year-old girl)

As years pass by, and violence is committed against a child, the child has less and less self-confidence.

(9-year-old girl)

### yes, please.

June, 2011

Dear Ms. René,

My name is Michael Elizabeth Marillynson. I am distantly acquainted with you through a woman friend whom I have known for more than 30 years. She speaks very highly of you and your work, and was particularly excited to tell me about the "Are We Leaving Our Men Behind?" article on your website.

You encourage feedback on the ideas on your website and thought I would share some of my perspectives on the issues you raise. I was excited to read this article, and want to thank you for speaking out on this subject. I want to be clear that I do so in absolute solidarity with you, and I hope how I say what I have to say is done with as much affection to you as I can.

I am a feminist. I am a 57-year-old white, upper middle class, privileged, heterosexual, married male. My unearned privilege matters and I attempt to take it into account as much as possible.

I would start out with your title, Are We Leaving Our Men Behind? We men are not behind you. We have never been behind you—in any way you want to take that statement. We have deliberately, skillfully, planfully, and always with violence and brutality made sure we are ahead of women—never behind. We have done so, as best as I can tell, since humans began walking on two feet.

When I hear men, usually, or women, whine about us men being left behind I know tat it is a ruse, a tactic, an obfuscation; yet another way to demonstrate devotion at the altar of patriarchy. I have learned patriarchy, like Mary Daly teaches us, is about reversals and lies and control of concepts and language. What bigger lie could there be than us men are being left behind by women? Is there one shred of evidence in human his-story that anything women do or have ever done was not summarily taken by us men **if we wanted it**?

Let's pretend for one minute we ARE being left behind. Just how are we being left out? What is it you, Ms. Rene, are doing in the myriad engagements of your life and work with women and girls I have asked to be involved in and you told me no? Have you ever experienced a man wanting to be involved in the global empowerment of women and girls just for its sake alone? Not because he wanted something else vile? Have any of your woman friends experienced this?

I have gratefully been invited into some "sacred" spaces by powerful women. I have also been excluded.

When I have been denied inclusion was I "being left behind?" Have I said, "Oh, I want to help women but you won't let me, you man-hater?" Would I have stopped caring about the foul stench of patriarchy and what we men are doing to this planet and sang the "poor, pitiful, abused me" song?

No means no. If I was told no I would have assumed one of two things: either I was not ready for it in some way, or it was inappropriate for me to be involved. Period.

I choose to understand I don't get to go anywhere I want to, or do anything I want to, because I am a privileged white male.

My non-negotiable treason to patriarchy doesn't stop because I don't what I want. It doesn't stop because something didn't go my way. It doesn't stop me grinding my teeth every day when I contemplate what we men are doing.

I will only be "left behind" because I don't care to walk in step with women and women's wellbeing. That's it. And to say it has anything to do with women "leaving us behind" is

214

a bald-faced, but extremely effective, lie perpetrated by patriarchy and His minions.

Regarding "reclaim your power as a woman and participate in the crescendo of female power on the planet so men can have a reaction in order to do their work of reclaiming the energy of the heart"—that will be the day.

First of all, we men don't have to wait to have you or anyone else do anything for us, to do what we should be doing in the first place. I have a button on all of my coats saying, "Men can stop rape." I don't have to have you "do your energy work" for me not to rape. I don't need women to invite me into their inner sanctum so I don't rape. I don't have to have anything to not rape other than a desire and commitment not to rape. And don't bother trying to talk me out of it because you can't. It is my commitment to myself. It is a hard-won loving commitment I have made to myself. My treason. Mine. It is not negotiable, nor dependent on circumstances.

Have you seen any marches down Main Street by men looking to reclaim their hearts? Call me jaded but I think that is because we don't give a shit, until you tell us we can't. Then you are going to hear, as Charles Dickens penned, "a chorus of scorched cats."

You said, "I see that the underlying sentiment is 'Oh, my God, we're going to be leaving our men behind!'" First of all, I see women, en masse, rejecting men/patriarchy as the first essential step in the right direction but, of course, it will be swiftly and brutally punished by men. Leaving your men behind is punishable by death the world over. Just look in

the newspaper. You will not leave us because we own you and no one else is allowed to own you. This is not negotiable in patriarchy.

Look at the holocausts women have endured when they made the slightest move toward solidarity with other women and said, "NO" to men. Think witch burnings. Think female genital mutilation. Think daily brutal rape. Women know "leaving their men behind" means economic hardship, social censure, ridicule, or death. Patriarchy has seen to it you know this and you police yourself.

"Some women wouldn't be comfortable living alone and being celibate" is, of course, true but to say this is about "comfort" is missing the point. Women's sexual and menial servitude to men/patriarchy is man-datory. It isn't about comfort, even though "comfort" might be in there somewhere for extremely wealthy, privileged women, but even there I'm not so sure.

"I'm about to completely unplug myself from the fear-based, male-dominated patriarchal system. I remember the terror that came up and how difficult it was for me to work with it and finally bring it to rest." It is gratifying you can "put this to rest" but I'm not sure how that could be possible. The patriarchy menace that impinges on you every day has not gone away. Patriarchy knows how to resurrect your fear and we men will do so if we feel it is worthwhile. I don't think this can be "put to rest" until patriarchy as we know it has been "put down."

"What strikes me first is that this is not a question asked by a woman standing in her power. This question is only of concern to a second-class

citizen. This question is fear-based." Lucia, my concern about this is it is victim-blaming. Some women may "enjoy" second-class citizenship, but the rest of women suffer third, fourth, fifth-class citizenship, if any citizenship at all.

To advance the notion women can "stand in their power" or "bring it to rest" means she just has to do x-y-z things and her plight in patriarchy is solved. Yet again, this tells her it is her fault. If she would only stand in her power everything would be hunkydory! This is the "C'mon, just smile for us honey" argument which, of course, is a sick game invented by patriarchy.

I certainly agree with you "It is time for women to reclaim their power and move forward onto the front lines of consciousness. This, of course, means throwing off their conditioning as second-class citizens, standing as the powerful beings they are, and speaking and acting their truth." Although I wish this could all be an inside job, I see no way women are going to save the human race if they don't speak and act their power, whether or not their consciousness changes. I'll gladly settle for women throwing off the yoke of patriarchal oppression, violently if necessary, even if their "consciousness" doesn't change.

You say "Men, on the other hand, need to reclaim the energy of the heart and, for most men, that will only be accomplished once they have processed their reaction to the crescendo of female power that is happening on the planet." I read this sentence as "... and, for most men, that will only be accomplished once they have blah, blah, blah, blah..."

215

It seems we men always have some good reason for being fucking assholes individually and collectively and if we would only… blah, blah, blah, blah… then something good would miraculously happen. I read this as yet one more sublimely insidious obfuscation and tactic of patriarchy. If you womenfolk can just help us wounded men find our feelings, or appreciate our feminine side, or help us forgive ourselves, or bond with our fathers, or whatever the flavor of the month is, we'll just be swell.

Guess what? Peekaboo! It's all bullshit! We don't "need" to do any of this to stop raping you. That's it. That's all there is. End of sentence. We don't "need" to do anything to stop raping you except decide to stop raping you. The reason we are not deciding to stop raping you has nothing to do with our enlightenment. It is because it is not in our interest to decide to stop raping you. It is ugly self-interest, but it is what it is. Men/patriarchy put lipstick on this pig.

"It is necessary to give each human the time and space needed to make that decision. And, unless someone seeks out your help, there's really not much you can do to assist him or her in making that choice." I couldn't disagree more. Tell the seven-year old her father needs space and time to decide to stop sexually assaulting her. Tell the Filipino woman trapped in sexual slavery in Chicago her pimps and rapists just need time to contemplate why it is they burn her with cigarettes and put their fists up her vagina.

And yes, we most certainly can "assist" him in making that choice. It's called laws and solidarity and shame and consequences. It's amazing how fast we men can change our behaviors when we see our own wellbeing in it. It's astonishing how quickly our "feelings" need expression when we are threatened with divorce or jail or public shaming.

"Sometimes, the kindest thing you can do for a drowning person is to put your foot on their head and push them back under the water!" I agree, although whether it is kind or not doesn't really interest me. If men/patriarchy responded accountably and mercifully to kindness, then kindness would interest me. But they don't, so it doesn't.

I do not care about men/patriarchy's wellbeing or existence. I am indifferent to a man/many men's drowning in their own vile poison. I see no evidence that putting my foot on His head, or removing my foot, makes any difference. I am interested in women's wellbeing and me deepening my understanding of my accountability as a man in patriarchy. It would be far better for all womankind if men were sent to another planet, including me if necessary, for women's wellbeing.

You say, "If we want to help the men in our lives, our best bet is to do our job as women really, really well, i.e., reclaim your power and stand in it as fully as you can." I say forget about "helping" the men; do this because it is good for you. It doesn't matter whether it is "good" for men or not. It is good for you. Do it for you. The men can drown or swim. Men can figure it out. We've more than proven that.

In solidarity,
Mike

Postscript—February, 2012: When I emailed Ms. Rene my thoughts on her website essay I did so because she eagerly invited responses to her writings, and she hinted she would post them. I never received any response (I included my email address) nor was my response posted. Patriarchy has a way of silencing even outspoken women.

# Speaking of Women

One can never consent to creep when one feels an impulse to soar.

~ Helen Keller
(1880–1968)

Powerful men often succeed through the help of their wives. Powerful women only succeed in spite of their husbands.

~ Linda Lee Potter
(1935–2004)

The slave is unconditionally accessible to the master. Total power is unconditional access; total powerlessness is being unconditionally accessible. The creation and manipulation of power is constituted of the manipulation and control of access. All-woman groups, meetings, projects seem to be great things for causing controversy and confrontation. Many women are offended by them; many are afraid to be the one to announce the exclusion of men; it is seen as a device whose use needs much elaborate justification. I think this is because conscious and elaborate exclusion of men by women, from anything, is blatant insubordination, and generates in women fear of punishment and reprisal (often well justified). The woman-only meeting is a fundamental challenge to the structure of power.

~ Marilyn Frye
(1941–)

I don't have the time every day to put on makeup. I need that time to clean my rifle.

~ Henriette Mantel
(1958–)

If the American white male-dominated society is based on violence and war, then if women really want to get ahead, that's the only route they can take. They can't try to reason. We've been trying to reason with men for thousands of years, and it doesn't work. Men are not reasonable people, for the most part—they're too territorial. So now it's time so say, "Well, this is our fucking planet. We gave birth to it, and it is in our likeness that it is created. You are fucking with us—so fuck you." Because that's the only language they can understand. They're not going to understand reasoning. Not at this late date.

~ Lydia Lunch
(1959–)

# pleas and promises

### an ode to my siblings

When the ruptured cords
of our sibling devotion
were laid bare
they betrayed
the hollow
pleas and promises
of trauma
long since lamented.

**ignorant, likeable, and androputriarchy-safe**

*i just don't understand – okay?*

I've done public education work on the topic of domestic violence prevention for many years. Among the various routine assertions I hear from audiences includes women who say, "I just don't understand why she puts up with that," and men who say, "I just don't understand why a man would hurt his wife."

I used to lament at how poorly we were educating the public about the dynamics of domestic violence when I heard these supposedly innocent and empathetic statements. I thought these were the exact people—sympathetic, eager to understand—we should but were failing to reach.

But after hearing them for the kazillionth time, and always with a tone that made me suspicious, I began to think more about my assumption of where the blame belonged.

I've concluded these assertions of so-called ignorance/innocence/naivety are, at best, self-promoting obfuscations intended to manipulate the listener's opinion of the speaker.

Consider:

These statements/questions do not reveal innocent ignorance. If I say, "I just don't understand how a woman can't do algebra," I'm telling you something very important about me, not any factual reality about any woman's algebra abilities.

There are many reasons why a particular woman might not be good at algebra. If I want to understand why that particular woman can't do algebra, or why a group of women, or even many women, can't do algebra, I can probably figure it out if I choose to investigate the matter.

There isn't a cosmic force field preventing me from understanding something that is easily understandable with minimal effort. This isn't about me being too stupid, ignorant, or having an inability to learn. This isn't about my being such a sweet and naïve person I couldn't possibly grasp the ugly truth about something all around me.

This is about purposely not understanding something I really don't want to understand. It is akin to not understanding exactly how cows are abused, slaughtered, and "processed" for our evening steak (I don't eat meat, by the way—another Androputriarchal institution I can do without). We could find out what happens in the slaughterhouse, but we really don't want to know.

These statements/questions do not reveal that our community's educational efforts are inadequate, or that we "just need to say it to people in a way they can understand it." They do reveal the speakers preference not to have a deeper understanding of the plight of women/girls in our homes, neighborhoods, cities, nations and all over the world.

We have been taught by Androputriarchy to feel sympathetic to the women who declare, "I just don't understand why she puts up with that," and the men who plead, "I just don't understand why a man would hurt his wife." Would we be so sympathetic to a woman or man who publically declares, in a health care conference, "I just don't understand why women would allow themselves to get so fat" or "I just don't understand why men would allow themselves to have erectile dysfunction."

To start with, would we really believe the person saying that? Even if it were true the person didn't understand, wouldn't we place the burden of attempting to understand squarely on them? Wouldn't we hear a statement such as this as blaming the victim, or at least insulting the victim?

These statements/questions do reveal the speakers priorities. That is, I choose not to know. I prefer to not know, because knowing makes me choose sides. Choosing sides is dangerous to my health and well-being.

Choosing sides means knowing domestic violence is about male privilege, male power, male hegemony, Androputriarchy, Androputriarchal institutions, and speaking openly about it means challenging those institutions. It means drawing a line and standing on one side of that line, which makes me the target of all the powerful people and institutions on the other side of that line. Who wants that?

These statements/questions do reveal the speakers desire to control what you think of him/her.

For example, the woman who says, "I just don't understand why she puts up with that," is trying to convince you, and probably herself, she is not a battered woman and could never become one. She is mentally counting the layers of protection she believes she has positioned between herself and men's violence so she can believe she is somehow safe. Those layers might include wealth, status, occupation, attachment to males, publically-declared devotion to Androputriarchy, the status quo, etc.

She is purposely distancing herself from battered women, as a group, because she doesn't want to be tainted by that dirty association. She feels good pleading ignorance—it puts her in a more favorable peer group.

By the way, no matter how convincingly she protests, the probability she has been battered and/or sexually assaulted by her father, step-father(s), grandfather(s), brother(s), son(s), boss(es), boyfriend(s), or husband(s) is pretty high. Sadly, it is also not her choice or within her control. If I walk up to you and slug you in the face, you've just become

a violence victim. If I dated you twice before I slugged you, you've just become a dating violence victim. If I moved in with you before I slugged you, you've just become a domestic violence victim. It's my choice, not yours.

The same is true with men who claim, "I just don't understand why a man would hurt his wife." It is in his interest to convince you he is not a batterer, has never battered, could not be a batterer, and cannot even conceive of such a thing. What better way to improve his reputation but in a subtle, indirect way by puffing himself up and speaking disparagingly and with "innocent ignorance" about batterers and their motivations? But who would know batterer's motivations better than men? This also reinforces the fact all men benefit from men's violence and oppression of women. Look at me, Ladies (Mommy), I am one of the good guys. I'm special.

By the way, no matter how convincingly he protests, the probability he has battered and/or sexually assaulted his mother, step-mother(s), grandmother(s), sister(s), daughter(s), girlfriend(s), secretary(s) or wife(s) is pretty high.

These statements/questions do reveal the speakers desire to identify with the aggressor, and all of the perceived privileges and safeguards inherent with that peer group association, and not with the victim. No man or woman who chose to remain loyal to the disempowered would ever take a position distancing her/himself from the disempowered.

Whenever we hear a person saying or doing something that estranges him/herself from the subject of domestic violence or the oppression of women, or from the plight of a particular battered woman, we are clearly witnessing a desire to distance oneself from the victim and her peer group.

# Speaking of Women

Ya Ummi (my mother), I cannot live my life with a woman who has no key to my mind and does not share my concerns. She cannot—will not—read anything. She shrugs off the grave problems of the day and asks if I think her new tablecloth is pretty. We are living in difficult times and it is not enough for a person to be interested in his home and his job—in his own personal life. I need my partner to be someone to whom I can turn, confident of her sympathy, believing her when she tells me I'm in the wrong, strengthened when she tells me I'm in the right. I want to love, and be loved back—but what I see is not love or companionship but a sort of transaction of convenience sanctioned by religion and society and I do not want it.

~ Ahdaf Soueif
(1950–)

Feminist consciousness-raising has not significantly pushed women in the direction of revolutionary politics. For the most part, it has not helped women understand capitalism—how it works as a system that exploits female labor and its interconnections with sexist oppression. It has not urged women to learn about different political systems like socialism or encouraged women to invent and envision new political systems. It has not attacked materialism and our society's addiction to overconsumption. It has not shown women how we benefit from the exploitation and oppression of women and men globally or shown us ways to oppose imperialism. Most importantly, it has not continually confronted women with the understanding that feminist movement to end sexist oppression can be successful only if we are committed to revolution, to the establishment of a new social order.

~ bell hooks
(1952–)

What [Sarah] Palin so beguilingly represented... was a form of female power that was utterly digestible to those who had no intellectual or political use for actual women: feminism without the feminists.

~ Rebecca Traister
(dates unknown)

She [Mary Daly] taught us not only to think outside the box but then to ask, who put this box here and why?

~ Linda Barufaldi
(dates unknown)

# hurricane
## (awakening from a dream on saturday morning, age 37)

he is there suddenly
lurching into my gut
a terrible derailed train engine
hot, steaming, screeching, too late to escape.
my world is electrified with panic
each hateful noise a claw to my skin
the irreversible chatter of my destruction
his steely grip crushing my neck
i flex my back
pretend away the pain and humiliation
every moment of his vicious attack
i must witness, breathe in, endure
warm urine, my own, my ally, mine
slowly flows down my thighs
darkening my blue jeans
painting my shame
in sleep my arms and legs scratch the bed
like my dogs snoozily chasing squirrels
only there can i scream
CALL THE POLICE!
I'LL KILL YOU!
I HATE YOU!
until my voice fails
i awake
screaming no sound
air hissing through my throat
groggily proud of myself
for resisting, for screaming, for hating
only in dreams
do i have the courage for action
a child, a boy, i hid, i disappeared, i became nothing
let the hurricane vent his fury
on the objects that resist him
i am weak and defenseless
i will be destroyed

©2014 Michael Elizabeth Marillynson LLC - from the book "Contrary to the Custom of Men: Field Notes on the Pestilence of Patriarchy from a Disloyal Son." For re-printing permission go to: con2men.info.

androputriarchy's pestilent pronouncements

# bravery and knavery

**Bravery**: having or showing courage, resolution, or daring under difficult or dangerous conditions; consciously rising to a specific test by drawing on a reserve of inner strength; to dare or defy.

Who is brave—the perpetrator of loathsome acts and crimes, or the survivor?

Is it brave to be vengeful or to be merciful?

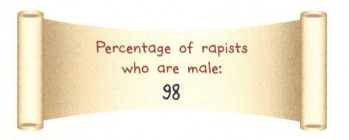

**Percentage of rapists who are male: 98**

Why is bravery always attached to a penis?

Why does bravery always come in military **men**, police**men**, and fire**men**?

We love to refer to military veterans as "humble and stoic" because they don't want to talk about their "war" experiences. It may be stoic, but is it humble? How many are ashamed to think about, let alone talk about, how they experienced intense fear and so-called "cowardess"—really, just self-preservation? How many don't want to reveal the awful things they perpetrated, watched others perpetrate, or ignored that were perpetrated on defenseless human beings? How many don't want to reveal the awful things perpetrated on them? How many don't want to think about how they were made violent, destructive pawns in corrupt Androputriarchy?

**Percentage of adolescent sex offenders who are male: 92**

What is bravery? Taken from various dictionaries, the definition above says nothing about a penis. It says nothing about a requirement for being a man or men. Why not?

Why do we always think of these types of men when we think of bravery?

**Percentage of victims of rape: Men = 13   Women = 87**

How did bravery become saturated with testosterone and covered in facial hair?

Who should be considered brave over the centuries—the women who have survived the brutality of men, or the men who have done the brutalizing?

223

> **Killed in the line of duty in the United States—2010:**
>
> Firefighters—87
> Police officers—162
> American soldiers—930
> (462 died in combat;
> 468 committed suicide)
> Wives/partners—1,200
> Prostituted women—2,229

Is it bravery to hold families and communities together with nurturing, caretaking and commitment, or to blow families and communities apart with selfishness, violence and abandonment?

Is it bravery to associate sexuality with intimacy, love and pleasure, or is it bravery to associate sexuality with violence, degradation, control over, and pain?

> **Percentage of sexual abusers who perpetrate against young children:**
>
> Men = 90    Heterosexual = 95

Why don't we have parades down Main Street every year for the women who work in child protective services organizations, or battered women's shelters, or family planning organizations, or midwifery services, or women killed by their husbands, or women raped in the American military by American soldiers, or women who protest sexual harassment, or women and/or girls being sexually assaulted and exploited by every type of man there is, particularly their family members?

Why don't we have statues of brave women in every town in America? Are we saying there have been no brave women? For every man honored for his so-called bravery in granite or bronze in America are we saying there were no women in his life or in his time or in his world who were not equally or more brave? Who did not put their own lives on the line for what this man is being feted for?

| **google search terms** (January 18, 2012) | **result** |
|---|---|
| "support our troops" | 12,600,000 |
| "support our police" | 2,670,000 |
| "support our firefighters" | 1,210,000 |
| "support our prostitutes" | 602 |
| "support our battered women" | 262 |
| "support our secretaries" | 9 |
| "support our exploited women" | 0 |

Veterans are lauded, respected, and given social and economic benefits far above the average person in the United States. Who and what is a veteran, exactly? Who got to decide in the first place? Are women who have survived the violence of their husbands and/or intimate partners, the discrimination and harassment of the workplace, and the exclusion from the leading ranks of their religion—yet, go on to raise a family and support the wellbeing of their communities—veterans worth recognition?

**Knavery:** dishonest or crafty dealing; an instance of trickery or mischief; a deceitful or dishonest act; dishonest conduct; fraud; acts of lying or cheating or stealing activity that transgresses moral or civil law.

# Speaking of Women

Can spirit from the tomb, or fiend from hell,
More hateful, more malignant be than man—
Than villainous man?

~ Joanna Baillie
(1762–1851)

My wish is to ride the tempest, tame the waves, kill the sharks. I will not resign myself to the usual lot of women who bow their heads and become concubines.

~ Trieu Thi Choi
(dates unknown)

They (women) have stabbed themselves for freedom—jumped into the waves for freedom—starved for freedom—fought like very tigers for freedom! But they have been hung, and burned, and shot—and their tyrants have been their historians!

~ Lydia Maria Child
(1802–1880)

... the soldier's business is to take life. For that he is paid by the State, eulogized by political charlatans and upheld by public hysteria. But woman's function is to give life, yet neither the State nor politicians nor public opinion have ever made the slightest provision in return for the life woman has given.

~ Emma Goldman
(1869–1940)

Marriage, laws, the police, armies and navies are the mark of human incompetence.

~ Dora Russell
(1894–1968)

## rotten fruit does not fall far from the infested tree

Androputriarchy, like Nazism, the Ku Klux Klan, the Taliban, and other hyper-Patriarchal movements, has the defining characteristic of being rotten to the core.

It is not that some men, or even a large part of men, are bad. It is Androputriarchy that is bad through and through. For men to have a chance at decency, they have to make a conscious effort to comprehend and resist Androputriarchy.

One of the ways Androputriarchy maintains its perfidiousness is by camouflaging men's sordid behavior with a mind-numbing fog that leaves everyone involved in a semi-comatose state.

A glaring example is when we read in the newspaper Joe So-and-So killed his ex-wife and their three children and all of the interviewed neighbors, family, and co-workers exclaim, "I can't believe he'd do something like that!"

When we hear such a thing, we are witness to the stuporous effectiveness and efficiency of Androputriarchy.

It is not exemplary or noteworthy, nor should it be surprising in an informed and rational world, any given man would use the tactics and tools Androputriarchy puts at his disposal for his own interests, like controlling, dominating, and/or assassinating his family.

Every man and boy under Androputriarchy is trained and coerced to bond with other boys and men around the campfire of women's degradation. Why would it then be a surprise to us when he does so?

In fact, the opposite is true: those men in human history who have had every opportunity to take advantage of their male privilege through hurting women and children and did not do so are the ones who are exemplary, unusual, and noteworthy. Imagine: a man exposing himself to harm from Androputriarchy because he concluded male privilege is wrong and immoral!

Given how our human family is completely poisoned by Androputriarchy, the newspaper article would be rational if it looked like this:

# MAN RETURNS TO HALF-EMPTY HOUSE— ACTS KINDLY AND GENEROUSLY TO DIVORCING WIFE

April 5, 2012, Detroit, MI—(AP) When George White came home today he was shocked to find all of his wife's possessions, and the children, gone. The shock didn't end there.

On the kitchen table he found a note from his now-separated wife saying she was tired of his selfish and immature behavior, she needed to take care of her family, and had filed for divorce.

After sitting and thinking about the situation for more than three hours, Mr. White called his wife, agreed with her assessment of his behavior, apologized, and asked how he could support her and the kids.

Afterwards he went to all his neighbors' homes and told them what had happened and apologized for the ways he had been disrespectful to his family, or to them.

When interviewed Mr. White said, "I can only be thankful to my wife for doing the right thing in taking care of herself and the kids, and giving me this wake-up call that I need to do some serious soul-searching. I will be seeking therapy first thing tomorrow morning. My goal is not to get her back, but to figure out how I let myself get to this point and what I need to do to respect myself."

Neighbors interviewed in this quiet, tree-lined suburban enclave expressed shock and dismay at their neighbor's behavior.

Mr. White's backdoor neighbor Frank Gibbons said, "I've known George and his family for 20 years. He was wealthy, arrogant and could have had anything he wanted. He is the last person I would suspect could be so accountable."

Similarly, Mr. White's neighbor across the street was shocked. "You hear about this type of responsible behavior in the papers once in a while, but you never think it could happen in your neighborhood. I would never have thought George was capable of being this conscientious."

# Speaking of Women

A woman fit to be a man's wife is too good to be his servant.

~ Dorothy Leigh
(?–c.1616)

If men cannot cope with women in the medical profession let them take a humble occupation in which they can.

~ Sarah Josepha Hale
(1788–1879)

The older I have grown, the more serious and irremediable have seemed to me the evils and disadvantages of married life as it exists among us at this time.

~ Harriet Martineau
(1802–1876)

In rebellion alone, woman is at ease, stamping out both prejudices and sufferings; all intellectual women will sooner or later rise in rebellion.

~ Louise Michel
(1830–1905)

We've begun to raise our daughters more like sons… but few have the courage to raise our sons more like our daughters.

~ Gloria Steinem
(1934–)

Patriarchy is itself the original men's movement, and the struggle to overthrow it must be a movement of men as well as women. But men can only be authentically a part of that struggle if they are able to acknowledge the injustice of their own historical privilege as males and to recognize the ongoing ideologies and economic, political, and social structures that keep such privilege in place.

~ Rosemary Radford Ruether
(1936–)

If women have colluded with men in their own oppression, then we must stop nurturing our oppressors, and recognize that men are our oppressors, that our oppression as women is not an "accident" but systematic and purposeful and will not end until we do what we must do to free ourselves.

~ Julia Penelope
(1941–2013)

Feminism as a force or intensity has to disrupt all officially charted maps— it calls for the remapping of relationships. Everything has to be called into question. Including the possibility of love. This is a big, ambitious, crucial project that breaks with what is traditional or ossified. Therefore it can't hearken back to a "natural" state. So in terms of "community," a truly thoughtful, demanding, relentless feminism would demand a re-charting of territorialities; the suspension of old-fashioned boundaries of what constitutes a state. What is required for the future is a remapping even of our unconscious topology. Therefore, no one in their right mind is even going to hope that the state will be the place where something grandiose will happen, community-wise. Nor are they going to expect justice from the state—nor from any typical or stereotypical and sclerotic institutional models.

~ Avital Ronell
(1952–)

some questions for you and the men in your life

father knows best (price for sex)

When prostitution and sexual slavery are being discussed—the rare times they are—Androputriarchy and perpetrators are left out of the chat: a **weave of absence**. Buried even deeper from prying minds is who those perpetrators actually are. They couldn't be our fathers, our brothers, our sons, our uncles, our nephews, our cousins, our bosses, our co-workers, our politicians, our police officers, our clergy, or our neighbors—could they?

It should not be surprising to any of us that statistics on how many women in the United States are being forced into prostitution are incomplete and "hard to find." When I researched the "number of prostitutes in the United States," I kept getting this type of response: "It is difficult to know the actual numbers because this population is so difficult to find and study."

Really?

It would appear men, serial rapists in this case, don't have the slightest problem finding prostituted women. Maybe we should give them pens and questionnaires to administer to the women they are raping.

We don't know how many because Androputriarchy doesn't want to know, and doesn't want us to know, and we're okay with that. It's easier—at least for us men—that way.

On the other hand, consider the facts we have accumulated about security guards in America. They are so much more important than prostituted women they have their own category at the United States Bureau of Labor Statistics. You can find out pretty much anything you'd want to know about security guard injuries, for example, at their website. Of course, there is nothing mentioned about the rate at which security guards are raped, which must set them apart as more noteworthy than prostituted women.

For example, the rate of fatal injuries (84) to security guards was 9.4 fatalities per 100,000 workers in 2007. This was an 8% increase from 2006. The rate in 2007 was more than twice the rate for all workers (3.8) that year.

51% (43 fatalities) of security guard fatalities were due to homicides. Of these 43 homicides, 47% (20 fatalities) were committed by a customer or client, 33% (14 fatalities) by a robber, and the remainder (9 fatalities) by an unknown assailant.

The median days away from work—a key measure of the severity of injuries and illnesses—was 8 days for security guards, compared with 7 days for all occupations.

Falls were the most common event leading to injuries with days away from work to security guards, occurring at a rate of 27.5 per 10,000 full time workers in 2007.

The rate of assaults and violent acts experienced by security guards was 14.4 per 10,000 full-time workers.

On and on the Bureau of Labor Statistics waxes poetic, detailing

**Weave of absence:** all of the purposeful tactics and strategies used by Androputriarchy, and their cumulative results, to make women and/or men invisible when it is in Androputriarchy's interest.

229

minutiae like what time of day security guards are most likely to be injured, what type of surface they are walking on, what day of the week it is, how the age of the security guard factors into their injuries, etc. Someone in Washington really cares about security guards.

Who knew the study of security guards in America was so much more important than the study of prostituted women, even though the occupation of security guards is so much safer than the daily torture and slavery of prostituted women? Just a coincidence, I guess.

But we just can't seem to figure out how many women are being prostituted in America because they are so difficult to find. Maybe they are all just as clever at hiding as Osama bin Laden. Oops, I forgot, we found him.

The data I could find estimates the population of prostituted women is between 100,000 and 1,000,000 in America, land of the free and the brave and the rapers.

Let's play with conservative numbers, as playing with conservatives is such a drag. 100,000 prostituted women (we won't even mention girls and boys at this point) being serially raped three times per day, 250 days per year (I'm giving them the weekends off), equal 75,000,000 rapes per year.

According to the U.S. Census of 2010, there were 71,074,531 adult males around to perpetrate these rapes, or about 1 rape per man. We've been busy, eh guys?

Who is doing all of this raping? Somebody is doing it. It's not all being done by my family, so somebody in your family must be contributing to the (non)statistics.

So if the United States Bureau of Labor Statistics won't ask the questions, I would like all of the rest of us to do it and then pass on our information to them (http://data.bls.gov/cgi-bin/forms/iif?/iif/oshcont1.htm).

From now on, at Thanksgiving, at Christmas, at Hanukah, at Groundhog Day, at Penis Day, I would like us to start asking questions of our own families. Here is a starter list of questions—feel free to add your own:

## For Dad/brother/uncle/son/nephew/husband/lover/manfriend:

- How much money have you spent in your lifetime paying for sex?
- How much sex did that get you?
- How many different women have you paid to have sex with you?
- How many girls (seventeen years of age or younger) have you paid to have sex with you?
- How far have you traveled to pay women and/or girls for sex?
- Were you ever injured with a woman or girl you paid to have sex with you?
- What was the race of the women/girls you paid for sex?
- Did you ever injure a woman or girl you paid to have sex with you?
- If you claim you haven't spent money to get women to have sex with you, why not?

- If you claim you haven't spent money to get women to have sex with you, what other males in our family do you think might have?
- How many times have you coerced/threatened/forced a woman and/or girl to have sex with you but didn't bother to pay them?
- Have you ever gone into a brothel or similar place and found a woman relative of yours? Or some other woman/girl you knew?
- How did you get along with the pimps of the women you used for sex?
- How much of the money you gave to the women went to the pimps?
- Did you give the money to the women/girls, or to the pimps?

If you answered "none" to all of these questions, did you do so because you'd like me to think we live in a very special family, or because you are not telling me the truth?

If no women were raped by any male in our family, what kind of family do you think is doing the raping?

Of the three "types" of people "named" in prostitution—the "prostitute," the "pimp," and the "john," which one has the least shameful name? Why do you say that?

Of the three "types" of people involved in prostitution—the "prostitute," the "pimp," and the "john," which one is the least likely to be arrested? Why do you think that?

## For Mom/sister/aunt/daughter/niece/wife/lover/womanfriend:

- Have you ever been forced into sexual acts to make money?
- How many of those times was it a relative of ours that forced you?
- Have you ever been under the control of a pimp?
- If so, was the pimp a relative of ours?
- Which of the women in this family do you think have been forced to give sex for money?
- If you answered "none" to all of these questions, did you do so because you'd like me to think we live in a very special family, or because you are not telling me the truth?
- What is it about the men in our family that would make you think they are different than the average raping family men?
- Who would you have sex with only because they paid you for it?
- Do you think prostituting yourself for money is an empowering activity? Why or why not?

## Questions for you to ponder (probably before Thanksgiving):

- What response are you anticipating if you ask these lists of questions to any of the men or women in your family or close to you?
- What would your family members' refusal to answer these questions tell you about your family?
- How would their treatment of you for asking them to answer these questions tell you about how they view or treat women?
- Is there someone in your life you absolutely trust you could show this list of questions, and your own answers, and feel completely supported, protected, and understood?
- Before asking any of these questions, do you think your family cares about the plight of prostituted women?
- After asking any of these questions, do you think your family cares about the plight of prostituted women?
- If a man wanted to further the power and control of Androputriarchy, would it be more efficacious for him to rape a prostituted woman, or a homecoming queen?
- What is the difference between a "rape camp" and a "brothel" from the women victims' perspective? From any woman's perspective? From your perspective?

# Speaking of Women

Marriage is for women the commonest mode of livelihood, and the total amount of undesired sex endured by women is probably greater in marriage than in prostitution.

~ Bertrand Russell
(1872–1970)

Alas! Why has the plain truth the power of offending so many people…?

~ Julia Kavanah
(1824–1877)

Whether our reformers admit it or not, the economic and social inferiority of woman is responsible for prostitution.

~ Emma Goldman
(1869–1940)

You can be up to your boobies in white satin, with gardenias in your hair and no sugar cane for miles, but you can still be working on a plantation.

~ Billie Holliday
(1915–1959)

A woman reading Playboy feels a little like a Jew reading a Nazi manual.

~ Gloria Steinem
(1934–)

Feminists are often asked whether pornography causes rape. The fact is that rape and prostitution caused, and continue to cause, pornography. Politically, culturally, socially, sexually, and economically, rape and prostitution generated pornography; and pornography depends for its continued existence on the rape and prostitution of women.

~ Andrea Dworkin
(1946–2005)

Pornography is the undiluted essence of anti-female propaganda.

~ Susan Brownmiller
(1975–)

Now, should we treat women as independent agents, responsible for themselves? Of course. But being responsible has nothing to do with being raped. Women don't get raped because they were drinking or took drugs. Women do not get raped because they weren't careful enough. Women get raped because someone raped them.

~ Jessica Valenti
(1978–)

Women aren't prostitutes. They are prostituted… by the pimps and johns that use them. Prostitution is something done to women.

~ Dictamus
(blog name)

Easy is an adjective used to describe a woman who has the sexual morals of a man.

~ Nancy Linn-Desmond
(dates unknown)

Prostitution isn't like anything else. Rather, everything else is like prostitution because it is the model for women's condition.

~ Evelina Giobbe
(dates unknown)

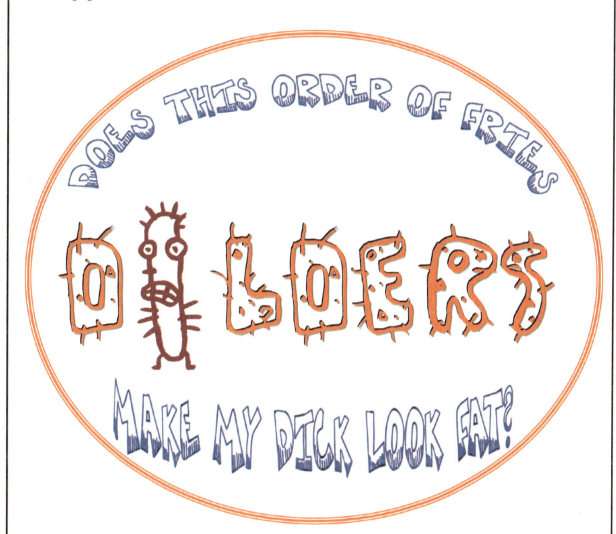

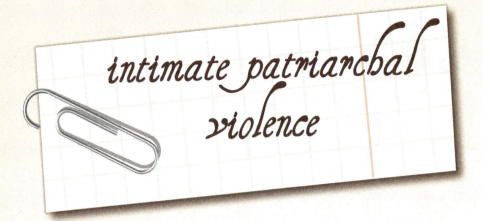

# intimate patriarchal violence

## so-called domestic violence, batterers, and sundry co-conspirators

In 1988 I was recruited to help establish a batterer intervention program for the reason most are begun: a place to hide men charged with assault and battery on an intimate partner so the courts can appear as if they take this sort of thing seriously. Oh, and to keep the jails less crowded for serious offenders like marijuana users. The judges and probation officers could then tell anyone who would listen what a good system it was, and the oh-so-helpful-and-nice-and-very-professional social workers and psychologists were thrilled with the court-mandated cash flow.

Even with all the grief I garnered over 11 years due to my constant, obnoxious insistence we be accountable to our primary constituency—women and children—I was quite the man of success. I was on television babbling on about batterer tactics, flown around the country presenting workshops, was a founding member of our state coalition, was named Michigan Social Worker of the Year, Eastern Michigan alumni of the year, blah, blah, blah.

All during that time I continually told my audiences, court systems, and everyone else I could about my deep concern whether we should be doing this work at all because of how it potentially put women and children at more risk. I can now say I have lost whatever skepticism I had, and am completely certain we shouldn't be doing it.

Given that I worked in the belly of this beast for many years, and am complicit in whatever damage was done, I offer some thoughts on the topics of so-called domestic violence, batterers, and sundry co-conspirators.

First, my definition:

**Intimate Patriarchal Violence (IPV):** a replacement for both "domestic violence" and the now-popular "intimate partner violence" because of how both of those terms obfuscate the perpetrator and His purpose: deliberate and pragmatic degradation, abuse, and violence used by men within the complicity and sanction of Androputriarchy to create and maintain male privilege at the expense of women. Intimate Patriarchal Violence is battering, and batterers are the perpetrators of Intimate Patriarchal Violence.

Intimate Patriarchal Violence is, in all instances, a choice of behavior(s) men make, and nothing but a choice, for their own calculated interests. No exceptions.

Battering is not the result of poor communication skills, lack of empathy, low self-esteem, powerlessness, changing male role models, loving too much or too little, anger issues, psychological problems, genetic or hereditary issues, medical issues, medications, family of origin, provocation, poverty, brain neurotransmitters or circuitry, psychiatric disorders, unemployment, low or high educational attainment, male or female hormones, stress, race, religion, class, disability, childhood trauma, jealousy, intoxication, drug or alcohol problems or addiction, bad relationships, loss of control, bad temper, disease, diminished intellect, mental illness, any external person or event, or any other male-privileged concoctions, misinformation, disguises, fabrications, sleight of hand, contrivances, prevarication, falsehoods, deceptions, obfuscations, fiction, concealment, evasion, myths, decoys, machinations, distractions, or window dressing.

IPV is an, if not the most, important form of political, social, and economic oppression of women individually and as a group.

IPV is a means for men to systematically, socially and institutionally dominate, control, devalue and disempower women.

Battering is always greater than an individual act; it supports the larger goal of the oppression of women. Battering is a lifestyle; never a singular event.

Battering is never justified, excusable, provoked, out of control, accidental, or an isolated incident with no further dynamics. The batterer is responsible for his behavior, not the person who is the target of the battering. Battering and abusive behavior is regulated by the batterer's estimation of the possible gains, weighed against the possible consequences, of his strategic behavior.

Battering behavior is prevalent across all lines of race, ethnicity, geography, education, social class, religion, and sexual orientation.

Men are responsible for at least 95% of the battering that occurs in the United States.

Men batter because they can and it serves as a means to an end. Our culture encourages, supports, condones, entitles, and expects men to dominate, degrade, and control women.

Battering is chosen behavior and, therefore, other choices can be made. Non-violent and respectful ways of participating in intimate relationships can, at all times, be chosen.

Battering has adverse, long-term psychological, emotional, physical, and economic effects on individual women and women as a group. When the newspaper says, "the nightmare is now over for these poor children" because the batterer is dead or in prison, this couldn't be further from the truth.

Physical violence irreversibly changes the dynamics of a relationship. Comprehension of this dynamic is imperative in the distinction between a "bad" relationship and one where the presence and/or history of violence exists.

Battering is not an addiction or disease. Men who batter are not powerless; battering is not a secondary "symptom" to alcoholism or addiction; intoxication and addiction are, among other things, tools of the batterer; battering and its consequences will not cease or go away just because the batterer gets sober/straight or "works a good drug/alcohol recovery program." Addiction/alcoholism recovery activities and requirements, and anything else he can lay his hands on, are frequently used by the batterer to manipulate, abuse, and control his partner/family.

As I have stated elsewhere, I used to be an "expert" in these things and both trained and critiqued batterer intervention programs and personnel. From what I can tell, there may be one or two programs in America that genuinely do their utmost to keep in mind it is their responsibility to:

1   Serve the interests of battered women and children, not batterers;

2   Hold men strictly accountable for their actions and not cater to their obfuscations;

3   Base their programs on the fact IPV is a political act of intimate and public terrorism perpetrated by men against women;

4   Hold themselves and their own programs to the highest level of public transparency and accountability;

5   Open their doors and solicit monitoring by women survivors/ women's shelters/the feminist community.

One of these programs, from what I can tell from the outside, is the VCS Community Change Project which uses the New York Model for Batterer Programs. Check them out at: http://www.nymbp.org/index.htm.

Delivery of intervention services to batterers in a community is always secondary to the empowerment and safety of women. The highest priority of batterer intervention programs must be to promote women's safety, empowerment and rights.

Batterer intervention programs must create and implement self-monitoring mechanisms that work to minimize batterers' ability to use the program as leverage against the survivors of their battering and/or the community intervention network.

Intervention programs for batterers must not be used as a substitute for arrest, conviction, probation, incarceration, or other legal sanctions. Batterer programs should never, ever, advocate for the interests of batterers in any milieu at any time, especially the criminal justice system.

Any so-called batterer program or person(s) that promote or use any of the following methods or arguments is at best incompetent, but more likely just lazy, sexist, stupid, self-interested, aligned with the batterer and the power structure that enables him, places money over women's safety, is politically-challenged, and should be publically and loudly discredited, resisted, and shamed in all ways possible:

- time-outs
- couples counseling
- anger management
- partner contact
- any kind of "treatment" or "therapy" or "rehabilitation"
- makes claims about the so-called success of their "program" or "model"
- claims batterer programs are better than no programs
- claims variety is the spice of life in batterer intervention, and "everybody can do their own thing" with batterers
- labels their batterer-participants "voluntary" or "involuntary" as there are, in fact, no "voluntary" men in batterer programs
- insists on the confidentiality of the batterers—a social-worky gimmick of entitlement that works against accountability
- advocates in any way for a batterer, particularly to a court, or anyone else on behalf of the perpetrator
- puts women in groups with men
- claims "it takes two to tango" (see the insightful quote by Ann Goetting next page)
- pays any attention whatsoever to "what she did" to supposedly cause/provoke his abuse

I'm sure I've overlooked some important factors; I've been out of this "work" for many years. Suffice to say 999 of the so-called batterer programs out of 1,000 in America have no intelligent idea of what they are doing, and are part of the problem and not part of an accountable solution.

Some of the above clear-thinking is derived from:

Pennsylvania Coalition Against Domestic Violence (PCADV) http://www.pcadv.org/

New York Model for Batterer Programs (http://www.nymbp.org/index.htm)

# Speaking of Women

Had God intended women only as a finer sort of cattle, He would not have made them reasonable. Brutes, a few degrees higher than... monkeys... might have better fitted some men's lust, pride, and pleasure; especially those that desire to keep them ignorant to be tyrannized over.

~ Bathsua Makin
(1612–1674)

... the day will come when men will recognize woman as his peer, not only at the fireside, but in the councils of the nation. Then, and not until then, will there be the perfect comradeship, the ideal union between the sexes that shall result in the highest development of the race.

~ Susan Brownell Anthony
(1820–1906)

Men, after much demur and hesitation, have given women liberty to write; but they cannot yet consent to allow them full freedom. They may flutter out of the cage, but it must be with clipped wings; they may hop about the smooth-shaven lawn, but must, on no account, fly.

~ Mary E. Bryan
(1838–1913)

In entering upon their new life they decided to be governed by no precedential methods. Marriage was to be a form that, while fixing legally their relation to each other, was in no ways to touch the individuality of either; that was to be preserved intact. Each was to remain a free integral of humanity, responsible to no dominating exactness of so-called marriage laws; a union was trust in each other's love, honor, and

# Speaking of Women

courtesy, tempered by the reserving clause of readiness to meet the consequences of reciprocal liberty.

~ Kate Chopin
(1851–1904)

Men renounce whatever they have in common with women so as to experience no commonality with women; and what is left, according to men, is one piece of flesh a few inches long, the penis. The penis is sensate; the penis is the man; the man is human; the penis signifies humanity.

~ Andrea Dworkin
(1946–2005)

What would it be to initiate an affirmative movement? To affirm certain values—not merely in protest and anger, but in almost serene determination because we've spent some time reflecting on things? Our methodology has been reactive—nothing has been affirmative. Is there the possibility of a genuine displacement, realignment, re-territorialization, that would not be so dependent on the very values we abhor? This would have to come from feminine intensity—I don't see where else it would come from. To start thinking about, initiating and instituting a genuine peace, or something, movement—again, we're stuck with words that are Paleolithic. We need a language change, which means, among other things, we have to actively affirm mutation.

~ Avital Ronell
(1952–)

I want my body
but it's never mine
it's only for creating babies
with a man's name on it.

~ Karen Finley
(1956–)

These political passions are born of a hunger so deep that it touches on the spiritual. Or they were for me, and they still are. I want my life to be a battle cry, a war zone, an arrow pointed and loosed into the heart of domination: patriarchy, imperialism, industrialization, every system of power and sadism. If the martial imagery alienates you, I can rephrase it. I want my life—my body—to be the place where the earth is cherished not devoured, where the sadist is granted no quarter, where the violence stops.

~ Lierre Keith
(1964–)

Battering takes two: a man and a patriarchy. Beating is not synonymous with battering, though it can be a part of the battering experience. Battering is an obsessive campaign of coercion and intimidation designed by a man to dominate and control a woman, which occurs in the personal context of intimacy and thrives in the sociopolitical climate of patriarchy. For the woman it is a terrifying process of progressive entrapment into an intimate relationship of subjection that is promoted and preserved by a social order steeped in gender hierarchy—where mainstream ideology and social institutions and organizations, including the criminal justice system, the church, social service and medical institutions, the family, and the community, recognize male privilege and accordingly relegate a secondary status to women. That is what battering is all about: a man using male privilege derived from a patriarchal social structure to coerce a woman, sometimes through fear for her very life, into an exploitive intimate relationship that holds her hostage and in servitude to his personal needs and desires. With the weight of society behind him, a man is able to gain deference, and all that goes with it, from a woman. It becomes clear that battering is control over women that thrives within the larger system of patriarchy; it reflects the patriarchal legacy of male ownership as it persists into romantic relationships, including marriage. Battering is the systematic abuse, by a man, of societally bestowed male privilege to exploit wife or other female intimate companion. Using this definition there can be no battered men: men can be treated unfairly and even brutally by women, but they cannot be battered because to be battered requires a social order antagonistic to one's particular gender.

~ Ann Goetting
(dates unknown)

# from the halls of montezuma to home sweet home

## isolating you makes androputriarchy stronger

There is a certain core of tactics Androputriarchy uses to perpetuate Himself and isolation is one of His favorite, most powerful, and devious instruments.

This isolation occurs at every level of a girl's and woman's life and reaps untold rewards for us men.

The purpose of Androputriarchal isolation is to keep women alone, weak, and vulnerable to predation, which we happily provide.

The bogus boys-only canards constructed to perpetuate isolation are—like all things in Androputriarchy—set up brilliantly for the general welfare of men.

When individual or collective women throw off an oppressive rule/tactic, they are not just objecting to this particular trap. They are, by Androputriarchy's induction, rejecting all of Androputriarchy and His malignant constructions, and therefore putting her treasonous soul at risk of Androputriarchy's mortal condemnation and punishment.

It should come as no surprise—but probably does to most people—even while we men like to puff ourselves up and pretend our national games with other men/nations—utilizing power and control tactics like war, torture, man-datory patriotism, posturing, and **rapism**—are only meaningful in and of themselves, they are merely a front for our borderless and universal agreement we are entitled to the enjoyment of subjugating women and children and we certainly will not let national borders get in our or any other man's or nation's way of that privilege.

While sniffing around the undead carcass of Androputriarchy, I have uncovered a few of His devices of isolation:

There is a **TRANSNATIONAL** covenant between men to fight with other nations over their arbitrarily-concocted versions of misogyny and female bondage as long as all men and nations agree male privilege is an inalienable entitlement of all men, regardless of borders or particular expression.

There is nowhere on Earth where women are not controlled and isolated, nor anywhere on Earth this isolation is safe to be named. Naming women's isolation is potentially punishable by death worldwide.

An example of this would be America's recent invasion of Afghanistan where, on a lark, my government invoked

---

Rapism: "the fundamental ideology and practice of patriarchy, characterized by invasion, violation, degradation, objectification, and destruction of women and nature; the fundamental paradigm of racism, classism, and all other oppressive –isms."

238

the pretense of rescuing Afghan women from their Taliban overlords as a reason to savage that country—as if we cared about Afghan women any more than we care about our "own." But it's always a nice bone to throw to those noisy broads when they make a fuss about war and stuff.

So-called Andropputriarchal "custom" and "tradition" and "folklore" and "myth" and "philosophy" and "dogma" and "institutions" and "rites" and "conventions" and "gospel" and "doctrine" and "theology" and "ideology" (male-made rules for—and enforcement of—male privilege) universally claim women should remain in the home for all sorts of ingenious, insipid, male-serving, and deadly reasons that isolate women. Keeping you "in your home" literally and figuratively keeps you ignorant of what us men are up to outside of the home; keeps you further away from the levers of power; keeps you less in contact with other women— especially those that might make revolution with you; and helps you doubt your abilities and confidence outside of the home were you ever so courageous to venture out.

Isolation is about men controlling the language and the conversation. Controlling the language includes centuries of men carefully tinkering with words/concepts like how "man" is the universal representation for "mankind," and is no accident, ladies. Nor is it benign.

Controlling the conversation is about how women's interests and oppression are invisible in 99.999% of any "serious" public discussion of politics, economics, or anything else. This is the Andropputriarchal Weave of Absence. Women's interests and oppression are invisible on television, radio, internet, in our churches, our hospitals, homes, workplaces, friendships, families, and in our politics. One way that is cleverly enforced is by men whining that men are victims, too, and how we must be "fair" to "everyone."

If you have any doubt about this, bring up women's interests and women's oppression at least once every day in casual conversation. Observe how you are treated.

**NATIONALLY**, men like their alcohol certain ways. They might like it cold or room temperature; watery tasting or as bitter as women's tears; they might drink to go raping or battering, or not drink at all because they have their hand directly on God's penis and know better than anyone God favors abstinence.

Similarly, nations have their unique and rich cultural "traditions" of *ischogyny*, woman-slaughtering, and

ongoing oppression with their own clever little twists. Hey, if you haven't travelled the world and visited those brothels with the saucy 12 year-old half-breed whores that will do anything for $5 USD then you've got to get out more, buddy.

In my country, America, we are a "developed" nation and we isolate women by deriding and assassinating lesbians, primarily so our hetero women will do what they're told. No wait, they do that everywhere. Okay, how about this one: in America we tell women that, if they want to get a man, they have to acquire "perfect" bodies and wear tight fitting clothes and shave their pubic hair so they look "good" (whatever that means) in a g-string bikini. If you don't, you are a lesbian and will die an old maid.

In other countries women are isolated by being told they have to wear burqa's that cover their bodies from the soles of their God-forsaken feet to the hair on their slutty heads. This is a great tradition that isolates them from just about everybody, but certainly from anybody who might help them escape their particular Andropputriarchal nightmare.

We men also make up all sorts of purposefully inane rules about what makes women in America—like all other countries—desirable. Note it is the very inanity and arbitrariness of the rules that make them so powerful and debilitating—to women. Yet another fun activity women are isolated from is the making up of these rules, and the rules are unpredictable and/or unattainable, hence making all women stupid losers, yet isolating them more. Are you beginning to see a pattern here?

Isolating women by controlling the conversation is evident when 1,000 times more women know what "NASCAR" is than what the "E.R.A." was. Men's control of the conversation is evident when ejaculation is jealously enfranchised

---

Ischogyny: [*ischo*, meaning suppression or restraint; *gyny*, meaning women] the series of interlocking self-created and self-serving myths held, and behaviors, tactics, and actions taken by men/Andropputriarchy, that enhance male bonding and male exaltation at the expense of women; the oppression of women. A replacement for "misogyny" which incorrectly concludes oppression of women is based on "hatred" of women, which it is not; so-called hatred is an incidental weapon.

by Androputriarchal religions and the point of all pornography; while menstruation, the necessary and sacred flow of life, is shameful, disgusting, isolated, and forbidden to speak of.

In America women are restricted to make, in their lifetime, $0.76 for every dollar a similarly-qualified man does; women are subject to sexual harassment and rape in the work place; women are not allowed combat roles in our military which then cuts off their ability to ascend to leadership positions. Poverty rates are higher for women than men in all racial and ethnic groups. Women are segregated into low-paying occupations, and occupations dominated by women are the lowest paid; women spend more time providing unpaid care-giving than men; eight in ten custodial parents are women; custodial mothers are twice as likely to be poor as custodial fathers; domestic violence is a primary cause of homelessness for women; and these truths are abject proof of Androputriarchy's deliberate and successful use of isolation.

Now we move to the **REGIONAL** level where, for example, you might be more likely to be butchered in Iowa for being identified as a lesbian, for being a white woman married to a black man in Mississippi, or for being a prostituted woman in Grand Rapids, Michigan. Aren't local customs quaint? All countries have regions where their ischogyny is expressed with colorful mischief.

When we start looking at the **NEIGHBORHOOD** level of isolation, we see how the single most dangerous place for women comes into play: the home. "What are you doing talking to the neighbor, you cheaten' bitch? If I catch you doing that again, I cut off your tits!" That sort of fun, isolating stuff.

> **Mistermanaged:** a replacement for "mismanaged" that reveals the completely volitional man-ner in which men purposefully and intentionally rig things for our own purposes and goals. For example, anger Mistermanagement: how men carefully use anger as a weapon and then cover it up as if it were unintentional or beyond our control.

Home is where the King is in His castle, and it's like a nation in miniature—this man controls His woman this way while across the street that man controls His woman that way. The two men might fight over the exact location of the property line between their homes but neither is going to get up from watching Law and Order: Special Victims Unit on the new 70" LED-backlit LCD television to interfere with the guy next door who is hammering His old lady. Hey, this is America godammit.

And, as always, the best payoff (besides the raping) is when we have taught you women to oppress **YOURSELVES**—AND YOU DO IT! This is where the isolating really pays off. The complete colonization of women's minds with our wretched poison. Women not trusting other women. Women fighting other women over men; over money; over employment; over religion; over anything.

Isolating women by telling them they are whores, and then blaming them when they aren't whores as we enjoy our pornography because they won't put out like the woman in the magazine. Convincing women the problem is THEM and they would be stupid to reveal their stupidity to anyone else. It doesn't get any better than this, fellas.

Women are afraid to leave their homes for fear of assault: so they stay home; afraid to go to work for fear of assault; go to "that" part of town for fear of assault; travel to this city or country for fear of assault; wear these clothes for fear of assault; object to how they are being spoken to for fear of assault; go anywhere at night for fear of assault; say "NO!" to their husbands for fear of assault; speak up for their rights the world over for fear of assault. This is abject proof of Androputriarchy's deliberate and successful use of isolation.

When I, as an individual man or as a representative of Parasitic Androputriarchy, destroy what you value and destroy what you are attached to and destroy your social connections, I make your world smaller, I make your desires and attachments painful, I make your self-reliance and self-acceptance atrophy. That, in turn, makes what I say important. It makes my values THE values.

Isolation is but one of the daily working tools of men, batterers, and **Mistermanaged** Androputriarchy.

240

# Speaking of Women

Few, save the poor, feel for the poor.
> ~ Letitia Landon
> (1802–1838)

I have been into many of the ancient cathedrals—grand, wonderful, mysterious. But I always leave them with a feeling of indignation because of the generations of human beings who have struggled in poverty to build these altars to the unknown god.
> ~ Elizabeth Cady Stanton
> (1815–1902)

Nagging is the repetition of unpalatable truths.
> ~ Baroness Edith Clara Summerskill
> (1901–1980)

The argument between wives and whores is an old one; each one thinking that whatever she is, at least she is not the other.
> ~ Andrea Dworkin
> (1946–2005)

The genius of any slave system is found in the dynamics which isolate slaves from each other, obscure the reality of a common condition, and make united rebellion against the oppressor inconceivable.
> ~ Andrea Dworkin
> (1946–2005)

An inheritance isn't something you simply ignore—it's part of you, part of the transmission system. But you have to negotiate with it and recognize its history—where it comes from, what it imposes on you, what kind of a frame it traps you into.
> ~ Avital Ronell
> (1952–)

Does giving birth make me a real woman? No, earning less than a man makes me a real woman.
> ~ Suzy Berger
> (dates unknown)

# taking everything personally

How do you dare to tell me that I'm my Father's son when that was just an accident of birth?
~ "Wind Up" by Ian Anderson

When I was 12 years old I was ordered to stay home one Saturday and help Mr. Gill work on his car's muffler in my dad's garage. After a couple of hours lying under his car, Mr. Gill was muttering to himself about how he was having difficulty getting something loose.

I jokingly said, "My dad would swear at it and throw tools to get it off." Mr. Gill politely replied, "That doesn't help fix a car."

For a few minutes, I thought about what Mr. Gill said. I could do that because Mr. Gill wasn't throwing tools, unlike my dad, and so the whole morning had been pretty boring. It didn't take me long to figure out what this meant: Mr. Gill obviously didn't know how to fix cars.

So goes the brain of an adolescent boy steeped in the sewage of one of the lesser Gods of Androputriarchy.

I grew up—no, scratch that—I became larger in a prototypical 1950's white, lower-middle class hetro family. Mom submissive, Dad a raging racist, terrifying abuser, and us four kids trying to survive in a constant ether of fear.

**Prepetrator:** a precedent for "perpetrator" and a replacement for "forefathers" this word describes the generations of men who established the social environment that now entitles and enables your male perpetrator to abuse you.

My dad liked to tell the story over and over of my **prepetrator**—his father—and how my grandfather threw him down the basement stairs for some minor infraction. This was meant to demonstrate how more lenient my father was with us and we should be thankful.

He liked to lecture me and my brother with his manly exploits as an adolescent—how he was a star athlete; had the most beautiful girls in high school on his arm; how he and his buddies would go out and beat up niggers and homos. An All-American boy.

Needless to say I was a huge disappointment to my father.

My brother and I were supposed to be quarterbacks on the football team, the ladies' men, and come home with a bloody nose because we got in a fight with some guy and set him straight. We fell a tad short of those expectations. In fact, my brother and I were basically sissies. Not even the boxing gloves my dad bought us for Christmas, or the staged fights he put us through, did any good. We didn't have the right stuff.

Talk about the wrong stuff: my brother ended up being a nurse and I ended up being a social worker. We might as well have been homos! He probably never grasped how he was the key factor in our career choices. Here I was, years after escaping my batterer, a social worker in a batterer accountability program. Thanks for the thoughtful preparation, Dad.

We had other charming, unique ways of doing things in my household. Like when my dad cut my mom's elbow open by throwing her through a glass storm door and she was shooting blood all over the place. My dad did what I assumed all families did: he called up his drunk dentist-friend Roger to come over and stitch her up. And stitch her up he did. It's great to have a dentist as a friend.

I share these heartwarming stories to ponder various mysteries: why didn't I pick up my father's calloused fists and carry on the tradition? What was it about me that I just couldn't be cruel like him? How did I somehow set the feminist, activist course my life has taken? Where did this book come from? Do we leave boys with only two choices: decide they will never be the loathsome beast their father is and do what it takes to not be abusive, or decide I will never be on the receiving end of abuse ever again and be the controller dishing it out?

I am 57 years old now and still can't say for sure, but I do think two factors are key: one, I was cursed/blessed to always identify with the victim/underdog and, two, I sought out and maintained close relationships with strong women.

I was married the first time for 28 years. Obviously this person meant a lot to me and we had many experiences over that time. But when I think about my developing accountability as a man, I remember two key events.

Shortly after I met my wife we were traveling somewhere and as she was driving, I "jokingly" threatened to throw a barrette of hers out of the window of the car. She let me know in no uncertain terms this was not a joke, it was the type of thing her former battering boyfriend used to do, and I was not to ever do it again.

The second event came about seven years later when we were again traveling home and she said something I didn't like and I yelled "SHUT UP!" at her. She turned and screamed "NO!" even louder than I had yelled. Her response scared me. This was the first and last time I ever said "shut up" to another human being.

Both of these situations frightened and shocked me and had a lifelong impact. She was absolutely right to

put me in my place on both occasions, and I am thankful she did. What I did in both cases was abusive, controlling, manipulative, and unacceptable. There is no doubt in both situations I was "fishing" to see what I could get away with and her overwhelming response were critical and enduring lessons for me.

I have also been in psychotherapy on at least a half dozen occasions in my life in an attempt to undo some of my father's damage. It has been very helpful generally. I regret none of those therapists grasped what domestic violence is or what its effects are, nor did they have a feminist analysis of the world that showed up in their work. They failed me in that way.

I found I spent as much time in therapy attempting to grasp my relationship with my siblings as I did with my parents. Aside from my father/tyrant, work was king in my family. You got credit as a human being based on how hard you worked. The dynamics of survival in my family led to us four kids being a tight pack; like a military unit. The chain of command was top-down (I was youngest) and you followed orders and demonstrated loyalty. It kept us as safe as we could be. Of course, all of this had implications for my adult life, which I continue to sort out today.

Then there are the larger issues of Androputriarchy altogether: how my father was its messenger, servant, and beneficiary, and the huge amount of time and energy it has required of me to see my father's, and my family's, smaller part in preparing me to be an obedient foot soldier of male privilege.

Just because I have been saturated in Androputriarchy like all other men doesn't necessarily mean my perspectives are representative enough to generalize out to my brethren. However, I have made most of my life's work a study of this subject and I do think it is likely that what I find operating in murky places in my brain is likely happening elsewhere in men. My struggles to figure out who I am, who I want to be, and how I want behave in the world has led me to writing this book. It has also had other results and revelations, which I share below.

## Targets

The "boys will be boys" practice of men, individually and collectively, leering and catcalling at women is a time-honored Androputriarchal ritual. It spans from "hubba hubba" to "you must wear a burqa so I am not tempted to rape you." I want to offer my perspective on the predatory nature of this behavior.

I was driving home from work through a small, rural town. As I drove by a combination car wash and laundromat I saw out of the corner of my eye a woman entering the door. I want to share what happened in the next instant in my brain. I instantly recognized many things in this scene: there was only one car there; the woman was alone; this is an isolated place; there is no one else around; I am much bigger than she is; I could control her; from her clothes and the fact she was at a laundromat she looked "lower class"—someone who is economically vulnerable. I could probably attack her and be "successful."

Now, why on earth would I be thinking all of these things? Why would I, Mr. Feminist Nice-Guy, be thinking these things? I have been trained, like all other men, in the foul, predatory sewage of Androputriarchy where men are predators and women are prey. I don't like it that my mind would instantly begin to survey a situation in this manner, but it does. I don't like it that I have some sort of post-traumatic stress disorder and have a hard time turning off intrusive visions of torture being inflicted by men.

This is the training I received as a boy/man and something I want to understand and be revealed—accountability is the best disinfectant. I want women to know we are trained to predate you, and it takes considerable ongoing effort not to do so.

## Necrophilia

Mary Daly, my shero, defines necrophilia thus:

> Necrophilia: the most fundamental characteristic and first principle of patriarchy: hatred for and envy of Life; the universal message of all patriarchal religion: death worship. Patriarchy is the prevailing religion of the entire planet, whose essential message is necrophilia.

I couldn't agree more.

This is another aspect of my, and men's, deeply ingrained personality I have to fight constantly. I see it first and foremost in my so-called "humor." My humor is all about death, destruction, injury, pain, mishap, emotional detachment, and victimization.

Most men find me endlessly hilarious; most women find my humor adolescent and obnoxious. I am inclined, like most men, to "show off" and brag about my destructive willingness and detachment.

For example, I like to joke about how, when our cat dies, I am going to make a purse out of his "pelt." Now this might possibly be funny once—if that. But when said over and over is just obnoxious and immature. This is my male-dumb showing: it's about showing how detached and brave and strong I am. It is sick and necrophilic.

But so-called "humor" is merely one place necrophilia is expressed in my life, and the lives of men. Because I/we were trained in this doesn't give us any excuse for worshipping it and continually expressing it.

## The fellas

When I think about how absolutely rudderless I was as a teen and young man, and how desperate I was to have meaningful relationships with men and be part of a "team," it is amazing I am not in prison or a cult.

I have sought out and had many male friends and mentors over the years. I have also had some of these men attempt to predate me for sexual or other interests. I'm not really sure how I protected myself, but I did.

My father threw tools; he didn't instruct me how to use them. My father had almost no interest in my life, and knew nothing about me. He didn't teach me anything other than to obey him. So I had to learn things on my own. Oddly enough, I spent a lot of time by myself in his garage teaching myself how to use his tools. I think I was very hungry for male mentorship at a young age, but never found it—at least not from men.

Fast forward to the mid-1980's when I had just completed graduate school and began my career as a social worker. I was invited to join a "men's group" which was quite the rage at that time. Join I did and I was a member of this group for 11 years. We met roughly once per month to talk, do sweat lodges, ceremonies, and other adventures. I really loved my men's group and enjoyed my time with these men, most of whom were social workers and half of whom were gay. I especially loved the physical affection I could share with the gay men.

The problem began in my ninth year with the group. At that point I was in my fifth year as a facilitator of the batterer accountability program, and my brain chemistry was changing due to that work. One day it occurred to me, if I was going to be true to my ideals of male accountability like I professed every day in my work, then I had to be consistent everywhere—including my men's group. That was the beginning of the end.

I began to talk about male privilege and entitlement in the group, and was vigorously scolded for bringing up the subject. I confronted the group about how two members had acknowledged, in our meetings, assaulting their female partners but none of us told them to report themselves to the police or get into a batterer accountability program. More scolding.

I reluctantly began to see this group of men was no different than any group of men—they protected their male privilege with the same vigor as batterers in my workplace. I was crestfallen—though I shouldn't have been. This was all about me wanting with all of my heart for this group of men to be different—to be the accountable men I've always wanted to know and be safe with. But they wanted nothing to do with the subject of male privilege and male accountability, and effectively silenced me. I made a commitment to myself to do everything I could to demand discussion of these issues, even though I knew it wouldn't happen.

Two years after I began this effort I left the men's group. The final straw, which the group thought was absolutely hilarious, was when I told them I couldn't stay in the men's group unless women were included as members and we would talk openly in front of them about our male privilege. Suffice to say that that was my last day in the men's group after 11 years with them.

### Princess Sheeping Beauty

Plenty of women have thought and written on the topic how Androputriarchy controls the subject of "beauty" and how women are subject to His tyrannical dictates.

My contribution to the subject is comprehending how one of the benefits of the myriad and ever-changing "beauty" demands from Androputriarchy allows men to be stupid, lazy, disrespectful, and arrogant about beauty.

That is, "beauty" is defined by the brotherhood of any given culture and the individual men in that culture need only lift only one brain cell to "measure their women" by it. You are supposed to look like X to be beautiful; you don't, so you aren't beautiful. I am entitled to go out and purchase or otherwise acquire a woman who is X. Oh, and you're an ugly pig.

This is an ingenious ploy so us men don't have to grow up and learn to develop a respect, reverence, and honor of women's beauty as it is in reality, and how it changes over time and circumstances.

Could it be women's beauty is not just about their appearance? Could it be I am responsible, as a maturing and intelligent man, to adapt my mind and appreciation to all the ways a woman is beautiful? Could it be my love for my life-partner's beauty becomes deeper and more profound as I age and reveals my own maturation and wisdom as a human being?

Number of public statues of individuals in the United States: 5,193
Number that depict women: 394, or 7.5%.
~ Harper's Index July, 2011

# Speaking of Women

...since the excessive tyranny of men prevails over divine right and natural laws, the freedom that was once accorded to women is in our day obstructed by unjust laws, suppressed by custom and usage, reduced to nothing. And so these laws compel women to submit to men, as conquered before conquerors, and that without reason or necessity natural or divine, but under pressure of customs, education, chance, or some occasion favourable to tyranny.

~ Heinrich Cornelius Agrippa von Nettesheim
(1486–1535)

I am a feminist because I dislike everything that feminism implies. I desire an end to the whole business, the demands for equality, the suggestion of sex warfare, the very name feminist. I want to be about the work in which my real interests lie, the writing of novels and so forth. But while inequality exists, while injustice is done and opportunity denied to the great majority of women, I shall have to be a feminist. And I shan't be happy till I get... a society in which there is no distinction of persons either male or female, but a supreme regard for the importance of the human being. And when that dream is a reality, I will say farewell to feminism, as to any disbanded but victorious army, with honour for its heroes, gratitude for its sacrifice, and profound relief that the hour for its necessity has passed.

~ Winifred Holtby
(1898–1935)

The Black female is assaulted in her tender years by all those common forces of nature at the same time she is caught in the tripartite crossfire of masculine prejudice, white illogical hate and Black lack of power. The fact that the adult American Negro female emerges a formidable character is often met with amazement, distaste and even belligerence. It is seldom accepted as an inevitable outcome of the struggle won by survivors and deserves respect if not enthusiastic admiration.

~ Maya Angelou
(1928–)

Thus far, our responsibility for how we treat chickens and allow them to be treated in our culture is dismissed with blistering rhetoric designed to silence objection: "How the hell can you compare the feelings of a hen with those of a human being?" One answer is, by looking at her. It does not take special insight or credentials to see that a hen confined in a battery cage is suffering, or to imagine what her feelings must be compared with those of a hen ranging outside in the grass and sunlight. We are told that we humans are capable of knowing just about anything that we want to know—except, ironically, what it feels like to be one of our victims. We are told we are being "emotional" if we care about a chicken and grieve over a chicken's plight. However, it is not "emotion" that is really under attack, but the vicarious emotions of pity, sympathy, compassion, sorrow, and indignity on behalf of the victim, a fellow creature—emotions that undermine business as usual. By contrast, such "manly" emotions as patriotism, pride, conquest, and mastery are encouraged.

~ Karen Davis
(1944–)

Feminism hasn't failed, it's just never been tried.

~ Hilary Mantel
(1952–)

Insofar as men gain time, ease, independence, or liberty from women's domestic labors, they lack incentive to change. Society will not crumble if men take a turn at the dishes.

~ Linda P. Rouse
(dates unknown)

It's hard not to be a fighter when you're constantly under siege.

~ Cassandra Duffy
(dates unknown)

GIFT BUTTON IDEAS FOR DADS, BROTHERS, HUSBANDS, SONS, UNCLES, YOU NAME IT

**GUNS**  **FOR TOTS!**

**ANGER MANAGEMENT**  **FOR MEN**

**YOU DON'T HAVE TO BE A FEMINIST**  **TO HATE PATRIARCHY**

**ASHAMED TO BE A MAN UNDER VILE PATRIARCHY**

**PIMP**  **THE WORLD'S OLDEST, OLDEST PROFESSION**

**THE PERFECTLY MANGINEERED WOMAN**

**MEN CAN STOP RAPE**

DOES THIS ORDER OF FRIES **OILOERS** MAKE MY DICK LOOK FAT?

**We Can Do It!**  **Think of Male Privilege and Sexism as Filthy Toilets.**

**FEMINISM** **Accept no imitations**

**Daddy's Little Feminist**

**FEMINISM** **Until the men grow up**

©2014 Michael Elizabeth Marillynson LLC - This poster is from the book "Contrary to the Custom of Men: Field Notes on the Pestilence of Patriarchy from a Disloyal Son." For re-printing permission go to: con2men.info. Images courtesy of Wikimedia Commons: desiree esposito; jacqueline godany; nasa; scott bauer; usla

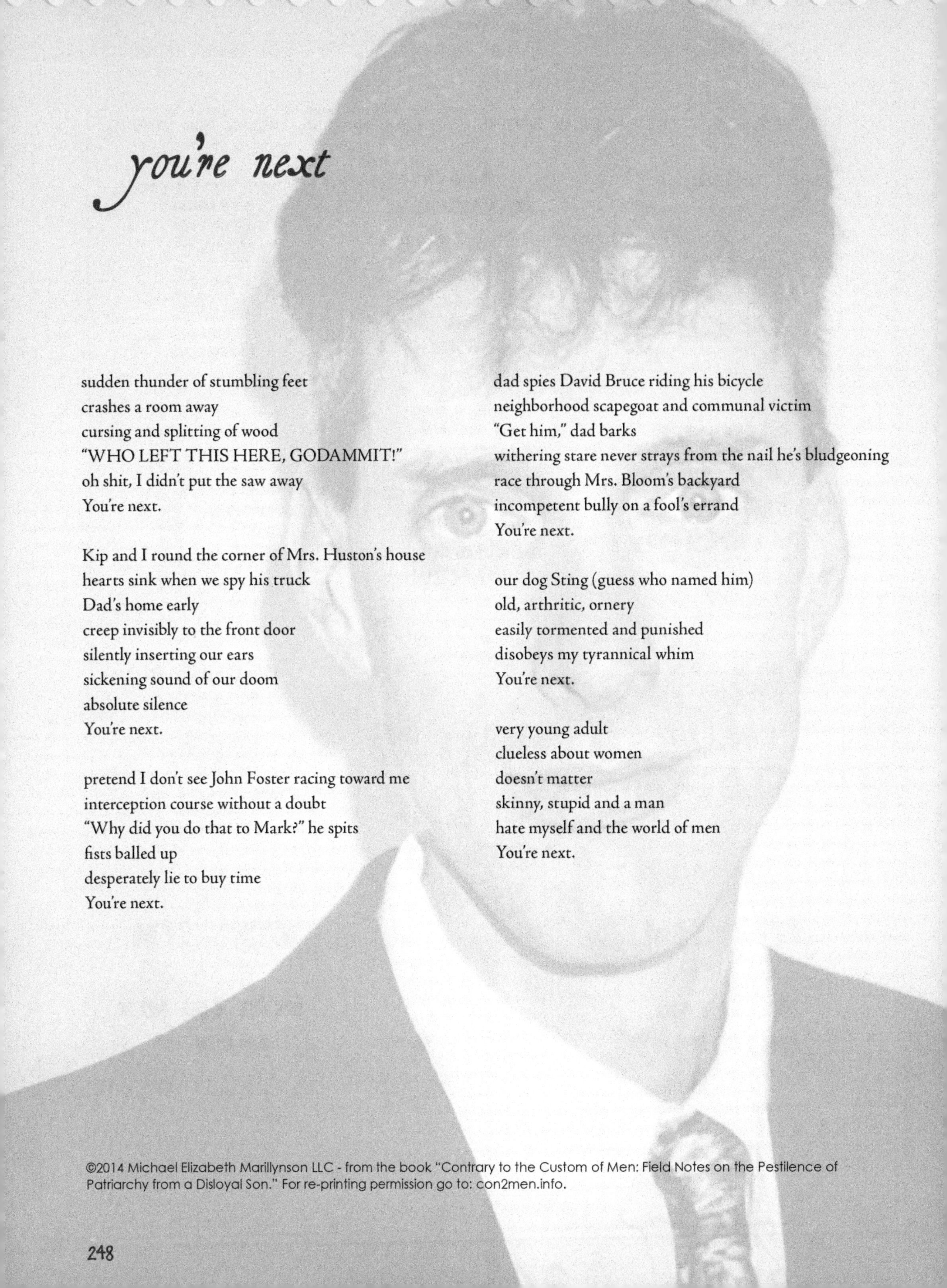

# you're next

sudden thunder of stumbling feet
crashes a room away
cursing and splitting of wood
"WHO LEFT THIS HERE, GODAMMIT!"
oh shit, I didn't put the saw away
You're next.

Kip and I round the corner of Mrs. Huston's house
hearts sink when we spy his truck
Dad's home early
creep invisibly to the front door
silently inserting our ears
sickening sound of our doom
absolute silence
You're next.

pretend I don't see John Foster racing toward me
interception course without a doubt
"Why did you do that to Mark?" he spits
fists balled up
desperately lie to buy time
You're next.

dad spies David Bruce riding his bicycle
neighborhood scapegoat and communal victim
"Get him," dad barks
withering stare never strays from the nail he's bludgeoning
race through Mrs. Bloom's backyard
incompetent bully on a fool's errand
You're next.

our dog Sting (guess who named him)
old, arthritic, ornery
easily tormented and punished
disobeys my tyrannical whim
You're next.

very young adult
clueless about women
doesn't matter
skinny, stupid and a man
hate myself and the world of men
You're next.

©2014 Michael Elizabeth Marillynson LLC - from the book "Contrary to the Custom of Men: Field Notes on the Pestilence of Patriarchy from a Disloyal Son." For re-printing permission go to: con2men.info.

# are all clouds tornadoes?

## am i saying all men are batterers?

I did much public speaking in my short-lived career (20 years) as a social worker. I was a favored presenter because I talked about our "interventions" with domestic violence perpetrators, which is a very salacious subject to the public.

If I had stood up in front of a gathering of 100 social workers and psychologists and said when warm air saturated with humidity meets an oncoming cold front tornadoes are possible, would it be reasonable to be angrily asked if I am saying all clouds are tornadoes?

If I had stood up in front of a gathering of 100 social workers and psychologists and said men have a nearly 50 percent chance of developing cancer in their lifetimes, would it be reasonable to be angrily asked if I am saying all men will get cancer?

If I stand up in front of a gathering of 100 social workers and psychologists and say 95% of batterers are men, and we have not yet gathered, to our absolute shame, the statistics to know what percentage of men will batter, would it be reasonable to angrily ask me if I am saying all men are batterers?

Yet this question: "So, are you saying all men are batterers?" was asked endlessly—and angrily—of me.

I never once in all of that time said all men are batterers. So why would so many learned professionals be complacent about clouds and cancer, yet want to pointedly challenge me with this accusation sloppily dressed as a question?

Why indeed.

What could be the reason to be asked such a question so often?

I suppose it could be asked by a person who just wasn't listening, or was listening selectively and wanted me to give a quick-and-dirty factoid.

It could be asked by a woman who desperately wants me to say "No." to reassure her it is possible to find a male partner who won't harm her. Or she could fear it might actually be the case all men are batterers—which very likely could be consistent with her personal experience.

It is most likely asked by men or women who want to discredit me (or anyone with a factual message about Androputriarchy and men) to get me and those like me to shut up. It is most likely asked by someone who wants to bait me into looking ridiculous for challenging men and male privilege, or to condemn me as an "extremist," or to get me on the defensive and back off. Silence the messenger.

And this reveals how Androputriarchy so subtly and effectively works—through intimidation, coercion, ridicule, and silencing through public pressure. This "questioning" is designed to, and results in, all of us doubting ourselves and fearing to speak truthfully about what we see and know to be true.

Now for my answer to this question.

For a number of years I made public presentations with a man who was court-ordered to the batterer intervention program I co-directed. He openly stated the woman he assaulted to get himself sent to our program was probably the 35th woman he had assaulted in his life. He was one of the few men I ever met in that program who took his own accountability, and all men's, seriously.

He would say, in public presentations, "All men are batterers until proven otherwise." This is not a statement which can be factually true or false, yet I wholeheartedly agree with him nonetheless. I also believe all snakes are poisonous until proven otherwise, and even though all electrical outlets may not be packing electricity, I won't shove a metal fork in one on the off-chance it isn't.

As to the question I am asked about batterers/men, as usual, the question reveals much more about the questioner than it does about the questioned.

# Speaking of Women

The custom of widow-burning (suttee) in India, the Chinese ritual of footbinding, the genital mutilation of young girls in Africa (still practiced in parts of 26 countries of Africa), the massacre of women as witches in Renaissance Europe, gynocide under the guise of American gynecology and psychotherapy—all are documented facts accessible to the tomes and tombs (libraries) of patriarchal scholarship. The contemporary facts of brutal gang rape, of wife beating, both overt and subliminal psychic lobotomizing—all are available. What then can the label anti-male possibly mean when applied to works that expose these facts and invite women to free our Selves? The fact is that the labelers do not intend to convey a rational meaning, nor to elicit a thinking process, but rather to block thinking. They do intend the label to carry a deep emotive message, triggering implanted fears of all the fathers and sons, freezing our minds. For to write an anti-male book is to utter the ultimate blasphemy. Thus women continue to be intimidated by the label anti-male. The courage to be logical—the courage to name—would require that we admit to ourselves that males and males only are the originators, planners, controllers, and legitimators of patriarchy. Patriarchy is the homeland of males; it is Father Land; and men are its agents. This deception/reversal is so deep that women—even feminists—are intimidated into self-deception, becoming the only self-described oppressed who are unable to name their own oppressor, referring instead to vague "forces," "roles," "stereotypes," "constraints," "attitudes," "influences." The point is that no agent is named—only abstractions.

~ Mary Daly
(1928–2010)

By placing human need above other social and political requirements and human life above property, profit, and even individual rights, female consciousness creates the vision of a society that has not yet appeared.

~ Temma E. Kaplan
(1942–)

Because gender is not really natural it requires constant enforcement and repetition.

~ Martha McCaughey
(1966–)

At the core of patriarchy, ideologically fundamental to the nation-state, is the belief that one builds a "self"—becomes more fully human—through competition and acquisition, a creed that culminates in standing armies, colonial expansion, and ridiculously large buildings that tower over slums, a creed which is nothing more, at bottom, than materialism itself.

~ Carol Flinders
(1970–)

A violent act pierces the atmosphere, leaving a hole through which the cold, damp draft of its memory blows forever.

~ Jane Stanton Hitchcock
(dates unknown)

## does resisting male privilege make you a feminist?

*all women are: brave! strong! beautiful!* *

**Feminist:** a woman (and maybe one or two men?) who, by thought or deed, resists the Androputriarchal scourge in solidarity with women.

I agree with Mary Daly, Andrea Dworkin, and other furies who astutely clarify Androputriarchy is "the prevailing religion of the entire planet, whose essential message is **necrophilia…**" and "characterized by invasion, violation, degradation, objectification, and destruction of women and nature."

With a nod to the much sought-after unified field theory in physics which would explain all fundamental forces and elementary particles in terms of a single field: patriarchy as we know and suffer under it on Earth is the unifying theory of all human oppressions.

Just as there is a "food chain" in the oceans where one organism feeds on another and is then eaten by another, no matter an organism's status in that chain, all oceanic life forms are subject to the properties of water—without exception.

Similarly, all women and girls are subject to, and oppressed by, Androputriarchy. Many girls and women are, indeed, destroyed outright by Him. Even those women at the apex of **Androconditional privilege** are subject to His whims.

To survive, all girls and women must find their own way to resist Androputriarchy's capricious and crushing intent. Given my definition of "feminist," all girls and women are feminists, as all are humans engaged in some form or resistance.

I remember participating in a "panel" presentation with two women in a college psychology class where the "resistance" light bulb switched on for me. We were there to talk

about the abuse we suffered as children from our fathers. After the three of us had given brief talks, the students began asking questions, making comments, and sharing aspects of their own childhoods.

One student talked about some awful things done to her and how she had been very assertive, even aggressive, in resisting her father's battering. As I was listening to her I felt ashamed about what a total wimp I was regarding my father-tormenter, whom I had never openly challenged in my life—even as an adult. As I sat there I thought, "How am I going to be able to respond to what this woman is saying when I was just a total wuss all of the time and never resisted my father? I'm supposed to be a role model!"

**Necrophilia:** [*necro* meaning the dead, corpse, dead tissue; philia meaning unnatural attraction, tendency]: "the most fundamental characteristic and first principle of patriarchy: hatred for and envy of Life; the universal message of all patriarchal religion: death worship."

**Androconditional privilege:** some of the benefits of male privilege, entitlement, and oppression being conditionally extended by Androputriarchy and/or His agents to those who do not normally qualify: that is, women. For instance, a white, heterosexual woman who enjoys much affluence and power due to her marriage to a wealthy white, heterosexual male who will lose those conditional privileges upon being discarded by him.

---

*  Poster title by Anke Feuchtenberger ~ (http://collections.vam.ac.uk/item/O191043/all-women-are-courageous-strong-poster-feuchtenberger-anke/). Also, please see "If I weren't a cunt" by Ms. Feuchtenberger from the Winter 1996 issue of On The Issues Magazine ~ (http://www.ontheissuesmagazine.com/pdfs/1996Winter_vol5.pdf)

All-of-a-sudden I had the moment of clarity and realization: I did resist my father—just in my way! The woman who was talking was just like my oldest sister—assertive, aggressive, and didn't take shit from anybody. But that was not me: I was just the opposite. I learned to survive my own way, right or wrong, and resist I did. My resistance took a passive, invisible approach. When possible I would show no emotion while my father abused or threatened me. This worked sometimes because my father's sadism was fueled by demonstrations of fear or begging. I was also very good at just not being noticed or quietly slipping away from conflict.

This was an invaluable lesson in my life—to understand my way of resisting tyranny was just as valid as anyone's; there is resistance going on all around me, and I could appreciate and respect everybody's way of resisting.

Resisting male privilege makes you a feminist by the mere fact of the resistance imperative for any woman or girl to survive under Androputriarchy. Hence, all women are feminists: whether they like it or not; whether it is safe to say so or not.

The F-word (feminist) can cost you a fortune, if not your life, so it is a brave woman who proclaims it publicly. This is one type of resistance. Of course, just because women don't publically proclaim themselves feminist doesn't mean they aren't. They may embrace their feminism in a quieter way.

I would make the distinction between what is actually resistance to Androputriarchy, and what could be confused as such: dissatisfaction with one's relative entitlement and privilege under Androputriarchy. My experience is women are being described in the first instance, and men in the latter.

# Speaking of Women

Because the revolutionary tempest, in overturning at the same time for the throne and the scaffold, in breaking the chain of the black slave, forgot to break the chain of the most oppressed of all—of Women, the pariah of humanity.

~ Jeanne-Francoise Deroine
(1805–1894)

Men's hearts are cold. They are indifferent. The militant, not the meek, shall inherit the earth.

~ Mother Jones
(1830–1930)

Be militant in your own way! Those of you who can break windows, break them. Those of you who can still further attack the secret idol of property... do so. And my last word is to the Government: I incite this meeting to rebellion. Take me if you dare!

~ Emmeline Pankhurst
(1858–1928)

At the ballot-box is not where the shoe pinches… It is at home where the husband… is the supreme ruler, that the little difficulty arises; he will not surrender this absolute power unless he is compelled.

~ Tennessee Claflin
(1845–1923)

Women are all female impersonators to some degree.

~ Susan Brownmiller
(1935–)

Heterosexuality, marriage and motherhood, which are the institutions which most obviously and individually maintain female accessibility to males, form the core triad of antifeminist ideology; and all-woman spaces, all-woman organizations, all-woman meetings, all-woman classes, are outlawed, suppressed, harassed, ridiculed and punished.

~ Marilyn Frye
(1941–)

Courage is relaxed by delay.

~ Aldrude
(fl. 1170s)

# This is your brain.

## This is your brain on Patriarchy.

## Any questions?

©2014 Michael Elizabeth Marillynson LLC - This poster is from the book "Contrary to the Custom of Men: Field Notes on the Pestilence of Patriarchy from a Disloyal Son." For re-printing permission go to: con2men.info. Images courtesy of Wikimedia Commons: alan denney; rawa (http://rawa.org)

# am i a man hater?

### aren't you?

A United States Marine returns home from war wondering how he will adjust to civilian life. He has been involved in bloody doings, some "legitimate" in his mind and others unquestionably wrong and immoral. He has seen other soldiers do things he wishes now he had tried to put a stop to.

His decision is to forget about what happened, put it behind him, and move on with his life.

The response from his adoring and patriotic family, community, and nation? He is a stoic hero due all of the respect, benefits, and honor veterans "deserve."

Another United States Marine returns home from war wondering how he will adjust to civilian life. He has been involved in bloody doings, some "legitimate" in his mind and others unquestionably wrong and immoral. He has seen other soldiers do things he wishes now he had tried to put a stop to.

His decision after much soul-searching is to publically acknowledge the atrocities he and his fellow soldiers perpetrated on innocent human beings. He makes public statements because he thinks being personally accountable for what he did, and what he saw others doing, is necessary for his own life and for some sort of justice to be served.

The response from his adoring and patriotic family, community, and nation? He is shamed and ridiculed. He is threatened with violence. He is called a liar. He is publically berated for harming all soldiers by being truthful and personally accountable. He is derided for "aiding the enemy." He is asked why he "hates the troops; hates freedom; hates our way of life; hates America."

As is obvious, the response from the so-called patriots to a soldiers' heartfelt reflections tells you much more about the hecklers than they wish to be aware of.

Of course, these are not questions at all, but accusations, derision, and threats meant to shut the man up.

In my corner of the world, I have many times been asked if I am a "man hater." Big surprise, eh?

I have been asked or accused of this when I speak publically about what I see in Androputriarchy. I am called a man-hater when I speak openly about the staggering violence, degradation and oppression perpetrated against women, children, animals, and nature worldwide by men on a daily and millennial basis.

What holds the more valuable revelation in this so-called question: my response to it or the reason it is being asked?

What answer would the "asker" prefer? What answer makes it easier for the questioner to disregard everything I have to say? What answer gives him more fuel to burn me with?

What answer might I give which helps or hinders the asker's commitment to stop men's violence and advocate for women's rights?

I was taught over time the important part of listening to such "questions" is the tone of the questioner, not necessarily the question. The "you stupid idiot" tone of the questioner. The status quo preservation tone of the questioner. The abusive attack tone of the questioner. The holier-than-thou tone of the questioner. The shut-the-fuck-up-or-else tone of the questioner.

The bottom line in Androputriarchy is always "shut up or else." This is where the so-called man-hater "question" comes from.

Oddly enough, I've come to see all people are man-haters. We all hate men to some degree and to some awareness, and for every good reason. Men have given us ample reason to hate and revile men and manhood. It is amazing to see the ways we silently twist our lives around the constant menace of men, like the well-trodden path around a coiled snake. It is easier, and much safer, to displace this burden onto women. In fact, it has been turned into a sport and religious imperative.

We dare not utter this truth. We have been so well indoctrinated into Androputriarchy and the worship of men it would be reckless to acknowledge man-hating. But there are the little things that happen every day that demonstrate how our fear, loathing, and hatred of men are saturated into every fiber of our consciousness.

## Speaking of Women

I ask no favors for my sex... All I ask of our brethren is that they will take their feet from off our necks.

~ Sarah Moore Grimké
(1792–1873)

The sight of women talking together has always made men uneasy.

~ Germaine Greer
(1939–)

Men have defined the parameters of every subject. All feminist arguments, however radical in intent or consequence, are with or against assertions or premises implicit in the male system, which is made credible or authentic by the power of men to name.

~ Andrea Dworkin
(1946–2005)

Man-hating is everywhere, but everywhere it is twisted and transformed, disguised, tranquilized, and qualified. It coexists, never peacefully, with the love, desire, respect, and need women also feel for men. Always man-hating is shadowed by its milder, more diplomatic and doubtful twin, ambivalence.

~ Judith Levine
(1952–)

She must learn again to speak
Starting with I
Starting with We
Starting as the infant does
With her own true hunger
And pleasure
And rage.

~ Marge Piercy
(1936–)

Why is a woman's lack of a husband so important to note?

~ Guerrilla Girls
Bitches, Bimbos and Ballbreakers: The Guerrilla Girls' Illustrated Guide to Female Stereotypes

# MEN ARE NOT PIGS.

## Pigs are gentle, sensitive and intelligent animals.

Men have always been afraid that women could get along without them.
~ Margaret Mead (1901-1978)

The men are much alarmed by certain speculations about women; and well they may be, for when the horse and ass begin to think and argue, adieu to riding and driving.
~ Adelaide Anne Procter (1825-1864)

©2014 Michael Elizabeth Marillynson LLC - This poster is from the book "Contrary to the Custom of Men: Field Notes on the Pestilence of Patriarchy from a Disloyal Son." For re-printing permission go to: con2men.info. Image courtesy of Wikimedia Commons: scott bauer

## accountability is the best disinfectant

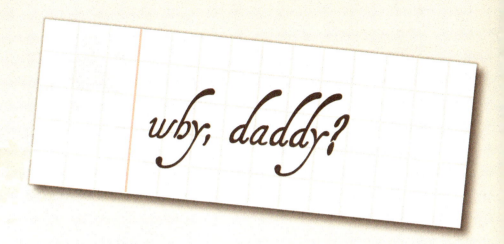

# why, daddy?

One thing I learned working in batterer accountability groups is accountability is the best lie detector.

The process of doggedly pursuing accountability is infallible, and always trips up the man attempting to obfuscate his actions, thinking, and purposes.

It is an ability all children are born with, before it is pummeled out of them by Androputriarchy.

Here is how Androputriarchy begins His brainwashing of a four-year-old:

"Daddy, why is Mommy crying?"

"Her head hurts."

"Daddy, why does Mommy's head hurt?"

"Because she bumped her head on the cabinet."

"How did Mommy bump her head on the cabinet?"

"Because she was arguing with me and fell."

"Daddy, why did Mommy fall?"

"Because she's stupid! Now stop asking questions and go to your room."

As a facilitator in a batterer accountability group I had a little more leverage, in general, than most four-year-olds. The assailants had good reason to answer my questions because if they didn't they could be discharged from the program and have to go back to the court and explain why.

So we would use the same "Why, Daddy" process with him.

"So George, you said you are unjustly in this program because you never touched your wife Jane; is that correct?"

"Yes."

"How did she bump her head?"

"We were talking and she just bumped her head on the cabinet."

"And when you say 'talking' do you mean talking like we are now, or were your voices raised like you were arguing?"

"More like we were arguing."

"What was the argument about?"

"I don't know. What does it matter?"

"Are you sure you don't remember?"

"Yes."

"Do you have memory problems, George?"

"No."

"But you say you don't remember what you were arguing about; on the other hand, you do remember that you didn't cause your wife to bump her head. Could you explain how your memory seems to work in one case, but not the other?"

"Why are you asking all of these stupid questions? We're just going around and around!"

"Yes, we are going around and around. I am following you, and will continue to follow you, and you seem to be going around and around. Now, back to your memory. Do you have a good memory or a bad one George?"

"My memory is fine."

"If your memory is fine, then I'm sure you can remember what you and your wife what were arguing about."

"I think it was about money."

"You think it was about money; was it or wasn't it about money?"

"It was about money."

"What about the money were you arguing about?"

"I thought she had more money than she had. I had given her $100 two days ago and she should have had $60 left over but didn't."

"Wow, your memory is good George. So how did a disagreement over $100 get your wife's head bumped into the cabinet?"

"She's clumsy."

"Oh, I'm sorry to hear that. How clumsy?"

"Very."

"How long has she been clumsy?"

"Her whole life."

"And how long have you known she was so clumsy?"

"Ever since I've known her."

"And how long is that?"

"Seven years."

"So why did the police arrest you for domestic violence, and the court send you here, just because your wife is clumsy?"

"She said I forced her into the cabinet."

"How close were you to your wife when she fell into the cabinet?"

"Pretty close."

"So did your wife fall into the cabinet because you were getting in her face and yelling?"

"Kind of."

"Well, is that what happened or not?"

"Yes."

"So you rushed up on your wife and she was afraid and jumped away from you and into the cabinet?"

"Yeh, but that doesn't make it my fault!"

"But George, you already told us you knew your wife was clumsy. If your wife is clumsy, and you rush up on her, didn't you know she might fall?"

"Maybe."

"We don't accept maybe here, George."

"I knew she could."

"Is this what the court said is the reason they sent you here?"

"Yes."

This is the type of story heard over and over again in accountable batterer programs—the few that exist. The key is to never stop asking why until you get to the truth. You'll know when you get there. I've never seen it fail if given enough time and commitment.

This process is equally effective outside of a batterer program, and is likely one of the reasons I was so often accused of treating judges, probation officers, therapists and attendees of my workshops "like a batterer." I naively figured that if accountability is good for batterers, then it is good for all of us, regardless of who you are, including me.

Also, it usually wasn't difficult to catch batterers in their lies due to the fact our world teaches and entitles men to use what I call the "two-step" argumentation process. Step one is: do what I tell you. Step two is: if you don't do what I tell you, I hit you.

That doesn't teach a person to be very facile in logic or argumentation. Hence, because batterers over-rely on that coercive style, and the very fact their abuse of others is founded on a dishonest and imbalanced interactional method, it is not difficult to catch them up in their own deceit.

However, I want to be perfectly clear: it may be possible for the police, courts, or some other official to use this process with a batterer. However, I am not in any way saying those whom he terrorizes—his wife/partner/children/victims—can or should do this with him. Absolutely not. It is not the person who is traumatized by the assailant who is responsible to stop him or to hold him accountable. It is the community's responsibility to do so, without exception.

Many so-called batterer "treatment" programs/facilitators (using the word "treatment" with batterers already tells you the "professional" engaged in that activity is a quack, at best) like to dress themselves up so they can look competent by doing social-worky stuff like psychological evaluations and that type of crap with batterers. Not only is this misbegotten busywork totally useless, it diverts everyone's attention away from the simple imperative of holding men/batterers accountable, and can be achieved simply by speaking with them.

I also discovered accountability for abusive or disrespectful behavior is, by definition, never convenient or easy. If the consequences chosen by, or for, a man who has been abusive or disrespectful does not raise noisy resistance from him it has missed the mark for real accountability.

# Speaking of Women

Men hate more steadily than they love.

~ Samuel Johnson
(1709–1784)

I am aware that many object to the severity of my language; but is there not cause for severity? I will be as harsh as truth, and as uncompromising as justice. On this subject, I do not wish to think, or to speak, or write, with moderation. No! No! Tell the mother to gradually extricate her babe from the fire into which it has fallen; but urge me not to use moderation in a cause like the present (slavery). I am in earnest—I will not equivocate—I will not excuse—I will not retreat a single inch—AND I WILL BE HEARD. The apathy of the people is enough to make every statue leap from its pedestal, and to hasten the resurrection of the dead.

~ William Lloyd Garrison
(1805–1879)

Women in general seem to me to be appreciably more intelligent than men… a great many of them suffer in silence from the imbecilities of their husbands.

~ Henry Louis "H. L." Mencken
(1880–1956)

Fear was my father, Father Fear.
His look drained the stones.

~ Theodore Roethke
(1908–1963)

All men are batterers until proven otherwise.

~ Rick Liska
(dates unknown)

## accountability— it's what's for breakfast!

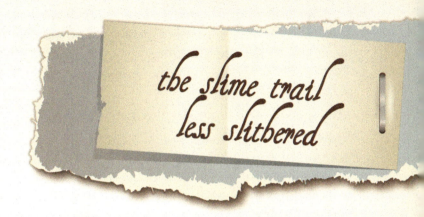

## the slime trail less slithered

Accountability for, by, and of men is the alpha-to-omega of what is necessary for men to atone for the past, acknowledge the conditions of the present, get out of the way of the future, and hopefully save our planet.

Don't be fooled by anyone attempting to pull you into the whiny pity-party parlor game of "women's" accountability. This is one of those dime-a-dozen Androputriarchal ploys meant to throw you off course. Men's accountability, and hence the accountability of Androputriarchy, is the only relevant issue. As Nancy Reagan said, with all of the wisdom at her disposal, just say no.

As I learned while working with so-called domestic violence perpetrators (men, that is), sunlight is not only the best disinfectant, but accountability cannot survive without it. That is one of the many reasons you will notice Androputriarchy is founded upon lies and lying, and its undead corpse is teaming with the maggots of fraudulence. That is why, as pointed out above, Androputriarchy does not intend to have this conversation about men's accountability and will do anything to stop it. Like whine about "women's" accountability, etc.

My experience with accountability as applied to men is it can be a soul-saving poultice, but the application brings great discomfort to the patient. As it should.

One way to quickly ascertain if a particular man or institution has an interest in personal/institutional accountability is simply to observe whether they avoid or embrace it. Any and all efforts made to avoid accountability should be taken at face value, no matter how much energy or violence is employed to change your mind.

Conversely, it is safe to say a quick way to ascertain if a particular man or institution does have interest in personal/institutional accountability is simply to observe whether they embrace it. You may recollect 1) men/Androputriarchy have been known to pretend as if they were doing the accountable thing to get out of trouble, and 2) repeat after me: Androputriarchy is founded upon lies and lying, and its undead corpse is teaming with the maggots of fraudulence.

So it may be a good thing a particular man/institution is speaking/behaving in an accountable manner, but time and sunlight will tell the whole story. When it comes to men and accountability, hope for the best and prepare for the worst. Keep in mind as well none of us has much experience with men being accountable, so it will be a new thing to behold and comprehend.

Be particularly wary of Trojan horses in odd places. For example, a man who chairs a women's studies program at a university. Hmmm… Male social work students who head up the annual Take Back the Night march. Hmmm… Men who insist they are feminists (yours truly included). Hmmm…

I've tried to figure out a simple formula for determining when male accountability is being exhibited, but there are approximately 3.5 billion boys/men infesting the Earth at this time and there would be that many versions of account-ability were that to actually happen. These numbers don't include the hundreds of millions of Androputriarchal institutions that exist solely to serve men's dangerous interests (the Catholic Church, for example).

Suffice it to say I personally use the "thirsty man in the desert" guide as a general rule.

Guys: don't come to me claiming you are seeking accountability unless you look at all times like a thirsty man in the desert desperately seeking water to save your life. You will go after accountability with all of the passion you can muster and will not be deterred by anyone or anything that would entice or threaten you to stop. You will go after accountability because you have determined it is the only chance you have to save your own life. You will persistently question everything you have ever been told and your former life and its trappings will fall away from you, sometimes violently, and it will cause you much pain. You will have to learn to live with isolation and loss. You will be mocked for your efforts by practically everyone you know, certainly all of the men, and you will have to put most if not all of the comforts and credentials you have worked for in your life at risk. You will do all of this without a pity party or expectation you be thought of as a hero by women because of it.

Enjoy, fellas!

## ~ Never, ever again?

As you already surmised, men's personal and herd accountability for Androputriarchy's crimes is a life-long undertaking at the very least. Realistically, it is a multi-generational commitment and task. To give some idea of the enormity of commitment that would be necessary from men, consider your own driving habits.

Assuming you've driven an automobile before, have you ever exceeded the speed limit? Even if it was by one mile per hour?

All right, that includes all of us.

Next, what are the privileges and rationalizations associated with your speeding?

---

## RATIONALIZATIONS
### (why I should speed)

little or no consequence
everybody does it
doesn't harm anyone
it's not really a crime
not likely to get caught
it's no big deal
it's efficient
it's a stupid law
nobody else gets a consequence for it
I can afford the ticket
I know what I'm doing
I know how to not get caught
the people who really abuse the privilege get caught
they should go after the really bad people

---

## PRIVILEGES
### (what I gain from speeding)

I get somewhere quicker
I save time in my day
I get to break the law
I am above the law
it just feels good

---

I suppose the "privileges" gained from speeding must be quite rewarding given the wholesale civil disobedience being perpetrated by American drivers. However, when looking at the list of "privileges" above, it does not seem very compelling. The list of "rationalizations" for this criminal behavior is a bit more substantial.

Now we get to the difficult part. What it would take for you to never, ever again break the speeding laws? No exceptions (unless you are an ambulance driver).

Is this a difficult question for you to answer? When I've asked this question of others, the answer usually boils down to, "If I had been speeding and I caused significant harm or death to someone because of it, I would never again break that law."

Is your answer instead, "I would stop speeding forever because I decided it wasn't the right thing to do?"

Allow me to take this notion back to men's accountability. I am suggesting men immediately begin demonstrating their accountability by cutting themselves off cold-turkey from their centuries-old insanely-generous male privilege Men's Heritage Foundation.

If we spent 30 minutes putting together a list of the "privileges" men reap from male privilege, sexism, and Androputriarchy, it's fair to say we would realize a much longer, deeper, and wider array of spectacular benefits men would be relinquishing.

So what is it going to take to convince men that abandoning all of their male privileges is worth doing? And even if all men, or even one man, decided to do so, what would it take?

I say none of this to make anyone feel sorry for men—no need for that.

As I've said elsewhere: half-assed, half-hearted and half-measures are to accountability as a fish is to a bicycle. Nothing less than complete accountability is required from men and this is the price tag men have inflated for themselves.

Image courtesy of Wikimedia Commons:
Basher Eyre

### ~ Batteries not included

If a man, a group of men, or all men decided they want to be completely accountable today for all of their and Androputriarchy's crimes since Neanderthal man dragged his knuckles out of the swamp, what are women responsible to do to help them with this Amazonian task?

Absolutely nothing. This is the simplest part of the discussion by far.

First of all, if men want to stop being King Baby Asshole they can do so immediately. No batteries required. We men make hundreds of decisions each day about many things, including how much of an asshole to be. We are competent to make our own decisions. And we can decide to stop being assholes right now—24/7/365.

Second, all men have to do is stop it. What to do instead will come to us if we shut the fuck up. Necessity is the father of not being King Baby Asshole. We'll figure it out. There is no mystery or magic elixir or thoughtful feminist model necessary.

If we men are serious, we will perfect being anti-assholes. We perfect everything else we set our pestilent minds to, so we have a proven track record. All other hand-wringing by men or women is avoidance of the task.

---

**Men's Heritage Foundation:** is about inheritance; men's inheritance from men and Androputriarchy. This inheritance might include money, but always includes exalted status, entitlement, power, economic advantage, political advantage, religious advantage, primary access to opportunity, and admission to the boys club. It is intergenerational male privilege. It is a King's crown handed to all boys at birth. Like a scrotum, it comes with the penis. Men's Heritage Foundation are those undeserved privileges men accumulate over decades and centuries of oppressive entitlement, inequitable accumulation of resources, and unearned advantage that is passed down to male sycophants/mercenaries.

# Speaking of Women

Cautious, careful people always casting about to preserve their reputation or social standards never can bring about reform. Those who are really in earnest are willing to be anything or nothing in the world's estimation, and publicly and privately, in season and out, avow their sympathies with despised ideas and their advocates, and bear the consequences.

~ Susan Brownell Anthony
(1820–1906)

A man's home may seem to be his castle on the outside; inside, it is more often his nursery.

~ Clare Boothe Luce
(1903–1987)

The man of today did not establish this patriarchal regime, but he profits by it, even when he criticizes it. And he has made it very much a part of his own thinking.

~ Simone de Beauvoir
(1908–1986)

We learned the hard way that even though we had all the law and all the righteousness on our side, that white man is not going to give up his power to us.

~ Fannie Lou Hamer
(1917–1977)

The discovery is, of course, that "man" and "woman" are fictions, caricatures, cultural constructs. As models they are reductive, totalitarian, and inappropriate to human becoming. As roles they are static, demeaning to the female, dead-ended for male and female both.

~ Andrea Dworkin
(1946–2005)

A woman needs a man like a fish needs a bicycle.

~ Irina Dunn
(1948–)

I think if more men started becoming the victims of rape—or castration—that might help redress the imbalance of sexual violence. Since women only commit 13.3% of all crimes, they should have their own subways, their own streets, their own cities, their own countries, their own continents, and eventually their own planet—yes! Run by and for women. Just for a change—just to see if it makes a difference.

~ Lydia Lunch
(1959–)

Not all men are annoying. Some are dead.

~ anonymous

what motivates men's allegiance to Androputriarchy is what would motivate them away from it

# how do we change men and androputriarchy?

I will use myself as an example.

Although I have taught myself to have a deep and abiding desire to respect women, be a witness to injustice, and use the power and tools available to me to make a difference, I don't think this is the "bottom line" necessary to change Androputriarchy, one man at-a-time or as a herd.

Fortunately or unfortunately, it comes down to selfishness. That is, Androputriarchal behavior is always initiated out of self-interest, and it only changes out of self-interest. To change men's behavior, values and lives, we have to change what He identifies as His self-interest.

Androputriarchal attitudes, sense of entitlement, and behavior aren't inevitable—just encouraged. We will have to encourage—insist, actually—in boys and men and girls and women, a completely different value system. This value system will teach boys it is heroic to use their powers to assure peace, mercy, and respect in their communities and to do otherwise is the ultimate shamefulness. As I have written elsewhere, what if masculinity were defined by mercies, not massacres?

This issue hinges on the self-interested continuum from heroism to disgrace.

In our present world, men's male-bonding is valued above all other bonding, identifications, and attachments. This bonding is predicated and constructed on the suffering and broken bones of women and the male-called "feminine."

Men are heroic, to other men, the more they prove themselves detached from women and from their own compassion. Conversely, men are shamed by other men and Androputriarchy for showing respect and compassion for women and, God forbid, bonding and identifying with women.

Therein lies at least some sort of way out of the swamp for the future.

A sane, safe, merciful, inclusive, healthy, and nurturing world would see boys and men affirmed and idolized for bonding with women and supporting women's self-actualization. Boys and men would be condemned, shamed and disgraced by other boys and men for acting in the manner we teach boys and men to act now.

It comes down to self-interest: I want to feel heroic and good about myself, and I don't want to feel ashamed and disgraced. Hence, I am in the self-initiated mind frame to learn and adjust and do what it takes to feel good about myself.

I like the notion of altruism, and I think it is attainable in some rare instances, but it has never changed one thing in human affairs and it is a total dead-end as far as eradicating the blight that is Androputriarchy. Altruism is not sustainable as a strategy—heroism and shame are.

# Speaking of Women

Most men are brave till courage has been tried, and boast of virtue till their price is known.
~ Mercy Otis Warren
(1728–1758)

Men, their rights and nothing more; women, their rights and nothing less.
~ Susan Brownell Anthony
(1820–1906)

The history of men's opposition to women's emancipation is more interesting perhaps than the story of that emancipation itself.
~ Virginia Woolf
(1882–1941)

Men are afraid that women will laugh at them. Women are afraid that men will kill them.
~ Margaret Atwood
(1939–)

Now, I know, in this room, some of you are the women I have been talking about. I know that. People around you may not. I am going to ask you to use every single thing you can remember about what was done to you -- how it was done, where, by whom, when, and, if you know -- why -- to begin to tear male dominance to pieces, to pull it apart, to vandalize it, to destabilize it, to mess it up, to get in its way, to fuck it up. I have to ask you to resist, not to comply, to destroy the power men have over women, to refuse to accept it, to abhor it and to do whatever is necessary despite its cost to you to change it."
~ Andrea Dworkin
(1946–2005)

Gay marriage is scary because it is a symbol of sex, and therefore women, eluding patriarchal control.
~ Martha C. Nussbaum
(1947–)

# ON THE JOB SAFETY BEGINS HERE

THIS OFFICE HAS WORKED ____ DAYS WITHOUT A **SEXIST** COMMENT OR ACT

THE BEST PREVIOUS RECORD WAS ____ DAYS.

DO YOUR PART TO MAKE A NEW RECORD. ____ DAYS REMAIN TO ACHIEVE OUR GOAL.

©2014 Michael Elizabeth Marillynson LLC - This poster is from the book "Contrary to the Custom of Men: Field Notes on the Pestilence of Patriarchy from a Disloyal Son." For re-printing permission go to: con2men.info.

# inoculating against androputriarchy

## the pestilence of which to be ever-vigilant

Androputriarchy has to go.

Fellowship could, someday, possibly, be permissible under a watchful eye.

The human race is teetering on the edge of destruction by men and the only hope we have is women no longer tolerating the plunder and destruction of men and Androputriarchy and save Mother Earth before it is too late.

At that point in the degradation of the human race, it will be painfully clear Androputriarchy is a destructive parasitic thugocracy that cannot be ignored, cured or left unrestrained. At that time in women's evolution—and begrudgingly by men only because we want our sorry asses to be saved—women will begin to put in place the safeguards and limits on men, men's behavior, and Androputriarchy needed to pull us back from the brink.

Androputriarchy has amply demonstrated He will not stop Himself. He will not stop Himself even if He is drowning in His own filthy bile and sewage. On top of that, He will call bile and sewage masculine perfume to be adored and worshipped. Matriarchy will be forced to be the tough parent and insist on vigilant controls and very, very tough love so Androputriarchy will no longer harm Himself, destroy property, or hurt others. Without this open and universally-acknowledged reality, the human race has no hope for survival.

Malarial mosquitoes, like males in Androputriarchy, are individually and collectively harmful parasites to women and children. Androputriarchy is no more "reformable" than malarial mosquitoes. They are what they are, whether you like them, loathe them, or are indifferent. A community, nation, or household as well as a nation is safest when prepared to prevent harm from them.

We exterminate mosquitoes, abort them, purposely destroy their habitat, and otherwise control them without thought to "reforming" them. Our efforts have never included "reasoning" with mosquitos, seeking "their higher self or appealing to their better nature" or making certain they are "included" in our efforts so they will not be "disrespected" or feel "left out."

Yet we feebly stumble over ourselves making up stories about how men in Androputriarchy are good souls with some minor flaws that just need reforming—as long as it doesn't encroach on their myriad privileges, depravities, and entitlements.

The fact is: malarial mosquitoes, left to their own devices, will suck the blood of warm-blooded mammals, causing untold hardship and death. Androputriarchy has not distinguished Himself from mosquitoes in this regard, even though He has had every opportunity to do so, and so must surrender to the consequences.

---

**Androputriarchy:** [*andro* meaning male, man; *putrere*, meaning rotten, or proceeding from decay; *archy* meaning ruler] an alternative for "patriarchy" that attempts to make clearer the corruption, malevolence, and destructive blight that male supremacy has been in human history and remains to this day.

I am not the go-to person for designing the future. For that you need: 1) women; 2) women smarter than I am; 3) very courageous women.

But I do have some suspicions about what a benevolent future would look like.

First of all, it will require feminist revolution/transformation, and not reform. As Elizabeth Cady Stanton said, "Reformers who are always compromising, have not yet grasped the idea that truth is the only safe ground to stand upon." Reform is a scrap of bread thrown from the gluttonous Patriarch's table to starving women to give the illusion of mercy, generosity and "progress." It is none of those things.

You will know true revolution/transformation by its byproducts: howling men; violence and intimidation perpetrated by men to quash insurrection; unity in women; clarity in women that the actions/goals/results are specifically about disempowering Androputriarchy and empowering Matriarchy.

If this begins to show some success, you will see more and more men peel away from Androputriarchy as they conclude it no longer favors them, thus putting to the lie the so-called exclusion notion. This is the inclusion women have been inviting men into for millennia and men have had no interest whatsoever because it did not serve their interests.

There will be Gender Truth and Reconciliation Commissions all over the world at every level of human organization: governmental, business, religion, medicine, military, etc. The more Androputriarchal a particular human organization has been, the more Commissions it will require. As has long been said, sunlight is the best disinfectant and Androputriarchy has left much sepsis to decontaminate. Hazmat suits required.

Quotas will be thought of and used as the merciful medicine desperately needed by a sick humanity. In fact, just as antibiotics are often dispensed in a manner where one takes a large dose at the beginning and then continues to take smaller doses long after the illness has seemed to subside, so will quotas and other remedies be applied socially. Quotas in politics, business, health care, religion, police forces, criminal justice systems, etc. will start out requiring at least a 51% representation of women—probably higher. This might be titrated downward towards 50% over the centuries if men prove themselves trustworthy.

Reparations will be another key element in healing the patient. This will be tricky as women are not the only social group to have been scourged by Androputriarchy. This will require a truthful and deep examination of Men's Heritage Foundation. That is, what undeserved privileges have men or other social groups accumulated over centuries of oppressive entitlement, passed down to their male sycophant/mercenaries, how has that harmed the human family, and what needs to be done about it?

Just as some places in America have mechanisms called "environmental impact statements" every Man and Republican hates, we will begin to institute similar impact analyses for women and children for all human activity. These analyses would, by definition, take into account our responsibility to be good stewards of Mother Earth and the environment upon which we are dependent, especially regarding animals.

Finally, it will require constant, invasive, mandatory, and ever-vigilant monitoring of men and men's gatherings by women in all aspects of life—particularly the home. This will be necessary as Androputriarchy has amply demonstrated His willingness to become belligerent and destructive at any moment when it appears to be in His interest.

The necessity of this monitoring and inoculating might be lessened over a few centuries when men have established a successful record of trustworthiness and women have instituted effective methods of monitoring effectively and humanely.

---

**Men's Heritage Foundation:** is about inheritance; men's inheritance from men and Androputriarchy. This inheritance might include money, but always includes exalted status, entitlement, power, economic advantage, political advantage, religious advantage, primary access to opportunity, and admission to the boys club. It is intergenerational male privilege. It is a King's crown handed to all boys at birth. Like a scrotum, it comes with the penis. Men's Heritage Foundation are those undeserved privileges men accumulate over decades and centuries of oppressive entitlement, inequitable accumulation of resources, and unearned advantage that is passed down to male sycophants/mercenaries.

It may be useful to consider how Androputriarchy has abundantly demonstrated His preference for maintaining a parasitic grip on women, and how this might help women design monitoring and safety methodology.

**Parasitism:** A type of symbiosis where two (or more) organisms from different species live in close proximity to one another and one (parasite) organism obtains food and other needs at the expense of the other (host).

**Mutualism:** A type of symbiosis where two (or more) organisms from different species live in close proximity to one another and rely on one another for nutrients, protection, or other life functions. Both (or all) of the organisms involved benefit from the relationship.

The styles, purposes and functions of different types of biological symbiosis have been deeply studied and documented. Many, if not all, of the tactics of parasites are the tactics of Androputriarchy. Knowing this, women could continually work to improve and provide inoculation to the human family so the genocidally virulent pandemic of Androputriarchy could not re-establish a significant toehold on Earth—or elsewhere.

## Speaking of Women

Wouldn't it be possible for us just to banish these men from our lives, and escape their carping and jeering once and for all? Couldn't we live without them? Couldn't we earn our living and manage our affairs without help from them? Come on, let's wake up, and claim back our freedom, and the honour and dignity that they have usurped from us for so long. Do you think that if we really put our minds to it, we would be lacking the courage to defend ourselves, the strength to fend for ourselves, or the talents to earn our own living? Let's take our courage into our hands and do it, and then we can leave it up to them to mend their ways as much as they can: we shan't really care what the outcome is, just as long as we are no longer subjugated to them.

~ **Moderata Fonte**
(1555–1592)

I have no idea of submitting tamely to injustice inflicted either on me or on the slave. I will oppose it with all the moral powers with which I am endowed. I am no advocate of passivity.

~ **Lucretia Mott**
(1793–1880)

... when women are the advisers, the lords of creation don't take the advice till they have persuaded themselves that it is just what they intended to do; then they act upon it, and if it succeeds, they give the weaker vessel half the credit of it; if it fails, they generously give her the whole.

~ **Louisa May Alcott**
(1832–1888)

The revolt against any oppression usually goes to an opposite extreme for a time; and that is right and necessary.

~ **Tennessee Claflin**
(1845–1923)

To free ourselves from patriarchy, we must all become pro-female and look at the costs to women of male power, male privilege, and male violence. Feminism—recognition of the imbalance of power between men and women, combined with a commitment to correct the imbalance—is the only solvent that will dissolve patriarchy and release all of us, women and men, from its power.

~ **Elizabeth Dodson Gray**
(1929–)

# Speaking of Women

In a better world, children will not be taught epics about men who are honored for being violent, or fairy tales about children who are lost in frightful woods where women are malevolent witches. They will be taught new myths, epics, and stories in which human beings are good; men are peaceful; and the power of creativity and love is the governing principle. In this world, our drive for justice, equality and freedom, our thirst for knowledge and spiritual illumination, and our yearning for love and beauty will at last be freed. And after the bloody detour of androcractic history, both women and men will at last find out what being human can mean.

~ Riane Tennenhaus Eisler
(1937–)

Men who want to support women in our struggle for freedom and justice should understand that it is not terrifically important to us that they learn to cry; it is important to us that they stop the crimes of violence against us.

~ Andrea Dworkin
(1946–2005)

Could there be a feminine intensity or force that would not be merely "subversive"? Because subversion is a problem—it implies a dependency on the program that is being critiqued—therefore it's a parasite of that program. Is there a way to produce a force or an intensity that isn't merely a reaction (and a very bad and allergic reaction) to what is? In other words, could feminism be a pointer toward a future of justice that isn't merely reproducing what is, with small reversals?

~ Avital Ronell
(1952–)

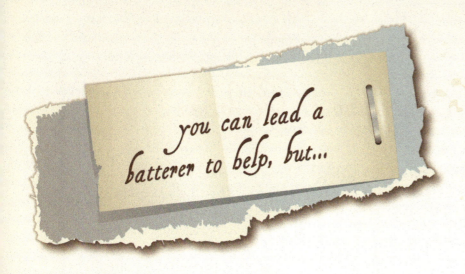

# you can lead a batterer to help, but...

## how do we help batterers?

Back in the day, when I offered public presentations regarding my work with Intimate Patriarchal Violence perpetrators, I would invariably ask the following question: How do we help batterers?

Below is a typical list of responses I would write on the chalkboard:

## How do we help batterers?

- get them into therapy
- get them into drug/alcohol treatment
- teach them anger management skills
- teach them communication skills
- teach them empathy skills
- help them get jobs and/or job skills
- work to boost their self-esteem
- get them into credit or budget counseling
- get them into marriage counseling
- explore their victimization as children
- help them admit they need help
- throw them in jail
- teach good impulse control
- reduce their inner sense of insecurity
- relieve their overdependence on their spouses
- get them a psychiatric evaluation
- replace irrational thought patterns
- tap into their own inner strengths
- relieve their abandonment anxiety
- get her to take responsibility for her part in it

All of these responses are revealing about the person(s) who offer them, and about how Androputriarchy and male privilege have demented our collective psyches and rationality. However, they have nothing to do with why men batter (although "throw them in jail" demonstrates the clearest vision about what is actually going on).

I facilitated these public presentations so often I could predict with some reliability the general motivations of the contributors.

For example, the suggestions that had to do with psychotherapy, psychological machinations, and social service programs came primarily from oh-so-helpful-and-nice-and-very-professional social workers and psychologists and probation officers. These people/professions had direct or indirect career/financial interests in their concocted theories.

Fabrications that had to do with men's innate "goodness" and having "lost their way" were usually offered up by heterosexual women who desperately wanted to believe it was possible to save and/or be in a relationship with a man who wasn't an abusive, immature asswipe.

You can guess which one of the inventions above is from the batterer(s) in the audience. At least I hope you can.

Immediately after getting our list written I would then turn to another question: "What are the characteristics of God?" Although most of my audiences were populated by people who apparently knew things about God, even the atheists demonstrated an interest in these exercises.

I would make the following heading and write all the responses on the chalkboard:

## Characteristics of God

- all-knowing
- omniscient
- omnipotent
- forgiving
- wrathful
- all-powerful
- male
- kind
- father
- vengeful
- just
- infinite
- eternal
- incomprehensible
- supreme
- sovereign
- transcendent
- omnipresent
- unchanging
- wise
- truthful
- loving
- merciful
- patient
- just
- righteous
- jealous
- morally perfect

I would then thank the audience and ask them to help me write one more list—"What are the characteristics of batterers?" I would make a point of starting this list directly next to the God list. It would only take a couple of examples before an uncomfortable laugh would move across the room as they saw these two "characteristics" lists were going to be similar, if not identical.

## Characteristics of batterers

- all-knowing
- omniscient
- omnipotent
- forgiving
- wrathful
- all-powerful
- male
- kind
- father
- vengeful
- just
- infinite
- eternal
- incomprehensible
- supreme
- sovereign
- transcendent
- omnipresent
- unchanging
- wise
- truthful
- loving
- merciful
- patient
- just
- righteous
- jealous
- morally perfect

Then the fun began: those people with the highest level of denial and the lowest level of understanding of what men's battering is about would say these lists cannot possibly be the same, because characteristics like "kind" and "loving" and "just" and "merciful" cannot describe batterers.

Interestingly, I never had to defend this exercise—at this point three or four women's hands would frantically shoot up wanting to respond to this denial. "Believe me" they'd say, "my batterer was all of these things. He was kind sometimes and vicious other times. It depended on what he wanted."

After the conversation went on for as long as time would allow, I would ask the audience to guess which characteristic on the list all of the (formerly) battered women I had ever spoken with said was the most powerful weapon their batterer used on them. Interestingly, the audience almost always chose the answer these women had given me, even if they had spent the last 20 minutes arguing about the list: loving. I would say, "Yes, that's right. These women told me "loving" was the tactic the man used to capture her into the relationship and what he used to keep her there, or re-capture her.

I would then offer some observations to the audience as a result of our discussion:

1) To the extent anyone in that room found it erroneous to think of batterers as anything other than merciful and punishing Gods in their homes is the extent to which they are (willfully?) ignorant of—or in denial of—the reality of men's battering.

2) To the extent anyone in that room found it erroneous to think of batterers as anything other than merciful and punishing Gods in their homes is testimony to how they think of the subject of Androputriarchy, male privilege, and men's violence from the perspective of the perpetrator, not the victim. When you see the world from the perspective of the perpetrator you are on the side of, and collude with, the perpetrator whether you think so, or want to, or not.

If you want to fundamentally and accurately understand Androputriarchy, male privilege, and men's violence, you have to be courageous enough to put on the x-ray glasses of the victims. Period.

Finally, I come full circle in the exercise: If you are God in your household; if you are all-knowing, omniscient, omnipotent, forgiving, wrathful, all-powerful, male, kind, vengeful, just, infinite, eternal, incomprehensible, supreme, sovereign, transcendent, omnipresent, unchanging, wise, truthful, loving, merciful, patient, just, righteous, jealous, and morally perfect—just exactly what do you need help with?

If you are God in your household, and you get what you want when you want it, what do you need help with? When you get sex on demand, laundering on demand, meals on demand, child care on demand, money on demand, apologies on demand, glorification on demand, alcohol on demand, excuses for abuse on demand, what do you need help with?

I remain convinced, as I have told countless audiences, the best advice on how to help a batterer is to hold his victim's arms behind her back while he beats her. But he already has this help by way of the generosity of Androputriarchal male-privileged culture. I don't know what else our Androputriarchal world could do to help men more. The whole thing is set up to help the three billion sub-Gods on this dying rock in every way imaginable.

The world is one giant men's club—haven't we helped men enough?

So, I would engage the oh-so-helpful-and-nice-and-very-professional social workers and psychologists and probation officers by pointing out their self-serving strategies and shamefully moronic theories. I never won a popularity contest in my years as a social worker.

I would assert it is the responsibility of all people with the power they have, especially the oh-so-helpful-and-nice-and-very-professional social workers and psychologists and probation officers, to oppose and resist and disempower the batterers—not help them.

My last question to all of the Androputriarchy and male-privilege apologists, lackeys and hangers-on: of the over 2,000 batterers I worked with in 11 years in various batterer intervention programs, how many do you think came to the program without any outside pressure to do so?

None. Not one. Zip, zilch, nada, zero.

Not one guy had ever gotten up one bright, sunny morning and said to himself, "I have become quite an abusive, insufferable, selfish, arrogant fuckwad and I want to change my life. I want to be accountable to myself and my family and the world and give up my authoritarian, unearned power, go through years of self-critical reflection, risk everything I now hold dear, and devote my life to justice for the disempowered. I'll get out the telephone book right now and see who can help me with this."

So all of this begs the question: if these batterers want absolutely nothing to do with "help," and do not need our help, why are we so determined to give it to them?

# Speaking of Women

The world has never yet seen a truly great and virtuous nation because in the degradation of woman the very fountains of life are poisoned at their source.

~ Lucretia Mott
(1793–1880)

I know that I am a slave, and you are my lord. The law of this country has made you my master. You can bind my body, tie my hands, govern my actions; you are the strongest, and society adds to your power; but with my will, sir, you can do nothing. God alone can restrain it and curb it. Seek then a law, a dungeon, an instrument of torture, by which you can hold it, it is as if you wished to grasp the air, and seize vacancy.

~ Amantine Lucile Aurore Dupin,
best known by her pseudonym George Sand (1801–1876)

Slavery always has, and always will, produce insurrections wherever it exists, because it is a violation of the natural order of things, and no human power can much longer perpetuate it...

~ Angelina Grimke
(1805–1879)

The right to vote will yet be swallowed up in the real question, viz: has woman a right to herself? It is very little to me to have the right to vote, to own property, etc., if I may not keep my body, and its uses, in my absolute right.

~ Lucy Stone
(1818–1882)

The suffering of either sex—of the male who is unable, because of the way in which he was reared, to take the strong initiating or patriarchal role that is still demanded of him, or of the female who has been given too much freedom of movement as a child to stay placidly within the house as an adult—this suffering, this discrepancy, this sense of failure in an enjoined role, is the point of leverage for social change.

~ Margaret Mead
(1901–1977)

The master's tools will never dismantle the master's house. They may allow us temporarily to beat him at his own game, but they will never enable us to bring about genuine change. And this fact is only threatening to those women who still define the master's house as their only source of support.

~ Audre Lorde
(1934–1992)

# LAKE PATRIARCHY

## The Cleanup is Mind Boggling

If we're lucky, the human race will survive to one day face the catastrophic fact of the reeking sludge and detritus hidden under polluted Lake Patriarchy. The submerged wreckage of Patriarchy's rape of our environment, animals, and people, and the horrific emotional and psychological condition of the human species, will beg for healing.

"He says that woman speaks with nature. That she hears voices from under the earth. That wind blows in her ears and trees whisper to her. That the dead sing through her mouth and the cries of infants are clear to her. But for him this dialogue is over. He says he is not part of this world, that he was set on this world as a stranger. He sets himself apart from woman and nature.

We are the bird's eggs. Bird's eggs, flowers, butterflies, rabbits, cows, sheep; we are caterpillars; we are leaves of ivy and sprigs of wallflower. We are women. We rise from the wave. We are gazelle and doe, elephant and whale, lilies and roses and peach, we are air, we are flame, we are oyster and pearl, we are girls. We are woman and nature. And he says he cannot hear us speak.

But we hear." ~ Susan Griffin, from Woman and Nature: The Roaring Inside Her

©2014 Michael Elizabeth Marilynson LLC - This poster is from the book "Contrary to the Custom of Men: Field Notes on the Pestilence of Patriarchy from a Disloyal Son." For re-printing permission go to: con2men.info. Image courtesy of Wikimedia Commons: fema/mark wolfe

were we ever to encounter such a thing

## what might male accountability look like?

Beautiful, light-as-air snowflakes flutter down to the Antarctic surface where they land on other snowflakes, which rest on top of others. Over millions of years the pile of snowflakes compresses down and forms ice that averages at least 1 mile (1.6 km) in thickness. One cubic foot of ice weighs 57 pounds. A one-mile-high tower of ice, only one square foot around, weighs 150 tons.

Men are the snowflakes of Androputriarchy, and our millennial contributions to the sorry state of the human condition are the glaciers that inexorably grind over the lives, aspirations, dignity, and bones of women and children.

For me, or any man, to guess as to what male accountability would look like for our long history of, and ongoing, sexist crimes should be contemplated with caution. Also, consider that we've rarely seen this phantom before, so we are groping around in the dark.

Regardless, I would like to give it a go. To stop the mighty inertia of the Androputriarchal glacier will take serious measures on a massive scale.

Before lighting this fuse I would like to clarify what I mean about accountability and consequences. In all of the ideas I offer below I do so with the assumption accountability is an inside job. Imposing consequences or punishment on a person may be necessary for the wellbeing of the community, but is not accountability. Accountability is self-initiated, and from my experience with men's accountability, it always includes the help, insight, and tough love of others.

For example, I am out in my backyard kicking around a ball and I accidently kick it against your window, shattering it. You are not home, and no one knows I broke your window. To be accountable for my actions I have to both 1) decide to acknowledge to you my responsibility for the damage, and 2) work out what I can do to enact the best possible solution FOR YOU to the problem.

Acknowledging my responsibility can, in many instances, be the easiest part of the process. What if I decide to have the glass replaced in your window before you even know about it, and then come to find out there was special glass in the window I didn't know about? Or, if I had talked to you, you would have told me you wanted to take care of it and just send me the bill. Or you may tell me you think I should have the entire window removed, costing hundreds of dollars, and not just the glass.

I may then want to go to a trusted friend and talk the situation over with them to see what they think. They might see a simple solution neither you nor I did. This is getting other people's help with my accountability.

I don't have to like accountability, or the demands you may make on me. But I may do what you ask anyway because I think it is the accountable thing to do and good for me as a person and as a man.

Hence, any/all of the suggestions listed below are offered with the notion we men would gladly propose/accept these measures as good medicine for us individually, as a group, and for our communities.

To be accountable for our actions we men would:

- identify with the victim's needs and interests, and not the perpetrators
- acknowledge our male privilege, how it benefits us, and how we collude in it
- listen to women and follow women's leadership

277

- acknowledge Intimate Patriarchal Violence cannot produce families, only hostages
- acknowledge Androputriarchy is a terrorist, corrupt organization
- acknowledge our physical abuse, sexual abuse, intimidation, social control, isolation, economic abuse, coercion, and emotional and psychological abuse of women and children
- accept ameliorative quotas and full affirmative action as determined by women as to gender, race, economic, employment, leadership and in all other ways to speed the process of making women whole; this would include mandatory 51% female representation in leadership in all human organizations until we sort things out
- provide universal and respectful health care for all women and children as a birthright entitlement
- provide adequate housing for all women and children
- comply with any sort of curfew as determined by women for the safety of the community
- prioritize environmental protection over private property

- entitlement, or so-called economic growth, as directed by women
- support lesbian/gay/bisexual/transgendered people's full and safe participation in the world community
- gratefully accept, support, and provide reparations to women
- fully participate in truth and reconciliation commissions led by women
- acknowledge the damage the worship of Androputriarchy, male-dumb, and men has done
- outlaw hate speech, pornography, and private handgun ownership
- produce a "home safety analysis," by each man for each home, which looks at the ways we will make every family member safe from ourselves
- support and be active in community and regional committees whose purpose is to establish and maintain constructive barriers against sexism, racism, heterosexism, ageism, appearancism, wealth inequality, unequal educational access, prostitution or any other degradation of women, etc.
- insist, until militaries are phased out, for every dollar spent on

- military, ten dollars must be spent on social service programs unrelated to military
- utilize Women and Children Impact Assessment Forms, like we use environmental impact forms today, to make sure our actions economically, socially, and politically protect women and children in all things
- consequence ourselves for behavior disrespectful to women or children
- actively practice responsible, proactive, meaningful environmental stewardship, including such things as reducing worldwide meat consumption by 95%
- implement economic policies that cap worker/owner pay discrepancies to a factor of 3, and usury laws with a maximum interest rate of 3% over costs
- limit men meeting together without female supervision and mentorship to two unrelated males at a given time
- equate so-called patriotism [Patriot: from Greek patrios, of one's fathers; from Latin pater, father, patria fatherland] with hate crimes and hate speech

# Speaking of Women

The time is fast approaching when to call a man a patriot will be the deepest insult you can offer him. Patriotism now means advocating plunder in the interest of the privileged classes of the particular State system into which we have happened to be born. The greater the state, the more wrong and cruel its patriotism, and the greater is the sum of suffering upon which its power is founded.

~ Leo Nikolaevich Tolstoy
(1828–1910)

Privilege is the greatest enemy of right.

~ Marie von Ebner Eschenback
(1830–1916)

Patriotism is as fierce as a fever, pitiless as the grave, blind as a stone, and irrational as a headless hen.

~ Ambrose Bierce
(1842–1913)

Patriotism is a kind of religion; it is the egg from which wars are hatched.

~ Henri René Albert Guy de Maupassant
(1850–1893)

True patriotism hates injustice in its own land more than anywhere else.

~ Clarence Darrow
(1857–1938)

Patriotism… is a superstition artificially created and maintained through a network of lies and falsehoods; a superstition that robs man of his self-respect and dignity, and increases his arrogance and conceit.

~ Emma Goldman
(1869–1940)

Nationalism is an infantile disease. It is the measles of mankind. Heroism on command, senseless violence, and all the loathsome nonsense that goes by the name of patriotism—how passionately I hate them!

~ Albert Einstein
(1879–1955)

The notion that a radical is one who hates his country is naïve and usually idiotic. He is, more likely, one who likes his country more than the rest of us, and is thus more disturbed than the rest of us when he sees it debauched. He is not a bad citizen turning to crime; he is a good citizen driven to despair.

~ Henry Louis "H. L." Mencken
(1880–1956)

Patriotism is an arbitrary veneration of real estate above principles.

~ George Jean Nathan
(1882–1958)

When fascism comes to America, it will be wrapped in the flag and carrying the cross.

~ Sinclair Lewis
(1885–1951)

I will fight for my country, but I will not lie for her.

~ Zora Neale Hurston
(1891–1960)

No matter that patriotism is too often the refuge of scoundrels. Dissent, rebellion, and all-around hell-raising remain the true duty of patriots.

~ Barbara Ehrenreich
(1941–)

**Synthesis:** The combining of separate elements or substances to form a coherent whole.

I know this book is riddled with sexism, racism, ableism, classism, ageism, genderism, heterosexism, and all of the other ignorances, arrogances, and self-delusions that are me.

How do I know? I am a White, upper middle class heterosexual male in good health born in 1956 in the nasty, racist, Republican Crackertown of Jackson, Michigan. I'm the fish who wrote it and, although I can't see what's in 95% of the putrid water, I do know it is water I have been swimming in all of my life.

I know the water needs changing. Desperately.

Speaking of desperation, I dearly wish to make this book better for future editions and/or whatever it is I am going to do on the internet (www.con2men.info).

## WOMEN

(or if you consider yourself intersexed, transgendered, or any other sexuality that happily survives the dualistic male/female dungeon):

I am interested in your reactions/thoughts on what I have written/created here.

Did I get all or part of it? Did I totally miss it?

Did I say it in a way that was unnecessarily offensive? Blatantly sexist or stupid?

Did I stop before I got to the bottom of the shit pile?

Are there ways I could better take my ignorance/privilege into account?

What do you have to say about Androputriarchy that I can broadcast?

## MEN

If your desire is to complain about what big victims you are, how men are not being treated fairly, how the feminists are taking over the world, how I am not being kind or forgiving or nice, how you are going to hunt me down and kill my family, or offer me touching stories of male-bonding, you have come to the wrong place. Go away.

I am only interested in your accountability as a man to women and what you are learning about how you are a beneficiary of Androputriarchy. If you have not leapt headlong into your accountability within the first sentence I will delete your submission and move on.

Send thoughts to: mantraitor@con2men.info.

I shall not grow conservative with age.

~ Elizabeth Cady Stanton
(1815–1902)

# arcanum

"At wch, with a strange and sodayne Musique, they fell into a magicall Daunce, full of præposterous change, and gesticulation, but most applying to their property: who, at their meetings, do all things contrary to the custome of men, dauncing, back to back, hip to hip, theyr handes ioyn'd, and making theyr circles backward, to the left hand, wth strange phantastique motions of theyr heads, and bodyes."

~ Benjamin Jonson, English playright (1572–1637), in describing the movement of the witches in his 1606 play "The Masque of Queens." The witches were the antimasque symbols of women's transgressive sexuality, anger, unruliness and dangerousness. At that time witchcraft was a crime punishable, under the orders and hands of men, by barbaric torture and death.

Image courtesy of Wikimedia Commons.

CPSIA information can be obtained
at www.ICGtesting.com
Printed in the USA
BVOW05s2104150617

487037BV00007B/8/P